PRAISE FOR *PHILANTHROPIC LANDSCAPES*

"A lifelong student of civil society and an outstanding practitioner of philanthropy, Charles Hamilton provides us with important reflections at a time when our society seems at its most divided and most hopeless. Here are valuable insights on how nonprofits and philanthropists need to listen to each other and work together with humility to address our most intractable problems and thus ensure our democracy. *Philanthropic Landscapes* is a timely collection that will have a significant influence on the field."
— *Phoebe Boyer, President and CEO, Children's Aid, NYC*

"In 1965, Richard Cornuelle published *Reclaiming the American Dream: The Role of Private Individuals and Voluntary Associations* and helped launch a resurgence of attention to the role of philanthropy and civil society in the workings of American culture. *Philanthropic Landscapes* continues this work on the theory, issues, and challenges that have confronted citizens, philanthropists, and scholars seeking to flesh out both the art and science of positive human action in civil society. Hamilton, whose career has gracefully united the world of ideas and the world of practical philanthropy, has done yeoman's work in helping us discern a more robust vision of civil society as a space of voluntary action that operates in different ways from either the world of markets (money-based trade) or politics (contestation for the control of government institutions and the policy-making process). Hamilton does not give us a view through rose-colored glasses, though. Instead, he asks us to travel with him through significant philosophical and institutional problems, addressing historical neglect, flaccid theoretical tools, the complex relationship of civil society both to political democracy (they are not equivalent) and markets (they are not equivalent), and the hubris of Big Money seeking Big Solutions. The citizen-reader who makes this journey will be enlightened and hopefully better prepared to act with reflection and choice, reminded that civil society is primarily a different way of seeing social activity in the world, a different way of doing things in the world, and applies different means." — *Lenore T. Ealy, Ph.D., President, The Philanthropic Enterprise*

"This wonderful collection of essays and articles provides both practical and inspirational guidance to current and future donors, family foundation board members, and anyone with an interest in ethical and effective multi-generational family philanthropy. As a donor, trusted advisor, and long-time observer of the field, author Charles Hamilton shares insights and context around timely (and timeless!) debates in family philanthropy including the question of perpetuity, options for strategic philanthropy, capacity building, hubris and power dynamics, governance, donor intent, and more. A must-read for anyone interested in understanding the role and potential of private philanthropy in civil society." — *Jason Born, Vice President for Programs, National Center for Family Philanthropy*

"This fascinating new collection of essays — many updated and expanded in interesting ways — provides a rare glimpse into a deep, subtle, and inquiring mind, one that has been ruminating for years on the enduring importance of philanthropy in free societies. Charles Hamilton is a seasoned practitioner who has sat on every side of the philanthropic table, and in many other chairs throughout civil society. Yet he has remained forever curious about the big questions behind the work, and forever hopeful about the positive potential for philanthropy and civil society despite some very difficult challenges. We need more voices like this to help us tackle those challenges!" — *Dr. Michael Moody, Frey Foundation Chair for Family Philanthropy, Dorothy A. Johnson Center for Philanthropy, Grand Valley State University*

Philanthropic Landscapes

The Value of Civil Society
&
The Practice of Philanthropy

Philanthropic Landscapes

The Value of Civil Society
&
The Practice of Philanthropy

Essays by
CHARLES H. HAMILTON

Founded 1973 @
Union Square W., NY, NY

Cover illustration, *Ascolta la Radio,* © 2018, by Francesco Campanoni, Milan and
Cortona, Italy. Francescocampanoni.com.

Book design and production editing by Sue Khodarahmi.
Cover design by Doris Halle.
Index and copyediting by Lorin Driggs.

Published by Free Life Editions
(Founded 1973 @ Union Square W., NYC)
Free Life Editions
#1102
1301 N. Tamiami Trail, Sarasota, FL 34236
Freelife-editions@outlook.com

Paperback and ebook - Kindle edition by KindleDirect Publishing Platform
Printed in the United States
First edition: August 2019

ISBN: 978-1-7330871-0-0 (paperback); 978-1-7330871-1-7 (ebook - Kindle)

To those most important to me:

Gregory, Douglas, Clara, and my smart/funny/lovely partner, Carol

CONTENTS

Philanthropic Landscapes

The Value of Civil Society
&
The Practice of Philanthropy

INTRODUCTION

THE CLAIMS OF CIVIL SOCIETY

[N]ot to recognize the claim of politics is taken to indicate some defect of character or sensibility.... The things political activity can achieve are often valuable, but I do not believe that they are ever the most valuable things in the communal life of a society. A limitation of view, which appears so clear and practical, but which amounts to little more than a mental fog, is inseparable from political activity. A mind fixed and callous to all subtle distinctions, emotional and intellectual habits becomes bogus from repetition and lack of examination, unreal loyalties, delusive aims, false significances are what political action involves.

The spiritual callousness involved in political action belongs to its character, and follows from the nature of what can be achieved politically. Political action involves mental vulgarity ... because of the false simplification of human life implied in even the best of its purposes ... to make it [society] live requires a social activity of a different and more radical character; and its life is as often threatened by political success as by political failure.

Political activity as I understand it, then, is neither the only adequate expression, nor the overwhelmingly most important expression of a sensibility for the communal interests of a society or of mankind.... Indeed, political activity involves a corruption of consciousness from which a society has continually to be saved. — Michael Oakeshott

Civil society refers to all institutions in which individuals can pursue common interests without detailed direction or interference from the government. — Reinhard Bendix

T his collection explores themes on the value of civil society and the practice of philanthropy. Indeed, they are related in critical ways. Section One focuses on the tradition of civil society, in contrast to and often in opposition to the state or government. Chapter 1 introduces various takes on the idea of civil society. Two new articles explore the unique contributions of Elinor Ostrom and Gene Sharp. Chapter 2 emphasizes civil society in greater detail from different vantage points. It suggests that there may be a way to measure how robust civil society is. And it looks skeptically at some key ideas pushing the increasing politicization of philanthropy. These pieces were explorations for a larger project on civil society and philanthropy that I was working on while a Visiting Fellow for two years at the Yale Program on Non-Profit Organizations in the 1990s.

In Section One and often throughout this volume, I have used philanthropy in the expansive sense that one of my mentors, Bob Payton, preferred: "as a comprehensive term that includes voluntary giving, voluntary service, and voluntary association, primarily for the benefit of others." It is a better term than common and limiting ones, like voluntary sector, independent sector, third sector, the voluntary impulse, etc. Section Two is devoted to philanthropic practice. There, philanthropy usually has a narrower meaning: giving and focusing money for social purposes by donors, foundations, and other vehicles. In any case, it should be clear by the context which meaning is intended.

There is a point of view in these essays. At the same time, I hold dearly to the basic liberal view about openness and the progress of knowledge that J. S. Mill captured in *On Liberty*. Often in disputes, he wrote, "conflicting doctrines, instead of being one true and the other false, share the truth between them; and the nonconforming opinion is needed to supply the remainder of the truth." Thus, "so long as popular truth is one-sided, it is more desirable than otherwise that unpopular truth should have one-sided asserters … to compel reluctant attention to the fragment of wisdom which they proclaim as if it were the whole." In this day and age, I make no claim I know "the whole," but I do believe that there is immense value in emphasizing the ideas and lens of civil society. This rich and complex tradition may appear to be "nonconforming opinions" now, when the politicizing craziness that infects all discourse is implicitly or explicitly *de rigueur*.

The Claims of Civil Society

It is a truth universally acknowledged that the state (government) and civil society are quite different. Historical sociologists, economists, historians, anthropologists, liberal theorists, conservatives, radicals, reactionaries, et al., all call upon the distinction in their thinking and work, whether it is to embrace or erase it. They come down on different sides about what history shows, the means each uses, the theoretical underpinnings and morality, and ultimately about the respective mix or predominance necessary for a good, free, and flourishing society. This acknowledged distinction, then, is only the beginning of a conversation that has been going on for centuries.

These essays (particularly in Section One) have a point of view. It is captured so well by Thomas Paine at the beginning of *Common Sense*: "Some writers have so confounded society with government as to leave little or no distinction between them; whereas they are not only different, but have different origins." The idea of civil society is a powerful lens for seeing human action and the role of social institutions. The distinction between the voluntary means of civil society and the coercive means of the state elucidates so much about our past, the present, and possible futures which would otherwise be distorted or opaque.

The Politicization of Society

However, we live in a world where nearly everything is seen through a political lens. As the economic historian Max Harwell put it, "Politicization can be defined as that now pervasive tendency for making all questions political questions, all issues political issues, all values political values, and all decisions political decisions." The complex, voluntary, and often unplanned nature of civil society in action is so easily overlooked, dismissed, and difficult to grasp. The simple assumption is made that no alternative exists except to seek the political procrustean bed without regard to consequences and social costs. These solutions are then tailored to one's particular ideology, so, as Jacques Ellul observed so many years ago, our time has become an "age of the intellectual organization of political hatreds."

Civil Society

Instead of "seeing like a state," to use James C. Scott's wonderful phrase, bringing civil society back into the discussion helps reveal the diverse means whereby voluntary action and institutions become a fertile — and alas fragile — cooperative bulwark against totalitarian presumptions abroad and here. The idea is open-ended and complex. Michael Walzer succinctly identified civil society as "the space of uncoerced human association." Historian Alan Macfarlane, in turn, presents a valuable description of the elusive nature and deep value of civil society in action in *The Making of the Modern World* (2002):

17

... the historical documenting of the accidental and artificial development of civil society, which for the first time [i.e., in the 19th century] became dominant in a world civilization. Democracy, liberty, equality and wealth all have their roots in this common, largely invisible, bed of associations. Its emergence was an accident, its survival precarious.... These little groupings had bodies, they were emotionally and organizationally more than the sum of the parts, yet they were also artificial bodies. They were not based on birth or inheritance, nor were they merely chartered off-shoots of the State. They were autonomous, yet regulated lightly, recognized yet largely ignored, "nobodies" in Maitland's phrase, yet they filled the teeming middle space of open, democratic societies. This multitude of associations were the bane of all authoritarians, they needed to be "bundled up" into the State according to those from Hobbes, through Rousseau, to Hitler and Mussolini. If they could not be incorporated into the body politic, they must be exterminated if possible. A world of State and citizen alone, with no cross-binding ties between citizens and not mediated through the State, was proclaimed.

That historical perspective suggests why the historical facts of civil society cannot be captured by a grand theory the way the state can be (or even the way that subset in civil society, the economy, can be). It is a nuanced idea. I should also note that civil society can be full of contractions and inhabited by nasty, anti-democratic strains. This important point is not the focus of the essays here and is wisely discussed by others.

Seeing civil society is also perplexing because we all tend to believe we can gain the knowledge to understand, control, and manage all human desires, actions, and contingencies. As Hayek points out in his justly famous article, "The Pretense of Knowledge": "To act on the belief that we possess the knowledge and the power which enable us to shape the processes of society entirely to our liking, knowledge which in fact we do not possess, is likely to make us do much harm." That rationalistic pretense leads us to codify our own hubris and limited knowledge, and to try to force it on others. Seeing like the state is always dangerous. Bringing civil society back in can add balance, and provides a better understanding of how human action works and can flourish.

Civil Society and Philanthropy

Philanthropy, in the expansive sense, is a major component of civil society. One might suppose that using and protecting civil society would be nearly second nature in philanthropy. Perhaps it once was. Whatever was off with the idea of charity, it worked within civil society to strengthen it and to provide. Whatever is right about the later idea of scientific philanthropy, it has reinforced hubris and the statist route for a grand "national purpose," as the progressive liberals like Herbert Croly sought. Alas, philanthropy by experts has deeply fractured both philanthropy and civil society, in part by driving out genuine pluralism, participation, and discovery of alternatives. So it is that philanthropy has increasingly been mesmerized by the same siren song of government panaceas. It has come to ignore or dismiss the means and possibilities within civil society. The politicization of philanthropy continues to distract us, waste gobs of money, and do great harm.

The 1980s and early 1990s represented a significant period for "bringing the state back in" and for pushing philanthropy further under the state umbrella. This was about the time that I began my research on civil society and philanthropy. In 1985, Peter Evans, Dietrich Rueschemeyer, and Theda Skocpol published *Bringing the State Back In*. It was an important work, but its tunnel vision reinforced the politicizing of social discourse and philanthropic goals. It advanced the state's "necessary claim to being the guardian of the universal interests of the society over which it has jurisdiction." It is not clear what sort of encompassing "general" public interest exists to be channeled through the state. It is a preternaturally contested notion. Rather than helping many diverse public interests in the competitive "marketplace" of civil society, the state tends to slip into an ideological vested interest guardianship "for reasons of state." Hobbes would be pleased. The brunt of that book assumes its own "dominant theoretical" paradigm that highlights "states as organizational structures or as potentially autonomous actors." By bringing "the state back in to its proper central place in explanations of social change and politics," the authors — not entirely on purpose, I suspect — rigidly rationalize politicizing civil society, and in its wake, philanthropy, too.

Ironically, as these renewed efforts were made to bring the state back in, there were different historical and historic trends trying to find room for an alternative that would keep the state outside and to bring civil society back in. In 1988, Polish dissident Adam Michnik gave voice to the struggle against the totalitarian state by civil society: "From the official point of view a civil society doesn't exist. Society is not recognized as capable of organizing itself to defend its particular interests and points of view.... The crucial problem is therefore to build a democratic society which renders totalitarianism impossible by altering the social mechanisms of power." And in his remarkable *Making Democracy Work* (1993), Robert Putnam found that civil society was the best explanation for successful democratic government: "Building social capital will not be easy, but it is the key to making democracy work."

Still, many writers and researchers on philanthropy and the nonprofit sector were eager to subsume civil society and philanthropy under the welfare state (though the theory works for any state regardless of adjective). For instance, in *Shifting the Debate* (1987), the authors stipulated that "the nonprofit sector is a dependent sector." This was less a topic for discussion and debate but was simply "the starting point for any serious consideration of the place of nonprofits in the American polity." Authors such as Lester Salamon developed theories for the dependence of philanthropy on government. Their phraseology biased and sanitized such politically slippery terms as voluntary failure, interdependence, and partnership.

These were complex positions that deserved credit and scrutiny — except that many of these writers didn't really countenance critical thinking from alternative viewpoints. A broader conversation was simply avoided by labeling all criticisms as a "reactionary political agenda" and "mythical." I, on the contrary, worried that their kind of political correctness was forcing philanthropy into the fold for state purposes; *that* was deeply reactionary. But this discussion was never full-throated and always adumbrated.

A Commonwealth of Citizenship Outside the State

One of the problems of exploring the contrast between civil society and the state (government) is how to measure it. There are measures for economic vitality and growth that are very important. But if philanthropy writ large is such an important part of civil society, shouldn't we be able to find reasonable proxies to measure and compare it? The third article in Chapter 2 looks at whether different concepts of citizenship can be helpful here.

When asked, most people will describe good citizenship as voting and participation in the political process. Whatever its virtues, it is a limited, passive idea of citizenship. There is another way to think about citizenship that is embedded in and supportive of civil society. The extent to which individuals volunteer and give — that is, the extent of philanthropy — may be a more active, engaged, and robust way that we discharge our responsibilities as citizens. The contrast is between political citizenship as voting, and social citizenship as seen through philanthropy. That difference can help us understand why it is so crucial to support, protect, and expand philanthropy and civil society, as indeed Robert Putnam discovered in his classic work on Italy. Perhaps "a commonwealth of citizenship outside the state" does strongly impact the vitality of political citizenship — you can't have the second without the first. Or, to put it differently, perhaps a hobbled or decaying civil society is a warning about a forthcoming crack-up of political citizenship and the deterioration of democracy. The questions and issues raised by such a contrast are fascinating and, in our current time, deeply troubling. They could also suggest roads to recovery.

The Practice of Philanthropy

Section Two shifts gears and focuses on the wondrous and messy practice of philanthropy — where practice is never perfect. Here the use of the term philanthropy is narrower and primarily about issues affecting giving, foundations, and donors, as well as the impact of this on the whole nonprofit community and its practice. For several decades I was employed as a foundation philanthropoid, a philanthropic advisor, and was also a small donor. A series of twenty-five articles look at some of the key issues and challenges I saw.

Hubris is endemic to the field. It has — to borrow one wag's wonderful phrase — no natural enemy in philanthropy. It is also often confused with leadership, because, I suppose, one believes one knows best and wishes to promote or otherwise prove we know best. Robert Greenleaf nicely sets leadership apart from hubris: "The servant-leader is servant first.... It begins with the natural feeling that one wants to serve, to serve first. Then conscious choice brings one to aspire to lead." For instance, for all the hype and even potential of strategic philanthropy, I have seen it sully intelligence and good intentions. Several articles in Chapter 3 address this. A greatly revised article takes a look back at, and forward from, a 2009 effort of NYC Mayoral leadership. What city leadership there was reflected badly on the lack of leadership from philanthropy and nonprofits. There was so little understanding, listening, and communication between the three of them that even the city's efforts were not very wholehearted or successful. It is chastening to look back.

Other articles cover such topics as capacity building for foundations, how philanthropy can tell its story well, and how it can be improved. The issue of foundation payout, perpetuity, and endowment spend out are recurrent quandaries. Decisions about them have a huge and underappreciated impact on foundation success and impact. The unintended consequences of decisions regarding them merited particular attention in several articles, as does the importance of aligning payout decisions with mission and investment policies.

The long history of the purported holy — and gold — grail from the current intergenerational transfer of wealth is not just about numbers. It has big implications for showing that philanthropy can do more. It looks like the hand-wringing that the philanthropic purse is too small is misplaced. The funds can be raised if nonprofits and philanthropy (1) communicate better cases for support; (2) listen more carefully to donors; (3) talk to donors about individual and social values while deemphasizing taxes; and (4) know how effective and efficient their organizations and programs are. A new article in Chapter 5 summarizes the "making" of and values behind the inter-generational transfer phenomenon.

Governance and board responsibilities are touched on in several articles, though the topic deserves so much more. My experience is that boards largely determine whether an organization succeeds or is a magnet for screw-ups.

Finally, I look past the different limiting political connotations that the phrase "donor intent" has accumulated. Used thoughtfully, a donor's intent can be a very important "helping hand" for family foundations that want to build and model a philanthropic legacy. Or it can become a disastrous cudgel in the hands of some overreaching donors and the eyes of some supersensitive successive generations. Importantly, a focus on donor intent and philanthropic legacy also improves accountability and impact.

About These Articles

This book is comprised of thirty-three articles, academic papers, and reviews. They were written on and off over approximately thirty years. They are largely presented as originally published in different publications and venues. Several articles have been combined for this volume. Since I was trying to work through different issues in different ways, there is repetition between articles. Five articles are greatly expanded and essentially new. Most of the articles have been lightly edited from the originals. Certain formatting and style issues were made consistent. I made sentences and points clearer, made corrections, and noted other reference materials. In a few pieces, the urge to revise got the better of me. I added material to address what seemed to be a major lacuna in the originals. The source notes at the end of each article indicate if significant editing was done. Some of these articles should have been updated, expanded, or even combined. Alas, that just isn't possible.

Personal Rationale

In 1957, William Faulkner was asked what a writer wants. He answered: "[T]he day will come when he must pass through the wall of oblivion, and he wants to leave a scratch on that wall." Just so; this collection is a scratch on that wall. It is made up of a series of "unfinished excursions" with a pattern of thought to all of it. For me, rereading the articles is like reading thirty-three pieces of a one-hundred-piece puzzle. On some issues, my views have changed a great deal in the intervening years. New issues enthrall and perplex me. (Philip Pearlstein once wrote, "Lucky artists are the ones who hook onto a problem beyond solution.")

My career in philanthropy and board service, a joyful addiction to books, the challenges of history and ideas, and my family and friends above all represent whatever legacy I may leave. This collection stands alone and puts my career, efforts, and contributions in a larger context. In his *Journals*, Thoreau wrote, "Every man thus tracks himself through life, in all his hearing and reading and observations and traveling. His observations make a chain." This volume somehow completes a life's circle for me.

Finally, then, I hope I have added to the body of work on the value of civil society and the practice of philanthropy. Most of all, I hope that some readers will be moved to use my narrow shoulders to do much better work of their own — in both words and deeds. Most of all, though, I hope these pieces encourage readers to turn to the ideas and authors I have learned so much from, and to learn from them, just as I do still.

Fini and Relevance

The ideas of civil society ebb and flow in the intellectual consciousness, but they remain more enlightening than ever. I am reminded of the sly — and serious — comment by André Gide: "Everything that needs to be said has already been said. But since no one was listening, everything must be said again."

So it is that the relevance of these ideas struck me anew when I read William Galston's fine 2018 work, *Anti-Pluralism: The Populist Threat to Liberal Democracy*. I have not met Galston, but he is always thoughtful, tolerant, and rational. I don't always agree with him, but in such a truly trying period as we find ourselves, one could not have a better intellectual companion.

He begins his book noting that: "In just twenty-five years, the partisans of liberal democracy have moved from triumphalism to near despair." He seeks a way out from two unsatisfactory alternatives: "illiberal democracy" or "undemocratic liberalism." I agree that we certainly are in an age of closed-minded elitism and closed-minded populism. We are, it seems, institutionalizing the onset of friendly fascism.

Yet his sensible approach as to why we are in this predicament and how we might revive liberalism and democracy are missing something. He identifies "the tension between politics and markets" as the most enduring problem of liberal democracy. That is surely a problem, but not, it seems to me, the problem.

On the one hand, the book's focus tends to be constrained by what is euphemistically called public policy. The problem was nicely phrased in an interesting critique of English think tanks that Noel Malcolm wrote in a

1991 issue of *The Spectator*: "Their most valuable effect of policy has been long-term and indirect.... The best achievements of the think tanks seem to come about when they are not trying to do the Government's work for it: once they start trying to find new solutions to the Government's problems, they start seeing things through the Government's own narrow viewfinder." There is a sense in which the arguments in *Anti-Pluralism* are too narrowly envisioned inside politics.

As a result, on the other hand, Galston does not engage the ideas and experiences of civil society: that "commonwealth of citizenship outside the state," in Frank Prochaska's felicitous phrase. Instead, civil society doesn't play much of a part in his diagnosis or treatment plan. What is necessary to ensure the vitality of civil society and not make it prone to festering? Does political populism go bad as civil society loses both its independence and robustness? Does populism also drain civil society of its flexibility, dynamism, and pluralism? And what role can — must? — civil society play in a revived liberal democracy? There are no easy answers here, but I would have valued Galston's analysis. I wondered how his analysis might have been different if there had been a chapter on the relevance of civil society.

This lacuna is uncharacteristic of much of Galston's work. Over the years, he has often added to our understanding of how civil society contributes to the problems and solutions of democracy. (Movingly, his book is dedicated to Vaclav Havel and Liu Xiaobo, two heroes for civil society in both their writings and actions.) And he participated in crafting the November 2018 American Charter of Freedom of Religion and Conscience, at a time when free speech, tolerance, and dialogue are attacked by both government and groups within civil society. The Charter is a meaningful expression from civil society. As Galston pointed out, "the public dimension of religion and conscience risks entangling the two with the state, to the potential detriment of both government and religious integrity. Averting this risk requires government to minimize its involvement...." He highlights the key roles that both civil society and government must play to balance competing rights and safeguard basic liberties of religion and conscience. The civil society part is largely missing in the book.

But Galston does hint that his political focus may be limiting: "Realism demands more than a narrow focus on the political order within which individuals can pursue their self-interest." That seems very right to me. He then ends his book with Lincoln's challenge from his 1862 Annual Message to Congress: "The dogmas of the quiet past are inadequate to the stormy present.... As our case is new, so we must think anew, and act anew. We must disenthrall ourselves.... We cannot escape history."

Perhaps we must disenthrall ourselves from the limiting focus on politics. In closing, then, I am reminded of Gene Sharp's comment in *Social*

Power and Political Freedom which was reviewed here: "If we are not to become helpless political automatons, or to be annihilated, we must find and implement effective means of control over the power of rulers.... We must deliberately act in ways which strengthen the non-State institutions of our society, and consciously refrain from increasing the concentration of effective power in the State." Surely seeing more broadly with the lenses of civil society is relevant, indeed necessary.

A Reader's Crib Sheet

These thirty-three articles, academic papers, and reviews were written on and off over approximately thirty years for different audiences and different purposes. Ten are new or essentially so. The topics range widely, and there are, inevitably, numerous repetitions.

Perhaps it would be helpful, then, to provide a personal list of what I consider the more interesting and helpful articles in this long book. Article numbers in bold below indicate new or greatly expanded articles.

Depending on the reader's goals, this list may help you focus and get into the topics of most interest.

Section One — The Value of Civil Society
Chapter 1, Civil Society: The Ties That Bind – articles **1, 2,** and **3**
Chapter 2, Bringing Civil Society Back In – articles 1, 2, and 3

Section Two — The Practice of Philanthropy
Chapter 3, The Hubris of Philanthropy – articles **1** and 2
Chapter 4, Notes on Philanthropic Practice – articles **1**, 3, and 5
Chapter 5, The Intergenerational Transfer of Wealth – article **1**
Chapter 6, The Payout Question – articles 2, 3, and 4
Chapter 7, Governance Matters – articles **1** and **2**
Chapter 8, Philanthropy and the State – article 1
Chapter 9, Donor Intent, Legacy, and Impact – articles **2** and **3**

SECTION ONE

THE VALUE OF CIVIL SOCIETY

Civil society is that set of diverse non-governmental institutions which is strong enough to counterbalance the state and, while not preventing the state from fulfilling its role of keeper of the peace and arbitrator between major interests, can nevertheless prevent it from dominating and atomizing the rest of society.... Civil society has at the very least two contrasts, and so its essence cannot be seized with the help of a merely bi-polar opposition between pluralism and monocentrism. We must try to understand that which we have suddenly discovered we possess and value. Many of us in the West took it for granted (some still do), as a kind of normal human condition, while those in the East learnt to love it more ardently by being so thoroughly deprived of it, and by seeing the utter falsity of the faith which declared it to be redundant and fraudulent. But we need to know just what it is we love. We can only identify it through characterizing the full variety of its historical contrasts. — Ernest Gellner

The experience of democratic orders has demonstrated that the antithesis between the state's monopoly of power and civil society's private associations must be maintained if democracy is not to degenerate into anarchy or dictatorship. — Reinhard Bendix

One of the characteristics of this world of associations is, of course, that if you are brought up in it and it surrounds you, it becomes invisible. Associationalism is now so "natural" to the British and Americans that it seems to need no explanation, and it would hardly be such peoples who discovered the power of association. It tends to be those who have lost or have weakly developed associationalism who first notice its importance.... Democracy, liberty, equality, and wealth all have their roots in this common, largely invisible, bed of associations. — Alan Macfarlane

CHAPTER 1

CIVIL SOCIETY: THE TIES THAT BIND

Civil society is a phrase with much resonance but little content; we have to put the meaning in. — Zhang Zhilian

The idea of a civil society — even one that avoids overtly political activities in favor of education, the exchange of information and opinion, or the protection of the basic interests of particular groups — has enormous antitotalitarian potential.... We must ask whether the idea of a civil society — however effective it was in helping to bring down communism — will turn out to be useless in the building of democracy. I do not think that it will.... In the end, a robust civil society offers the best prospects for overcoming the divergence of state and society and bringing citizens into active engagement with public life. Only under such conditions can democracy be made secure. — Bronislaw Geremek

What must be in the space between individuals and the state are mediating organizations. Their existence will not guarantee the presence of a satisfactory civil society, but their absence guaranties its absence. — Anne Firor Scott

T his chapter introduces a theme — in six tidbits — running throughout this collection: that civil society and philanthropy are intimately connected. I have always thought that they are immensely valuable ways for thinking about and making sense of society, freedom, and the state. What Frank Prochaska alludes to about civil society applies as well to philanthropy: "Civil society is among the most fertile, if amorphous, concepts in history, for it deals with the possibilities of sociability and the boundaries of politics." For definitions, let us start with

> *Civil society*: "social institutions such as markets and voluntary associations and a public sphere which are outside that direct control, in a full or in a mitigated sense, of the state." — Víctor M. Pérez-Díaz

> *Philanthropy*: "a comprehensive term that includes voluntary giving, voluntary service, and voluntary association." — Robert L. Payton

A short review introduces the idea of civil society. Other brief articles discuss aspects of the history of philanthropy. I suggest a more robust idea of citizenship coming from civil society and philanthropy. And I consider how the important work of Gene Sharp (on nonviolent action) and Elinor Ostrom (on voluntary governance) enrich our understanding of how civil society and philanthropy work.

Thomas Paine's *Common Sense* in 1776 was "the first political essay in modern times to make and defend the distinction ... between civil society and the state," as one biographer noted. That distinction has been valued and contested since then.

In the 1970s and 1980s civil society reappeared: a valuable perspective used by American social commentators and by Eastern European dissidents. Philanthropy blossomed, perhaps a bit aimlessly. Alas, as the politicization of society reasserted itself, these two realities may have lost some of their earlier attention and luster. But I continue to believe that civil society and philanthropy provide remarkable lens by which to "see" social reality. They can together largely redeem the enduring values of liberalism through, and its emphasis on, individual liberty and voluntary cooperation.

1. The Idea of Civil Society

The idea of civil society gained historical immediacy in the two decades before this review of Adam Seligman's *The Idea of Civil Society* was originally published. The turmoil around the breakup and search for an alternative to communism in the 1970s through the 1980s reverberated through the world.[1] The Reagan years led many to wonder, Is that it? Is that the best we can do? Ironically, each failure highlighted aspects of the same problem: that humanity cannot be perfected through government, no matter what kind of government. Many scholars and policy analysts started saying once again that government cannot solve all problems.

On the one hand, we can see that the progressive politicization of society causes cascading layers of government failure: from the inefficient, annoying, and deeply invasive, to more tragic and bloody circumstances.[2] On the other hand, the idea of an alternative has always been in the "ether" of recent policy thinking. See, for instance the original 1977 and 1996 twentieth-anniversary editions of *To Empower People*.[3] They straddle the 1994 publication of the book reviewed here. What, then, is an alternative sphere of human action to which we can repair?

"Civil society" is an inviting term that can help us think about these issues. It is vaguely classic, properly amorphous, and, well, civil. Not political in the usual sense, nor individualistic, nor communalist. It also has a very long and deep tradition in the historical and political economy literature. We still need to appreciate and understand the language, history, and possibilities of civil society. Many years ago, Polish dissident Adam Michnik presented the dilemma that still applies today:

> The problem faced by Polish society is that from the official point of view a civil society doesn't exist. Society is not recognized as capable of organizing itself to defend its particular interests and points of view.[4]

Civil society is simply the arena of voluntary action. It encompasses a myriad of institutions both formal and informal — churches, schools, businesses, voluntary associations, communities, clubs, and so forth — where people pursue their individual and common goals: moral, spiritual, and material. The modern condition, writes Adam Seligman, is characterized by "a fundamental crisis of representing society."[5] What binds society together? he asks. And how do we "constitute a sense of community among and between social actors?" (p. 204). This is one of the most basic questions in the broader social sciences, and one that bedevils us still. Innumerable commentators have reflected upon how to organize life and conceptualize the social order: how to reconcile, yet again, the political and the social/economic, the private and public, the individual and communal, the egoistic and altruistic.

In the first few chapters, the author provides a "clear exposition of the developing idea of civil society, its historical antecedents, the social context of its emergence and transformation (in the eighteenth and nineteenth centuries), and its continuing relevance to the problems and crises of modern existence" (p. 4).

However, one of the best, nuanced views of civil society is in Víctor M. Pérez-Díaz's fine history of post-Franco Spain, *The Return of Civil Society*. It is worth quoting at some length because he defines two meanings of civil society, which give a dynamic sense to historical experience. In a narrow sense, civil society represents:

> Social institutions such as markets and voluntary associations and a public sphere which are outside the direct control, in a full or in a mitigated sense, of the state.

The development and emergence of civil society in this sense prepares the way for and strengthens an overall more robust sense of civil society and the body politic, including the state and government. The further value of this broader definition is that it places civil society in some sense prior to and necessary for a sociopolitical society of liberal democracy, free markets, and open discourse. This larger sense entails:

> A set of sociopolitical institutions including a limited government or state operating under the rule of law; a set of social institutions such as markets (or spontaneous extended orders) and associations based on voluntary agreements among autonomous agents; and a public sphere in which these agents debate among themselves and with the state about matters of public interest and engage in pubic activities.[6]

Seligman takes on the idea of civil society in several ways. There are hints of a coherent meaning and development of the idea if one reads carefully. First, the author gives a selective summary of the intellectual tradition that has brought civil society to the twentieth century. He starts with Grotius and the important natural law tradition. John Locke is a fleeting, transitional figure. The author is quite right to move on quickly to the Scottish Enlightenment of Francis Hutcheson, Adam Ferguson, and Adam Smith. With them the idea of civil society becomes firmly grounded.

Adam Ferguson, in his 1767 classic *An Essay on the History of Civil Society*, establishes civil society as the modern social change away from barbarism. The ancient assumption that political participation in the polis was everything and individual action nothing no longer held. Not only was society based on individuals, but it didn't need a visible hand organizing, controlling, and forming everything. There was, by contrast, a natural human propensity for voluntary cooperation and social development, imperfect though it was always held to be. Civil society was, in Ferguson's famous phrase, "the result of human action, but not the execution of any human design." As Kant made perfectly clear later, civil society was not merely the realm of economic interests. It fully incorporated the moral individuality of mankind.

Seligman goes on to mention, but fails to develop, two opposing traditions that follow from the Scottish Enlightenment view of civil society. The first rests on Hegel. Deeply influenced by the Scottish Enlightenment, Hegel clearly established private ownership of property and the marketplace as preeminent features of civil society. Many have also argued that, with Hegel and certainly Marx, civil society lost a relatively independent image and was ultimately folded back into political society. Later in the nineteenth century, various ideas of citizenship further trivialized the idea of civil society. Citizenship came to be encompassed more and more within the narrowing confines of political participation (is voting really the sole criterion for good citizenship?). It thereby served to institutionalize "the idea of civil society in the polity."

A more distinctly sociological and historical tradition was built upon the work of Tocqueville, Durkheim, and Weber. It emphasized the fluid separation of the idea of civil society as a complex of autonomous and voluntary institutions from the idea of the political, as state and government. This was not just theoretical musing. The United States was an exceptional example of this perspective, as Tocqueville famously knew:

> Americans of all ages, all stations in life, and all types of disposition are forever forming associations.... They can do hardly anything for themselves, and none of them is in a position to force his fellows to help him. They would all therefore find themselves helpless if they did not learn to help each other voluntarily.[7]

As one reads on in Seligman's book, however, the reader might easily become confused about the notion of civil society. The author concludes that his book is "an argument on the inadequacy of the idea of civil society" (p. 199); that indeed "the concept of civil society seems to add little to existing ideas of democracy or of citizenship" (p. 203). I don't see that. It is not at all clear why that is, except that he clearly views civil society as necessarily subsumed under the political, precisely the tragedy that Michnik warned about above. My own sense is that the author also became bollixed up in his own biases as he covered much too much ground with much too much academic jargon and theorizing. What is one to make, for instance, of a sentence such as this: "The institutionalization of civil society in terms of citizenship implied the representation of society in terms of the workings of a universal-abstract reason, which, in the public realm, was embodied in the idea of universal citizenship" (pp. 145–146). He mangles any conceptual and historical essence that the notion of civil society may have.

Perhaps most important, he doesn't "see" the value of the idea of civil society for understanding historical experience and the value of voluntary action by itself for addressing the human predicament. Since Aristotle's pronouncement that "man is a political animal," there has been a tendency for anything outside of the "political" to be invisible: to assume that anything "social" can only work under the direction of the political. Seligman seems intent upon placing civil society within the procrustean bed of politics.

There has always been an uneasy relationship of independence, mutual antagonism, and dependence between state and society in theory and practice. Boundaries blur. But the two are different, relying at least on different means. It had been a common, albeit largely lost, tradition to "see" beyond the political and the state. That tradition gives clear standing to civil society. For instance, Daniel Boorstin observed that "in America, even in modern times, communities existed before governments were here to care for public needs."[8] It was common to see the institutions of civil society and the political state as largely independent. A limited rule of law was essential, but intrusions into how people peacefully pursued their moral values and their economic interests were destructive of progress and civilization. As George Unwin observed in his *Studies in Economic History*: "The expansion of England in the seventeenth century was an expansion of society and not of the State. Society expanded to escape from the pressure of the State."[9]

While the American exceptionalism expressed by Boorstin and often attributed to Tocqueville may be comforting, it diminishes the truly radical and rich universality of associational life that has too often existed under the radar. Earlier observers like Jean-Baptiste Say and Max Weber noted this. The "*corps intermédiaires*" of Montesquieu and the "little platoons" of Burke have too often been ignored or belittled in the East and West. The local, informal, slow-acting — and sometimes messy — actual workings of civil society institutions make them invisible. And there is a wealth of historical work that is rediscovering civil society.[10] In recent decades, efforts by people in central Europe, the former Soviet Union, China, and innumerable other countries are trying to fill the vacuum of corrupt polities and failed states that have systematically destroyed most elements of civil society — except the church in some countries. Nationalism and ethnic violence have become a favored, and disastrous, way to fill the void. In the West, civil society has been ignored in favor of an unstable amalgam of extreme individualism and a modern version of the ancient polis on a national scale. Sadly, the highly touted "partnership" of the nonprofit sector and government has obscured the progressive politicization of society.[11] And that is no answer to our societal problems.

Seligman was quite right that these problems have risen to crisis proportions: even more so now. This is not evidence, however, that "the idea of civil society itself becomes the problem rather than the solution of modern existence" (p. 198). On the contrary, these difficulties make thinking about things in terms of civil society even more important. Doing so presents no panaceas, but it is illuminating. Beyond the historical record, for example, there is a rich tradition of contemporary thinkers who have written within the tradition of civil society. A very few examples might prove to be useful starting points, such as Robert Putnam (*Bowling Alone*); Michael Oakeshott (*Rationalism in Politics*), with his brilliant discussion of civil association; Robert Nisbet (*The Quest for Community*), with his emphasis on the dangers of individualism out of touch with intermediate institutions; Edward Shils (*The Virtue of Civility*), with his development of the idea of civility and a focus on our common collective self-consciousness; and James C. Scott (*Seeing Like the State*), with his remarkable critique of simply "seeing like a state."

If the ancient polis, a leviathan, or individualism can neither free nor perfect humanity, where does one go? Our modern condition remains what every "modern" condition has been since at least Adam Ferguson's time. The ties that bind people must be both voluntary and political, incorporating civil society and the state. But there is a delicate balance to it all. Indeed, civil society may arguably be the key to holding back the growth of authoritarian states of whatever political hue, even especially in a democracy such as ours is supposed to be. Political participation (political freedom) is necessary, but it is far from sufficient. It seems nearly incontrovertible in our time that too great an extension of the political is self-defeating. The idea (lens) of civil society is much more important than Seligman believe.

Of course, these two traditions of "seeing" social activities remain with us. The blurring of the distinction between the political (the state and government) and society effectively makes the idea of civil society disappear from public discourse. Perhaps its voluntary methods are not only messy and frustrating. They may hold great promise in helping society and individuals flourish and limiting authoritarian impulses of whatever political kind.

Throwing out or subsuming civil society impoverishes out thinking and our solutions to society's problems. Additional consideration of the history and concept of civil society is desperately needed.

This review has been revised and expanded somewhat for this volume. It was originally published in The American Scholar, *Winter 1994, as a review of* The Idea of Civil Society, *by Adam Seligman (New York: The Free Press, 1992). Reprinted here by permission of* The American Scholar.

---

[1] See Daniel Siegel and Jenny Yancey, *The Rebirth of Civil Society* (New York: The Rockefeller Brothers Fund, 1992) and *The Idea of Civil Society* (Durham: National Humanities Center, 1992).

[2] See, for instance, Kenneth Templeton, editor, *The Politicization of Society* (Indianapolis: Liberty Press, 1979).

[3] Peter Berger and Richard John Neuhaus, *To Empower People: From State to Civil Society* (Washington, DC: American Enterprise Institute, 1996). This expanded twentieth-anniversary edition includes twelve new contributors to the original 1977 version.

[4] Adam Michnik, "Towards a Civil Society: Hopes for Polish Democracy," *Times Literary Supplement*, February 19–25, 1988, p. 188.

[5] Adam Seligman, *The Idea of Civil Society* (New York: The Free Press, 1992). p. 57. Subsequent pages numbers are in the text.

[6] Víctor M. Pérez-Díaz, *The Return of Civil Society* (Cambridge: Harvard University Press, 1993), pp. 57 and 53.

[7] Alexis de Tocqueville, *Democracy in America*, translated by George Lawrence (New York: Harper and Row, 1966), pp. 485–486.

[8] Daniel J. Boorstin, *The Decline of Radicalism: Reflections on America Today* (New York: Random House, 1963), p. 46.

[9] George Unwin, *Studies in Economic History* (London: Macmillan and Co., 1927), p. 341.

[10] Alas, here is not the place to begin a bibliography. I would merely mention Geoffrey Finlayson, *Citizen, State, and Social Welfare in Britain* (Oxford: Oxford University Press, 1994), which is reviewed later in this volume; Peter Clark, *British Clubs and Societies: 1580–1800* (Oxford: Oxford University Press, 2000), on England; Robert Putnam, *Making Democracy Work* (Princeton: Princeton University Press, 1993), on Italy, also reviewed in this volume; David Beito, *From Mutual Aid to the Welfare State* (Chapel Hill: The University of North Carolina Press, 2000), on the U.S.

[11] See, for instance, my paper in this volume, "Of Voluntary Failure and Change."

2. A Nobel Prize for Civil Society: Elinor Ostrom Shows the Way

A few words about the 2009 Nobel Prize and its continuing importance to philanthropy and for civil society. No, this isn't about the 2009 Peace Prize to President Obama, which may have been a timely, but alas a fraying and momentary reminder of the value of hope.

By contrast, the 2009 Nobel Prize in Economic Science recognizes something more important: insights of considerable real-world relevance to the philanthropic enterprise. It was awarded to Dr. Elinor Ostrom[1] for her decades of groundbreaking research on "economic governance": demonstrating how ordinary people do create useful, enduring rules, and a plethora of voluntary institutions that enable a sustainable and equitable management of shared resources. This is the essence of a robust civil society.

Over the years, several different foundations have funded her research, which has been encouraging. Too much of the intellectual and practical policy relevance of her remarkable work has escaped the notice of practitioners. Her insights could significantly change the way we do things.

I first wrote about Ostrom's work when the 2009 Nobel Prize was announced. Ten years on and its importance is even greater. Ostrom's window on human action can help philanthropy shed some of its hubris and redirect some of its emphasis and resources. Her work can reinvigorate the voluntary sector's ability to devise viable, diverse, and humane approaches to otherwise intractable problems — in other words, to help the institutions of civil society flourish. This is an opportunity to recalibrate much of philanthropy. Four elements of her work stand out here.

Active Citizens Can Manage

Much of Ostrom's work elucidates the Tocquevillian and classical liberal insights about the value and efficacy of active citizens and their voluntary associations. It is interesting to see how Ostrom's vast empirical oeuvre is so grounded in such vigorous, wide-ranging intellectual traditions. These insights are contrary to the all-too-common, implicit and explicit views among policy analysts and philanthropoids that citizens are really "only passive consumers of political life." Referring to how policy analysis is usually taught, she further notes, "We have robbed citizens of almost any kind of active political life in our textbook renditions of democracy other than going to the polls."[2] Despite protestations to the contrary, this bias unwittingly imbues much of what philanthropy tries to do with a hubris about and hidden disdain for people actually "muddling through" their own challenges of collective action (to use Charles Lindblom's wonderful phrase).[3]

Some may object that philanthropy has a long history of supporting grassroots activity. True and to be applauded. Many of these efforts are misplaced, however. First, too much of that activity has gone to corralling support for external government interventions, or a "corporatist economy," to use Edmund Phelps' terms for "a system in which the business sector is under some kind of political control."[4] Whatever the ideological goals, these programs in the end rely on and encourage citizen passivity. This is not empowerment. Second, too little has been done to support — and too much to thwart — local knowledge and local institution building. They are messy and often don't conform to preconceived models, but they succeed as Ostrom's work has amply demonstrated.

Ostrom's many grassroots empirical studies have focused on how people peacefully organize themselves to manage "the commons": common property and resources. The conventional wisdom is that common property will be poorly managed, so it must either be regulated by central authorities or privatized. In her groundbreaking 1990 book *Governing the Commons*, and in her subsequent work, Ostrom has empirically shown us that there is a third way, in addition to markets and government. What does this mean? Civil society or the independent sector can successfully address many more challenges than given credit for.

It turns out that in many different contexts common resources can be and are managed successfully through robust voluntary institutions and often sophisticated rules devised by those very individuals who use and have — often conflicting — stakes in preserving the resource. Cases come from around the world, such as fisheries, forests, pastures, lakes, lobster grounds, and water resources. For instance, private property is the norm for farmlands in a Swiss village, but the pastureland has been managed as common property for hundreds of years. There are lands in Japan held by thousands in common. Successful examples also include ancient communal irrigation systems, modern water systems, and community property forests.

These solutions to common resource problems are not merely small-scale possibilities for certain environmental issues. These phenomena have broader, larger-scale implications encompassing the complexity and challenges of social life and the third sector: "Problems of the commons exist in a wide variety of settings ranging in size and complexity from the family (e.g., the household budget and kitchen sink) to the global scale (e.g., loss of biodiversity and global warming)."[5]

It turns out that common resource or property situations are — pardon the pun — quite common. It turns out that this third sector, this civil society, can often develop more successful approaches than government or the market.

Not all commons issues can be managed successfully in these ways, of course. There are real tragedies where managing common resources leads to overuse and degradation. Private solutions and government efforts certainly have their place and they can bring on their own large-scale tragedies. But there are also many successful alternatives to the usual stale, elitist solutions that are proffered by most policy wonks and foundations of all stripes.

Towards the end of *Governing the Commons*, Ostrom writes: "if this study does nothing more than shatter the convictions of many policy analysts that the only way to solve common pool resource problems is for external authorities to impose full private property or centralized regulation, it will have accomplished one major purpose."[6] Her work demonstrates that civil society or the third sector has its own, independent methods worth cultivating. Philanthropy's shift to greater understanding, experimentation, and funding of these truly voluntary approaches would yield more robust, citizen-centric approaches and even better institutional solutions.

Going Beyond Panaceas

The search for "panaceas" blinds policy thinking from looking deeply at how people can solve their problems and how philanthropy can really help. Ostrom's work is a trenchant critique of that kind of intellectual hubris: the belief "that universal institutional panaceas must be imposed by external authorities to solve small-scale, but still complex, uncertain, and difficult, problems."[7] It is a hubris, starkly, that assumes human actions are stupid and experts are prescient. It seems to be a natural human tendency to find and impose unitary solutions to the diverse challenges of society, all inimical to a robust civil society. In a 2002 article titled "Policy Analysis in the Future of Good Societies," Ostrom writes eloquently about the need to "overcome our addiction to overly simple solutions to complex problems."[8] As she and a co-author wrote in *The Encyclopedia of Earth*:

> It is difficult to craft successful, sustainable and robust local institutional arrangements by imposing of rules from external authorities or through the influx of funds from external agencies. Unfortunately, many policy analysts have not recognized this problem. All too often, analysts enthusiastically propose blueprint, cookie-cutter approaches to community conservation. These approaches are based on relatively simple, even somewhat simplistic models, of what they consider to be "community" management applied across multiple contexts.[9]

This search for simple conceptual and institutional panaceas infects the halls of foundations as much as it does academia. And philanthropic dollars make the conceit even more dangerous. The penchant for building logic models is a perfect example of how philanthropy can revel in being out of touch with reality. Indeed, to borrow wonderful wording used by Tony Proscio in a different context, the constant search and presentation of panaceas seems still to have "thrived most spectacularly in the groves of philanthropy — pastures in which, evidently, the word has no natural predators and so can multiply at will."[10]

Philanthropy is often too eager to "do" something rather than "understand" something: to "get on with it"; to outline a "rational logic model" that may not be grounded in real life; and to go directly to imposing a solution. In this understandable but overwrought eagerness, the processes of diagnosis, monitoring, and learning this third way are severely short-changed in philanthropic thinking and actions. Thus, intellectual constructs and institutional procrustean beds are imposed from outside and above, impoverishing civil society and the people and institutions that make real change (and have to live with externally imported "solutions").

In my experience, philanthropy as a field doesn't really do a good job of listening or supporting people "muddling through" to their own solutions. When one has money and therefore power, it is too easy to be self-important and revel in the faux-brilliance attributed to you by supplicants. I am not suggesting that this is the fault of grantees, for we encourage this. (I remember that when I took my first job as a foundation executive director, an experienced nonprofit leader took me aside and said, "That is great, Chuck. And remember, this is the last time you will ever tell a bad joke, get a bad meal, or get an honest compliment." With rare exceptions, he was right!)

We need to do a better job of developing and testing a richer set of policy ideas, encouraging a more diverse discussion, and then supporting the discovery process that can lead to viable solutions developed within civil society.

Embracing Institutional Diversity and Not Government Failure

"Diversity" is a term one often finds in Ostrom's work. Engaging different perspectives is critical to studying and celebrating "the diversity of institutional arrangements that humans have crafted to cope effectively with different settings and problems."[11] Social problems are usually complex, dynamic, contentious, and not solved by a retreat to omniscience, logic models, or canned panaceas. Yet the natural penchant of policy wonks and philanthropoids of all stripes is to assume government holds the means for solutions to nearly all problems. It becomes the end; it is the "go-to" refuge when complexity gets in the way. Ostrom quotes at length cognitive and behavioral economist Robert Sugden's view of this intellectual procrustean bed:

Most modern economic theory describes a world presided over by a government (not, significantly, by governments), and sees this world through the government's eyes. The government is supposed to have the responsibility, the will, and the power to restructure society in whatever way maximizes social welfare; like the US Cavalry in a good Western, the government stands ready to rush to the rescue whenever the market "fails," and the economist's job is to advise it on when and how to do so. Private individuals, in contrast, are credited with little or no ability to solve collective problems among themselves. This makes for a distorted view of some important economic and political issues.[12]

Failures of government, markets, and the voluntary sector are often real. Perhaps the larger, systemic failure is this assumption that all things must and can be solved by government. As Ostrom noted of one analyst's views, "the only policy actor she sees as being relevant is the amorphous, fictitious, and omnicompetent entity called 'the government.'"[13]

This tends to be all too common in the halls, minds, and actions of philanthropy and the nonprofit sector. Much of the literature about the third sector contains a conceptual haze (it almost seems like a smokescreen at times), going back decades. The literature still presents the state looming large as a puppet master. We see that in Jon Van Til's early work *Mapping the Third Sector* and Lester Salamon's important *Partners in Public Service*.[14] The vaunted "partnership" language between government and voluntary sector interactions is rarely and unevenly a partnership. What we see is that much work on the nonprofit sector is an effort to subsume civil society under a government weltanschauung. When that is the only way one can conceive of the sector, alternative institutions and solutions are invisible. As important, they are not funded or supported in their efforts to grow and learn. This is put very well by Beresford and Croft when they acknowledge the state's ironic standing with the nonprofit sector: it is "a different kind of intervention.... The state will be involved in organizing, supervising, extending, and even reinterpreting our own self-help."[15] Ostrom's extensive empirical work questions the assumed efficacy of the state's presumed priority. Without eliminating its role when appropriate, it is just that "appropriate" should be earned, tested, and not presumed. Encouraging intellectual and institutional diversity is important.

How Do We Know Things and Resolve Challenges?

A large part of Ostrom's theoretical and empirical work helps provide a better grounding for "our" sector. Her work is different and less politicized.

It is a very sophisticated and empirical understanding of civil society or the third sector. "The presence of order in the world," Ostrom writes, "is largely dependent upon theories used to understand the world. We are not limited, however, to only the conceptions of order derived from the work of Smith [markets] and Hobbes [states]." We need a theory that "offers an alternative that can be used to analyze and prescribe a variety of institutional arrangements to match the extensive variety of collective goods in the world."[16] In this, Ostrom joins a large group of thinkers developing a rationale for a genuine third or nonprofit sector, which is different from market and state.

From philosophy and a wide empirical base, she has made a case for the ways in which knowledge is produced and can be used in civil society. Instead of "seeing like a state," as James C. Scott puts it in his magisterial book, Ostrom shows us that we can see "through" a clear lens of civil society. And to do so truly empowers people and produces creative and flourishing institutional forms that fit the circumstances.

But civil society is not a "thing." Civil society is primarily a different way of seeing social activity in the world, a different way of doing things in the world, and applies different means. That emphasis, without ignoring the relevance of markets and government, make her lesson particularly useful to philanthropy and the future of civil society. As James C. Scott puts it:

> I make the case for the indispensable role of practical knowledge, informal processes, and improvisation in the face of unpredictability: a case for the resilience of both social and national diversity and a strong case for the limits, in principle, of what we are likely to know about complex, functioning order.... Formal schemes of order are untenable without some elements of the practical knowledge that they tend to dismiss.... What has proved to be truly dangerous to us and to our environment, I think, is the combination of the universalist pretensions of epistemic knowledge and authoritarian social engineering.[17]

Nurturing Civil Society

Philanthropy has a special place in American civil society. And yet it has too often ignored or worked against a robust civil society. That is true across the political spectrum, in part because of the assumption that "policy" must entail central models and plans, which requires the state's oversight. Elinor Ostrom's well-deserved Nobel Prize is a welcome reminder of what we should really value in the philanthropic endeavor, and how we can honor and help civil society accomplish more and better. Her research on a third way to resolve common resource issues and her desire for more diversity in the opinions about and solutions to society's challenges reinforce each other. They have allowed her to "see" differently. As she noted in a 2003 interview:

> How can fallible human beings achieve and sustain self-governing entities and self-governing ways of life? ... Self-governing democratic systems are always fragile enterprises. Future citizens need to understand that they participate in the constitutions and reconstitutions of rule-governing polities. And they need to learn the "art and science of associations." If we fail in this, all our investigations and theoretical efforts are useless.[18]

As a thought experiment, consider how different our philanthropy, our programs, and the "solutions" we fund might be if we started thinking and seeing through the lens of civil society and used the tools and means attuned to it that Elinor Ostrom did so much to reveal and explain.

This is a much-expanded version – actually a new article – of one of my contributions to the Smart Assets blog of Philanthropy New York. Originally published November 15, 2009, it is reprinted with permission from Philanthropy New York.

---

[1] Elinor Ostrom is the only woman to win the Nobel Prize in Economic Science. She was a faculty member at Indiana University from 1965, including Professor of Political Science in the College of Arts and Sciences, and professor in the School of Public and Environmental Affairs. In 1973, she co-founded the Workshop in Political Theory and Policy Analysis with her husband, Vincent Ostrom. She served as president of the Public Choice Society from 1982 to 1984 and president of the American Political Science Association from 1996 to 1997. Ostrom was selected as one of the *Time "100 for 2012"* annual list of the world's 100 most influential people. She passed away in June 2012, at the age of 78.

[2] "Policy Analysis in the Future of Good Societies," *The Good Society*, V. 11, No. 1, 2002, p. 46.

[3] See Charles Lindblom's classic, "The Science of 'muddling through'," *Public Administration Review*, Spring 1959. Another valuable work by Lindblom and David K. Cohen is a fine primer on the intellectual humility and empirical rigor in the study of human action that animates Ostrom's work: *Usable Knowledge: Social Science and Social Problems Solving* (New Haven: Yale University Press, 1979.)

[4] Edmund Phelps, *Mass Flourishing: How Grassroots Innovation Created Jobs, Challenge, and Change* (Princeton: Princeton University Press, 2013), pp. 26 and 141.

[5] Elinor Ostrom, "Building Trust to Solve Commons Dilemmas: Taking Small Steps to Test an Evolving Theory," in S. A. Levin, editor, *Games, Groups, and the Global Good* (New York: Springer, 2009), p. 208.

[6] Elinor Ostrom, *Governing the Commons: The Evolution of Institutions for Collective Action* (Cambridge: Cambridge University Press, 1990) p. 182.

[7] *Governing the Commons, op. cit.*, p. 183.

[8] "Policy Analysis in the Future of Good Societies," *op. cit.*, p. 42.

[9] Harini Nagendra and Elinor Ostrom, "Governing the Commons in the New Millennium: A Diversity of Institutions for Natural Resource Management," published in the on-line *Encyclopedia of Earth*, August 12, 2008.

[10] Tony Proscio, *In Other Words: A Plea for Plain Speaking in Foundations* (New York: The Edna McConnell Clark Foundation, 2000), p. 28.

[11] "12 Questions…to Elinor Ostrom", *GAIA*, V. 15, No.4 (2006), p. 246.

[12] Robert Sudgen, *The Economics of Rights, Co-operation, and Welfare*, (Oxford: Blackwell, 1986), p. 3.

[13] *Governing the Commons, op. cit.*, p. 216.

[14] Jon Van Til, *Mapping the Third Sector* (New York: The Foundation Center, 1988), and Lester M. Salamon, *Partners in Public Service* (Baltimore: The John Hopkins University Press, 1995)

[15] Peter Beresford and Suzy Croft, *Whose Welfare?* (Brighton, England: The Lewis Cohen Urban Studies Center at Brighton Polytechnic, 1986), p. 149.

[16] Quoted by Paul Dragos Aligica in "Elinor Ostrom on the Market, the State, and the Third Sector," *Reason*, October 12, 2009.

[17] James C. Scott, *Seeing Like a State: How Certain Schemes to Improve the Human Condition Have Failed* (New Haven: Yale University Press, 1998), pp. 6,7, and 340. Other important works on the value of local knowledge and citizen agency include John McKnight, *The Careless Society: Community and Its Counterfeits* (New York: Basic Books, 1995), and John Kretzmann and John McKnight, *Building Communities From the Inside Out* (Evanston, IL: Asset-Based Community Development Institute, 1993).

[18] Interview with Elinor Ostrom, "Rethinking Governance Systems and Challenging Disciplinary Boundaries," Mercatus Center at George Mason University, 2003.

3. Gene Sharp on Social Power and Political Freedom

Walking through the streets of Hiroshima in 1946, a Japanese soldier muttered, "If only we'd been born in a country, and not a damn-fool state." The quotation is a stark reminder that nuclear war is the ultimate symbol — and reality — of political violence. It also succinctly identifies the key distinction between country (or civil society) and state, which is so central in Gene Sharp's continuingly important 1980 book, *Social Power and Political Freedom*. In my view, it is his most radical book.

Introduction and Personal Note

The original review from which this longer article developed is based was published in 1981. Gene Sharp passed away on January 28, 2018, as I was preparing the essays for this book. I got to know Gene in 1974, when I published a new edition of Étienne de La Boétie's famous work, *The Politics of Obedience: The Discourse of Voluntary Servitude*. La Boétie was a sixteenth-century political philosopher who sagely saw that people could cut the bonds of political habit, corruption, and obedience by withholding their consent — the quintessential definition of nonviolent direct action. I had asked Gene if he would write an introduction. He demurred, saying he had neither the competencies nor time. But he did write a fine blurb. *The Discourse*, he wrote

> ... is a significant essay on the ultimate source of political power, the origins of dictatorship, and the means by which people can prevent political enslavement and liberate themselves.... [It] should have a prominent place in the history of political theory, and also of the development of the power analysis in which the technique of nonviolent struggle is rooted.

The same can certainly be said of Gene's oeuvre.

I would occasionally see Gene after that. We had several spirited conversations around some of the key themes that appeared in *Social Power and Political Freedom*. In early 1983, I organized and moderated a full-day conference in New York City on "The Politics of Nonviolent Action," with a keynote address by Gene and presentations by seven speakers, co-sponsored by the Center for Libertarian Studies and The Voluntaryists. Then, in early 1984, Gene asked me to become the founding executive director and a member of the board of directors of the Albert Einstein Institution, Cambridge, Massachusetts. It was founded to support his work and to "advance the worldwide study and use of strategic nonviolent action in conflict." For a bit over a year, I prepared the business plan, organized an office, hired an assistant, and implemented some successful fundraising and public outreach programs. I helped coordinate a major research project and several studies the Institution funded at the Center for International Affairs at Harvard University. To this day, the Institution continues to promote the work and methods Gene did so much to highlight.

Gene was studying nonviolent action early in the early 1950s; he was an imprisoned conscientious objector; he was secretary to A. J. Muste; and he was an editor of *Peace News* in the later 1950s. While doing graduate work at Oxford in the early 1960s he "rubbed minds" with the Oxford Anarchist Group and wrote several articles for *Anarchy* magazine. One can see the anti-statist and voluntarist influence in *Social Power and Political Freedom*, though Gene was very critical of anarchism's failure to give adequate thought "to the practical problem of how to achieve such a society and to the need for realistic means of social struggle which differ in substance from those employed by the State." Gene was always a hardheaded pragmatist. He was clear that the means mattered greatly.

It is not surprising, then, that his 1973 magnum opus was the very important 900-page book on precisely the methods of nonviolent action: *The Politics of Nonviolent Action*. It was the first comprehensive study of the nature and history of nonviolent struggle as a means for regime change and social change. Many books and pamphlets followed. He was nominated four times for the Nobel Peace Prize. That is a flash-in-the-pan, however, compared to the ongoing legacy of his works. People throughout the world and in the United States continue to use the social power of nonviolent action to claim their rights against political power and corruption.

The Impact of Nonviolent Action

Gene taught generations to "see" the impact that nonviolent direct action could have. This was based on his combination of historical and conceptual scholarly work and his keen practical perception of what was really happening in world events. His short 1993 handbook, *From Dictatorship to Democracy*, has had an outsized impact around the world. The *Times* of London ironically noted, "Not, perhaps, since Machiavelli has a book had such impact in shifting the balance of power between the rulers and the ruled." Over thirty translations have been made, with innumerable printed and Xeroxed editions. *The Wall Street Journal* called him an "American Revolutionary." He was "honored" to be an enemy of the state in Iran and Venezuela. Gene's influence has been felt in the opposition to, and often toppling of, totalitarian and autocratic governments around the world. A short list would include Eastern Europe during the fall of communism;

Nepal and China; Pakistan and Afghanistan; Palestine and Iran; Serbia and Ukraine; Venezuela and throughout Latin America; and in the uprisings known as the Arab Spring. The same can be said of many causes and nonviolent demonstrations in Europe and the United States.

Over the last forty years fifty-plus autocratic regimes have fallen through the use of nonviolent direct action. Such activity isn't always successful and immediate. There is nothing easy about it. It often has provoked retaliation. But think about it: hundreds of different methods of nonviolent action have had a remarkable impact throughout history. There are lingering questions, however, such as, What is it that lies behind nonviolent action and its methods? What makes it conducive to a free society?

Gene attempted to work through those questions in an endearingly personal way in *Social Power and Political Freedom*. Many of the themes in this book appear scattered in his other works, but they have a special resonance here, which allows for a closer look beyond — or under the hood of — the methods of nonviolent action. We are observers as Gene looked at and tried to work through what undergirded the method. He developed a view of how nonviolent means are based on opposition to state violence and grounded in the very nature of what many would now call civil society.

Four chapters in his book focus on these themes: "Rethinking Politics," "Social Power and Political Freedom," "The Societal Imperative," and "Popular Empowerment." In fact, with a good introduction, these 140 pages would make a quite useful, short book. Many of the other chapters (such as 3–10 and 12) touch on these broader themes while serving as a good summary of Sharp's earlier compendium, *The Politics of Nonviolent Action*. Also included in this collection are two thought-provoking essays on Hannah Arendt's *Eichmann in Jerusalem* and *On Revolution*.

Rethinking Politics

Gene sought to understand the underpinnings of his own, more practical work of advancing and refining the methods of nonviolent action. The essays are important, surprising and challenging. Here he stepped back a bit and urged us to join him to "rethink politics." He challenges us to question the political means:

> If we are not to become helpless political automatons, or to be annihilated, we must find and implement effective means of control over the power of rulers.... We must deliberately act in ways which strengthen the non-State institutions of our society, and consciously refrain from increasing the concentration of effective power in the State.

The power of what Gene was exploring is that he places nonviolent direct action as integral to civil society. What he calls social power is an alternative for the violent and naked reality of political power. It is a "weapon" in opposition to the political means. His critique of politics and the implications of this way of thinking are meant to be profoundly discomforting to the many "self-chosen elites" who still assume there is no alternative outside of the state and the politicization of all of society. Gene is hard on the utopians, the reformists, and the revolutionaries for not understanding power (or tragically, for being seduced by it). They seek it for their own ends — however disguised — while "the people themselves remain as excluded and powerless as ever." The alternative is the diffusion of social power:

> ... groups and institutions capable of independent action are called "loci (or places) of power" ... When power is effectively diffused throughout the society among such loci, the ruler's power is most likely to be subjected to controls and limits. This condition is associated with political "freedom."

This view comes across initially as standard political stuff, almost Burkean or Madisonian. But Gene didn't stop there. His understanding of politics was deeply intertwined with (but not solely so) a strong anti-statism: the realization that politics is, well, primarily based on the use of force and violence. And that is the reason nonviolent direct action is often necessary. More important, Gene made clear that the resort to political power to oppose political power is self-defeating: neither the best means to nor the proper end for the goals of a good society. Political power is volatile, dangerous, and quick to turn against what may have originally been good goals:

> The institutionalized capacity for political violence, once established for any purpose, can be shifted to other purposes not originally intended, and that this shift can be made essentially at the will of the person in command of those institutions.

The application of political violence, Gene argued convincingly, even for good or necessary reasons, carried with it the tendency to brutalize, to centralize, and to disenfranchise individuals and society. Corruption festers in its wake, much as Lord Acton noted: "Power tends to corrupt, and absolute power corrupts absolutely." While almost everyone agrees that the use of violence is pernicious, this is often forgotten in the immediacy of the moment. But violence, used as political expediency, becomes a norm, leading to the betrayal of legitimate social goals. Political violence is not politically neutral nor self-limiting. It feeds on itself. Political violence as a means usually morphs into an "end" that devours its children.

In broad outlines, then, rethinking politics begins with a philosophy that undermines political authority and envisions an alternative. Gene wasn't always crystal-clear in these essays, in part because he was thinking through the issues from the standpoint of means, not ends. But what can be more genuinely radical than seeing that a government's power rests, first, in the consent given by citizens and, second, that viable and humane alternatives exist primarily in the voluntary means of civil society different from the state?

Withholding Consent

Violence may keep a regime in power, but crucially, violence is not really the basis of state authority. Rather it is legitimacy and the tacit consent (and acquiescence) to state power. That is the true reason why nonviolent direct action is necessary. That is one method by which people demonstrate their withdrawal of consent. When consent is withheld, the power and legitimacy of a government will tend to crack and dissolve: rarely, though, without a fight. This was the key insight for nonviolent direct action. Gene referred to Étienne de La Boétie's *The Politics of Obedience* as one of "the most vivid expositions of the theory that tyrants can be controlled, and freedom restored, if only the citizens refuse to give them the necessary sources of power." As La Boétie put it:

> But if not one thing is yielded to them, if, without any violence they are simply not obeyed, they become naked and undone and as nothing, just as, when the root receives no nourishment, the branch withers and dies…. Resolve to serve no more, and you are at once freed. I do not ask that you place hands upon the tyrant to topple him over, but simply that you support him no longer; then you will behold him, like a great Colossus whose pedestal has been pulled away, fall of his own weight and break into pieces.

This perspective on consent removed the magic from tyranny and opened grand vistas for a multitude of nonviolent techniques of social change. There is, of course, nothing easy about withholding consent from tyranny, and Gene continually made that clear. It is also worth remembering that consent both underlies the rationale for the effectiveness of nonviolent action and is also the basis of all democratic theory and practice.

Civil Society and Social Freedom

But if consent is withheld, then what? What else is there than the next, "new" political regime? This is where Gene tried to avert the exchange of one tyranny for a different political tyranny that seems to be the only alternative that utopians, reformers, and revolutionaries can think of. When he wrote that democracy is "based upon the inner strength of the society," he was emphasizing what has long been called civil society. Why Gene didn't use that common and robust term is a mystery to me. It would have, to my way of thinking, clarified much for him and his readers. Indeed, "civil society" is not in the index of this book or his *The Politics of Nonviolent Action*. It is, after all, a vibrant liberal and radical term.

And yet, in common usage certainly since Adam Ferguson's *An Essay on the History of Civil Society* in 1767, civil society has been richly discussed as the arena of voluntary action outside of the political. It encompasses a myriad of institutions both formal and informal — churches, schools, businesses, voluntary associations, communities, clubs, and so forth — where people pursue their individual and common goals: moral, spiritual, and material. The means of action in civil society are voluntary means. Thus, the interrelatedness of civil society and the methods of nonviolent action are necessary aspects for there to even be social and political freedom. Adopting the language and tradition of civil society would have helped clarify his case for the methods of nonviolent direct action by grounding them in the fundamental nature of social action.

A few years after Gene collected these essays, the Polish dissident Adam Michnik succinctly identified the dichotomy Gene was working on here. Political tyranny — indeed, any centralized government of left or right — works to ensure that civil society does not exist. As Michnik noted:

> The problem faced by Polish society is that from the official point of view a civil society doesn't exist. Society is not recognized as capable of organizing itself to defend its particular interests and points of view.

Indeed, the language of civil society had a tremendous impact of helping Eastern European dissidents "see" their options differently, and to use nonviolent direct action so effectively. Nonviolence and civil society go hand in hand.

While Gene's development of the idea of social power would have benefited greatly from the tradition of talking about civil society, Gene did make a particularly important contribution to our understanding and appreciation of civil society. Make no mistake about that. He took the idea of civil society out of the reified world of a seemingly vacuous concept and gave it a practical, operational meaning: "realistic means of social struggle which differ in substance from those employed by the State." By focusing on the appropriate means — the "social power" of nonviolent direct action — Gene identified the major ways civil society can and does engage political power, which are consistent with and embody the open and voluntary elements of what can make civil society so robust. This is a huge contribution to be found in the interstices of his book, which has rarely been appreciated. Nor have the implications of his thinking about this been teased out. Gene's musings are an invitation to do so:

> Nonviolent sanctions have several characteristics which contribute actively to decentralization and the diffusion of effective power capacity in the society.... [they advance] the growth of the non-state institutions of the society.... It is the distribution of power throughout the society's structure as a whole which determines the de facto power of the ruler, regardless of the principles which are avowed for the system or its institutional forms.

If One Takes Care of the Means, The End Will Take Care of Itself

What are the necessary conditions for social and political freedom? Those conditions, he believed, are (1) the degree of diffusion of decision making throughout many different institutions in civil society, versus the centralization of state power; (2) withdrawal of consent; and (3) the degree to which conflicts are resolved through nonviolent means versus through violent political means. This understanding led him to develop the underlying social and political power analysis in which the techniques of nonviolent struggle are rooted.

Rethinking politics means questioning the assumption that the role of the state must always be expanded to meet all the various needs of society. The conditions for freedom and social justice are best assured by giving priority to voluntary action — and using nonviolent techniques when necessary — for they are more than mere techniques. This does not mean always avoiding politics and force. Remember, Gene was not an anarchist. But these voluntary and nonviolent means carry with them the seeds for diffusing power in society, for empowering people, for institutionalizing humane forms of conflict resolution, and for promoting sane, eternal vigilance. As Gene realized:

> To the degree that we can, step by step, vitalize, expand, and even create important substitute non-State institutions and lower levels

of participatory government to meet the social, economic, and political needs of the society, we can reverse the extraordinary gravitation of effective power to the large corporations and the central State apparatus.

The temptation to "make all this happen" through politics is always dangerous. There can be ways in which that might make sense. Gene has written about the need for governments to develop a civilian-based defense and a nonmilitary equivalent to war. This is important and has worked successfully at least on a small scale when the society has been strong and the state has been weak. But there can be a downside. For instance, would a large and centralized state, like the United States, really develop and allow techniques inherently detrimental to its own internal hegemony (as Gene's analysis suggests), or would it turn around and employ such methods to destabilize opposition?

Similarly, a department of civilian-based defense (which Gene suggested in one essay) or a state-supported national peace academy (which others have favored) would most likely be put to nefarious uses. Without a broader understanding of the imperatives of, and differences between, civil society and the state, these nonviolent methods could easily be trivialized into another tool of state oppression. The most important contribution of *Social Power and Political Freedom* is to show how social freedom and the methods of nonviolent action are integral to civil society and wonderfully inimical to state power.

Gene would be the first to agree that this ability of nonviolent means to be used for diffuse ends — value pluralism, as Isaiah Berlin and others have discussed it — can be one of the great advantages of nonviolent direct action. But it also reminds us that we must always keep the ends in mind. We must recognize that there can often be complex, multiple, positive, and incommensurate ends — a plea made so well by the Israeli peace activist Amos Oz:

> [in this] battle between fanatics, who believe that the end, any end, justifies the means, and the rest of us, who believe that life is an end, not a means … "compromise" means life. And the opposite of compromise is not idealism, not devolution; the opposite of compromise is fanaticism and death.

We must, then, not only embrace nonviolent direct action for its immensely valuable means, but we must also attend to the ends we want to advance. The means and the ends must be consistent with one another. That is the great reminder that Gandhi gave us: "If one takes care of the means, the end will take care of itself." A multitude of legitimate ends and the ability to compromise must also be part of our quiver. At the same time, however, Gene rightly notes that some ends are preeminent. Freedom, for instance:

> The relationships between social and political structures and sanctions may be far more significant then we have realized, and indeed may be intimately related to some of our most serious problems. We also need to think again about the nature of freedom.

Conclusion

In addition to this being his most radical book, one of the things I like about this book is that it was clearly a personal working out of important issues. He was humble about asking others to join him in doing the same. It is a pleasure to read a book so devoid of cant and fuzzy ideology and yet so committed to rethinking politics and promoting ways to act responsibly in a violent world. Gene could be obstreperous and difficult in person, and he was always a consummate teacher. And so, although published nearly 40 years ago, this book has only become more important. As Gene never tired of saying:

> Basic to this effort is that we think.... This exercise in rethinking politics points toward a process ... in which people are acting to shape the present, and simultaneously are increasing their ability to act to determine their future.

Gene's views evolved over time and no doubt my takeaways are different from what others may take away. But Gene's work deserves our continuing attention and thanks. By connecting civil society and nonviolent action in an appreciation of social freedom, he gave us a way to think about political freedom without always surrendering to political violence and authoritarianism. Nonviolent means are deeply embedded in and part of civil society. They are truly, to use Paul Goodman's wonderful phrase from his novel *The Empire City*, "weapons that we have that do not weigh one down."

This article is new, based on a short review originally published in The Progressive, *Vol. 45, No. 6, (June 1981), as a review of* Social Power and Political Freedom, *by Gene Sharp (Boston: Porter Sargent Publishers, 1980). Reprinted with permission of* The Progressive.

4. Invisible Aid

In the early 1930s, there was much discussion — as there is today — about how best to alleviate and then resolve the suffering among us. Walter Gifford, chairman of the Organization on Unemployment Relief, worried that the "invisible aid" provided by charitable individuals and organizations would be driven out if government relief became the norm. Both books under consideration here reveal the extensive nature and remarkable successes of "invisible aid" throughout American history. They ask challenging questions about where philanthropy and voluntarism are today.

Women's Associations

Historian Anne Firor Scott's topic in the first book reviewed here, her *Natural Allies: Women's Associations in American History,* is the doubly invisible aid proffered by women's voluntary associations from the 1790s on. Often ignored by, or barred from, traditional male bastions, women have shown an astonishing "contagion for organizing." Thousands of women's voluntary organizations have spontaneously arisen for all sorts of purposes. They "lay at the very heart of American social and political development." They have been forums to develop independence, managerial and political skills, and strategies for social change. This remains an exciting story.

Women's organizations often saw themselves concerned with morality, religion, and compassion. Over the decades, how that concern was expressed changed. A predominance of localized charities emphasizing individual efforts ("slum angels," for instance) gave way to large-scale reform efforts through national organizations. The early benevolent societies helped individuals in need in concrete ways, such as: "Mrs. Bowen: 2 shirts, 2 flannels, 2 gowns, 6 napkins." They were later joined by moral reform, anti-slavery, and then soldiers' aid groups during the Civil War. After that, there was a remarkable swelling of missionary organizations, temperance groups, as well as literary and self-development societies. By the turn of the century, the emphasis shifted again, this time as the "municipal housekeeping" movement. The rise of social justice groups faced the tough nature of urban-industrial society by promoting reform and legislative initiatives.

In addition to her sweeping summary of these women's voluntary organizations, Scott has many wonderful detailed digressions, such as a short history of the Boston Fragment Society from 1812 to today; a review of the Woman's Christian Temperance Union; and a summary of the remarkable organizing and networking by women around the Chicago World's Fair of 1893. Sadly, Scott's narrative rather abruptly dwindles and then ends shortly after the ratification of the Nineteenth Amendment.

By the end of the book, one gets the unfortunate and misleading sense that all this voluntary organizational effort was merely a prelude to suffrage — as if, to use Susan B. Anthony's words, "what they were waiting for is the ballot." This view might be a holdover from Scott's important work on suffrage. It is also due to the need to organize and place limits upon a vast amount of material for this book. But it also reflects a common tendency to see all voluntary institutions as simply baby steps towards politicizing all of society. So much of the history of voluntarism that Scott discusses has been invisible in most histories. That is why her work is so important. Sadly, the enduring value and methods of civil society are ultimately relegated to invisibility, too, as this book ends. If we are left appreciating the "end result" of suffrage more than this remarkable outpouring of voluntarism, we will miss important lessons Scott's history has for all of us. We should appreciate what she has set out before us and then look ever more closely at the methods and results of what a vibrant civil society can bring to us now. In their own right, these immensely diverse organizations make a difference in the lives of members and of those they help.

Finally, though, the same year her book was published, Scott succinctly expressed exactly why her work and the work of innumerable women's associations has been and remains important:

> What must be in the space between individuals and the state are mediating organizations. Their existence will not guarantee the presence of a satisfactory civil society, but their absence guaranties its absence.

Compassionate Care

Scott's detailed introduction does not dwell on the concrete accomplishments of women's voluntary organizations. That robust history of voluntary organizations is still to be written. More recent work by scholars such as David Beito (*From Mutual Aid to the Welfare State*) and Peter Clark (*British Clubs and Societies: 1580–1800*) would be just two works to peruse. The second book reviewed is helpful here. *The Tragedy of American Compassion* by Marvin Olasky provides a suggestive and flawed attempt at about the same time Scott penned her book. The volume focuses on the largely "invisible" attitudes and accomplishments made in the nineteenth century in the name of compassion — when compassion meant "suffering with." His work is not confined to women, but women, of course, figure prominently as both organizers and recipients.

Olasky's message is simple: the problems of need and poverty today remain remarkably like those of the nineteenth century. The attitudes and methods used then were surprisingly successful, even though most people don't know that. There is, then, a need to apply their lessons in our time. Olasky contends that government anti-poverty efforts in this century have made the problems more intractable. Bad government programs have driven out good, voluntary charity. His critique is wide-ranging, encompassing the approaches of government, foundations, and most private welfare agencies, as well as the attitudes both conservatives and liberals have about compassion and poverty. He is as unyielding in his criticism of Social Darwinism as he is of the Social Gospel.

The fascinating history of nineteenth-century compassion provides a sense of realism for Olasky's prescriptions. The perspective and results gathered by such observers and practitioners as Jacob Riis and Josephine Lowell are most interesting, in Olasky's telling. Riis describes how a "handful of women ... accomplished what no machinery of government availed to do. Sixty thousand children have been rescued by them from the streets." He further notes that over eight years, one charity had raised "4,500 families out of the rut of pauperism into proud, if modest, independence, without alms." His enthusiasm makes us want to believe him and to get additional corroboration.

Olasky presents seven marks of true compassion, which he neatly condenses into an A-through-G listing: Affiliation, Bonding, Categorization, Discernment, Employment, Freedom, and God. His description is extensive, and it boils down to several key points: emphasizing involvement and responsibility on the part of both givers and recipients; paying attention to the ties of family, friends, work, and community; distinguishing among the different types of need; facing the hard questions about whether the need is real; and focusing on spiritual needs as much as material. This successful model is contrasted with our current failure that has institutionalized entitlements and depersonalized dependence. Today, sadly, a professionalized bureaucracy that is crassly materialistic operates in philanthropy and government through rigid categories. A human element is lost.

His selective history is a lesson in some things that did work at one time. What now works and how is what we should seek to discover. Have we developed a truly compassionate system of aid that fails while it ameliorates our feelings of obligations towards others through a false sense of compassion? Olasky says yes in a somber challenge to each of us.

There are ideologically constrained commentators who have not given Olasky's book credit, and some who have uncritically accepted its story. The tragedy of American compassion will be exacerbated if we don't take his book seriously and critically. We need to get beyond a misuse of charitable resources and a grandiose trust in public policy. The direct personal involvement that was the hallmark of much nineteenth-century compassion has something important to teach us still. Olasky quotes the century-old wisdom of Nathaniel Rosenau of the United Hebrew Charities: "If every person possessing the capability should assume the care of a single family, there would not be enough poor to go around."

Conclusion

These two books deserve careful reading because they illuminate the earlier (and imperfect) soul of American civil society and philanthropy. Their respective points of view ache to be expanded upon. They show the capabilities of a remarkably robust civil society that is largely unknown today, taken for granted, or simply rejected. While invisible aid may remain invisible, it desperately needs to be recovered. What Scott says for women's organizations applies in general: "The more we learn [about women's voluntary associations], the more we will understand about the society that has shaped us all." And Olasky challenges us to apply true compassion: "It's time to learn from the warm hearts and hard heads of earlier times, and to bring that understanding into our own lives."

Nearly 26 years after this manuscript was written, we have seen astonishing examples of the invisible aid in civil society that blooms on the other side of terrible disasters. Sadly, however, our understanding is still not what it should be. We are still too quick to resort to political machinations. Our political class neither sees nor trusts the vitality of civil society. Too often they ignore the everyday acts of citizenship as well as those who would benefit most from compassionate care. Luckily, there is much scholarly work that has been done since these two books were published. There is much work still to be done.

A truncated version of my original manuscript appeared in Foundation News, *Vol. 34, No. 4, July/August 1994, reviewing only* Natural Allies: Women's Associations in American History, *by Anne Firor Scott (Urbana, IL: University of Illinois Press, 1991). The full manuscript included another book:* The Tragedy of American Compassion, *by Marvin Olasky (Washington: Regnery Gateway, 1992). For this volume, I have used the full, original manuscript.*

Foundation News Book Editor Richard Magat called the manuscript a "very fine review." It was paid for and then disappeared for seventeen months. When published, the portions on the Olasky book were excised. Foundation News staff disliked his conservative perspective. Dick and I were appalled by the political correctness and anti-intellectualism. I thought Olasky's book too political and simplistic. But challenging perspectives should be discussed. The book was extensively reviewed in other venues.

PHILANTHROPIC LANDSCAPES

About the time I submitted this manuscript, Dick decided to leave as the book editor. He wrote Editor Arlie Schardt recommending me: "a guy I think would be ideal to take over the book section.... He is very broad-gauged and broad-minded, and knows philanthropy, and writes well, and edits well." They clearly didn't want "broad-minded."

5. Citizenship and Voluntarism

Citizenship in America is an ever-changing notion. These Tanner Lectures on Human Values are a nice "brief sketch of American democratic citizenship as standing," that is, in terms of status. Those of us working in the voluntary sector will be stimulated by the respected political theorist's reflections. Nevertheless, we will then need to go beyond that idea to develop a richer understanding of the relationship of voluntarism to citizenship and vice versa.

For Shklar, American citizenship is defined by two characteristics: the ancient notion of participation in the polity, and the complex modern notion of participation in a civil society outside the political process. Shklar reduces these two ideas to "voting" and "earning," devoting a chapter to each. She develops her views along several familiar contrasts: equality and exclusion, principle and practice, and finally, "standing" and the "stigma of inferiority" as expressed by Frederick Douglass. Over two centuries, ideas on American citizenship have moved in fits and starts toward what Shklar calls inclusion: greater recognition, dignity, and the independence of individuals within society.

In her view, the struggle for American citizenship has been most dominated by the legacy of slavery, and more generally by the quest for equal rights. She addresses the slow, painful process of attaining universal suffrage in two ways. First, she provides a quick summary of concepts of citizenship from Aristotle and Machiavelli, through Hobbes, Rousseau, and Locke. Second, she considers how slavery and voting were constant themes throughout American history.

One key to citizenship, then, is equal participation in the political process. True enough. But I would argue that view of citizenship is too narrow and passive. Perhaps it has become even worse than that. The fine British historian Geoffrey Finlayson has talked about "the citizenship of entitlement," which seems horribly apposite today. More significant is one's part in civil society writ large. This is the private and public sphere outside the political process, consisting of myriad institutions and relationships — commerce, culture, voluntary action, and community. What if, for instance, one compared levels of giving and volunteering in America as a proxy for citizenship as engagement in civil society and levels of voting as a proxy for engagement in political society?

There are definitional problems and inconsistencies around what data universes one is using. But the general conclusion I draw is that more people do give and volunteer than vote. This doesn't mean that voting is unimportant. But it does suggest that this other definition of citizenship based on membership in civil society (i.e., giving and volunteering) is much bigger and more robust than the way Shklar defines it. She unfortunately limits this complex idea of participation in civil society to "earning": productive work which is crucial for self-respect, independence, and public concern. It is true that her observations about rights to work will be revealing, helpful, and infuriating for those dealing with inadequacy and need in American life. However, her limited focus doesn't honor the importance of the deeper, lived experience of citizenship in society.

Seeing citizenship through the lens of civil society provides a much more active and robust definition. It needs to be flushed out in a much more comprehensive manner. Thoreau succinctly captured the idea when he famously observed in *Civil Disobedience*, "Even voting for the right [thing] is doing nothing for it." Voting is cheap, easy, expressive, and seriously limited by voting for very limited options. Or, as some say, voting is actually voting against. Giving and volunteering represents a different kind of real affirmative commitment.

Thus, different notions of citizenship may emphasize different things. Citizenship through civil society is the lifeblood of any civilization. There is an always uneasy and often antagonistic relationship between it and the political process. The breakup of communism, and the rise of newly authoritarian regimes and violent failed states (Venezuela is merely one of many examples) have certainly revealed a corrupt politics where citizenship in the political sense no longer exists. Years earlier, these same regimes had sought to hamper or eliminate the threat of civil society. (Russia and China are vivid current examples.) It seems clear — and Eastern European dissidents knew this decades ago — that only through building a strong civil society will civilization and a democratic political process succeed. The challenge is that civil society is not very good at protecting societal or political concepts of citizenship — as Eastern European dissidents also discovered. It is precisely on this topic that Gene Sharp's empirical and conceptual work on nonviolent direct action is so important. (See the third article in this chapter on Sharp's work.)

Closer to home, voluntarism and giving are a robust, distinguishing feature of American citizenship, an observation well anchored by a diversity of opinions. In fact, from the Founding period on, Paine and others had developed a vision of citizenship largely separate from the state. It was grounded in participation in the multifarious institutions of civil society. Shklar largely misses the vitality and role of civil society by focusing narrowly on earning. Voting and work have much to tell us about citizenship, but they are essentially static when viewed primarily as lending status to people.

The innovative and robust character of American citizenship is still sustained by the strength of its multitude of voluntary actions and associations that give vitality to any civilization. It is revealing — and indicative of where future research should focus its attention — that the

American public may exhibit good citizenship more through voluntary action (commitments of time, money, and belief) than it does through the passive act of voting. Perhaps a vibrant and democratic political citizenship flourishes only when citizenship in civil society is flourishing.

This is a slightly revised review originally published in Foundation News, *Vol. 33, No. 2, (March/April 1992), as a review of* American Citizenship: The Quest for Inclusion, *by Judith Shklar (Cambridge: Harvard University Press, 1991). Reprinted by permission of* Foundation News.

6. Markets and Philanthropy

The remarkable productivity and efficiency of free markets are well understood. Yet there remains a nagging uncertainty about the moral credentials of capitalism. This seems especially true in the philanthropic community, which often takes pains to set itself apart (even above), claiming that its work rests on fundamentally separate values. While there are differences, business and philanthropy are tied together. They operate within a common context of civil society: voluntary action and participation in the private sector. They are synergistic. Discussing the moral stature of markets can be instructive to philanthropy and philanthropic practice.

The book reviewed here by H. B. Acton, *The Morals of Markets*, was originally published in England in 1971. It is one among many books now available making the case for the morality of capitalism. It remains timely because hide-bound ideas about the marketplace remain so common. This edition adds four additional essays to the original book. Note that Acton and many advocates of free markets make a clear distinction between free market "capitalism" and what is variously called state capitalism, corporatism, etc., in which the state plays a determinative role.

There are many thought-provoking nuggets in this meaty little book. But the general thrust shows how free markets are an integral part of any free society. The author points out that there are three ways to obtain what another individual possesses: one can offer something in exchange for it; one can take it; or one can ask for it ("but then … he has no say in precisely what it is that he obtains"). Stated this plainly, the free market system has straightforward moral advantages:

> [T]here is absolutely nothing in the complaint that markets are by their very nature immoral or amoral, although many of those who participate in them cheat or would cheat if they dared.… Competitive markets … give more scope for intellectual and moral excellence.… [I]n a society where competitive markets prevail it is not only trade, but also thoughts and men that are free.

While not a systematic treatise, this book makes one think and appreciate philosophically the complex world of both free markets specifically and civil society more generally. The author organizes his many insights around five general topics:

> *The profit motive.* It does not lead to avarice or selfishness. Not only are payment and trading for goods moral, "in competitive markets, individuals, whether firms or persons, provide for others in working for themselves."

Competition. Acton describes capitalism as a "system of mutual aid." Competition is not a zero-sum game. Striving after what one wants peacefully (an activity everyone would applaud in other spheres of life) is cooperative. This important point also applies to the "methods" of civil society more generally.

The welfare state alternative to markets. In the marketplace, coercion is at a minimum. A welfare state must progressively lead to the authoritarian imposition of state-controlled decision making and morality (which is not a morality at all).

Reflections on planning and prediction. Far from making markets obsolete, the rise of technology, complexity, and even charity make markets more necessary. As economist Israel Kirzner and others know, human action is a knowledge problem and markets harness information.

Distributive justice. Acton discusses the justice of a market in supplying consumers and shows that the idea of distributive justice is a rhetorical slogan. It is a smokescreen for the imposition of a single rule by a controlling distributor, surely a far cry from a moral concern.

The Morals of Markets also has many wise things to say about the philanthropic endeavor. Any economic system, for instance, has what Acton calls "casualties of a system." Importantly, he rightly condemns involuntary help: "There is no morally defensible reason at all for forcing some individuals, irrespective of their incomes or circumstances, to give pecuniary help to beneficiaries whose incomes and circumstances have not been inquired into. The existence of this system is a sign of moral abdication, and those who oppose its abolition can have no concern for justice." This is the beginning point that should underlie philanthropy's exploration of its own moral standing, but it is often ignored.

Throughout this book, the idea of personal responsibility stands out as one characteristic that must be nurtured in every quarter of society. As Acton presents it:

> We must now consider the argument that some needs are so fundamental that their satisfaction should not be left to the market but should be provided publicly. This amounts to saying that in what concerns their basic needs people should not be left to fend for themselves.

Pointing out that single moral conundrum is an invaluable service. Acton's point, I think, is not to embrace a completely "hands-off" position when it comes to helping others. Rather, it is a reminder that there are different ways to help. The market is one arena that requires individual responsibility. Philanthropic activity or public provision when necessary must also seek to enhance it. If this notion were fully appreciated and applied, it could change the way philanthropy helps. Indeed, more and more corporate giving programs, foundations, donors, and nonprofits are finding those programs that truly help are ones that encourage (and require) individual responsibility. There are many such interesting and controversial points in this book that deserve full discussions.

Thus, the moral foundations of free enterprise are also a big part of the moral foundations of civil society. And they provide a chunk of the basis for the moral and practical tasks of philanthropy. As F. A. Hayek put it:

> It is ... an old discovery that morals and moral values will grow only in an environment of freedom.... It is only where the individual has choice, and its inherent responsibility, that he has occasion to affirm existing values, to contribute to their further growth, and to earn moral merit.

The tasks of the marketplace and philanthropy are complementary. The moral foundations for each rest on voluntary action, personal responsibility, cooperation, and mutual aid. That is the essence of a flourishing and caring civil society.

Originally published in Philanthropy, *Vol. 7, No. 2, Spring 1993, as a review of* The Morals of Markets and Related Essays, *by H. B. Acton, edited by David Gordon and Jeremy Shearmur (Indianapolis: Liberty Fund, Inc., 1993). Reprinted by permission of* Philanthropy.

CHAPTER 2

BRINGING CIVIL SOCIETY BACK IN: CITIZENSHIP AND PHILANTHROPY

Some writers have so confounded society with government as to leave little or no distinction between them; whereas they are not only different, but have different origins. — Thomas Paine

We need to discover an appropriate social distance between governmental and voluntary agencies ... the search is essential if pluralism and voluntarism are to be preserved in the welfare state. — Ralph M. Kramer

Of all the problems in social policy none is more harassing, more complex, and perennial than that of determining the proper relation of the state to privately managed charities within its borders. This is the sore thumb of public administrative policy. — Alexander Fleisher

The lessons from the great civil revolutions of our time is that the institutions of civil society are the sources of a country's political will, the creators of common ground, and the repository of legitimacy for all public institutions, including the state. — David Mathews

For decades, we have invested political thought and policy with our hopes and energies only to discover that politics and politicization are pretty sterile and incomplete ways of looking at human action. Perhaps Jorge Luis Borges got it right: politics is "the most miserable of human activities."

After decades of trying to "bring the state back in," we need to renew the effort to "reinvent society" from the dual sources of theory and practice: to "bring civil society back in."

I started as adjunct research associate at the Center on Philanthropy at Indiana University in Indianapolis in 1992. In addition to a variety of projects for the Center, I wanted to explore the dual nature of citizenship: as a citizen within political society *and* as a citizen within civil society. Citizenship is almost exclusively perceived as constricted within political society. But that has seemed much too limiting and a bit of an ineffective charade. The second was messy, robust, and largely invisible to our political eyes. It seemed to me that philanthropy and volunteerism — the extent to which people give and volunteer — were useful proxies for this idea of citizenship.

I received two small grants and considerable encouragement as I got started. In 1994, I was appointed as a Visiting Fellow at the Program on Non-profit Organizations (PONPO) at Yale, intent upon devoting myself to this project. I read a great deal and started to organize my thoughts and my intellectual/historical "to-do" list. The five articles in this chapter were written while at Yale. Alas, life intervened. I was offered the position of director and chief operating officer at the J. M. Kaplan Fund in New York City. The chance to combine my intellectual interests with the practical challenges of grantmaking was catnip to me.

In the years since these drafts were written, the dichotomy between political and civil society seems more important and still needs much more work. These five articles represent initial working papers toward a fuller project. They were written for different audiences, each with a different emphasis (but with considerable overlap). I hope that this work retains some resonance and may be of help to others to *see* civil society. These are the unfinished fruits of a very fruitful two years at PONPO.

1. Making Democracy Work
Co-authored with Dr. Julie Fisher

Terms like *civil society, community, civic culture,* and *social capital* now clutter the academic landscape. As Emmett Carson said of the idea of civil society at the 1993 Association for Research on Nonprofit Organizations and Voluntary Action (ARNOVA) meeting, "If my mother doesn't know what it is, it won't work." Fair enough. And yet these terms attempt to capture a dawning paradigmatic change of academic and practical import. This is due to a combination of factors, including the fall of communism, the failures of public policy on the Left and Right, yearnings for some kind of togetherness, an abhorrence of powerlessness, and the worldwide explosion of nongovernmental organizations (NGOs) and other alternative institutions. Everywhere, it seems, people are rediscovering the social ties that bind people together.

For decades, we have invested the political process with our hopes and energies only to discover that politics may be more the effect of other social forces than the cause of basic social change. Something has been missing. Put another way, after several decades of "bringing the state back in" to what had become pretty sterile social science, we are now seeing an effort to reinvent society from the dual sources of theory and practice.

During the 1970s, Latin American intellectuals, reacting against tired Marxism as well as dictatorial states, began to write about *sociedad civil.* Harkening back to Adam Smith and Hegel, the term *civil society* reappeared in the literature of Central and Eastern European dissidents as they tried to carve out an understanding of social process that could stand in opposition to the state while being broader and more humane than simply "the market." The proliferation of NGOs throughout the world has also advanced understanding of what Michael Walzer has called "the space of uncoerced human association."[1] Increasingly, the idea of civil society has figured prominently in more and more works; of particular note are those by Víctor Pérez-Díaz and Ernest Gellner.[2]

The best book of the lot is Robert Putnam's *Making Democracy Work* (co-authored with Robert Leonardi and Raffaella Y. Nanetti).[3] It is beautifully written, based on twenty years of research. It is held together by the creative use of many different theoretical threads (collective action, game theory, the new institutionalism, etc.). It is a scholarly bestseller, having already sold nearly 20,000 copies in the nearly three years since its publication. It has had a remarkable impact on several disciplines. Its themes have garnered great journalistic attention, and we know of at least two foundations that have made major shifts in their funding priorities because of the book. The Kettering Foundation has begun a series of Civil Investing Seminars for foundation executives to explore giving strategies focusing on strengthening civil society.

Making Democracy Work is an important book for researchers and practitioners in the voluntary sector. The book is ostensibly a specific study of democracy in modern Italy. More important, this is a remarkable exploration of the crucial importance of social capital, that is, the "features of social organization, such as trust, norms, and networks, that can improve the efficiency of society by facilitating coordinated actions" (p. 167). That complex discussion enriches the whole concept of a voluntary sector and is tantalizing in its suggestions about what makes society work or not work so well. Yet the same researchers and practitioners in the voluntary sector have important contributions and corrections to make on precisely the topics Putnam has raised.

The book had its origins in 1970 when the Italian government began to implement a constitutional provision to set up regional governments. Although Putnam draws on evidence from all twenty regions, six regions that represent the vast diversities of Italy are singled out. Human action offers few such opportunities to systematically study institutional development and the impact of social context over many years. Putnam and his colleagues were there at the beginning; the results of their inquiries make for fascinating reading. The early chapters focus on twenty years of development, policy formulations, and implementation, attempting to chronicle and measure the contrasts long remarked on between northern and southern regions in terms of their institutional performance. All of this leads the author to ever-wider circles of inquiry.

Although Putnam's original inquiry grew out of the stark differences in regional governmental performance that began to develop during the 1970s, he found the usual explanations for those differences wanting. He began to suspect alternative explanations outside of the usual political science lexicon. The link between performance and the character of civic life — what he terms "the civic community" — became particularly important (p. 15). The differences in the level and vitality of civic life turn out to have a determining role in explaining differences in institutional success. Although business and government have a role to play, social capital, according to Putnam, "is the key to making democracy work" (p. 185). This is civil society, though Putnam does not use the term.

Perhaps even more fascinating are the historical roots of the ability of the North to use the opportunities of governmental decentralization and the failure of the South to do likewise. The story Putnam tells begins in the twelfth century when northerners responded to political anarchy by creating workingmen's guilds, while southerners welcomed the autocratic order provided by Norman invaders for the very same reason. In the city-states of the North, communes sprang from voluntary associations based on groups of neighbors committing to mutual assistance. Eventually, this led to the professionalization of city administration. Economic guilds were organized, and credit was invented, "one of the great economic revolutions in world history" (p.128). Although northern Italy continued to be plagued by poverty and factionalism, horizontal networks moderated conflict and social mobility was high.

In southern Italy, in contrast, the Norman kings reinforced the feudal rights of barons who provided them with military backing. Although the Normans also promoted religious tolerance and commerce, southern towns and cities that showed any desire for autonomy were subjugated by a network of officials responsible to the king.

Making Democracy Work starts out to "explore the origins of effective government" (p.15), but ends up somewhere else: exploring the foundations for an effective society, which is different from the state. Putnam's exploration of why political, economic, and social development seems to flourish differently in areas of similar political decentralization inexorably moves toward the key importance of the local, voluntary associations that make for civil society. Although Putnam does not specifically say it, civic community is also linked to civility. Not only is "collective life in the civic regions ... eased by the expectation that others will probably follow the rules" (p. 111), but people in northern Italy are less concerned about the need for strong top-down authority.

Note that the real core of democracy may not be "political" in the usual sense of the term, but profoundly social. It is the tension in that subtle shift in emphasis from the political to the social as it unfolds in Putnam's research that makes his intellectual odyssey so interesting and his book so important. For those of us researching and working on aspects of the voluntary sector, the point is especially salient. We, as reviewers, think it valuable to look anew at what makes a society work or not work by asking four questions about civil society that arise from Putnam's book:

1. What is civil society?
2. What is the relationship of civil society to government performance?
3. What is the relationship of civil society to democracy?
4. What is the relationship of civil society/social capital to socioeconomic development?

What Is Civil Society?

There is some debate about what civil society or, in Putnam's words, "civic community" means. And Putnam does not specifically define it. Michael Walzer's definition quoted above is a good beginning. Other observers are more explicit and include the for-profit as well as the nonprofit sector in their definitions. Pérez-Díaz, for example, defines civil society as "markets, associations, and a sphere of public debate."[4] Businesses, as well as nonprofit organizations, help mediate between the citizen and the state. Moreover, businesses and nonprofits are often more than just unrelated members of the same civil society. Just as the craftsmen's guilds formed in northern Italy a thousand years ago were economic in character, so also development NGOs as diverse as the Grameen Bank in Bangladesh or the Foundation for Economic and Social Initiative in Poland are promoting for-profit enterprises. They also work with grassroots organizations such as rotating credit associations, which, as Putnam points out, are found throughout the world.

The importance of a "sphere of public debate" to civil society is clearly understood by grassroots organizations in the Philippines that use large community blackboards as local newspapers. In contrasting the strength of civil society in northern Italy with its weakness in the South, Putnam uses newspaper readership as one of four civic community indicators. Even a partially independent media can help a country move from deference to autonomous, active civility.

Most discussions of civil society, including some of Putnam's, focus on vertical relationships, down to the citizen and up to the government. Putnam's "tale of detection" (p. xiv), however, also led to "astonishingly deep historical roots" characterized by stronger or weaker horizontal bonds. So much of our lives and theory are implicitly vertical. But as Putnam points out, "the relevant distinction is not between the presence and absence of social bonds, but rather between horizontal bonds of mutual solidarity and vertical bonds of dependency and exploitation" (p.144). His study measures the dramatic differences between the strength of civic community in northern Italy (where civic bonds are largely horizontal) and southern Italy (where they remain vertical).

Instead of focusing on definitions of civil society or civic community, Putnam and his colleagues put their energies, over twenty years, into a largely successful attempt to measure it. In addition to the incidence of newspaper readership, they measured the vibrancy of associational life, turnout for referenda, and the incidence of preferential voting for a particular candidate versus picking from the party list (as a negative indicator). They found that the four indicators were "highly correlated" (p. 96) with each other, as well as with support for political equality. Moreover, this "civic community index" was highly correlated with another index of civic community involvement developed for the period 1860–1920. This historical index included the strength of mass parties, the incidence of cooperatives, membership in mutual aid societies, electoral turnout, and local associations founded before 1860. No doubt variations on Putnam's method should be tried on other areas.

The Relationship of Civil Society to Government Performance

What makes government responsive and accountable? What makes for good government in some places and bad government elsewhere? Putnam and his collaborators ran detailed assessments of regional government success using twelve diverse measures. This created a composite measure of performance, including cabinet stability, budget promptness, and statistical and information services as measures of policy processes; reform legislation and legislative innovations as measures of the content of policy decisions; and seven measures of policy implementation, including day care centers, family clinics, industrial policy instruments, agricultural spending capacity, local health unit expenditures, housing and urban development, and bureaucratic responsiveness. Not only was there high consistency among these twelve indicators, but his team did two separate indicator analyses in 1978 and 1985 that were highly consistent with each other.

Not surprisingly, he found that there was a strong correlation between regional governmental performance and the strength of the civic community. More remarkable, the success or failure of regional governments in the 1980s was strongly correlated with the team's historical civil society index. Putnam and his team have, in other words, been able to move beyond correlation toward causality. Equally important were some of their negative findings. For example, the success or failure of regional governments was "wholly uncorrelated with virtually all measures of political fragmentation, ideological polarization and social conflict" (p.117). The highly civic community, in other words, is not necessarily free of strife.

In answering the question of why the relationship between civic community and government performance is so strong, Putnam focuses mainly on political culture. He found, for example, that contacts between citizens and governments in the South are more likely to be personalistic than those in the North. Northerners, whether they be political leaders or ordinary citizens, are more committed to equality and compromise than their counterparts in the South. Implicit in his argument is the assumption that political culture can only develop slowly, over many years.

Yet evidence from other parts of the world throws doubt on the generalizability of Putnam's powerful Italian findings. In the Third World, for example, the "why" question is being addressed more directly than in Italy. NGOs operate within an historical context close to that of southern Italy, yet in dealing with issues such as development or human rights, they often have a more direct impact on governments than the choral societies or sports clubs of northern Italy. Third World NGOs are sometimes able to subvert ineffective bureaucratic behavior because some government employees are smart and opportunistic, if not as well educated as NGO leaders. In India, for example, many development ministries and bureaus are collaborating with NGOs, even though the security ministry harasses them. Ties between NGOs and poorly funded subnational governments in many countries are increasingly common because NGOs can provide human and even financial resources. Many Brazilian cities, for example, work with both grassroots organizations and intermediary grassroots support organizations. In Sao Paulo alone there are over 1,000 neighborhood associations collaborating with the city government on community gardens and sanitation.[5]

In the Third World, let us go a little deeper and focus on the major factors associated with direct, positive NGO influence on government policy. The dramatic growth of NGOs is already having some impact on political culture, and thus a long-term cumulative impact on governments. Even so, it is those NGOs with a high degree of organizational autonomy that are having the strongest impact on government policy. To quote a Philippine NGO leader:

> In dealing with government it is important to make sure that you participate on your own terms. This means you do not access money from governments, nor do you sit down just to be coopted. You must be able ... to enter into relationships where you can participate in the conceptualization and onward to the implementation of every project.[6]

This may, of course, be more difficult in Central and Eastern Europe, where even nonpartisan organizations may be viewed as political opponents.

Measuring local performance and decentralization may be misleading without reference to a larger political context. What, for instance, is the true extent of the decentralization promoted by the Italian government? By the early 1990s, the regional governments were spending 10 percent of gross domestic product. Yet, with total government spending in Italy as high as it is, one wonders how important and robust even the northern regional governments really are. Indeed, a huge central governmental sector has to have a dampening effect on both economic development and social capital. Thus Putnam's "central question: ... What are the conditions for creating strong, responsive, effective representative [political] institutions?" (p. 6), may be answered quite differently at the national level. Without reference to the larger political and economic framework, including the nationally oriented nonprofit sector, regional governments can appear to take on an unsubstantiated importance.

BRINGING CIVIL SOCIETY BACK IN

What Is the Relationship of Civil Society to Democracy?

It is curious that, despite the book's title, and Putnam's substantially unassailable assumption that effective government must be responsive, accountable, and, therefore, democratic, the word *democracy* does not appear in the index. To be sure, civil society and democracy are closely intertwined. Indeed, except for a few very small islands in the Pacific and the Caribbean, it is hard to conceive of a democracy not based on a strong civil society. Yet civil society and democracy are not coterminous. Some observers, most notably Pérez-Díaz in his discussion of recent Spanish history, have concluded that the development of a strong civil society typically precedes the emergence of a democratic political system. Civil society may grow stronger under a dictatorship, although conflict is probable. Fragile democratic governments can be overthrown even though civil society has grown stronger, although civil society will often become a target as well. Yet, in support of Putnam's findings, a growing civil society can also strengthen democratic institutions or circumscribe the options of dictatorships.

How should we be thinking about these processes that advance civil society, responsive democratic government, and, ultimately (Putnam's question), effective policy implementation? A look back at the topic of "political development" is appropriate. In the 1960s, political development was as hot a topic in political science as "civil society" is today. By the 1970s, however, it had been eclipsed by "realistic" writings on topics such as the inevitable rise of bureaucratic authoritarianism and the apparent decline of democracy, particularly in Latin America. Ironically, this shift in political science occurred just as those writing about development were emphasizing local participation for the first time. With the explosion of NGOs in the developing and transitional countries and with the return to democracy in many countries, students of civil society need to look back at the political development literature. Political development can be defined as an interactive public decision making and learning process based on power creation and power dispersion within and between government and civil society. It leads to increased autonomy from below and responsiveness from above.[7] (This definition grew out of a reexamination of the political development literature.)

The toughest issue is, of course, the content of interaction between society and state. But previously excluded groups, newly organized into associations, can enhance the dimensions available for problem posing and problem solving.[8] Attempts to define political development need to focus on process recognition, but need not, indeed should not, imply that change is inevitable. It is a process that may start and be derailed, especially if civil society is only incipient or fragile. Nor is it occurring everywhere. Putnam's findings, however, buttress the view that it is usually propelled by the long-term growth of civil society. But in the developing and transitional countries, there is considerable evidence that short-term deliberate cultivation of civil society can also contribute to political development. In Cambodia, for example, where there were almost no NGOs even ten years ago, a small women's rights organization called Ponleu Khmer has, with international NGO support, become a major player in the national human rights dialogue, as well as an important organizer of an NGO network.

Regarding civil society's relationship with government performance and democracy, then, Putnam's analysis leads us in interesting directions. He assumes that political institutions shape policy and that they are shaped by history. Between these two assumptions, however, Putnam argues that the "practical performance of institutions ... is shaped by the social context within which they operate" (p. 8). Putnam does not undermine the common assumption that institutional change can influence civic culture. That is what he expected to find with the decentralization of Italian government. Yet, to Putnam's initial surprise, the strength in the opposite direction became the real crux of his argument: "Civic context matters for the way institutions work. By far the most important factor in explaining good government is the degree to which social and political life in a region approximates the ideal of the civic community" (p. 120).

The Relationship of Civil Society to Social and Economic Development

In addition to being predictive of effective regional government, Putnam's historic civic community index was much more predictive of current levels of socioeconomic development than were earlier levels of socioeconomic development:

> When we use both civic traditions and past socioeconomic development to predict present socioeconomic development, we discover that civics is actually a much better predictor of socioeconomic development than is development itself (p. 156).... Over the two decades since the birth of the regional governments, civic regions have grown faster than regions with fewer associations and more hierarchy, controlling for their level of development in 1970. (p. 176)

Again, Putnam has surpassed correlation with significant evidence of historical causality.[9] Yet, as Putnam himself points out, civic community in northern Italy embodies a dense mixture of economic, social, as well as political associations that foster competition as well as cooperation. More specifically, he argues that such "social capital" can overcome the proverbial free rider. Rotating credit associations, for example, also ubiquitous throughout the Third World, are based on strong norms of "generalized reciprocity," unsustainable by vertical networks. Moreover, economic institutions such as guilds were part and parcel of the growth of preindustrial civil society in northern Italy.

What Do We Make of This? Where Do We Go from Here?

The unsettling news about social capital in this book relates to Putnam's historical determinism. Indeed, as he notes somewhat pessimistically in the concluding chapter, with respect to social capital, "them that has gets" (p.169). He also finds that:

> [T]he southern territories once ruled by the Norman kings constitute exactly the seven least civic regions in the 1970s.... At the other end of the scale, the heartland of republicanism in 1300 corresponds uncannily to the most civic regions of today, followed closely by the areas still further north in which medieval republican traditions, though real, had proved somewhat weaker. (p. 133)

Although these stable and prosperous medieval societies were replaced by autocracies in response to the Black Death and the Hundred Years War, northern rulers still accepted civic responsibilities and relied upon civil associations. Putnam points out that the concept of a "patron of the arts" originated in northern Italy. The nineteenth century saw the use of the "principle of association" (p. 138) as a central element in the ideology of the *risorgimento,* and the emergence of cooperatives throughout the North. "By 1904, Piedmont had more than seven times as many mutual aid societies as Puglia, in proportion to population" (p. 148).

Why were the northern Italians already more prone to organize themselves in the year 1100? The answer, says Putnam, may be "lost in the mist of the Dark Ages" (p. 180). Despite Putnam's persuasive historical determinism, one is tempted to answer his query with the observation that guilds were originally organized because a few people voluntarily decided they were a logical response to a chaotic and threatening environment. By the same token, the dramatic organizational explosion that began in the Third World only twenty-five years ago — there are now between 35,000 and 50,000 intermediary NGOs in Asia, Africa, and Latin America — was a self-conscious response to worsening poverty, high-level unemployment, government corruption, and the increased availability of voluntary foreign assistance. To be sure, the new intermediary NGOs or grassroots support organizations were also able to link up to preexisting member-serving organizations at the local community level.

Even historical determinism, in other words, must have a starting point. It seems to be in the individual choices and values, the small-scale organizing, and the trust that people can develop in their daily lives. This had to be true during "the mist of the Dark Ages." It was also described by Tocqueville in *Democracy in America* and is now visible in the rise of NGOs in the developing countries.[10] So, although we agree with Putnam that history can be terribly tenacious, "history" does not fully determine. What Putnam's research does suggest is that context and culture are more stubborn in some places than in others. In places such as southern Italy, historical context may be "harder for would-be reformers to manipulate, at least in the short run, so our research is not likely to suggest shortcuts to institutional success" (p. 10). NGO organizers in the developing and transitional world, however, have some inherent advantages over the original Italian organizers of guilds and mutual aid societies. In 1100, it was hard to communicate, even between northern and southern Italy. Today international travel and the communications revolution tend to preclude the possibility of the isolated historical accidents that influenced an Emilia Romagna or a Calabria for a thousand years. Today international and Third World NGOs are not just letting civil society sprout by chance. They are cultivating it rather deliberately. One value of Putnam's book is that his analysis reinforces the dicey and delicate difference between cultivating civil society and proclaiming or co-opting it from above. It is also a reminder that newly sprouted civic cultures are inherently fragile.

On the plus side, one suspects Putnam is right: Civic traditions "have remarkable staying power" (p. 157). To be sure, civil society can be destroyed pretty thoroughly by dictatorial regimes of both the Left and the Right. And American society in recent decades has seen a decline in civility by most accounts. Yet traditions and something bordering on an associational "collective self-consciousness" persist and can be drawn upon. In addition, people seem to be quite deliberately creating civil societies in many parts of the world. If civil society in most of the developing and transitional countries is not yet as strong as it is in northern Italy, it is arguably stronger than in Sicily or Calabria. Moreover, unlike Italy, where choral societies and sports clubs were the most common forms of association, NGOs are tied more closely to socioeconomic results because they are specifically focused on local development and national development policies.

This conclusion provides us with hope that three major trends occurring throughout the developing countries — the growth of development NGOs, the continuing vitality of the informal for-profit sector, and the movement for human rights and democracy — are not just fads. They have the long-range potential to reinforce each other. This process of reinforcement and convergence can be accelerated by NGOs focusing on microenterprise development, governments willing to facilitate the widespread creation of new wealth rather than protecting economic exploitation, and political entrepreneurs aware of the need to challenge authoritarian governments.

Civil societies, an informal economy, and concern about democracy are also emerging in the transitional countries of Central and Eastern Europe and the former Soviet Union. Although educational levels are higher in the transitional countries than in much of the Third World, only the continuing growth of civil society can help people challenge habits of economic and political dependency.

What Kind of Research Makes Sense? Twenty Years on Local Organizations?

It is certainly true that nonprofit research can add much to the discussion about civil society. Putnam's book, we think, lacked something because he did not focus more directly on the voluntary sector. And yet, in a recent article called "Bowling Alone," Putnam reminds us that there are dilemmas in focusing too much on the voluntary sector: "To identify trends in the size of the nonprofit sector with trends in social connectedness would be another fundamental conceptual mistake."[11] Much voluntary sector research has emerged from advocacy, and it may not always focus on issues of bureaucratization or self-serving behavior. Nonprofits, just like government, business, and other forms of human interaction, can destroy social capital. Ironic, isn't it?

However, as researchers, we are paradoxically timid about our place. That the third sector comes in "third" underscores the point. Putnam's book, it seems to us, suggests a more upbeat and ambitious research agenda. His exploration of political institutions uncovers the central role that social capital plays in economic and political development for society as a whole. Italy became a case study for a perspective that has relevance domestically and internationally.

We need more works with the larger context provided by Putnam: the big studies more directly and immediately focused on the role of associational life, trust, and the voluntary sector in building democracy and civil society. Microstudies with a sectoral emphasis based on data collection must continue, of course. Yet we require more daring scholars in the tradition of, say, Tocqueville and Max Weber. In the coming years, we would hope to see research begun and other research finally concluded that will give us the longitudinal studies of NGOs and domestic institutional development we need.

"Bowling Alone" allowed Putnam to use some of his insights about America's declining social capital through a discussion of the decline in organized bowling leagues. There is room for serious disagreement about the extent to which this is true.[12] Some people are more inclined to see that we are just going through a process of shifting forms of community (for instance, the rise of a kind of "Internet community"). There is bound to be much disagreement over the causes of any decline in civil society. These are precisely the questions we need to look at. Can we, for instance, develop surveys of civic involvement over time? We need better tools that can measure dependency attitudes and participatory attitudes: perhaps using the work of Ellen Langer and others on learned helplessness. In that way, we could begin to see whether government policies, foundation grants, and voluntary associations actually strengthen civil society or lead to the destruction of social capital or encourage empowerment.

Putnam is eloquent in his description of this emerging American dilemma. As he writes in "Bowling Alone," "more Americans than ever before are in social circumstances that foster associational involvement (higher education, middle age, and so on), but nevertheless aggregate associational membership appears to be stagnant or declining."[13] We suspect that this dilemma afflicts many developed countries today, even as civil society becomes stronger in the developing and transitional countries. Whether we are interested in voluntary sector research, or what makes for a good society, or the state of associational life, a close look at Putnam and others who write about civil society can and should inform our discourse. As Putnam concludes his book, "building social capital will not be easy, but it is the key to making democracy work" (p. 185).

Originally published as a review of Making Democracy Work: Civic Traditions in Modern Italy, *by Robert D. Putnam, Robert Leonardi, and Raffaella Y. Nanetti (Princeton, NJ: Princeton University Press, 1993) in* Nonprofit and Voluntary Sector Quarterly, *V. 25, No. 1, March 1996. Reprinted with the permission of NVSQ and the kind permission of my co-author, Dr. Julie Fisher, a consummate scholar and activist for civil society around the world. Julie and I worked on this review while we were with the Program on Non-Profit Organizations at Yale University, she as a Scholar in Residence and I as a Visiting Fellow. She subsequently was a longtime program officer at the Kettering Foundation, and did distinguished work as an independent consultant. Her books include* Non-governments: NGOs and the Political Development of the Third World *(W. Hartford, CT: Kumarian Press, 1998) and* Importing Democracy: The Role of NGOs in South Africa, Tajikistan, and Argentina *(Dayton, OH: Kettering Foundation Press, 2013).*

[1] Michael Walzer, "The Idea of Civil Society," *Dissent,* Spring 1991, p. 293.

[2] Ernest Gellner, *Conditions of Liberty: Civil Society and Its Rivals* (New York: Viking Penguin, 1994) and Víctor Pérez-Díaz, *The Return of Civil Society: The Emergence of Democratic Spain* (Cambridge, MA: Harvard University Press, 1993).

[3] Robert D. Putnam, Robert Leonardi, and Raffaella Y. Nanetti, *Making Democracy Work: Civic Traditions in Modern Italy,* (Princeton, NJ: Princeton University Press, 1993). Page citations are included in the text.

[4] Pérez-Díaz, *op. cit.,* p. 456.

[5] See Julie Fisher, "Local Government and the Independent Sector in the Third World," in K. McCarthy, V. Hodgkinson, R. Sumariwalla, and Associates (Eds.), *The Nonprofit Sector in the Global Community: Voices from Many Nations* (San Francisco: Jossey-Bass, 1992).

[6] See Julie Fisher, "Cultivating Civil Society: NGOs, Donors and Governments in the Third World" (Unpublished manuscript, 1995).

[7] Fisher, Julie, *The Road from Rio: Sustainable Development and The Nongovernmental Movement in The Third World* (Westport, CT: Praeger, 1993), p. 17.

[8] See D. Goulet, "Three Rationalities in Development Decision-Making," *World Development* 14, No. 2, 1986, pp. 301–31, and S. Brown, "The logic of problem generation: From morality and solving to de-posing and rebellion," *For the Learning of Mathematics,* 4, No 1, 1984, pp. 9–20.

[9] For a recent, wide-ranging look at how and why social capital creates prosperity, see Francis Fukuyama's *Trust: The Social Virtues and the Creation of Prosperity* (New York: Free Press, 1995).

[10] See Fisher, 1993, *op. cit.*

[11] Putnam, R. D. "Bowling Alone," *Journal of Democracy,* No. 6, No. 1, January 1995, p. 71.

[12] "The Solitary Bowler," *The Economist,* February 18, 1995, pp. 21–22.

[13] "Bowling Alone," *op. cit.,* p. 73.

2. Recovering Voluntarism from the Dustbin of History

In the early 1930s, Walter Gifford, chairman of President Hoover's Organization on Unemployment Relief, voiced concern over the status of the "invisible aid" of charity in the social fabric. Gifford was an alumnus of Hull House, a board member of the Rockefeller Foundation, and president of AT&T. He spoke during a period when continuing efforts were being made to rationalize and professionalize charity and philanthropy. The state was increasingly seen as both the engine and instrument for the voluntary impulse.

These trends remain with us, and sadly, the sector we study — at least its historical dimension — remains largely invisible. For instance, one would be hard-pressed to find more than a few references to philanthropy, voluntarism, charity, and related topics in the third edition of *The American Historical Association Guide to Historical Literature*. Even in the nonprofit sector itself, historical understanding is a poor relation. The 1993–1994 edition of *Research in Progress* details 293 projects, only 19 (less than 7 percent) of which are captured by the keyword *history*. Such quick and dirty searches suggest that the visibility and viability of voluntarism have escaped historians whose work, in tum, contributes to the invisibility among sector scholars generally. [Now, nearly twenty-five years later, the situation is both better and worse. More historians are doing important research on philanthropy and the nonprofit sector — *and* the understanding of the relationships and tensions between voluntarism and the state are still too fraught with unquestioned assumptions.]

The two books under consideration here are important and complementary efforts to explore the history of an elusive topic. *Inventing the Nonprofit Sector* is a collection of nine essays (anchored by the title essay and "Cultures of Trusteeship in the United States," which together take up half the text, and include over seventy pages of valuable footnotes). The overall book focuses on three major themes. They provide a sketch of "an emerging institutional order" (p. xi). We are also treated to a remarkable effort to sketch out a historically sensitive and geographically grounded paradigm of trusteeship. Finally, the last three chapters present a series of provocative reflections on scholarship's own ambivalent role in developing the idea of the nonprofit sector.

Like Hall, Geoffrey Finlayson combines command of historical sources with a cautionary tale about the limited, politically tinged, and often teleological visions of historians. He avoids the well-worn assumption that the history of welfare must lead inevitably to the state. That insight opens an unusually rich sense of the remarkable extent and variety of voluntarism in the provision of social welfare in Britain from 1830 to 1990. We also have a subtly drawn study of the constantly shifting boundaries between voluntarism and the state.

Hall is a well-known *bête noire* among voluntary sector scholars. He is constantly reminding us that history matters and shows us here how it does. He uneasily accepts the idea of a "nonprofit sector" and uses it to remarkable effect as the axis from which he develops his three major themes and their various subthemes. The term has well-known limitations: it is a modern term that defines by exclusion and asserts its distinctiveness only by reference to commerce and the state. Many of the book's strengths and limitations, then, come from a term that Hall admits has a lot of unhelpful historical and theoretical baggage.

The invention of the nonprofit sector arose out of the self-conscious advocacy work of various commissions, researchers, and foundations starting in the early 1950s with the Cox Committee's investigation of foundations. It reached some form of conclusion with the work of the Filer Commission in the mid-1970s. Hall's summary of these efforts is fascinating and should be required reading for understanding both the history of the sector and the growth of its self-awareness. The first three essays in the book are the historical core which includes "Inventing the Third Sector," some reflections on religion and philanthropy in history, and a critique of the crisis of public policy regarding the nonprofit sector during the Reagan period.

Hall provides detailed and wide-ranging looks backwards to the American founding and forward through the Reagan era. That way, we can see the unfolding of this element of American democracy. Of particular importance throughout these accounts is the interpenetration of sectors, which over time has changed to become a relationship of "dependency" in theory and practice. We have, in these chapters, the best historical overview of this sector in America (as well as a model for bringing it up to date).

Hall shows great sensitivity to institutional themes, and this strength gives the book special salience for non-historians. (Hall credits the important work of Louis Galambos, "the dean of the history of organization," but his name is left out of the index.) The second three chapters present the historian at work on a theme of organizational and managerial trends. In particular, "Cultures of Trusteeship in the United States" is a very important effort to bring history, geography, an understanding of organizational behavior, and a sociological imagination to a topic of great relevance to scholars and practitioners. He sees four different leadership styles or cultures developing in the history of nonprofit organizations. This is in strong contrast to usual efforts among organizational theorists to posit an ahistorical ideal. The most important contrast is between an elitist model of "civil privatism" associated with Boston, and a more cooperative, federative, and associational model coming out of the Midwest. This is a rich chapter of applied history and is being subjected to various empirical tests in the literature.

The last three chapters seem less finished and less pointed. They also raise a very important and troubling topic that Hall has addressed elsewhere as well. He begins to probe from various angles the effects of the "patronage relationships" that often funds research agendas and may bias them, even unintentionally. (I remember Peter's story of sending a letter of inquiry to the Lilly Endowment and, willy-nilly, getting a huge grant.) The invention of the nonprofit sector out of advocacy research remains a serious challenge to scholarly advances in this field. Indeed, Finlayson's book is a gentle but major critique of a different kind of vested-interest scholarship. This is a topic that requires much more discussion, even though "biting the hand that feeds you" is a problem.

The history of the sector's self-definition provides additional dilemmas and obstacles for future research. The term "nonprofit sector" may be fundamentally different from what may be more broadly a voluntary sector. A methodology based on the idea of a nonprofit sector (whether applied to history, economics, or social theory) may fundamentally blind us to varieties of, and connections between, voluntary social action and related social phenomenon. This needs to be continually restudied, and any future research will have to stand on Hall's thoughtful work and address its assumptions. We can only hope that future explorations of this and other issues are done with the same commitment to careful thought and scholarship.

Collections of essays, of course, are always a problem. There is repetition, and coherence suffers. The themes that run through the book are present in Hall's shorter articles, but this shouldn't stop anyone from rereading his work often and appreciating the depth of the historical record in these essays. There is no doubt that a connected historical narrative would have been preferable, as Hall himself admits. Although there are always definitional issues inherent in the use of the term "nonprofit" that makes a full-scale history problematic, let me suggest a short-term alternative: Hall and his publisher could have considered revising and integrating the first two historical chapters into a single whole and published it as an outline for understanding the history of nonprofit organizations in the United States. It would be, I expect, a very valuable 150-page book.

Geoffrey Finlayson provides a broad, connected historical narrative to powerful effect. The brunt of this work brings visibility to the truly vast voluntary infrastructure for welfare provision that existed in Britain from the 1830s. His is a crucial overview of a broad topic that is getting more granular attention now. To do so, he had to jettison the nearly universal assumption that there is an upward "welfare state escalator" in historical development. This lack of a simple straight line also applies to the more recent period of 1949–1991. In fact, this book will give little comfort to either the left and socialist observers who want the "up" escalator, or to the ideologues of Thatcherism and the right who have their own view of an anti-welfare state "down" escalator going in the opposite direction. Neither approach works.

Voluntarism is portrayed broadly as neither a Victorian triumph over evil nor as a pathetic rear-guard action. Finlayson posits three sectors within voluntarism: First and primarily, there is a voluntary sector that includes self-help and mutual aid organizations as well as more traditional charitable and philanthropic entities. Second, there is the unstructured informal sector that includes relations between family, friends, and neighborhoods. And third, there is a commercial sector that might include commercial insurance and pension plans as well as, for instance, pawn shops. The book is divided chronologically under four general constructs: 1830–1880, self-improvement and paternalism; 1880–1914, collectivism and convergence; 1914–1949, war and welfare; and 1949–1991, participation and pluralism. That framework is very loosely applied since Finlayson values the historical record over any table of contents.

Finlayson's assumptions and framework are almost transparent in their simplicity, yet they fit the history and thinking of all sides and work well as organizing principles. The challenges facing any historian trying to uncover "invisible aid" can be daunting. The extent, variety, and depth of voluntarism's efforts at welfare provision revealed in this book will surprise almost everyone. Each chapter addresses the vast variety of what is known about each aspect of voluntarism; the successes, failures, foibles, and difficulties are laid out for the reader. Finlayson's summary and critique of the available data on voluntary activity, friendly societies, giving, and other charitable activity is a valuable exercise in "seeing" civil society at work. We also follow the ebb and flow of the controversies and interactions among intellectuals, politicians, and especially practitioners about what voluntarism and the state respectively could and should do. The constantly evolving efforts to find different mixes between voluntary and statutory provisions of welfare from 1830 through the Thatcher years is a series of constant adjustments within the context of a democratic *modus vivendi*. It is the character and not the amount of government involvement or funding that is important.

Finlayson's overview could use some of Hall's emphasis on institutional issues. The quotations and citations are very valuable. However, one gets only a hint of the internal organizational struggles, political battles, personal interests, and social forces that must have been driving forces in the historical process. The role of uncertainty must have been huge: uncertain funding, uncertain legal status, and the ups and downs of the economy and technology (as laws and regulations ate away at the voluntary sector's status). Future histories of welfare and voluntarism will owe a great deal to Finlayson's approach. And because of his work, they can go well beyond it with deeper historical analyses, as well as more sophisticated theories of voluntarism and the state.

From an editorial and production standpoint, both books have their problems. Finlayson unfortunately died just as the book was being completed. This is a great loss. It also means that the book's last 100 pages (covering the 1949–1991 period) lack finishing touches. They also suffer from occasional quotations with no citation and/or sources in the notes or bibliography. Hall's book suffers from too many typographical errors and at least one case where several lines and a footnote were dropped.

Finlayson begins his book with an observation from Robert Titmuss: "When we study welfare systems we see that they reflect the dominant cultural and political characteristics of their societies." Both books under review show great sensitivity to precisely this issue in their own extensive historical reporting. They also go a long way to revealing what Hall called "a universe of philanthropy and voluntarism that is bewildering in its complexity." Taken as a package, they highlight how deep and important this "invisible aid" is and why knowing the historical context is crucial.

Perhaps more important, both books caution us to be aware of and question the dominant cultural and political characteristics of our work and the work of others. Assumptions of all sorts, including pat categories and political blinders, can easily get in the way of reading history. Sometimes, crucial elements about philanthropy, nonprofits, and voluntarism are truly invisible to, or ignored by, us. In these two cases, Hall and Finlayson vastly improve our historical knowledge and the level of the discussion about what exactly we are "seeing" and needs to be studied.

Originally published in Nonprofit and Voluntary Sector Quarterly, *V. 24, No. 3, Fall 1995, as a review of two books:* Inventing the Nonprofit Sector and Other Essays on Philanthropy, Voluntarism, and Nonprofit Organizations, *by Peter Dobkin Hall (Baltimore, MD: Johns Hopkins University Press, 1992) and* Citizen, State, and Social Welfare in Britain, 1830–1990, *by Geoffrey Finlayson (Oxford: Oxford University Press, 1994). Reprinted with the permission of* NVSQ.

3. On the Vitality of Civil Society: Citizenship and Philanthropy

Introduction

For this paper, I hope to contribute to a better understanding of the importance of philanthropy (broadly defined as Bob Payton did as "voluntary action for the public good," which included the whole nonprofit sector) by addressing several issues that plagued us in 1994 and flummox us still. I do so by making broad and strong statements at odds with many of the assumptions that drive philanthropy and drive out openness to alternative viewpoints and facts. If anything, my contribution is in the tradition of Isaiah Berlin's classical liberalism: an invitation to an ongoing intellectual adventure and discovery process. Viewpoints should be contestable and varied; discourse should be open, diverse, and civil. What I am trying to do is suggest some points that deserve a "seat at the table," and exploration by others better able to do so than I. When this paper was first written the idea of civil society was vibrantly alive in theory and action. It has faded since then as new fads arise. I hope I may contribute a bit to showing how important a way of seeing it is.

I develop this paper around two basic themes:

Bringing civil society back in. The idea of civil society as distinct from government or the state is a very important lens through which to see. Philanthropy is a major but not the only component of civil society. It is the one I am interested in. And yet so much of the sector is primarily mesmerized by the siren song of government action and shies away from the support, means, and possibilities within civil society. The politicization of society has done great harm.

A different view of citizenship. When asked, most people will describe good citizenship as voting and participation in the political process. Whatever its virtues, there is another way to think about citizenship, as embedded in and supportive of civil society and philanthropy. The extent to which individuals volunteer and give may be a more active, engaged, and robust way we discharge our responsibilities as citizens. A large part of the paper considers how we might begin to look empirically at these two different views of citizenship: comparing and contrasting the data on the extent of volunteering and giving (as an expression of citizenship within civil society) with the extent of voting, and political participation (as an indication of citizenship through the political process). I believe the former turns out to be remarkably interesting and robust. The questions and issues such a contrast suggests are fascinating and troubling.

The Politicization of Society

During Vice President Gore's 1993 hearings on reinventing government, one invited guest was asked to comment on contracting out and public/private partnerships. The speaker raised some significant issues about liberty, individualism, and equal opportunity by suggesting, "We have to look back to Tocqueville." The published transcript, however, read, "We have to look back to the Tolk Bill."[1] Surely an obscure piece of legislation!

That at once hilarious and horrifying error of transcription captures an assumption that pervades so much social and public policy thought: All problems seem to be political problems which require coercive governmental solutions. This tendency applies equally well across the political spectrum; all sides of the debate about the kind of society we want are too quick to repair to politics.

As part of what has been called the politicization of society,[2] the voluntary sector has also been given a subservient role, and it has largely accepted such a role. For years voluntary action seemed largely invisible: irrelevant and ineffective.[3] Or voluntary action is seen to be the dependent younger sibling swaddled in state directives and funding. It has been theorized either as a bulwark of the welfare state or the saving grace of the conservative polity.

Foundations often rationalize their programs by expecting that the state will take them over. At least since the New Deal, reformers have believed "that the aim of the tradition of private philanthropy was the absorption by government of the responsibility for generating and administering reform.... The implication, too, was that whatever foundations and private philanthropy had been doing, government could do better."[4] While it is easy and dangerous to exaggerate what the voluntary sector does or can do, we have, I think, gone way too far in the other direction. Significantly, we have stopped exploring what the voluntary sector can do. Have scholars and practitioners been seduced by a politicized world? Too little knowledge about what the voluntary sector has accomplished leads to placing little importance on what may be unique about voluntarism. That, in turn, becomes a negative feedback loop, hampering a vision about what the voluntary sector can do. We need to reassess the challenge Ralph Kramer made many years ago: to find "an appropriate social distance between governmental and voluntary agencies."[5] Perhaps accentuating that distance between the public and private (including both the voluntary and commercial "sectors") has considerable value today.[6]

I want to situate philanthropy in the larger social context of civil society, thereby suggesting a workable alternative to the assumption that all social problems require political solutions. Philanthropy should not primarily be the handmaiden of politicization. The broad outline of such a framework is centered on the idea of civil society. Recovering what Vaclav Havel has poetically called "the independent life of society"[7] was both the stunning reaffirmation of modernity and the more recent key to the downfall of communism and continuing struggles around the world. Exploring the idea of civil society — with particular emphasis on philanthropy and the dynamics of citizenship based on voluntary social action — will reveal interesting perspectives and issues about the sector we study and work in, and about the locus of social change in society.[8]

Bringing Civil Society Back In

This is not the place to write a history of the politicization of American society nor of its impact on philanthropy. Reminding ourselves of the relative shift from independence to dependence — that there was life before politicization — may be useful, however.

It has been almost *de rigueur* since the Filer Commission to quote Daniel Boorstin's famous comment that "In America, even in modern times, communities existed before governments were here to care for public needs.... Philanthropy — our charitable spirit — in its transformed American shapes has become the leading feature of our relation to the world."[9]

Boorstin's comment contains a fundamental insight continually confirmed by much recent historical and theoretical work from around the world. Not only are government and society different. More important, in the continuum between them there can be a relative moral and practical preeminence given to voluntary social action as opposed to the coercive nature of state action. Consider, for instance, the article in this chapter on Robert Putnam. He and his co-authors unintentionally discovered this in their seminal *Making Democracy Work*. Other examples are given throughout this book.

Our last two centuries have been quite different. The radical vision of voluntary action that animated Tocqueville's *Democracy in America* has been transformed. We now live in the shadow of Herbert Croly's politicized *Promise of American Life*: "No voluntary association of individuals, resourceful and disinterested though they be, is competent to assume the responsibility" for America's national destiny."[10] Croly's call for a singular "National Purpose" required political centralization and social regimentation. Contestability of viewpoints and diverse purposes were out. His influence remains immensely strong and is one telling example of a thread of hostility to voluntary associations that runs through American history.[11] Indeed, there are important personal and intellectual connections between Croly and some of the leading early writers on philanthropy — for instance, Eduard C. Lindeman — that need to be explored someday.

The move from relative reliance on voluntary social power to reliance on political power is quite subtle, marbled with layers of admirable and dangerous tensions.[12] It certainly lionized executive power and expert bureaucratic control, eschewed voluntarism, gave moral sanction to coercion. It has infantilized social institutions. There was also an admirable emphasis on democracy that was a crucial aspect of American political development. A darker side existed as well. Emphasizing centralization placed democratic political processes squarely in the crosshairs of virulent political factions above all other social mechanisms. And there is a large literature on how "political citizenship" in the form of voting was essentially a passive act which deflected more robust citizen actions. Notions of liberty, the good society, citizenship, and social action became centered on the state.[13] A larger social and democratic vision, or what one writer has called "a commonwealth of citizenship outside the state," was rejected. [14]

As one would surmise from this adumbrated view of politicization, philanthropy was deeply afflicted, too. Voluntary action and voluntary associations were relegated to secondary importance or became highly suspect.[15] However interdependent our lives are, in much of the literature, philanthropy comes to the table as a junior partner, a young, weak sibling, subsumed under essentially political means. Or it is eager to get into the game and willing to sell its soul. Even the mediating structures that Berger and Neuhaus celebrate, for instance, are a means to an end — "alternative mechanisms" for more effective social planning of a conservative type. One does not get the sense that these structures are accorded enough independence, importance, purpose, or vitality of their own.[16] The point is rather similar in the important 1987 book *Shifting the Debate*, from a different frame of reference. It is not the conservative polity which is central, but the welfare state: "[T]he voluntary sector ought not be defined in such a way that it is in competition or opposition to the welfare state."[17] Van Til is quite right that defining by negatives is to denigrate any independence of the voluntary sector. The brunt of his argument, however, is to subsume the voluntary sector under the state. I will argue in the next paper in this chapter that Lester Salamon's seminal article on "voluntary failure" is incomplete and misleading precisely because it assumes the sector is derivative in the context of superior and presumably benign state action.[18] Without a fuller theory of the state and civil society, interpreting his work is difficult.

Jennifer Wolch, in *The Shadow State*, brought to philanthropy a clever and important switch in perspective. She also employed a state-centered approach to the study of the voluntary sector, by "bringing the state back in."[19] But, she argues:

the emergence of the shadow state is fundamentally linked to recent transformations in the welfare state. These changes were made possible because of the long-standing institutional interdependence of voluntary organizations and the state, which both enables and constrains voluntary action ... the transformation of the voluntary sector into a shadow state apparatus could ultimately shackle its potential to create progressive social change.[20]

It certainly does, in the form of a sleight-of-hand that brings philanthropy into the halls of government by recognizing it as a self-interested and elitist pressure group. Wolch's critical analysis is invaluable, but it too is incomplete. Indeed, when philanthropy acts that way, isn't it part of the problem? A "theory of state policy toward the voluntary sector" cannot stand alone, for it unduly focuses on the state. There is no theory of a "countervailing" civil society or social power. This point is brought out cogently in some recent work on Third World development, but the point applies to philanthropy as well. Joel Migdal has written about the difficulties encountered by state-centered theories:

> [N]ot only is the claim open to empirical verification, the theoretical assumption has frequently led to the tendency to strip the other components of society of their volition or agency, portraying them as malleable putty in the hands of the most powerful element of society, the state ... although the important point that "states matter" has now been made — and, to repeat, it needed to be made — there is no getting around the mutuality of state-society interactions. Societies affect states as much as, or possibly more than, states affect societies.[21]

Philanthropy, then, needs to see the world and be in the world in a much broader way than the dependency assumption or state-centered theories that have prevailed and still do. The term "civil society" is a popular term used to incorporate that social context. It has a great — though often invisible — historical and theoretical pedigree of contemporary relevance. Such a broad understanding of voluntary social action will give philanthropy the volition and agency that it often does not have. When the idea and history of civil society is fully developed, one hopes we would know better the unique aspects of philanthropy, the conflicts and differences that animate interactions with the state, and areas of true synergy necessary for the perpetuation of a good society.

PHILANTHROPIC LANDSCAPES

For Instance: Abandoning Civil Society and Getting "Bumped" into Social Security

A very brief digression on the history of Social Security may help make the distinction between problem-solving within civil society and solutions arising out of a rigid politicization of a problem.

Frances Perkins was secretary of labor for FDR and a principal architect of Social Security. The following is from a 1962 address. She makes two points that are striking: (1) voluntary action — though largely invisible — was doing the job before Social Security; and (2) that the terrifying impact of the Great Depression "bumped the American people" into state action and into Social Security as the only — visible — option (particularly telling, since much research has suggested government failures were a very significant element in bringing on and exacerbating the Depression). She wrote:

> I suppose the roots — the idea that we ought to have a systematic method of taking care of the material needs of the aged — really springs from that deep well of charitableness which resides in the American people, and the efforts and the struggles of charity workers and social workers to handle the problems of people who were growing old and had no adequate means of support. Out of this impulse to be kind to the poor sprang, I suppose, a mulling of ideas about social insurance for the aged. But those people who were doing it didn't know that it was social insurance. They just kept thinking that something definite, something that people could look forward to, would be a great asset and a great assistance to them in their work. Even de Tocqueville, in his memoirs of his visit to America, mentioned what he thought was a unique state of mind of the American people: that they were so honestly concerned about their poor and did so much for them personally. It was not an organization; it was not a national action; it was not a State action; it was not Government. *It was personal action that de Tocqueville mentioned as being characteristic of the American people. They were so generous, so kind, so charitably disposed* [emphasis added].

> Well, I don't know anything about the times in which de Tocqueville visited America. That was long ago, and I know little about the psychological state of mind of the people of this country at that time. But I do know that at the time I came into the field of social work, these feelings were real. *It was surprising what we were able to do through volunteer work — by the volunteer support of organizations who help the poor, and particularly the aged poor* [emphasis added]. Just look over the country at the old ladies'

homes and the old couples' homes and the old members' homes that sprang up because aged people had necessities that had to be met. In each case, somebody got money together and established these homes. And life went on for the aged, after a fashion, as recipients of a kind of charity. These things have been going on for years.

But actually, of course, the beginning of widespread interest in Social Security through the use of an insurance technique began in a serious way shortly before the Great Depression of 1929 ... *the real roots of the Social Security Act were in the Great Depression of 1929. Nothing else would have bumped the American people into a social security system except something so shocking, so terrifying, as that depression* [emphasis added].[22]

If the economic situation and the policy focus had been different, would an imperfect, creative, diverse voluntary system continued to meet the needs *and* have been continually improving over decades by encouraging innovation within civil society and the economy? We can't know, but we can ask ourselves now if Social Security has met its promises and whether institutional changes and innovations within both civil society and the economy may afford us different and better options now outside of a calcified, politicized, and increasingly bankrupt state system.

Civil Society

The intellectual task of "bringing the state back in" has been done. In fact, one could argue (but not here) that bringing the state back in and then throwing it out again — back and forth, again and again — has been a major thread in political thought.[23] Much less common is the idea of "reinventing society" or "bringing civil society back in." Infighting about the state is meaningless without reference to an alternative. There needs to be a positive, relatively independent alternative, broader than but including the market. The idea of civil society can meet that need. It had been reintroduced by the revisioning of the term in the 1980s as Eastern Europe tried to find a different way to vanquish communism. And yet it is a term with a plethora of fuzzy meanings.[24] At the 1993 ARNOVA meeting, Emmett Carson gave a genuinely cogent critique of the term: "If my mother doesn't know what it is, it won't work."

We need to rediscover civil society and apply its lens and its methods, rather than limit our vision arguing solely about limiting or expanding government and the state. My particular focus here is on the relationship of philanthropy to the idea of a vital and civil society (a "civil citizenship," if you will). Looking at the interconnections of civil society and philanthropy will enrich both ideas and our future.

The ideas of civil society and political society have often been conflated in political thought. From about the time of the Scottish Enlightenment and the writings of Adam Ferguson and Adam Smith, a different tradition did develop. Civil society was taken to be a sphere of voluntary and "spontaneous" human action different and largely separate from the coercive nature of the state and political society. Hegel was important in giving further meaning to the idea. For him, civil society included market forces, individual self-interest, and the myriad of social associations and institutions. Marx, Gramsci, and others later used the term in various ways but in large part folded the idea of civil society back into the state. How civil society really worked seemed amorphous enough that it never really gained the critical attention that it needed. In any case, the importance of this idea of civil society cannot be underestimated. Ernest Gellner has expressed this beautifully:

> Prior to the miracle of Civil Society, human societies habitually lived under coercive and superstitious systems, and generally took such a condition for granted.... Then, on one occasion, something rather strange and unusual happened. Certain societies, whose internal organization and ethos shifted away from predation and credulity to production and a measure of intellectual liberty and genuine exploration of nature, became richer.... What had been the normal social condition of man in the traditional world — government by fear and falsehood — was felt to be inherently illegitimate and avoidable. They [the *philosophes*] preached its modification and transformation. Astonishingly, the regime in which oppression and dogmatism prevailed was not merely wicked, but actually weaker than societies which were freer and more tolerant! [25]

The German historical sociologist Franz Oppenheimer's little book *The State* succinctly set out in clear terms how different were the means contrasting the political (coercion) and the economic (voluntary action).[26] Civil society refers to those social relations we have that are voluntary and cooperative, whereas the state is a sphere of action based on organized force. And one of the most useful and nuanced perspectives on civil society is provided by Víctor Pérez-Díaz in his excellent book on the emergence of democratic Spain. It is worth quoting at some length because he defines two meanings of civil society, which give a dynamic sense to historical experience. First, in a narrow sense, civil society represents:

> Social institutions such as markets and voluntary associations and a public sphere which are outside the direct control, in a full or in a mitigated sense, of the state.

The development and emergence of civil society in this sense prepares the way for and strengthens an overall more robust sense of civil society and the body politic, including the state and government. The further value of this broader definition is that it places civil society in some sense prior to, and necessary for, a sociopolitical society of liberal democracy, free markets, and open discourse. This larger, second, sense entails:

> A set of sociopolitical institutions including a limited government or state operating under the rule of law; a set of social institutions such as markets (or spontaneous extended orders) and associations based on voluntary agreements among autonomous agents; and a public sphere in which these agents debate among themselves and with the state about matters of public interest and engage in pubic activities.[27]

Many commentators and especially economists have rightly emphasized the importance of commerce and the marketplace to a vital civil society. Some have noted, however, how that narrow market focus limits the idea of civil society.[28] Following Tocqueville, I wish to stress the underappreciated force of the voluntary impulses of the institutions of philanthropy.

There is an invaluable interdependence between civil society and the state in the good society. However, one cannot assume the state is a benign or neutral presence. There are plenty of times when increasing the power of one results in impoverishing the other: increases or decreases in social power accompany decreases or increases in state power. This is the sad legacy of the communist experiments and myriad kaleidoscopes of totalitarian regimes, where enshrining state power crippled social power, leading all too often to totalitarian regimes. Recognizing a strong element of antithesis between the state's monopoly of coercive force and civil society's voluntary associations is crucial if democracy is to be maintained.[29]

Perhaps recognition of these differences is also a primary responsibility of philanthropy. Philanthropy is not only where "the moral agenda of society is put forward."[30] Philanthropy also embodies the voluntary human and financial means necessary to address many of the tragic problems all societies face. Keeping this distinction between political and social in mind does not necessarily preclude the much-valued philanthropic "partnerships" with government. But seeing them as simply a step towards governmental assumption of responsibilities suggests a client relationship rather than a partnership. And partnerships are more problematic than generally acknowledged. Any true partnership requires an appreciation of differences and dangers as well. In our politicized world, that is rare. Much of the progressive and radically democratic potential of philanthropy may be lost in a trade-off for greater politicization. The challenge is, to what extent does philanthropy support civil society?

Two Sectors Are Better Than Three

It is the accepted — albeit uneasy — practice to discuss philanthropy as one of three or more sectors in society.[31] Though useful in many ways, there are also attendant, well-known problems. Many such models are unconnected to any larger social theory. Perhaps coming up with finer and finer distinctions has resulted in a loss of perspective. This article suggests two is better than three: civil society, on the one hand, and the political system or the state on the other. Civil society itself is conceptualized, then, as including the broad philanthropic world of voluntary associations as well as other voluntary and commercial relationships. From a theoretical standpoint, this model has the advantage of being connected to a long tradition of political and sociological thought introduced above. It helps us see our history better.

Establishing a conceptual space for "the independent life of society" gives civil society putative powers and responsibilities. It underscores the need for the institutions of civil society (philanthropic and commercial) to see, respect, and support their own voluntary, diverse roots and means. It also suggests that the necessary interdependence of the two sectors is as fraught with dangers as it is open to synergistic possibilities. It is all too easy to decrease social power and drain people of active citizenship. Understanding the differences between these two sectors, for instance, may provide a cautionary note to those from different sides of the political spectrum. For instance, vouchers for private schools or a national service program — as ways to strengthen civil society — may be, as they say, self-referentially inconsistent, if overly politicized.

Conceptualizing philanthropy and the marketplace *within* civil society may avoid old controversies about differences between them that haven't been all that productive. Looking at the similarities may raise its own set of interesting points or troubling issues. Many practitioners and fundraisers see considerable similarity between them (for good and ill) as fundraising practices change and different revenue streams are developed. Researchers and policy makers try to stake out similarities and differences. The effort sometimes seems to be a non-issue. For many people, their often-justified distaste for commerce has led them to draw moats around philanthropy. In any case, looking at the "forest" in this way promises to raise many interesting issues in slightly new ways.

Some economists have tended to subsume all voluntary action and civic institutions into a procrustean bed of market relationships, or at least to preference the latter. A facile reading of Hegel and others (taking their lead from the Scottish Enlightenment) has led many to emphasize the marketplace and private property as the preeminent voluntary aspects of civil society. They have missed, for instance, the sophisticated arguments by Adam Smith and others about voluntary and cooperative action generally. One can make much too much of the view that equates civil society and the marketplace.

Just as philanthropy becomes "invisible" in some views of the welfare state, so it can for some market theorists. It should be noted that the critics of economics have been quick to take up and further caricature these views. This is too limited a view and subject to ideological interpretations, which are destructive. Whatever the differences, the point stands that civil society does embrace the voluntaristic similarities of market and philanthropy. Most economics embrace this even as they may not really understand the full dynamics of philanthropy. Ultimately, then, the two-sector conception marks a clear distinction, porous as it may sometimes be, between civil society — including philanthropy, markets, etc. — and the state. I believe seeing history and theory in that way is very valuable.

Bringing Philanthropy Back In, We Hope

After nearly a century of relative disuse, civil society was reaffirmed by the dissident intellectuals of Eastern Europe in the 1980s.[32] This was not only an intellectual weapon against totalitarian regimes, it was an effort to envision a less political alternative. We owe a great debt of gratitude to their brave words and actions. They reminded us that voluntary institutions are the lifeblood of social existence and individual liberty. The idea of civil society became a very powerful conceptual tool for a very real problem: how to carve out an area of social action independent from an all-encompassing state. As the Polish dissident Adam Michnik lamented:

> From the official point of view a civil society doesn't exist. Society is not recognized as capable of organizing itself to defend its particular interests and points of view.... The crucial problem is therefore to build a democratic society which renders totalitarianism impossible by altering the social mechanisms of power.[33]

Tentative though it was, this is exactly what happened with the August 1980 agreement between the Polish state and the Solidarity workers at Gdansk. Again, Michnik:

> For the first time organized authority was signing an accord with an organized society…. For the first time in the history of communist rule in Poland "civil society" was being restored, and it was reaching a compromise with the state."[34]

In subsequent years, it became clear that no compromise was possible. The moral and material poverty of totalitarian regimes began to disintegrate in the light of an idea. It remains to be seen if the resulting painful void will be filled with civility or new terrors. Twenty-five years later and the results are bracing. The state *is* at constant war with civil society institutions that are often too weak.

Nevertheless, the reality that the Eastern European intellectuals found themselves in underscores the point that we need a sphere of human action that is largely separate from the state. And their point still reverberates over decades (not always successfully, of course). Efforts continually bubble up and down in Russia and other former communist countries. Current examples would include in China, the Arab Spring, throughout South America, and in a myriad of small community efforts.

Though we don't like to admit it, there is a similar, subtle form of antagonism between voluntarism and both a welfare state or a conservative polity in the U.S., just as there is in the centralized regimes of the world. Society in America is frustrated by a progressively politicized perspective (while we demand more politically as well). The much-ballyhooed dissatisfaction of the American voter with Washington and "politics as usual" is shouted from the rooftops every election year. Reporting on the disillusionment of the American public with politics has been going on for some time.[35] A June 1994 Gallup poll found that 17 percent of the respondents said they can trust Washington to do what is right all or most of the time. This is down from a high in 1964 of nearly 76 percent. Think of what the numbers are now, in 2019!

Ironically, though, the loud calls for "change," are ironically framed as a need for more political solutions. They are at best palliative. At worst, the political "solution" will sacrifice democratic freedoms in progressively more intrusive ways, without changing what is in most need of change: the division of power between civil society and government. It is time to see that politicization — at current levels and regardless of the political label attached to it — will continue to exacerbate the political problems and impoverish society. Perhaps we will see that we need to conceptualize and embrace the "independent life of society" that Havel and others reaffirmed in their attacks on totalitarianism. This was, of course, part of the perception that Tocqueville had long ago: "There are no countries in which associations are more needed to prevent despotism of faction or the arbitrary power of a prince than those which are democratically constituted."[36]

Thank goodness, one might exclaim, for the American tradition of philanthropy. Perhaps this is how civil society will be reinvigorated. Consider some thought experiments. Pick an issue that seems mostly solvable through the political system: Social Security, the Equal Rights Amendment, etc. First, ask if the issue has been solved that way. And then ask what would have happened if much more of the thinking, time, and money over the years promoting the issue had been spent on setting up diverse and rich responses and associations within civil society. I am not suggesting either/or, but rather that we too quickly repair to political solutions when the voluntary actions of citizens can and do offer innovative and robust approaches.

The world of nonprofits today may provide only partial relief, for it is part of the problem. One of the most troubling questions — again, regardless of one's political persuasion — is, Has philanthropy itself become so politicized that there is precious little independent life left in it? A large and growing proportion of funding for nonprofit organizations now comes from government. In 1989, government funding accounted for 31 percent of income to nonprofit public benefit organizations.[37] A whole series of problematic effects follow. The plethora of nonprofit advocacy and public policy groups spend much of their time promoting their own brands of special needs to the government.[38]

James Madison's fear of faction is upon us with a vengeance, and voluntary associations are partly at fault. So many now exist in such large measure promoting their interests to government and to receive its largesse. This is the point in Jonathan Rauch's *Demosclerosis*: The silent killer of American government is us, through our own political associations as opposed to civil society organizations. A 1990 survey found that seven out of ten Americans belong to at least one association, and that "half the respondents said that the main function of most associations is to influence the government."[39]

Until we gain a broader sense of philanthropy within civil society, progress against these problems and for the needs of society will be compromised. Depoliticizing philanthropy, in a sense, may be liberating. The separation of church and state has certainly allowed for a vital religious institutional presence to flourish, especially in education and the social services. One critic has even suggested the need for a Constitutional separation of philanthropy and the state.

From Tocqueville to Pérez-Díaz, there is a long tradition of thought and history suggesting that the development of a robust civil society prepares the way for and sustains political democracy. It is not the other way around. The importance and relevance of the idea of civil society has been underscored by recent historical work that focuses on civil society as "a much-needed corrective to an exclusive emphasis on the formal institutions of government..."[40] Whether it is the lessons of Eastern Europe and the former Soviet Union, Robert Putnam's book on modern Italy,[41] Víctor Pérez-Díaz's work referred to above, James Given's comparative study of medieval Europe,[42] or Elinor Ostrom's studies on collective action,[43] there is a common thread. The institutions of civil society are of commanding importance. It is beginning to become apparent that our voluntary institutions are not derivative, not "third" anything, not merely "mediating."

Though often unrecognized, Pérez-Díaz's point about Spain has a more general relevance for us, too: "the gradual emergence of liberal democratic traditions of institutions and values in civil society *preceded*, and prepared the way for, the political transition of the 1970s" [emphasis added].[44] Democratic political institutions are certainly crucial to the strength of civil society and the health and extent of a society's philanthropic efforts. There is emphatically much more to it than that. In the rush to solve all problems through political means, have we brought on a decay of democracy, an uncivil society, and atomized individuals by ignoring or subjugating civil society? The point is not, of course, that state versus civil society is an all-or-none proposition. The point is that civil society has not gotten the independence, attention, and support necessary for it to flourish.

One last marker about philanthropy's own failure to live up to its possibilities and responsibilities to the civil society that has produced it: This is a topic that threads through this book, but it needs extensive, sophisticated documentation, discussion, and amplification way beyond the focus of this article or book. Suffice it to say that in my over thirty years in philanthropy, it has been continually seduced to focus on government and not on civil society. The challenge before philanthropy is to take responsibility and reverse that unquestioned emphasis. Let me conclude this section, then, with a comment about this written in white-hot clarity by Henry Suhrke, the remarkable and underappreciated advocate and critic of philanthropy who was founder/editor of *Philanthropy Monthly* from 1968 to 2002:

> It's not a pretty sight: leaders who have been living off of Tocqueville quotes for years, retreating frantically and loudly from the real possibility of putting their long and glorious heritage to work. The pronouncements and the ideas are uniformly negative. Philanthropy has its list of "Gimme's" but is

eager to proclaim that it must not be expected actually to bear societal responsibilities.

If philanthropy itself only claims marginal roles — supplying highly egocentric venture capital, criticism of society, and expertise on who to redistribute income and as a conduit for tax-derived funds (minus administration costs, of course) — it seems likely that public policy will accommodate these claims accordingly. That is the only conceivable outcome of the current daily litany of reasons why private charity ought not to be counted on for a major independent role in social policy.... The ultimate [result] is to lose the tradition for want of trying. How bizarre that so many leaders (?) now seem bent on the latter course.[45]

The Commonwealth of Citizenship Outside the State

Tocqueville was not only right about the America of his day. He set down observations of enduring relevance. There is indeed a certain independence, difference, and even preeminence to civil society that requires acknowledgment and then thoughtful theoretical and practical support.

Philanthropy has a special place within the sphere of civil society. It is through our philanthropic associations that we acknowledge and act out our values in a "commonwealth of citizenship outside the state."[46] Unfortunately, the power and vitality of this view of citizenship is vastly underestimated and difficult to measure. On the one hand, the good citizenship of everyday life is so natural it is "invisible." On the other hand, citizenship today is almost exclusively seen in a political context, as a bundle of political rights, for instance.[47] Desmond King notes the clear theoretical and normative bias: "There is a significant tradition of state intervention built around the idea of citizenship for which there is no real equivalent to underpin voluntary activity."[48] We need a different perspective on citizenship.

If philanthropy is, to some considerable extent, "voluntary action for the public good," then the extent to which we as a nation engage in voluntary actions and institutions says something about the vitality of our civil society (in the same way that voting is seen as a proxy for the vitality and legitimacy of a political system). What might a comparison show? This could be a useful rhetorical and substantive pursuit. Is this a contrasting view of citizenship that might serve to highlight the distinction between state and civil society in useful ways? I think so.

On the one hand, 55 percent of the voting age population cast ballots in the 1992 presidential election. That reversed a 30-plus-year decline in voting rates. Voting is no doubt important, but it is specifically limited to the political system and has peculiar benefits, as Wolfinger and Rosenstone noted in their book *Who Votes*: "[T]he most important benefit of voting ... is expressive rather than instrumental: a feeling that one has done one's duty to society ... and to oneself."[49] A similar attitude was beautifully expressed by Henry David Thoreau: "I cast my vote, perchance, as I think right; but I am not vitally concerned that that right should prevail. I am willing to leave it to the majority. Its obligation, therefore, never exceeds that of expediency. Even voting *for the right* is *doing* nothing for it."[50]

Giving and volunteering, on the other hand, are different kinds of commitments; it is doing something for the right as one sees it. Voting is focused on majority rule and is often a contentious zero-sum affair. Philanthropic involvement is a form of what one might call engaged and dispersed "civil sovereignty." Each philanthropic "vote" or action counts. This is "active" citizenship.

The data on giving and volunteering is incomplete and often suffers from definitional differences. Some very tentative comparisons with voting are possible though. A major 1985 survey, *The Charitable Behavior of Americans*, indicated that 89 percent of Americans age 18 or older had made contributions in 1984, averaging $650. Eight-one percent believed that it was the responsibility of people to give what they can to charities. What is equally significant is that 38 percent of those surveyed thought they should be giving more.[51]

There were approximately 190 million Americans 18 years and older then. Using the rough percentages mentioned above, 104.5 million voted in the last presidential election, and approximately 169 million donated money or volunteered that year. I don't want to make too much of this "quick and dirty" comparison. There are lots of subtleties and other issues that I have to leave for others to explore. This is certainly suggestive, however. Nevertheless, the contrast is striking, especially considering the real "cost" to individuals of giving and volunteering, which is absent to a considerable extent in voting. The point is simply that citizenship through philanthropy suggests a civil society that is both extensive and robust. Estimates made at Independent Sector suggest that the potential for dramatic increases in giving and volunteering is actually quite high and at hand.[52] (See, in particular, the first article in Chapter 5, "The Making of the Intergenerational Transfer.") As an engine of progressive social action, as well as for charitable care, philanthropy offers great potential for expressing the diverse, pressing, and competing conceptions of the good society that a large population inevitably holds. The center of that ideal of citizenship is in philanthropy.[53] Note that the decreasing trends in associational life since this article was written may be the canary in the mine, foreshadowing the progressive loss in civility and a dangerous increase in politicization.

Conclusion

The vitality of our society depends especially on the vitality of our institutions of civil society as much, and likely, I have suggested, more than anything else. Emphasizing the qualities of independence and importance of civil society is meant to question the usual imbalance by suggesting a different way of "seeing." This is especially true and needed within the philanthropic world.

I have questioned politics and the politicization of society as the best and primary mechanism to resolve problems. The idea of civil society provides a different way of seeing. It is a new starting point for discussing a different view of citizenship that is embedded in civil society and that can be imperfectly measured by the level of engagement in philanthropy. So many of the interventions of the state to improve society — be they "left" or "right" — have been found wanting.

That is why it seems to me that the civil society tradition of seeing a more robust form of citizenship in what Frank Prochaska felicitously termed "the commonwealth of citizenship outside the state" is an idea worth pursuing. And there is an interesting way to imperfectly compare and measure citizenship in civil society versus political citizenship as measured by voting.

This is not, however, an uncritical paean to philanthropy. On the contrary, what has happened to civil society and philanthropy is its own damn fault. It is sadly reminiscent of the downfall of the old regime as Tocqueville understood it. When we see

> so many ridiculous, ramshackle institutions, survivals of an earlier age, which no one had attempted to co-ordinate or to adjust to modern conditions and which seemed destined to live on despite the fact that they had ceased to have any present value, it was natural enough that thinkers of the day should come to loathe everything that savored of the past and should desire to remodel society on entirely new lines, traced by each thinker in the sole light of reason.[54]

It is natural enough that Herbert Croly and many others have sought solace and the promise of American life through solutions endlessly proffered through the state. I believe that philanthropy has in a very real sense failed its own nature by acceding to political answers and ignoring the possibilities of progress through the voluntary means of civil society. This point is clearly part of why I found the writings of Gene Sharp and Elinor Ostrom so valuable (see the relevant articles on them in Chapter 1).

I have suggested seeing social interactions less politically. But seeing and doing are different. I believe there is ample historical and other empirical evidence to validate the power civil society has. That is beyond this paper and has been taken up by many scholars. So it seems clear to me that within the messy and robust parameters of civil society there exists a powerful and unfulfilled potential in philanthropy, if we but see it and commit to it. We have powerful tools — means — long underutilized.

At the end of his novel *The Empire City*, Paul Goodman considers the human plight philosophically:

> Somewhere there is the enemy. What strength and weapons will he have to meet him with? Horatio tickets them off his fingers, *the weapons that we have that do not weigh one down*.... Also, there is the force that is in the heart of the matter, that, as if stubbornly, makes things exist rather than be merely dreams or wishes. [emphasis added][55]

People are looking for new, positive approaches to address their human problems, but fail to consider their own active citizenship in their everyday world. Perhaps we need to embrace more fully those weapons of civil society: weapons that do not weigh one down but do require thought and a different kind of civil-society-centric effort.

We need a few among us to claim philanthropy *can* do so much more, to even reject government help (as the Red Cross did in 1931)[56] as a defense of a civil society, and actually to act in creative and progressive ways to defend and extend a robust civil society. By doing so, we recognize and accept our responsibilities to our society and others through voluntary action. We need to experiment with how to support, protect, and ensure a flourishing civil society. Now that is a goal complex and diverse enough for philanthropy to discuss *and* tackle.

This paper was originally written for and presented at the Annual Meeting of the Association for Research in Nonprofit Organizations and Voluntary Action, Berkeley, CA, October 20–22, 1994. I would like to thank the Indiana University Center on Philanthropy and the J. M. Kaplan Fund for their financial and intellectual support. The paper was started while I was an adjunct research associate at the Center of Philanthropy, and finished while I was a Visiting Fellow at the Program on Non-profit Organizations at Yale.

[1] National Performance Review, Reinventing Government Summit, Philadelphia, PA, June 25, 1993. Testimony of Peter Cove, p. 30.

[2] See, for instance, Jacques Ellul, *The Political Illusion* (New York: Alfred A. Knopf, 1967); Kenneth S. Templeton, Jr., editor, *The Politicization of Society* (Indianapolis: Liberty Fund, 1979); and T. Halper and R. Hartwig, "Politics and Politicization: An Exercise in Definitional Bridge-Building," *Political Studies 23,* 1975.

[3] For instance, when John Kenneth Galbraith wrote *The Affluent Society* in 1958, he saw American society composed solely of a governmental and a commercial sector. In 1962, Milton Friedman simply saw voluntary cooperation as "the technique of the market place" in *Capitalism and Freedom* (Chicago: The University of Chicago Press, 1962), p. 13. Ten years later, Rose and Milton Friedman acknowledged more in *Free to Choose*, "Voluntary cooperation is no less effective in organizing charitable activity than in organizing production for profit." (New York: Harcourt Brace, 1972), p. 37.

[4] Barry D. Karl, "Philanthropy, Policy Planning, and the Bureaucratization of the Democratic Ideal." *Daedalus*, Vol. 105, No. 4, Fall 1976, p. 140.

[5] Ralph M. Kramer, *Voluntary Agencies in the Welfare State* (Berkeley: University of California Press, 1981), p. 292.

[6] It should be noted that the implicit critique of the voluntary sector presented here applies equally well to commerce.

[7] Vaclav Havel, "The Power of the Powerless," in *Open Letters: 1965–1990* (London: Faber and Faber, 1991), p. 177.

[8] We see the assumption that voluntary action is essentially derivative in the terminology we use: 1) a *third* sector; 2) a *non-X* sector that is a residual beneficiary of what government or profit-making industry can't do; and 3) a *mediating* structure or *intermediate* institution, all suggesting a lack of purpose and vigor of its own. I will avoid here most of the usual terms for the sector we study precisely for this reason. I use the term "philanthropy" following Robert Payton, as a "comprehensive term that includes voluntary giving, voluntary service, and voluntary association, primarily for the benefit of others." *Philanthropy: Voluntary Action for the Public Good* (New York: American Council on Education/Macmillan Publishing Co., 1988), p. 32.

[9] Daniel J. Boorstin, *The Decline of Radicalism* (New York: Random House, 1969), pp. 46, 68.

[10] Herbert Croly, *The Promise of American Life* (New York: The Macmillan Company, 1912), p. 24.

[11] See Peter Dobkin Hall, *Inventing the Nonprofit Sector: And Other Essays on Philanthropy, Voluntarism, and Nonprofit Organizations* (Baltimore: The Johns Hopkins University Press, 1992) for a flavor of that hostility in American history. His first two chapters offer an outstanding history of the "sector." See my review, which is the second article in this Chapter.

[12] Gene Sharp develops this contrast in valuable ways. See my review of his *Social Power and Political Freedom* in Chapter 1.

[13] One sees this tension in democratic theory underneath Isaiah Berlin's famous "Two Concepts of Liberty." In positive liberty, the locus of personal development and social change is the state under positive liberty while negative liberty sets the general rules and both means and ends are left outside politics. Isaiah Berlin, *Four Essays on Liberty* (Oxford: Oxford University Press, 1970). Two of the best earlier statements trying to establish a balance are the famous French classical liberal Benjamin Constant in his 1819 speech, "The Liberty of the Ancients Compared With that of the Moderns," in *Benjamin Constant: Political Writings*, edited by Biancamaria Fontana (Cambridge: Cambridge University Press, 1988), and Wilhelm von Humboldt's 1852 *The Limits of State Action* (Cambridge: Cambridge University Press, 1969). Both works have a great deal to offer those interested in a broader rationale for civil society and philanthropy.

[14] Frank Prochaska, "But the Greatest of These...", *Times Literary Supplement*, January 15, 1993, p. 15.

[15] See, for instance, Theodore J. Lowi, *The End of Liberalism*, 2nd ed. (New York: W.W. Norton and Co., 1979).

[16] Peter L. Berger and Richard John Neuhaus, *To Empower People: The Role of Mediating Structures in Public Policy* (Washington DC: American Enterprise Institute, 1977; Second Edition, 1996).

[17] Susan Ostrander, Stuart Langton, Jon Van Til, editors, *Shifting the Debate* (New Brunswick: Transaction Books, 1987), p. 130.

[18] Lester M. Salamon, "Of Market Failure, Voluntary Failure, and Third-Party Government: Towards a Theory of Government-Nonprofit Relations in the Modern Welfare State," in *Shifting the Debate*, pp. 29-49.

[19] See, for instance, Peter B. Evans, Dietrich Tueschemeyer, and Theda Skocpol, editors, *Bringing the State Back In* (Cambridge: Cambridge University Press, 1985); Michael Mann, *The Sources of Social Power*, 2 volumes (Cambridge: Cambridge University Press, 1986 and 1993); John A. Hall, editor, *States in History* (Oxford: Basil Blackwell, 1986).

[20] Jennifer R. Wolch, *The Shadow State* (New York: The Foundation Center, 1990), p. 15.

[21] Joel S. Migdal, Atul Kohli, and Vivienne Shue, editors, *State Power and Social Forces* (Cambridge: Cambridge University Press, 1994), pp. 20 and 2.

[22] Frances Perkins, "The Roots of Social Security," U.S. Government Publication Office, 1963. On October 23, 1962, Frances Perkins addressed the General Staff Meeting of the Social Security Administration.

[23] Consider two rather classic approaches: C. J. Friedrich, "The Deification of The State." *The Review of Politics*, V. 1, No. 1, January 1939; and William O. Reichart, "Anarchism, Freedom, and Power," *Ethics*, V. 79, No. 2, January 1969.

[24] The literature on the idea of civil society is extensive and diverse. The following are particularly useful starting points: Víctor M. Pérez-Díaz, *The Return of Civil Society: The Emergence of Democratic Spain* (Cambridge: Harvard University Press, 1993); Ernest Gellner, *Conditions of Liberty: Civil Society and its Rivals* (New York:

Viking Penguin, 1994); Krishnan Kumar, "Civil Society: An Inquiry into the Usefulness of an Historical Term", *The British Journal of Sociology*, V. 44, No. 3, October 1993; Michael Walzer, "The Idea of Civil Society," *Dissent*, Spring 1991; Charles Taylor, "Modes of Civil Society," *Public Culture*, Vol 3, No 1, Fall 1990; *The Idea of a Civil Society* (Research Triangle Park NC: National Humanities Center, 1992); Jean Cohen and Andrew Arato, *Civil Society and Political Theory* (Cambridge: The MIT Press, 1992). A collection of important essays on civil society by Edward Shils should also be mentioned, *The Virtue of Civility: Selected Essays on Liberalism, Tradition, and Civil Society*, edited by Steven Grosby (Indianapolis: Liberty Fund, 1997).

[25] Gellner, *Conditions of Liberty, op. cit.*, pp. 32 and 33.

[26] Franz Oppenheimer, *The State,* Introduction by Charles Hamilton (New York: Free Life Editions, 1973).

[27] Víctor M. Pérez-Díaz, *The Return of Civil Society* (Cambridge: Harvard University Press, 1993), pp. 57 and 53.

[28] See, for instance, Richard Cornuelle's lovely little piece published several years after I delivered this paper: "New Work for Invisible Hands," *The Times Literary Supplement*, April 5, 1991.

[29] "The experience of democratic orders has demonstrated that the antithesis between the state's monopoly of power and civil society's private associations must be maintained if democracy is not to degenerate into anarchy or dictatorship." Reinhard Bendix, "State, Legitimacy and 'Civil Society'," *Telos*, No. 86, Winter 1990–91, p. 150.

[30] Payton, *Philanthropy, op. cit.*, p. 119.

[31] See Jon Van Til, *Mapping the Third Sector* (New York: The Foundation Center, 1988).

[32] Here again, the literature is extensive. Consider, for instance, Zbigniew Rau, editor, *The Reemergence of Civil Society in Eastern Europe and the Soviet Union* (Boulder, CO: Westview Press, 1991) and Chandran Kukathas, David Lovell, and William Maley, editors, *The Transition from Socialism: State and Civil Society in the USSR* (Melbourne, Australia: Longman Cheshire, 1991).

[33] Adam Michnik, "Towards a Civil Society: Hopes for Polish Democracy," Times *Literary Supplement*, February 19–26, 1988, p.188.

[34] Adam Michnik, *Letters from Prison and Other Essays* (Berkeley: University of California Press, 1985), p.124.

[35] See, for instance, David S. Broder, *The Party's Over* (New York: Harper and Row, 1972), E.J. Dione, *Why Americans Hate Politics* (New York: Simon and Schuster, 1991), and Kevin Phillips, *Arrogant Capital* (Boston: Little, Brown and Co, 1994).

[36] Quoted in Robert Nisbet, *Twilight of Authority* (New York: Oxford University Press, 1975) p. 23.

[37] Lester M. Salamon, *America's Nonprofit Sector: A Primer* (New York: The Foundation Center, 1992) p.26.

[38] Between the lines, Christopher Jencks' book on *The Homeless* (Cambridge: Harvard University Press, 1994) provides a scary look at how advocacy groups can manipulate the "facts" to promote their politicizing agendas.

[39] Jonathan Rauch, *Demosclerosis: The Silent Killer of American Government* (New York: Times Books, 1994) p. 48.

[40] Robert Putnam, "The Prosperous Community: Social Capital and Public Affairs," in *The American Prospect,* No.13, Spring, 1993, p 41.

[41] Robert D. Putnam, *Making Democracy Work: Civic Traditions in Modern Italy* (Princeton: Princeton University Press, 1993). And see the review Julie Fisher and I wrote of the book, reprinted as the first article in this chapter.

[42] James Given, *State and Society in Medieval Europe* (Ithaca: Cornell University Press, 1990).

[43] Elinor Ostrom, *Governing the Commons: The Evolution of Institutions for Collective Action* (Cambridge: Cambridge University Press, 1990). Also see my article on Ostrom, when she received the Nobel Prize in Economic Science, reprinted in Chapter 1 of this book.

[44] Pérez-Díaz, *Return, op. cit.*, p. 3.

[45] Henry Suhrke, "Maxims for Philanthropy: Give Us the Tools and We'll Do the Job," *Philanthropy Monthly*, May 1995, p. 5 and 6.

[46] Frank Prochaska, "But the Greatest of These...," *The Times Literary Supplement*, January 15, 1993, p. 15.

[47] See T. H. Marshall and Tom Bottomore, *Citizenship and Social Class* (London: Pluto Press, 1992).

[48] Desmond S. King, "Voluntary and State Provision of Welfare as Part of the Public-Private Continuum," in Alan Ware, editor, *Charities and Government* (Manchester UK: Manchester University Press, 1989), p. 29.

[49] Raymond Wolfinger and Steven Rosenstone, *Who Votes* (New Haven: Yale University Press, 1980), p. 8.

[50] Henry David Thoreau, "Resistance to Civil Government," in *Reform Papers*, edited by Wendell Glick (Princeton: Princeton University Press, 1973) p. 69.

[51] *The Charitable Behavior of Americans* (Washington DC: Independent Sector, 1985).

[52] See Virginia Hodgkinson's remarks at the 1993 ARNOVA meeting.

[53] Peter Drucker suggests something alone these same lines in "Citizenship Through the Social Sector," in *Post-Capitalist Society* (New York: Harper Business, 1993).

[54] Alexis de Tocqueville, *The Old Regime and the French Revolution* (Garden City, NY: Doubleday and CO, 1955), p. 140.

[55] Paul Goodman, *The Empire City* (Indianapolis: The Bobbs-Merrill Co, 1959), p. 620.

[56] Cf. Cornuelle, *American Dream*, p. 67.

4. Of Voluntary Failure and Change

Toward a New Theory of Voluntary-Government Relations

I present here a perspective on voluntary organizations centered on "bringing civil society back in." I place particular focus on starting to unpack the slippery ideas of voluntary failure and partnership. This paper was presented in 1996. I tried to add some theoretical and historical vitality — and a different perspective — to our usual understanding of the changing roles of voluntary associations in modern society. While no one theory of the nonprofit sector applies in all circumstances, current theories may read too selectively from the past, explain too little of our present, and help us too meagerly for the future. This was clear in the spring 1995 issue of *Nonprofit and Voluntary Sector Quarterly,* which was largely devoted to the theory of the nonprofit sector by major scholars such as Jon Van Til and Lester Salamon. While these are important perspectives, the tendency to emphasize the presumption for government action over voluntary action is badly biased. It avoids understanding the theoretical and practical distinction between civil society and government.

Relations between the voluntary sector and government are a given. But the nature and tensions of that relationship, the toll politicization can take on citizens and civil society, need much more study. The exploration of the interdependency of voluntary organizations and government has too often taken a bad turn. It has led to such an unquestioned, politicized view of human action that voluntary organizations are seen to be (and, it is claimed, should be) inherently ineffective and also deeply dependent upon the welfare state. Much of the voluntary sector has come to accept this. Opposite claims for the independence of the sector can similarly be off. Both approaches ignore the "embeddedness" of all organizations in social structures and relations. I accept the interdependency account to a point. I question its overuse as an excuse for claims of voluntary failure and the use of the idea of partnership to hide power.

The theory of civil society and of the state is crucial for my presentation and was the topic of a paper given at the ARNOVA annual meeting in 1994, which is included in this chapter. All of this needs more research and clarity. While this paper shows its age, the issues remain as salient as ever. And since this was a general exploration of several important issues, I believe it is still relevant as a stepping-stone to a better understanding that can be carried on by others. Many important works since 1995 have continued to elucidate aspects of voluntarism and civil society in helpful ways, such as those by Geoffrey Finlayson, David Green, Robert Putnam, John McKnight, David Beito, James C. Scott, and many others. They need to be integrated into our larger understanding of voluntary action, democracy, and the state.

We need to alter our perspective, emphasis, and vision by understanding the independence, methods, and contributions of civil society — what Vaclav Havel called "the independent life of society" — to our understanding of interactions of the voluntary sector and government.

The Sore Thumb of Public Policy

Americans have always appreciated the difference between civil society and the state while we also want to fit them into a Procrustean bed where the progressive politicization of society seems to obsess every political persuasion now. Nowhere has the uneasy relationship between society and the state been more vexing than in relation to the voluntary sector. It had been almost *de rigueur* since the Filer Commission to quote Daniel Boorstin's famous comment that

> In America, even in modern times, communities existed before governments were here to care for public needs. There were many groups of people with a common sense of purpose and a feeling of duty to one another before there were political institutions forcing them to perform their duties.... Philanthropy — our charitable spirit — in its transformed American shapes has become the leading feature of our relation to the world.[1]

And yet the tension of the political over the social has gotten a whole lot messier and one-sided this century. When Frank Dickinson wrote a major study on philanthropic giving (for the years between 1929 and 1959), he took special note of the great expansion in what he called "public philanthropy." The evidence caused Solomon Fabricant to pose several questions in his introduction: "[I]s there any need to support private philanthropy when government is taking over more and more of the burden of helping the needy?...[S]hould not private philanthropy be expected to retire from the scene — except as the chief support of religious activities...?"[2] A few years later, it was reaffirmed that the state was a major "philanthropist."[3] What had happened was a major "interpenetration of government and the voluntary sector."[4] Of course, there has always been government intervention with both the voluntary and market sectors for good and ill.[5] The interpenetration between government and the commercial sector has been widely studied.

However, what might be called a conquest of the voluntary sector by government has in fact gone largely unquestioned. We need more sophisticated studies comparing the history and impact of government intervention with the efforts by the voluntary sector. Ironically, during the period when government seemed to grow so much, defenders of the voluntary sector seemed in such a minority. A different interpretation of the voluntary sector and government interaction took hold. Why this happened is still not fully understood. We owe Lester Salamon a great deal for highlighting this strange fact of modern American life:

> the fact that the set of social institutions that most vividly embodies the distinctive American penchant for private solutions to public problems has experienced its most dramatic growth during precisely the period of most rapid expansion of the state.[6]

Governmental "funding and direction" had helped produce the explosive growth and shape of the voluntary sector in the U.S. in the last seventy years. Sectoral cooperation is necessary, and great strides have been made identifying and understanding the relationship. This has become one of the hallmarks of the American welfare state. Recognition of this close relationship has, however, further encouraged a tendency to blur the distinction between sectors. This mirrors a common predilection among some political scientists:

> So great is the interpenetration between the public and private sectors that this basic distinction — on which the political rhetoric and dialogue of modern times has rested — has ceased to be an operational way of understanding reality.[7]

One must wonder whether a valuable insight into the relations of government action and voluntary action has proven too much. Have we become stuck in an attitude that assumes too much for the political process, de-emphasizes a myriad of social costs, and relegates the voluntary sector to tertiary importance? I believe that new "faults in the conceptual lens"[8] through which we see the voluntary sector have become apparent. We need to develop additional ways of looking at the relationship. The challenge is still, as Ralph Kramer set forth many years ago, to find "an appropriate social distance between governmental and voluntary agencies ... if pluralism and voluntarism are to be preserved in the welfare state." But most public policy starts with the state (as if that were the sole embodiment of the public and its public goods), and thus tends to ignore or denigrate civil society and the differences between them. The welfare state may be neither the appropriate starting point nor the final goal.

Taking a very broad perspective for a moment, we must ask the questions: Have state intervention, power, and vested interests stifled positive change and made matters worse? Are there reasons to believe society's institutional resilience through individual and social actions and preferences hold out better means and outcomes in many cases? The remarkable theoretical and empirical work of Nobelist Elinor Ostrom is a sophisticated, positive answer to this question. See my article on her in Chapter 1. This has been especially poignant in the struggles for emergent civil societies from communism, totalitarianism, poverty, and even in our own democracies.

Narrowing our vision back to our topic, it may very well be that a vital voluntary sector is required not only for the well-being of those less fortunate and for institutions of arts and culture. We are beginning to appreciate that the vitality of our whole civil society *and* our political democracy may depend on the vitality of the voluntary sector. [9]

But if "the evolutionary or unilinear model has failed, we still lack a new model that explains how and why the boundaries between market, state, and voluntary agencies in the provision of social welfare change over time and across countries...." In fact, perhaps "each constituent of the system cannot be reduced beyond a certain point." [10]

There is a common view, as Salamon and Anheier put it, that "a deep-seated ideological current posits a fundamental conflict between the nonprofit sector and the state and discourages cooperation between the two." [11] No doubt that is partially true. However, an equally strong case can be made that it is more accurate to say a deep-seated ideological current posits a necessary partnership between the welfare state and the nonprofit sector. Indeed, that idea of partnership tends to hide the presumption that the state action trumps voluntary social action. That assumption of partnership debases and subsumes the voluntary sector and overly emphasizes the impact of politics and power. Are the possibilities of voluntary action in turn ignored? Are the means and ends of voluntary action greater and more important than they are given credit for? We need a more carefully considered exploration of the differences between and relationships involving government and the voluntary sector.

Nationalizing the Idea of the Voluntary Sector

Finding an appropriate social distance between sectors requires understanding the prevailing intellectual lens supplied for studying the voluntary sector. Since at least the time of Herbert Croly and the progressives, public policy and much work on the voluntary sector itself have relegated the voluntary sector to a *means* for government policy. That is not to say that there weren't those tendencies before, but the radical vision of voluntary action that animated Tocqueville's *Democracy in America* was transformed. We live firmly in the shadow of Croly's politicized *Promise of American Life*: "No voluntary association of individuals, resourceful and disinterested though they be, is competent to assume the responsibility" for America's national destiny.[12] Croly's call for a singular "National Purpose" required political centralization, expert control, and social regimentation. It required a singular purpose and the political power to implement it. His influence remains immensely strong and is highlighted here as one telling example of how voluntary associations have been perceived as pesky distractions through American history.[13] (Indeed, important connections between Croly and some of the leading early writers on philanthropy — for instance, Eduard C. Lindeman, Croly's "closest intellectual companion during the last years of his life.[14] — need to be explored.) Continuing through the New Deal, reformers have believed "that the aim of the tradition of private philanthropy was the absorption by government of the responsibility for generating and administering reform.... The implication, too, was that whatever foundations and private philanthropy had been doing government could do better."[15]

It was generally assumed that philanthropy, voluntary action, and the sector as a whole was at best an incubator or passive implementor of government designs. Even Peter Berger and Richard John Neuhaus contributed to the depreciation of the voluntary sector by developing a powerful conservative defense of mediating institutions. They began their influential (and in many ways, very good) 1977 monograph *To Empower People* by contrasting two tendencies in American public policy concerning the "proper" relationship between society and state. There was "a continuing desire for the services provided by the modern welfare state" and a "strong animus against government." Berger and Neuhaus suggested that the contradiction was only apparent: "we suggest that the modern welfare state is here to stay, indeed that it ought to expand the benefits it provides — but that alternative mechanisms are possible to provide welfare-state services."[16] In that view the state decides and funds, and the voluntary sector merely "provides" the services. "Mediating structures" become largely a passive means used by state action. They would appear to have no intrinsic purposes, agency, or dynamism of their own. In their later 1996 edition, Berger and Neuhaus saw things differently and lamented that "The modern welfare state is arguably the most important case of an enormous exercise of power, by and large motivated benignly, yet having developed into an instrument of oppression as well as corruption."[17]

Berger and Neuhaus's original perspective is joined from a different frame of reference in the important 1987 book *Shifting the Debate*. It is not the conservative polity which is central, but the welfare state: "... [T]he voluntary sector ought not be defined in such a way that it is in competition or opposition to the welfare state."[18] An issue is defined away. In both cases, dependency has become an operative descriptor in the study of the voluntary sector. Peter Dobkin Hall writes:

> The starting point for any serious consideration of the place of nonprofits in the American polity is to accept the policy implications of the scholarly recognition of sectoral interpenetration: that the nonprofit sector is a *dependent* sector, not an independent one. The choices that lie before it — and before the public as it seeks to redefine the role of government and its relation to the universe of private institutions — have primarily to do with the types and consequences of various kinds of dependency.[19]

This is key. The difference between civil society and government is defined away. For all the increase in size of the voluntary sector and our societal interdependence, in most of the literature, the voluntary sector tends to be conceptualized as a junior partner, a young, weak sibling, subsumed under essentially political means. Such a limited image of the voluntary sector certainly influences our assumptions, studies, and practice. It became a self-fulfilling image.[20]

The long trek from relative reliance on social power to reliance on political power can be quite subtle over time, including admirable and dangerous tensions. There is an admirable emphasis on democracy that was a crucial aspect of American political development. I don't emphasize that here, but it is a very important and well-studied part of the whole picture. A darker side, less well studied, exists as well. Emphasizing political centralization and control places democratic political processes in the hands of the "winning" political elites and the administrative state above all other social mechanisms. It lionizes executive power and bureaucratic control, eschews voluntarism, and gives moral sanction to coercion. All social processes become a zero-sum game: Diversity disappears. Consideration of the nature of and strengths of voluntary associations is crowded out. Notions of liberty, the good society, citizenship, and social action became mediated only through the state.[21] As a result, a larger democratic vision, or what one writer has called "a commonwealth of citizenship outside the state,"[22] is impoverished by our increasingly politicized view of the world.

Do We Need to Talk of Difference and Dependency?

Maintaining some clear sense of the separateness and differences is key. We are then better able to understand and dissect the interactions and respective strengths, means used, and weaknesses of the relationship. In his critique of ideological politics, Edward Shils seeks a way to maintain civility and hope. His is the valid and telling cautionary tale of liberalism, that the "elevation of one value … to supremacy over all others, and the insistence on its exclusive dominion in every sphere of life" leads to tyranny. Part of the answer for him (as Isaiah Berlin and other classical liberals emphasized) is to maintain an appreciation of the separateness. The recognition of separateness is relevant to any discussion of the voluntary sector:

> A renewal of the old idea, fundamental to modern liberalism, of a separation of the spheres is needed. It can, of course, be realized only very incompletely; economic life cannot be completely independent of government and politics, and vice versa; religion and politics cannot be completely separated; culture and politics cannot be completely separated. Nonetheless, while acknowledging and accepting their necessary collaboration and affinity, it is very important that the guardians, practical and intellectual, of each of the spheres should be aware of the desirability, in principle, of their separateness. This would be a bulwark against the romantic — and ideological — insistence on the universal application of a single set of standards. The separation of the different spheres of life would not please those ideological politicians and intellectuals who seek complete consistency. Without it, however, civility would be extinguished, and our best intellectual traditions would be frustrated.[23]

While there are plenty of times when true positive cooperation occurs between government and voluntary associations, recognizing the contrast is crucial if democracy is to be maintained. Increasing the power of one tends to weaken the other. As Reinhard Bendix put it: "The experience of democratic orders has demonstrated that the antithesis between the state's monopoly of power and civil society's private associations must be maintained if democracy is not to degenerate into anarchy or dictatorship."[24] And exploring the contrast allows us more fully to appreciate the nature of the relationship between government and the voluntary sector. It also allows us to understand the unrealized potential of voluntarism.

Keeping the State In

Jennifer Wolch, in *The Shadow State*, brought to philanthropy a clever and important switch in perspective. She did so by overemphasizing a state-centered approach to the study of the voluntary sector by "bringing the state back in."[25] She argues that

> the emergence of the shadow state is fundamentally linked to recent transformations in the welfare state. These changes were made possible because of the long-standing institutional interdependence of voluntary organizations and the state, which both enables and constrains voluntary action.... [T]he transformation of the voluntary sector into a shadow state apparatus could ultimately shackle its potential to create progressive social change.[26]

It certainly does, in the form of a sleight-of-hand that brings the voluntary sector into the halls of government by recognizing it as a self-interested and elitist pressure group. Wolch's critical analysis is invaluable, but it, too, is incomplete. Indeed, her "theory of state policy toward the voluntary sector" stands things on its head and the voluntary sector becomes an embedded part of that state. In a backdoor sort of way, she acknowledges that the voluntary sector has lost independence. There is no theory of a countervailing civil society or social power. This point is brought out cogently in some recent work on Third World development, but the point applies to the voluntary sector as well. Joel Migdal has written about the difficulties encountered by state-centered theories:

> ... not only is the claim open to empirical verification, the theoretical assumption has frequently led to the tendency to strip the other components of society of their volition or agency, portraying them as malleable putty in the hands of the most powerful element of society, the state.... [A]lthough the important point that "states matter" has now been made — and, to repeat, it needed to be made — there is no getting around the mutuality of state-society interactions; societies affect states as much as, or possibly more than, states affect societies.[27]

Ironically, the focus on the state in theoretical studies, even from those inimitable to the state, has meant no real alternative perspective is available. Being "anti-state" is not being "for" anything. Just as "bringing the state back in" revealed many of the tensions that the previously dominant pluralist theories glossed over, much more remains to be done (theoretically and empirically) on the interaction. Because of its theme, even this presentation, while it set out to make more space in our thinking for civil society and the voluntary sector, put too much focus on the political. It opens the door to bringing civil society back in, but doesn't explore the means, actions, and results of civil society itself. The previous article — as well as other articles throughout this book — do go into the idea of civil society in greater detail.

When the usual conception of the sectors tends to preference the state, the voluntary sector is ignored or diminished. Much is thereby lost or obscured. David Schmidtz offers a perfect example of how such assumptions skew one's perspective:

> Richard M. Titmuss extols the virtues of voluntary activity driven by community spirit rather than by market forces. Apparently missing the point, Peter Singer infers from Titmuss's finding that "it is only the intervention of the state which can guarantee that everyone who needs blood will receive it." But this was not Titmuss's conclusion, nor is such a conclusion supported by Titmuss's study. On the contrary, the importance to the community of this voluntary activity weighs as heavily against turning the process over to government as it does against turning the process over to the market.[28]

Let us then go on to consider whether we make too much of the history of the welfare state. What are we to make of the idea of voluntary failure? And is "partnership" really the right word?

From the Welfare State

It can hardly be surprising that we would construct a history and a public policy paradigm that assumed the permanence — even permanent expansion — of the welfare state. Neoconservative Irving Kristol proclaimed in 1993 that "the welfare state is with us" no matter one's political affiliation.[29] The Democratic president at the time later proclaimed that "the era of big government is over," but expanded government, thus affirming Kristol's point. In the United States, the interactions of government and nonprofits are well developed. Thus, the politicization of society engulfs our sector and our thinking. It is ironic that the increasing "craziness" (there is no better word) and polarization within the welfare state over the last dozen years exacerbates government's inability to govern. But the politicization grows apace because different interests must wrest control rather than compromise. And there seems to be no alternative. Civil society seems rather quiescent in ways that had surprised me. This has all underscored the importance of investigating anew what the relationship is and should be between the government and the voluntary sector.

It is difficult to take a fresh look at these issues when "welfare state expansion was for social science not a puzzle, but a given."[30] We are told that the welfare state and the voluntary sector are indissolvably linked. To some extent this is true, since nonprofits can do some of the business of the government well. As Ralph Kramer has put it, "the uncertain future of the voluntary sector is now linked, for better or worse, to the fate of the welfare state."[31] And yet our current image of the welfare state and the voluntary sector rests in part upon assumptions about the historical inevitability of the welfare state, which betrays a factual selectivity and teleological hubris that is not justified.

Much more historical and interdisciplinary work is needed to fill out this suspicion. It is true that the sector doesn't know its history very well. Still, evidence exists. This is particularly clear in England, where social history is much more advanced than in the United States. Geoffrey Finlayson's fine history of social welfare, *Citizen, State, and Social Welfare in Britain, 1830–1990*, as well as Peter Clark's magnificent *British Clubs and Societies, 180–1800: The Origins of an Associational World*, are remarkable summary beginnings in this regard. Finlayson observes "that books which have been written on the history of social welfare provision over the past twenty to thirty years have, almost without exception, linked the word 'welfare' to the word 'state.'"[32] Thus, the history of caring for others morphs into welfare, which is further assumed to be the development of the welfare state. It is easy to project into the future and see that welfare must continue to be linked directly to the welfare state. What has happened, simply, is the annexation of caring into the welfare state.[33] The short section on Social Security in the previous article is suggestive. Such presumptions demand serious skepticism.

The actual history of the matter is much more complex, as Finlayson (and many others) chronicle. Instead, the real interaction between philanthropy and the state was comprised of a constant refrain of compromises and conflicts. There is no teleological necessity here:

> The linear development *from* voluntarism *to* state reduces the contribution of voluntarism to welfare to insignificance or sees it as a positive hindrance; it concentrates on all the demerits of voluntarism as stated above. It distorts the role of voluntarism by seeing it through collectivist spectacles. Equally, it ignores the ways in which voluntarism itself changed, and does not take into account the complex relationship between voluntarism and the state which ran through all the periods....[34]

A Place for Civil Society

Civil society — and the voluntary sector in particular — had a remarkable ability to respond to welfare needs, the most difficult needs, presumably, to be addressed outside the state. This includes rich associational efforts, families, individuals, and commercial efforts that provided an amazing safety net we forget existed. David Green, for instance, has written on the English tradition of "communal liberalism" and "reassessing the voluntary social institutions that had emerged under its influence by the end of the last century."[35] E. G. West has researched the history of non-state educational efforts in England from the Industrial Revolution on.[36] The friendly societies were a remarkable network and conglomeration of mutual aid societies. David Beito shows the same for the U.S.[37] They show that citizens — and networks of voluntary associations of their own design and making — can do a remarkable amount to provide for their own health and welfare. Is there reason to think those possibilities still exist in modern society? I believe the honest answer has to be yes as well as no. We need a fuller hearing and presentation of the evidence, rather than the lop-sided presumption that only state control and action is the answer. The idea of civil society and its robust history is powerfully behind much of the comments in this article.

The Capacity of Philanthropy

As a quick aside, one of the perennial limits perceived to hobble philanthropy and rationalize government funding has been limits in funding. This is a challenge but perhaps an overwrought and under-reached one. Consider the following description of English philanthropy:

> Enormous sums have been contributed, representing a massive redistribution of wealth.... Eighteenth- and nineteenth-century families at almost every level of the social scale commonly tithed their income to charitable causes. A study of middle-class households in the 1890s established that on average they spent a larger share of their income on charity than on any item in their budget except food. A survey of working-class and artisan families in the same decade showed that half of them subscribed weekly to charity and about a quarter of them also made donations to church or chapel. Even after the beginning of this century the sums contributed each year, not including church and chapel collections and unremembered alms, far exceeded government expenditures on poor relief. Philanthropic receipts

for London alone, observed *The Times* in 1885, were greater than the budgets of many European states.[38]

The expected and massive intergenerational transfer of wealth that could go to philanthropy from baby boomers brings this point up to date. See, for instance, my review of this phenomenon in Chapter 5. It may well be, as William Diaz and his co-authors noted in 1996:

> What difference can individual and organized philanthropy make? The answer requires both an estimate of the capacity of individuals and organized philanthropy to fill any gap and also a sense of strategy about how organized philanthropy might use its funds and influence to address the issue.... The future will have to be pieced together from disparate sources, but the capacity is there. What is needed is leadership, will, and the incentives to produce such changes.[39]

Much more research is necessary to parse the data over time of philanthropy's capacity.

There has always been, in Finlayson's words, "a mixed economy of welfare, in which there was a voluntarist and a statist presence."[40] On the one hand, there has been tremendous opposition to significant state intervention. And significant failures and inefficiencies. Some interventions were certainly appropriate; others, not so much. On the other hand, state action has rarely been merely passive or benign. Unintended consequences and the snowballing effect of more interventions to address those consequences are all too common. Voluntary associations have had to defend themselves against rival welfare efforts by the state as well as a host of other regulatory efforts to suppress and control them. The telling of this history is still, alas, in its infancy. Sadly, knowing and learning from history seem not a skill valued so much today.

The rise of the welfare state has also had a marked displacement effect that was understood early. For instance, C. S. Loch expressed a very common viewpoint in England in the era from 1830 to the 1880s: "To shift the responsibility of maintenance from the individual to the State is to sterilize the productive power of the community as a whole, and also to impose on the State ... so heavy a liability ... as may greatly hamper, if not also ruin, it. It is also to demoralise the individual."[41] It is probable that the rise of government transfer programs contributed to a substantial decline in the practice of mutual aid. This view still resonates.

For instance, in the United States, government programs "may have weakened networks of support within inner cities, transforming the experience of poverty and fueling the rise of homelessness."[42] Unfortunately, we don't yet have a full history like Finlayson's.[43] David Beito suggests what might have been lost and does need to be more fully researched:

> It is fairly clear that among white and African Americans, weakened mutual aid coincided with the growth of government's social-welfare role.... Even though the correlation between rising governmental involvement and declining mutual aid is clear, a cause-and-effect relationship remains to be proven. Nevertheless, common sense, if nothing else, dictates further inquiries into possible connections between these two trends.... The shift from mutual aid and self-help to the welfare state involved more than just a simple bookkeeping transfer of service provision from one set of institutions to another.... The rise of the welfare state not only accompanied the eclipse of indigenously controlled mutual aid institutions, but left impersonal bureaucracies dominated by outsiders in their place.[44]

Prevailing assumptions about state provision of welfare, independently or through control of nonprofit funding and missions, shouldn't stand as they are. There is good evidence that the welfare state suppresses incentives and innovations within civil society to solve problems and engage in solutions. Philanthropy and civil society can be broadly effective grounds for experimentation as opposed to the shifting winds, or calcifying impact, of politics and bureaucracy within a state system. And there is evidence that the voluntary sector *can* do more. Needless to say, while these issues need exploration, the work must be careful and critical. We don't need work that makes the same presumptive assumptions, but now in favor of some kind of perfect voluntary sector. The voluntary sector is no white knight. But we do need the openness to explore these issues.

What About Voluntary Failure?

We return to the "great displacement," as Kramer describes it, "in which governmental support has become a more important source of revenue in the social services than all private giving combined. Why are voluntary agencies used by government to carry out a public purpose?"[45] Kramer suspects it is not from rational analysis of the pros and cons but comes about largely for "pragmatic" reasons. Many years earlier, Frank Fetter called the "subsidy method" "not a policy; it is an accident."[46] No doubt this is partially true. But the intellectual and political currents in England and the United States, for instance, were clearly enthralled by the progressive possibilities of political control and money. The voluntary sector provision of services was a perfect object of attention for many reasons from both sides of the political spectrum. The idea of "voluntary failure" seems to explain so much: after all, the sector needed help. And yet it misunderstands the true nature of voluntary social action and becomes an excuse for intervening.

One must be careful when flinging about the idea of "failure." It can be a happy and often vacuous explanation for something one wants changed. Market or government failures, for instance, have often been invoked to explain a necessary role for voluntary associations. Lester Salamon is quite right that theories of the nonprofit sector based on correcting market and government failure ironically make the voluntary sector derivative and secondary,[47] though not necessarily dependent. But the idea of voluntary failure has been used by him to try to establish that the voluntary sector is endemically lacking. Voluntary institutions and their work therefore become, practically speaking, in need of and dependent upon government.

Salamon sees "voluntary organizations as the primary response mechanism" to market failure.[48] Taking this tack seems to turn the usual failure argument around. Government must step in and become "the derivative institution responding to 'voluntary failure,' and the inherent limitations of the voluntary or nonprofit sector"[49] While sometimes helpful, however, the idea of voluntary failure is too vague. It fails to explain why this great displacement seems to be of relatively recent vintage. It may also seem a bit odd for government to enter the scene to resolve voluntary failures by contracting to the voluntary sector. (In the end, the true failure of the voluntary sector seems to be lack of funding and incorrect direction, each at least contestable as I have suggested above. And see the first article in Chapter 3 of this book for more on funding the voluntary sector.) I think "failure" tends to involve preconceived ideas of the proper ends and means of voluntary and state actions. There is an additional presumption that voluntary action is inefficient and ineffective while there is a neat presumption of state efficiency and effectiveness. State action is seen beneficent, and the quest for power and unintended consequences (forms of government failure?) are not important considerations.

How can we know when there is voluntary failure? Since the idea is such a static snapshot in time, it can't establish failure since a more dynamic and longer-term perspective is needed to accurately do so. By ignoring longer-term correcting actions, one assumes that the sector cannot or will not respond. In the end, voluntary failure assumes what it is looking for, is too imprecise, and could apply to just about anything.

The voluntary sector, of course, has its fulsome fair share of failures and stupidities. But I would posit for further thinking and empirical work, that civil society and, specifically, the nonprofit sector have their own self-correcting mechanisms embedded in the very idea of choice and voluntarism.

Over time, one learns from mistakes and adapts. It is also possible that if certain needs are not met to someone's satisfaction, the need or the resources are not that much of a "public good." Different people have difference preferences. It is not necessarily a failure if the voluntary sector reflects different preferences in different ways. If a voluntary institution or effort does fail, there are presumably voluntary alternatives to try, unless voluntary failure is a general condition, and that hasn't been proven.

Failure explanations — as James Douglas pointed out about market and government failure — have some explanatory power, but they don't help to "identify the theoretical limits on the instrumentalities of government."[50] This is true of voluntary failures. Examples do not automatically prove a need for interventions. Indeed, intervention can easily interrupt or change natural adjustments. Thus, the mere assumption of failure is the driving force for it. The assumption seems to be that government intervention is the required answer without limits to its applicability. This ignores the self-aggrandizing possibilities of power, logrolling, and bureaucracy. It does not follow that specific voluntary failure — even if we could identify it — is thus a rationale for assuming government activity. Finally, there remains the question of comparing the impacts of sector failures. A voluntary failure might be relatively pale in comparison with an attendant government failure (and vice versa, of course).

If imperfections in the voluntary sector are viewed as natural rationales for government intrusion, what about government failure? It would appear that voluntary failure is looked at in a vacuum. There is the implicit assumption that the state is a relatively benign and passive responder to exogenous failure. In fact, social reality is much more complex. Governments are themselves an active participant in the social process. Presumed problems may be the result of government action or inaction, or a voluntary failure may actually be the result of government intrusions.

Looking at the idea of market failure is helpful when thinking about voluntary failure. One legacy of welfare economics from the 1920s on has been a host of theories of market failures: where public goods are not provided or "free-rider" problems exist, or where externalities exist so the actions of individuals affect others in positive or negative ways. While real issues, these theories are often incomplete in three basic ways. First, they unfairly compare static real-world market situations to some utopian ideal of equilibrium. When the static real world doesn't live up to the ideal, "failure" is posited. Failure is assumed to be a purely market phenomenon. More likely it is a result of many factors. Most important, the world of human action is not static. Nothing is so powerful in the relatively free marketplace than the self-corrective mechanisms of individuals and institutions. Second, upon identification of failure, it is assumed that government intervention is called for as an effective corrective. In addition, government intervention is usually assumed to be neutral, conforming to a rather benign view of motive and action where unanticipated consequences are downplayed. This is a rather utopian view of government action where power, self-interest, and coercion are their own contributing factors. Government actions have a good, long history of introducing failures of greater kinds, with the related tendency of repeating the process, world without end. Third, there is no comparison of the magnitude of effects of respective failures between sectors. Nor are there comparisons of corrective mechanisms embedded in each sector.

Over the years, the theory of market failure has been subjected to considerable work and criticism.[51] Presumed market failures are frequently not failures at all, but — to use an old saw — market opportunities. Policy prescriptions of government action often do not logically follow. While there is no common agreement, an appreciation has developed that not only are imperfections natural, but over time they provide the information necessary to help bring about corrective action within the marketplace. Much in these analyses of the failures of the theory of market failures applies to the idea of failure as applied to civil society, and specifically to the voluntary sector.

It seems at least highly plausible, then, that voluntary failure theory should be used with much greater care and not as a simple — and obscuring — excuse. It is too often a knee-jerk, go-to excuse when things are not as one likes them. It may, of course, be used to identify real problems, but it so easily glosses over the strengths of the voluntary sector and leaves out the often predatory nature of state action. Rather than a failure, such cases are more likely signals that change and adjustment are necessary. Perhaps the last word is best expressed by Chandran Kukathas of the LSE: "It will simply not do to assume that because markets or other social mechanisms produce imperfect results a central authority will produce better ones."[52]

So, does it really hold up as a rationale for government action? It may be that David Schmidtz's conclusion to his exploration of the public goods argument applies as well to the use of voluntary failure: "The public goods argument by itself can justify more than a minimal state, perhaps, but not a great deal more. The justification of big government requires a different kind of argument."[53] By quickly assuming voluntary failure and then moving on to the idea of a necessary "partnership" between government and nonprofits as the "fix," the theory wipes out the need for this broader consideration of the complex nature of social and political interaction. Voluntary associations are quickly relegated to ineffectualness except through governmental direction. In this, the theories of voluntary failure and partnership are mostly a repackaging of the politicizing legacy of Herbert Croly.

"Partnership" or Dependency?

When all problems seem to demand political solutions, civil society generally and the voluntary sector specifically are relegated to doing the bidding of the powers that be. Political power trumps all. This view can seem rather harsh. One clever way to bridge this has been to talk more about "interdependence" and "partnership" between government and the nonprofit sector. Those terms can be useful and describe something of the interactions between sectors, but only with care. As a matter of theory and fact, however, interdependence and partnership are too often misnomers masking dependency, when the government sector is much more "equal" than the voluntary sector.

As Kramer noted years ago, "the division of responsibility between governmental and nongovernmental organizations will continue to be determined primarily by the political process."[54] (After many years as a grantmaker in New York City, no truer words were written, as evidenced by the travails foisted on nonprofits, by city, state, and federal politicos and regulations, all of which seemed uninterested in and ignorant of, the nonprofits who were allegedly their partners. Some of this is evident in my look at NYC, in the first article of Chapter 5.) Indeed, Smith and Lipsky suggest that one way to look at the voluntary failure theory convert it "into one that responds primarily to political stimuli and impulses."[55] One should never underestimate the power behind political decision making.

Things were very different when, for instance, Amos Warner and Alexander Fleisher wrote their critiques of "public subsidies of private charities."[56] Their critiques touch on many of the same relevant issues today that are echoed in the works of Salamon, Smith, and Lipsky, and others. While they often saw the alternative as government service provision, these earlier subsidies to charities were quite different. They were made to support extant programs of charities with funds only. There tended to be little policy direction or implementation of specific government programs. The change we see today includes heavy "funding and direction," and that is a crucial difference: an explicit, politicized intrusion of the state. As Peter Beresford and Suzy Croft put it in a more contemporary context:

> [W]hile patch and welfare pluralist philosophies are framed in terms of giving a greater role to voluntary organizations and informal effort in place of statutory provision, it is the *state* which is seeking to mobilise such non-statutory and unpaid caring. [This is a] different kind of intervention. Instead of primarily providing services to meet our needs, the state will be involved in organising, supervising, extending and even reinterpreting our own self-help.[57]

What is the extent to which this different kind of government action beyond "neutral" funding changes the nature of the nonprofit's work? Or more baldly, does it change who decides these things? Kramer, among others, reported little change in mission for organizations getting government funding.[58] There are other studies, however, that suggest missions are greatly affected. In 1970, a survey of charitable organizations in Chicago by the Commission on Foundations and Private Philanthropy found concerns among the recipients that the strings attached to increasing government funding would subject them to political whims and government bureaucracy.[59] In 1988, the Rockefeller Institute of Government surveyed nonprofits receiving significant funding from the state of New York:

> Among those interviewed, however, there was general agreement that the "scale of interdependence" is clearly tipped toward nonprofit dependence on government.... Just under half the nonprofit survey respondents ... agreed that nonprofit organizations are too dependent on government funding and that receipt of state funds has significantly changed the program priorities of voluntary agencies. Even more important, more than a third felt government financing has actually changed their mission.[60]

Mission and programs often change as a result of government funding and direction, i.e., government funding is clearly not neutral. One must be careful not to inadvertently mask the actual power relationships that exist here. I am not suggesting that the relationship is only one-sided; perhaps Smith and Lipsky's term "unbalanced reciprocity" applies best. Indeed, foundation funders often engage in the same exercise of power with grantees. It is perhaps less heavy-handed. They don't have the same kind of coercive power and wallet. Nor am I suggesting such changes are always bad.

It is often assumed that the locus of power in the political process is democratic and therefore somehow "good." The tie between government and the voluntary sector is thus perceived as the common pursuit of the collective good. One of the legacies of the scientific management and social engineering perspective of earlier decades has been the presumed advantage of the expertise and objectivity in the professionalization of society. No doubt expertise and professionalism (bureaucratization) can be good. It can easily lead to elitism and hubris. It can be as biased as loaded dice and as blind as a bat. There are clashes where it is assumed there can only be one collective good and one public interest. Government does not lend itself to a diversity of public goods. The diversity of civil society and the voluntary sector is a one of its strengths.

Demonizing the political process is not my intent. And yet it is so common to assume good things from politics and leave it at that. I would suggest that looking at government and voluntary sector interactions through the lens of public choice theory is valuable here. Public choice uses economic analysis to study political behavior:

> The public choice model of politics and democracy is actually quite simple. Politics is assumed to be a system consisting of four groups of decision-makers — voters, elected officials or politicians, bureaucrats, and interest groups. Individuals are assumed to be rational utility-maximizers who seek benefits from the political system.[61]

Public choice theory can be valuable, though not always flattering or corrective, especially when it comes to government relations with the voluntary (and the market) sector. It remains true, as Daniel Moynihan used to say, that "the problem now is that citizens won't leave government alone."[62] Why? Because it can satisfy public needs *and* it satisfies private interests. We cannot understand the nature of the "unbalanced reciprocity" of government and voluntary sector until we understand more fully the motives, interests, and actions of the actors. As Mitchell and Simmons put it: "There is little evidence that a sense of community is what drives political participation outside the local community. There is, however, strong evidence that much political participation is based on a calculation of personal advantage."[63] We cannot assume, as a default position, that government action (or the actions within the voluntary, market, or "academic" sectors) is disinterested and in the interest of all for all the right reasons.

Who, then, will protect us from the negative effects of such self-interested partnerships? Public choice theory suggests this is difficult without a more thoroughgoing reform of the rules of engagement. Clarity about the independence of the sectors is key, as well as an understanding of the relative differences in means used by them. Balance the reciprocity.

The evidence both within the nonprofit sector and the commercial sector suggests that it is very difficult. Providing funds and direction is nothing new. It is little different from the provision of subsidies, regulations, etc., mandated by government within the market sector, but it had previously been less noticed in the voluntary sector. In both cases, "failure" is very often an excuse for control. In the private sector, rather than discuss third-party government and partnerships, one might just as often speak of collusion or corporate welfare.

The general catch-22 of the voluntary sector is nicely laid out by Maria Brenton's summary of the British experience. The role of the voluntary sector, she concludes, is twofold: first as a provider of services (presumably also including as a subcontractor), and second, in a "watchdog role over the main-line provisions of the welfare state."[64] In the American "partnership" context, this means combining in many cases the role of supplicant/beneficiary and disinterested watchdog, which is actually co-opted and politicized by the supplicant role. That kind of conflict-of-interest role is very difficult to play well and in the public interest, because the public interest begins to seem more and more like one's own personal bias and interest. The point is not that partnerships can't exist or aren't good, but simply that they are very difficult. Decision-making power is usually quite unequal. They are not partnerships at all, and quite often are not in the public interest despite the rhetoric.[65]

Conclusion

During Vice President Gore's long-ago hearings on reinventing government, one speaker was asked to comment on contracting out and public/private partnerships. The guest raised several critical issues, suggesting, "We have to look back to Tocqueville." The published transcript, however, read, "We have to look back to the Tolk Bill."[66] That hilarious — you just can't make it up — error of transcription is also horrifying in that it wonderfully captures an assumption that pervades much social thought and policy analysis. Problems are assumed to require governmental solutions; civil society takes the hindmost. This tendency applies equally well across the political spectrum; all sides of the debate about the kind of society we want are too quick to repair to politics, and to assume that it is a good and costless fix.[67]

That same tendency to focus on the state is particularly common in our thinking about and research on the relationships between government and the voluntary sector. It shows up in the assumptions we have about sector independence and the appropriate social distance — especially lack of — between government and voluntary agencies. It shows up in the one-sided teleological vision we have of the welfare state. Indeed, the voluntary sector and civil society become largely invisible, as the Tolk Bill story shows.

Words matter in all of this. They can elucidate or obscure a great deal. That shows up in our use of such imprecise terms as voluntary failure, third-party government, interdependence, and partnership. Those terms can be useful and describe something of the interactions between sectors. As lenses through which to engage theory and practice, however, these terms tend to rationalize state actions, impoverishing and biasing explorations of what is, or can be, important about the voluntary sector and the larger idea of civil society. Our limited conception of the voluntary sector has obscured the past and the possibilities of the future.

The potential of civil society and an "unleashed" voluntary sector addressing the problems that face society may be much, much greater than we assume (acknowledging, too, its self-inflicted and politically imposed failures). Voluntary failure is too often an excuse for interventions while hobbling sector innovations. Government partnership in nonprofit relations in modern society may be quite costly — and more restraining — than is commonly believed. The unbalanced subservience in the relationship is downplayed, as are the unintended consequences. Certainly, any public choice analysis of the forces and interests involved on all sides would lead one to a more sober outlook of politics as would, for instance, a look at the results of the Reagan and Thatcher years.[68] Finally, the idea of interdependence, while valuable in some contexts, has tended to remove distinctions, denigrate the nature and processes of the voluntary sector, and thus made these words and much theory subservient to the heirs of Croly's progressive and statist "promise of American life."

This short paper and all of the articles in this chapter raise a number of questions about how we see the sectors. Even though dated, I have tried to suggest a different way of seeing by "bringing civil society back" into the discussions about this "sore thumb of public administrative policy" — that is, the relations between state and nonprofits. I am not claiming they are right, but that serious consideration is called for.

With Massimo Paci, I believe that "behind contemporary appeals to revise the organizational form of the welfare state, which the current expansion of voluntary and market sectors tends to imply, there is a venerable impulse that cannot simply be denied. While the forces of conservatism are hardly likely to do so, this impulse must also be comprehended and supported by the progressive forces that have been traditionally identified with the welfare state and its conquests."[69] Perhaps we can begin looking at the "the voluntary impulse" within civil society for what it has been, what it is, and what it can be.[70] A candid look at this impulse without the biasing wordplay of such ideas as voluntary failure and partnership opens the possibility for a more complex and important discussion. Perhaps we can then see more clearly for our society what is humane, diverse, and free. That would be a radical project.

This paper was presented at the Annual Meeting of the Association for Research on Nonprofit Organizations and Voluntary Action, at the panel on "Voluntary Action in Modern Society", with Lester Salamon as the discussant, NYC, November 7–9, 1996. The paper was subsequently published as Working Paper #10, January 2004, by The Philanthropic Enterprise. *It has been slightly updated for this publication.*

[1] Daniel J. Boorstin, *The Decline of Radicalism* (New York: Random House, 1969), pp. 46 and 68.

[2] Frank G. Dickinson, *The Changing Position of Philanthropy in the American Economy* (New York: National Bureau of Economic Research, 1970), pp. 28-29.

[3] "The State as a Major 'Philanthropist'." In *Giving in America: Toward a Stronger Voluntary Sector*. Report of the Commission on Private Philanthropy and Public Needs, 1975.

[4] Steven Rathgeb Smith and Michael Lipsky, *Nonprofits for Hire: The Welfare State in the Age of Contracting* (Cambridge: Harvard University Press, 1993), p. 19.

[5] cf. Peter Dobkin Hall, *Inventing the Nonprofit Sector: And Other Essays on Philanthropy, Voluntarism, and Nonprofit Organizations* (Baltimore: The Johns Hopkins University Press, 1992). Also see, for instance, Jonathan R. T. Hughes' history of the role of nonmarket controls and the control bureaucracy in American history, *The Governmental Habit* (New York: Basic Books, 1977) and Robert Higgs' look at the growth of government, *Crisis and Leviathan: Critical Episodes in the Growth of American Government* (New York: Oxford University Press, 1987).

[6] Lester M. Salamon, *Partners in Public Service: Government-Nonprofit Relations in the Modern Welfare State* (Baltimore: The Johns Hopkins University Press, 1995), p. 1.

[7] Bruce L. R. Smith, editor. *The New Political Economy: The Public Use of the Private Sector* (New York: John Wiley and Son, 1975). Quoted in Jon Van Til, *Mapping the Third Sector* (New York: The Foundation Center, 1988), p. 95.

[8] Salamon, *op. cit.* Chapter 2, "Of Market Failure, Voluntary Failure, and Third-Party Government", p. 35.

[9] See, for instance, Robert D. Putnam, *Making Democracy Work: Civic Traditions in Modern Italy* (Princeton: Princeton University Press, 1993); Ernest Gellner, *Conditions of Liberty: Civil Society and Its Rivals* (New York: Penguin Press, 1994); and Víctor M. Pérez-Díaz, *The Return of Civil Society* (Cambridge: Harvard University Press, 1993).

[10] Massimo Paci, "Long Waves in the Development of Welfare Systems," in *Changing Boundaries of the Political*, edited by Charles S. Maier (Cambridge: Cambridge University Press, 1987), p.181.

[11] Lester M. Salamon and Helmut K. Anheier, *The Emerging Sector: An Overview* (Baltimore: The Johns Hopkins University Institute for Policy Studies, 1994), p. 102.

[12] Herbert Croly, *The Promise of American Life* (New York: The Macmillan Company, 1912), p.24.

[13] See Peter Dobkin Hall, *Inventing the Nonprofit Sector: And Other Essays on Philanthropy, Voluntarism, and Nonprofit Organizations* (Baltimore: The Johns Hopkins University Press, 1992) for a flavor of that hostility in American history.

[14] David W. Levy, *Herbert Croly of The New Republic* (Princeton: Princeton University Press, 1985), p. 281.

[15] Barry D. Karl, "Philanthropy, Policy Planning, and the Bureaucratization of the Democratic Ideal." *Daedalus*, Vol. 105, No. 4, Fall 1976, p. 140.

[16] Peter L. Berger and Richard John Neuhaus, *To Empower People: From State to Civil Society*, Second Edition. Edited by Michael Novak (Washington: The AEI Press, 1996), pp. 157 and 158.

[17] Berger and Neuhaus, p.146.

[18] Susan Ostrander, Stuart Langton, Jon Van Til, editors, *Shifting the Debate* (New Brunswick: Transaction Books, 1987), p. 130. This was originally an issue of *NVSQ*, V. 16, nos. 1-2, 1987.

[19] Peter Dobkin Hall, in *Shifting the Debate*, p.19.

[20] Heny Suhrke, the insightful, wonderful and now sadly forgotten founder and editor of *Philanthropy Monthly*, made the following white-hot observation in the May 1995 issue: "It's not a pretty sight: leaders who have been living off of Tocqueville quotes for years, retreating frantically and loudly from the real possibility of putting their long and glorious heritage to work."

[21] One sees this tension of social versus political in democratic theory in Isaiah Berlin's famous "Two Concepts of Liberty." The locus of personal development and social change is the state under positive liberty while negative liberty sets the general rules, and both means and ends are left largely outside politics. Isaiah Berlin, *Four Essays on Liberty* (Oxford: Oxford University Press, 1970). Two of the best earlier statements trying to establish a balance between the social and the political are the famous 1819 speech by French classical liberal Benjamin Constant, "The Liberty of the Ancients Compared With that of the Moderns," in *Benjamin Constant: Political Writings* (Cambridge: Cambridge University Press, 19887), and Wilhelm von Humboldt's 1852 *The Limits of State Action* (Cambridge: Cambridge University Press, 1969). Both works still have a great deal to offer those interested in a broader rationale for voluntary action.

[22] Frank Prochaska, "But the Greatest of These..." *Times Literary Supplement*, January 15, 1993, p.15.

[23] Edward Shils, *The Intellectual and the Powers and Other Essays* (Chicago: University of Chicago Press, 1972). p 67 and 68.

[24] Reinhard Bendix, "State, Legitimacy and 'Civil Society'," *Telos*, #86, Winter 1990-91, p. 150.

[25] See, for instance, Peter B. Evans, Dietrich Tueschemeyer, and Theda Skocpol, editors, *Bringing the State Back In* (Cambridge: Cambridge University Press, 1985); Michael Mann, *The Sources of Social Power*, 2 volumes (Cambridge: Cambridge University Press, 1986 and 1993); John A. Hall, editor, *States in History* (Oxford: Basil Blackwell, 1986).

[26] Jennifer R. Wolch, *The Shadow State* (New York: The Foundation Center, 1990), p. 15.

[27] Joel S. Migdal, Atul Kohli, and Vivienne Shue, editors, *State Power and Social Forces* (Cambridge: Cambridge University Press, 1994), pp. 20 and 2.

[28] David Schmidtz, *Rational Choice and Moral Agency* (Princeton: Princeton University Press, 1995), p. 177. Italics added.

[29] Irving Kristol, "A Conservative Welfare State," *The Wall Street Journal*, June 14, 1993.

[30] Jill Quadagno, "Theories of the Welfare State," *Annual Review of Sociology*, 1987, Vol. 13, p. 110.

[31] Ralph M. Kramer, "The Future of the Voluntary Sector in a Mixed Economy," *The Journal of Applied Behavioral Science*, Vol. 21, No. 4, 1985, p. 377.

[32] Geoffrey Finlayson, *Citizen, State and Social Welfare in Britain, 1830-1990* (Oxford: Oxford University Press, 1994), p.1. See Peter Clark, *British Clubs and Societies, 1580-1800: The Origins of an Associational World* (Oxford: The Claredon Press), 2000.

[33] See, for instance, Norman Barry's history and critique of the concept of welfare and its transformation into the domain of the welfare state. *Welfare* (Buckingham, UK: Open University Press, 1990). Also see the classic collection, *The Welfare State,* edited by Charles I. Schottland (New York: Harper and Row, 1967).

[34] Finlayson, *op. cit.*, p. 418.

[35] David G. Green, *Reinventing Civil Society: The Rediscovery of Welfare Without Politics* (London: IEA Health and Welfare Unit, 1993), p.3. Also see his, *Community Without Politics: A Market Approach to Welfare Reform* (London: IEA Health and Welfare Unit, 1996).

[36] E. G. West, *Education and the State: A Study in Political Economy* (Indianapolis: Liberty Fund, 1994); and *Education and the Industrial Revolution* (Indianapolis: Liberty Fund, 1994).

[37] David Beito, *From Mutual Aid to the Welfare State: Fraternal Societies and Social Services, 1890-1967* (Chapel Hill: The University of North Carolina Press, 2000).

[38] Frank Prochaska, "Philanthropy," *The Cambridge Social History of Britain 1705-1950*, edited by F. M. L. Thompson (Cambridge: Cambridge University Press, 1990), pp. 357-358.

[39] William Diaz, Dwight Burlingame, Warren Ilchman, David Kaufmann, Shawn Kimmel, "Welfare Reform and the Capacity of Private Philanthropy," *Capacity for Change? The Nonprofit Work in the Age of Devolution* (Indianapolis: Indiana University Center on Philanthropy, 1996), pp. 129 & 145.

[40] Finlayson, p. 398.

[41] C. S. Loch, quoted in Finlayson, p.101-102.

[42] Michael B. Katz, *The Undeserving Poor: From the War on Poverty to the War on Welfare* (New York: Pantheon, 1989), p. 190-191.

[43] See, as one instance, David Beito's suggestive article, "Mutual Aid, State Welfare, and Organized Charity: Fraternal Societies and the 'Deserving' and 'Undeserving' Poor, 1890–1930." *Journal of Policy History*, Fall, 1993. Also see his important From Mutual Aid to the Welfare State: Fraternal Societies and Social Services, 1890–1967 (Chapel Hill: The University of North Carolina Press, 2000).

[44] David Beito, "Mutual Aid for Social Welfare: The Case of American Fraternal Societies," Critical *Review*, Fall, 1990. p. 726-729.

[45] Kramer, "The Future of the Voluntary Agency in a Mixed Economy," *op. cit.*, p. 379.

[46] Frank Fetter, "The Subsidizing of Private Charities," *American Journal of Sociology*, V. 7, 1901-1902, p. 384. Amos Warner takes the same view in *American Charities: A Study in Philanthropy and Economics*, originally published in 1894, (New Brunswick: Transaction Publishers, 1989) p. 417.

[47] Salamon, "Of Market Failure....", *op. cit.*, p. 44.

[48] Salamon, "Of Market Failure....", *op. cit.*, p. 45.

[49] Salamon, "Of Market Failure....", *op. cit.*, p. 44.

[50] James Douglas, *Why Charity: The Case for a Third Sector* (Beverly Hills: Sage Publications, 1983), p. 160.

[51] For a discussion of failure within the nonprofit context, see Chapter 9 of *Economics for Nonprofit Managers*, by Dennis R. Young and Richard Steinberg (New York: The Foundation Center, 1995); James Douglas, *Why Charity*, op cit., David Prychitko and Peter Boettke, "The New Theory of Government-Nonprofit Partnership: A Hayekian Critique of the Salamon Paradigm," The Philanthropic Enterprise, *Working Paper No. 1*, September 2002, and The Study of the Nonprofit Enterprise, edited by Helmut Anheier and Avner Ben-Nur, (New York: Kluwer Academic/Plenum, 2003). For discussions on market failure, see, for instance, the collection edited by Tyler Cowen, *The Theory of Market Failure: A Critical Examination* (Fairfax, VA: George Mason University Press, 1988), *Market Failure or Success: The New Debate*, edited by Tyler Cowen and Eric Crampton, (Cheltenham, UK: Edward Elgar, 2002). Also see William Oakland. "Theory of Public Goods" *Handbook of Public Economics, Vol. 2* edited by A. Averbach and M. Feldsein (New York: North Holland Press, 1987), and Richard Cornes and Todd Sandler, *The Theory of Externalities, Public Goods and Club Goods* (Cambridge: Cambridge University Press, 1986).

[52] Quoted in *The Voluntaryist* Email Group essay, by Carl Watner, July 8, 2012.

[53] David Schmidtz, *The Limits of Government: An Essay on the Public Goods Argument* (Boulder, CO: Westview Press, 1991), p. 160.

[54] Kramer, "The Future of the Voluntary Agency in a Mixed Economy," *op. cit.*, p. 387.

[55] Steven Rathgeb Smith and Michael Lipsky, *Nonprofits for Hire: The Welfare State in the Age of Contracting* (Cambridge: Harvard University Press, 1993), p. 30.

[56] Alexander Fleisher, "State Money and Privately Managed Charities," *The Survey*, October 31, 1914, p.110; and Amos G. Warner, *American Charities: A Study in Philanthropy and Economics*, (New York: T.Y. Crowell, 1894).

[57] Peter Beresford and Suzy Croft, *Whose Welfare?* (Brighton, UK: The Lewis Cohen Urban Studies Center at Brighton Polytechnic, 1986), p. 149. Quoted in Van Til, p.123.

[58] Ralph Kramer, *Voluntary Agencies in the Welfare State*, (Berkeley: University of California Press, 1981), p. 291.

[59] Commission on Foundations and Private Philanthropy, "The Role of Philanthropy in a Changing Society," in Brian O'Connell, editor, *America's Voluntary Spirit* (New York: The Foundation Center, 1983), p. 296.

[60] Sharon Dawes and Judith Saidel, *The State and the Voluntary Sector* (Albany and New York: The Nelson A. Rockefeller Institute of Government and The Foundation Center, 1988), pp. 52-53.

[61] William C. Mitchell and Randy T. Simmons, *Beyond Politics: Markets, Welfare and the Failure of Bureaucracy* (Boulder CO: Westview Press, 1994), p. 41. This is a good introduction to public choice in general. Also see the revised edition of the classic work on public choice by Dennis C. Mueller, *Public Choice II* (Cambridge, Cambridge University Press, 1989). Nonprofit and voluntary research needs a good introduction to public choice theory geared for the field.

[62] Daniel P. Moynihan, "The New Science of Politics and the Old Art of Government," The *Public Interest*, Winter 1987, p. 27. Quoted in David W. Brown, *When Strangers Cooperate: Using Social Conventions to Govern Ourselves* (New York: The Free Press, 1995) p. 4.

[63] *Beyond Politics*.), *op. cit.*, p. 25.

[64] Maria Brenton, *The Voluntary Sector in British Social Services* (London: Longmans, 1985). Quoted in Van Til, *op. cit.*, p. 123. Ira Glasser makes a similar point in his "Prisoners of Benevolence: Power Versus Liberty in the Welfare State," in *Doing Good: The Limits of Benevolence*, (New York: Pantheon Books, 1978).

[65] One more recent look is David Prychitko and Peter Boettke, "The New Theory of Government-Nonprofit Partnership: A Hayekian Critique of the Salamon Paradigm," *Working Paper # 1*, September 2002, The Philanthropic Enterprise.

[66] National Performance Review, Reinventing Government Summit, Philadelphia, PA, June 25, 1993. Testimony of Peter Cove, p.30.

[67] See, for instance, Jacques Ellul, *The Political Illusion* (New York: Alfred A. Knopf, 1967); Kenneth S. Templeton, Jr., editor, *The Politicization of Society* (Indianapolis: Liberty Fund, 1979); and T. Halper and R. Hartwig, "Politics and Politicization: An Exercise in Definitional Bridge-Building," *Political Studies 23* (1975).

[68] See, for instance, Paul Pierson, *Dismantling the Welfare State? Reagan, Thatcher, and the Politics of Retrenchment* (Cambridge: Cambridge University Press, 1994).

[69] Paci, *op. cit.*, pp. 195-196, in Maier, *Changing Boundaries of the Political*.

[70] See Frank Prochaska's fine little book, focusing on modern Britain, *The Voluntary Impulse: Philanthropy in Modern Britain* (London: Faber and Faber, 1988).

5. The Commonwealth of Philanthropic Citizenship

Background

This article combines different early efforts to develop my project on citizenship and philanthropy, all produced about the same time. I tried here to outline a tentative table of contents for a book on the subject.

Admittedly dated, repetitious, and incomplete, the views sketched here — a set of lenses to help make sense of the world and its noise — has been useful and revealing for me. It is a structure of an argument and approach to difficult issues that I hope may be helpful to others who can develop a much fuller exploration.

Introduction

The institutions of civil society are sustained not only by civility but also by rational reflection on the benefits they confer on the pursuit of interests. — Edward Shils

If democracy is to maintain a society of free men, the majority of a political body must certainly not have the power to "shape" a society.... [I]t is the spontaneously grown network of relationships between individuals and the various organizations they create that constitutes societies. Societies form but states are made. This is why so far as they can produce the needed services, or self-generating structures, societies are infinitely preferable. — F. A. Hayek

This project grew out of my belief in philanthropy writ large. It was my career. I was also continually troubled because donors, foundations, nonprofits, and the commentators and policy wonks who swarm about it didn't seem to understand. I felt philanthropy was untethered to anything greater than being a mere instrumentality. It was either a wallet or a service provider. I often saw it as quite ineffective. On the foundation/donor side, it was commonly afflicted by bouts of tone-deaf hubris. As many others have noted, it seemed to be its own fault, which philanthropy itself could reform. It needed to be embedded in something larger and serving a larger purpose.

Exploring the nature of civil society and situating the philanthropic and nonprofit world within the context of civil society served three purposes. First, it gave greater content and context to what we mean by civil society. Otherwise the term is too amorphous. While the market is a necessary and crucial aspect of civil society, I wanted to limit my focus to the "new work for invisible hands" in the way Richard Cornuelle urged.[1] Second, looking at the extent to which we engage in philanthropy (i.e., giving and volunteering) may give us a robust view of what Frank Prochaska eloquently described as "the commonwealth of citizenship outside the state."[2] The contrasts between the extent of voluntarism and philanthropic activity and the data on voting strike me as enlightening. Third, the contrast between civil society and the state (or government) can and should never be total. But highlighting the differences in means, power, support of diversity, etc., gives philanthropy space to operate successfully with greater responsibilities. In sum, all of this builds towards a way to look at philanthropy and voluntarism differently while demanding more of it. Perhaps we can see better how best to be "civil" citizens in every sense of that term and be able to act more freely and fulsomely as citizens.

I do not want to suggest that civil society is the panacea. Nor that philanthropy is in any sense perfect. But I do believe philanthropy needs to refocus much more attention on missions and programs that remain in and respect civil society and its means. As a valuable thought experiment, though, perhaps the first question as we look at problems is what are the goals, means, and solutions that honor civil society and its "nature," as hackneyed as that may sound. (The short article earlier in this book on Elinor Ostrom's work is highly suggestive here.) If we can't do that, then it is a failure of vision — a failure of our own making. Perhaps this work can shed some insight on the troubling question of what erodes both civil society and philanthropy, and how we might build up social capital to nurture a civic culture. What David Mathews wrote at a "better" time seems ever more difficult and necessary today:

> The lesson from the great civil revolutions of our time is that the institutions of civil society are the source of a country's political will, the creators of common ground, and the repository of legitimacy for all public institutions, including the state. *To put it bluntly, the state or government is more dependent on civil society than anyone ever imagined a decade ago.* Only the civil society, or the public through civil institutions, can do certain things. If the public or civil society doesn't do its job, the institutions of society cannot do theirs. (emphasis added)[3]

The Problem of Philanthropy

In one of my favorite movies, an offbeat 1966 classic titled *Morgan*, the protagonist is warned, "You better watch it!" He responds coyly, saying, "Yeah, but what is it?" That is the feeling one often gets when discussing what is variously called the third sector, the independent sector, the voluntary sector, the nongovernment sector, the nonprofit sector, the public sector, or even the invisible sector. I prefer, for simplicity's sake, the more encompassing generic term *philanthropy*. In his 1895 play *An Ideal Husband*, Oscar Wilde described philanthropy as "the refuge of people who wish to annoy their fellow creatures." Ambrose Bierce's *The Unabridged Devil's Dictionary* defined a philanthropist as "a rich old (and usually bald) gentleman who has trained himself to grin while his conscience is picking his pocket." There is certainly some truth in each of those. But I use philanthropy the way Bob Payton did: to mean, broadly speaking, "voluntary giving, voluntary service, and voluntary association, primarily for the benefits of others."[4] Used in that way, philanthropy today is big, it is important, and it is in trouble.

Philanthropy is big and getting bigger. When this outline was written, formal philanthropic institutions numbered approximately one million. Estimates ranged from two million to six or seven million if less formal associations are included. Indeed, in 1992, researchers counted the number of nonprofits in New York City. They found 19,500, twice the number they thought existed.[5] Beyond that, what is one to make of a portion of society that 1) employs at least nine million people, with volunteers contributing the equivalent of approximately another nine million jobs; 2) generates revenues of at least $535 billion ($437 billion excluding volunteers); and 3) has operating expenses of $455 billion ($357 billion excluding volunteers). Giving and volunteering by individuals is also widespread. In 2018, these numbers are mostly much larger now. In addition, as I discuss in Chapter 5, the capacity and likelihood of a huge intergenerational transfer of wealth is upon us in 2018 and for the next several decades, which could mean a massive increase in available resources.

Philanthropy is important. Besides the sheer numbers, there is a pervasiveness to philanthropy. It is one of the great unsung engines of moral and social progress. We all know about the centrality voluntary associations played in Tocqueville's America. There is a vast, poorly known literature that attests to this. American society has always been perceived that way. Reality is more nuanced. Visitors from the former Soviet Union, for instance, are more astonished by 4-H clubs and the voluntary associations of our lives than they are by our big combines and flashy cars. More telling, they thought they could do even more with it than was being done in the U.S.![6] Philanthropy has always had a significant charitable dimension: witness the astonishing but not altogether surprising outpouring after natural disasters. Philanthropy, most vividly through churches, is a teaching ground for caring and citizenship. It brings people together; provides for ourselves and others in many ways; encourages action, diversity, and pluralism; and is a testing ground for innovations of all kinds. For better and worse, philanthropy is also the place (to use a physical metaphor) where much of America's moral and political agenda is raised, discussed, and promoted, where individuals, through their giving and volunteering, express their moral concerns. While the philanthropic impulse is common throughout the world, its depth and inherent role in American society makes it special on our ground.

Finally, philanthropy is in trouble. It is much too often ineffective and inefficient. It seems arguably the handmaiden of the government. Major funding for many nonprofits comes from government sources. It has been estimated that 31 percent of the income for nonprofit public benefit organizations comes from government. Is that voluntary? Fifty-one percent of the income comes from fees, service charges, and other income from their own business enterprises?[7] Is that nonprofit? Is that charitable giving? Charitable organizations and foundations have been under attack in recent years for a variety of real and imaginary sins: big salaries, political action from all political sides, amassing of wealth, sleazy tactics, loss of charitable mission, etc. In the 1990s, there were impressive calls for philanthropy to do more, but they seemed to me mostly vacuous and inexperienced.

As these previously published essays are being prepared for publication, there are new, serious, and disturbing criticisms of philanthropy. They highlight very important issues. Lord knows that philanthropy needs serious criticism. But there are assumptions throughout many of these critiques that privilege the state and hubristic elitism over civil society, that could only lead to a far greater politicization of philanthropy not seen before. These need serious responses, too.[8]

The source of much of the trouble with philanthropy is conceptual, I fear. Philanthropy is constantly in the throes of defining itself. "Yeah, but what is it?" Although there is general agreement that it is vitally important, we can't seem to agree on its relationship to, and uses for, society. The world of philanthropy is in danger of losing its way through lack of attention to what makes it special. It is in danger of becoming an ideological whip. It remains in danger of becoming almost an off-the-books way of supporting the further politicization of society, whatever the political ax.

And it has largely accepted such a role. Henry Suhrke, the insightful, wonderful, and now sadly forgotten founder and editor of *Philanthropy Monthly* from 1968 to 2002, captured this in a white-hot observation after attending a most depressing meeting of major philanthropy players:

> It's not a pretty sight: leaders who have been living off of Tocqueville quotes for years, retreating frantically and loudly from the real possibility of putting their long and glorious heritage to work. The pronouncements and the ideas are uniformly negative. Philanthropy has its list of "Gimme's" but is eager to proclaim that it must not be expected actually to bear societal responsibilities.

If philanthropy itself only claims marginal roles — supplying highly egocentric venture capital, criticism of society, and expertise on who to redistribute income and as a conduit for tax-derived funds (minus administration costs, of course) — it seems likely that public policy will accommodate these claims accordingly. That is the only conceivable outcome of the current daily litany of reasons why private charity ought not to be counted on for a major independent role in social policy.... The ultimate [result] is to lose the tradition for want of trying. How bizarre that so many leaders (?) now seem bent on the latter course.[9]

Philanthropy, then, needs a much broader perspective of its role and standing if we are to understand both its strengths and weaknesses. Dependency on state-centered theories that currently prevail just don't cut it. I believe the term "civil society" provides a different lens. On the one hand, such a broad understanding of voluntary social action will give philanthropy the volition and agency that often does seem to be there. A model of philanthropy that is grounded in the idea of civil society may shed light on many of the contentious issues always facing it. On the other hand, it gives much greater content and meaning to an often amorphous term.

The Politicization of Society

There are many theories of society. Some seem almost to ignore philanthropy.[10] But mostly, it seems to me that all sides of the debate about the kind of society we want (and about philanthropy) are too quick to repair to politics. We live in a politicized world, where all problems are political problems and all solutions need political solutions. We live in a world that surely needs politics, but we should heed the warning James Madison gave us in 1794 about "the old trick of turning every contingency into a resource for accumulating force in the government."[11] This tendency applies equally across the political spectrum; all sides of the debate about the kind of society we want are quick to repair to politics and the state.

The "democracy in America" grounded in voluntary action that animated Tocqueville had been transformed into Herbert Croly's deeply politicized "promise of American life." We continue to live in the shadow of Croly's 1909 progressive dictum against voluntarism: "No voluntary association of individuals, resourceful and disinterested though they be, is competent to assume the responsibility." But there is no one "American national purpose." Nor can it be encompassed in a political Procrustean bed. That is the point: Only philanthropy and civil society can take on the vast diversity of purposes that a free, robust, diverse, and innovative society has.

The politicization of society deforms philanthropy even as it embraces its subservience. The purpose of this proposal is to further the effort to revive and develop the contrast between society and the state; to find a true balance that appreciates the role of philanthropy as "voluntary action for the public good." The emphasis here will be on the nature and possibilities of "civil" society rather than the evils and consequences of statist interventions. It is not enough to change the perception of the role of government; we need to provide a vision (and examples) of nongovernmental alternatives that go beyond what many see as merely narrow free market answers. I have no settled answers but want to add something to the discussions about philanthropy, citizenship, and a good society. The politicization of society should never be accepted.

Civil Society

We need to reassess the challenge Ralph Kramer made many years ago: to find "an appropriate social distance between governmental and voluntary agencies."[12] Accentuating that distance between the public and private (including both the voluntary and commercial sectors) has considerable value today. To follow that line of inquiry requires a conceptual framework derived from political and social theory, a grounding in historical works and contemporary trends, and a practical frame of reference that will help make philanthropy "visible" and relevant in a fuller context.

The idea of civil society gives both heft and a kind of independent existence to social phenomena that have otherwise been sucked into the politicization of society, philanthropy included. The historical sociologist Reinhard Bendix gives a good initial definition for a wonderfully complex notion: "*Civil society* refers to all institutions in which individuals can pursue common interests without detailed direction or interference from the government."[13] Michael Walzer viewed civil society as "the space of uncoerced human association."[14] Civil society encompasses all the institutions through which individuals and groups of individuals act primarily voluntarily, outside of and distinct from the government: property and markets, families, schools, churches, clubs, communities and neighborhood groups, businesses, and so on. Today, "distinct from government" might seem almost inconceivable. Yet not so many years ago, most human action that was productive was voluntary and cooperative, rather than compulsory and politicized. And as such, it was robustly democratic and pluralist.

The term was much in vogue when I started this work; it faded and is now flabbily used. I return to it in this article where I want to look at civil society in two ways. There is, first, the common dichotomy made between state and civil society, and then there is a fuller positive perspective emphasizing civil society's content, voluntary means, and rich texture.

State Versus Civil Society

The important 1987 book *Shifting the Debate* is still indicative of much of this work on the voluntary sector: "the voluntary sector ought not be defined in such a way that it is in competition or opposition to the welfare state."[15] Lester Salamon's valuable work on "voluntary failure" is similarly flawed by assuming a very benign view of state action and a derivative voluntary sector.

And yet civil society refers to those social relations we have that are voluntary, whereas the state is a sphere of social action based on organized force. The distinction rests in large part on the different *means* employed and on the different ways decisions are carried out.[16] Decision making in political systems, for instance, is collective (in democracies anyway) and usually universally applied. Other forms of human action within civil society bask in a wide sea of choice and diversity.

Not only is civil society different from, but indeed, it is prior to, government. This is the burden of Tocqueville's great work. Daniel Boorstin has echoed the same viewpoint:

> In America, even in modern times, communities existed before governments were here to care for public needs. There were many groups of people with a common sense of purpose and a feeling of duty to one another before there were political institutions forcing them to perform their duties.... Philanthropy — the charitable spirit — in its transformed American shapes has become the leading feature of our relation to the world.[17]

We tend to forget the extent to which there were truly vibrant civil societies in the United States and a number of countries down to this century. A. J. P. Taylor gives a particularly evocative and rich description of civil society in England of the early 1920s:

> The most influential figures in public life were indeed voluntary workers.... The public life of England was sustained by a great army of busybodies, and anyone could enlist in this army who felt inclined to. Though most of its members came from the middle class, they were joined in this period by trade union officials and by self-educated manual workers. These were the active people of England and provided the ground swell of her history.[18]

For nearly a century, the idea of civil society nearly disappeared, only to be reintroduced with powerful effect by the dissident intellectuals of Central Europe and the former Soviet Union. They were prescient in knowing they didn't want a political solution that replaced one tyranny with a state using the same means but perhaps more humanely for the moment. They tried to conceptualize a sphere of human action independent of the state. Domestically, the crumbling of the welfare state and the erosion of our civic culture also led to a reintroduction of the idea of civil society in an effort to find alternative and effective answers to social problems.

In both cases, the idea of civil society became a very powerful conceptual tool for a very real problem: how to carve out an area of social action independent from an all-encompassing state. As the Polish dissident Adam Michnik lamented, "From the official point of view a civil society doesn't exist. Society is not recognized as capable of organizing itself to defend its particular interests and points of view."[19] This is exactly what happened with the August 1980 agreement between the Polish state and the Solidarity workers at Gdansk. Again Michnik: "For the first time organized authority was signing an accord with an organized society…. For the first time in the history of communist rule in Poland 'civil society' was being restored, and it was reaching a compromise with the state."[20] Comparatively speaking, then, civil society is sharply distinguished from the state.

The well-known three-sector model of voluntarism — as the third part of a triptych including business and government — is very widely used.[21] The three-sector view is, I believe, a misleading distraction.

The Qualities and Means of Civil Society

We cannot leave the matter as a simple dichotomy, however, first because describing civil society solely in opposition to the state gives it only a negative connotation and no independent importance. Second, as a comparative term alone it easily becomes an ideological ping-pong ball of limited usefulness. If civil society is the space between the individual (or family) and the state, and if opening up that space is a valuable moral and policy goal, then the focus should be on what makes civil society attractive, exciting, and distinctive.

The English political philosopher John Gray has written that civil society refers to "the domain of voluntary associations, market exchanges, and private institutions within and through which individuals having urgent conceptions and diverse and often competitive purposes may coexist in peace."[22] A civil society is where people join in diversity, pluralism, and choice, where the freedom to try things, initiate, succeed and fail are common responsibilities. A civil society, in turn, requires tolerance, individual responsibility, civility (Ms. Manners would approve), and agreement on the general rules of the game. As many historians and political philosophers have noted, these qualities also make a limited government and democracy possible.[23]

These qualities of a civil society are precisely the ones that also describe the best of philanthropy: voluntary giving, voluntary service, and voluntary association. For me, then, there is a special and obvious place at the center of civil society (its moral center, anyway) for all the voluntary associations that make up the world of philanthropy.

Nonetheless, civil society is, rightly, a contestable concept with lots of ambiguity. Sadly, it is also easily ignored because it notes a series of phenomena in human action that are difficult to see. Hayek caught that aspect when he wrote that "societies form but states are made." Thus, recovering what Vaclav Havel has called "the independent life of society" was both the stunning breakthrough of modernity and the more recent key to the downfall of communism.

Civil society reentered the lexicon of political discourse largely through the need to reinvent and rethink the bases of the social contract, political legitimacy, citizenship, and individual conscience. It is too easily taken for granted, too much ignored and left unexamined. It is suggestive of an alternative to the fetishism for politics and markets. By its nature, civil society is ambiguous. The task is to understand better the mechanisms and means available from the nature of civil society. Just as the mechanism of markets is very well researched and theorized, the same has to be done if we are to see the possibilities — perhaps even the necessity — of relying more on the innovations within civil society. Indeed, the complexity and globalization of society may suggest such a necessary realignment between civil society and government. As Ralf Dahrendorf wrote:

> What we are learning is that certain tasks — which, in many countries, have "traditionally" been regarded as belonging in the public sphere — are now so immense that government cannot conceivably cope with them by applying public expenditure and the conventional machinery of public administration.[24]

That was in 1992. It is a lesson we must continually relearn. If we have learned nothing else about public policy, it is that politicization crowds out considering other options. The sad reintroduction of totalitarian governments in Eastern Europe suggest how fragile all of this is and how important it is for us to understand and advocate for civil society.

PHILANTHROPIC LANDSCAPES

The Two Forms of Citizenship

Consider the idea of citizenship. A closely reasoned discussion of the idea of civil society and the role the philanthropic sector plays will fall on deaf ears unless there is a practical and empirical way to also define and measure it. When one thinks of citizenship, there is usually the assumption that good citizenship involves participation in the political process; it tends to be reduced to voting. We are subjected to this view every couple of years. While important, that is much too limited a view. There is another way to look at citizenship. Let me introduce it through the contrast presented by the French classical liberal Benjamin Constant in an important speech in 1819. Two views of citizenship (or liberty) are presented which follow the classic distinction between (civil) society and the state. On the one hand, Constant takes the ancient idea of liberty or citizenship to be participation in and through the polis, "in an active and constant participation in collective power." In our time, this would be captured primarily in voting. Modern liberty is for him, on the other hand, a vast sphere outside direct political participation. It is, in large part, the right of everyone:

> to express their opinion, choose a profession and practice it, to dispose of property, and even to abuse it; to come and go without permission, and without having to account for their motives or undertakings. It is everyone's right to associate with other individuals, either to discuss their interests, or to profess the religion which they and their associates prefer, or even simply to occupy their days or hours in a way which is most compatible with their inclinations or whims.[25]

What, then, are these two different senses of citizenship? There is often an implicit assumption that a single periodic action of voting fully discharges one's responsibility as a citizen. It is certainly true that important thinkers like Hannah Arendt and Judith Shklar focus very heavily on political participation and voting.[26] Wolfinger and Rosenstone comment that "the most important benefit of voting ... is expressive rather than instrumental: a feeling that one has done one's due to society ... and to oneself."[27] It becomes a bundle of political rights and entitlements, which are usually essentially passive actions. Of course, a similar attitude was expressed more negatively by Henry David Thoreau: "I cast my vote, perchance, as I think right; but I am not vitally concerned that that right should prevail. I am willing to leave it to the majority. Its obligation, therefore, never exceeds that of expediency. Even voting *for the right* [thing] is *doing* nothing for it."[28]

The literature on voting behavior and rates over time is very good. There is much interesting material on the role of voting in legitimating political arrangements. There is research suggesting that as political initiatives succeed, there is a decrease in the choice and vitality of alternatives available within civil society.

The idea of civil society suggests that the responsibilities of citizenship are greater and more robust: not entirely fulfilled by political participation. Rather, citizenship is a more complex everyday affair. It is through awareness of one's connectedness in society and through everyday actions that citizenship is expressed. Citizenship, in any full sense, is a more integral part of our lives. It may be, then, that involvement in civil society is a more important indicator of full citizenship. Analyzing the extent of philanthropic activities and voluntarism may be one good way to determine the vitality of civil society.

A particularly eloquent brief statement described civil society as "the commonwealth of citizenship outside the state."[29] "Yeah, but what is it?" What does that mean? I started this article by suggesting that the idea of civil society can give a richer meaning and context to philanthropy. Now it is time for philanthropy to return the favor. For I think involvement in philanthropy can be a very good proxy for a richer and empirical view of good citizenship. If philanthropy is "voluntary action for the public good," then the extent to which we as a nation engage in it says something about the vitality of our civil society (in the same way that voting is seen as a proxy for the vitality and legitimacy of a political system). What might a comparison show? This can be a useful substantive question to explore.

Measuring Citizenship

Comparing data on the extent of giving and volunteering with rates of voting yields imperfect but fascinating comparisons. The contrast suggests a convenient paradigm and a way to measure the health of our civic and our political cultures.

In the 1992 presidential elections, 55 percent of the voting age population cast ballots. That reversed a thirty-plus-year decline in voting rates. Voting is important, but it is specifically limited to the political system. Giving and volunteering is a different kind of commitment; it is doing something for the right as one sees it. Whereas voting is focused on majority rule and the imposition of particulars among the various public goods, philanthropic involvement is a form of what might be called civil sovereignty (to borrow from the economic idea of consumer sovereignty), in the sense that each philanthropic "vote" or action counts in the most pluralistic and democratic way.

The data on giving and volunteering is more problematic and incomplete. Some suggestive comparisons are possible, however. For giving, in 1991, 72 percent of American households reported contributing to one or more charitable organizations. Churches, of course, were the major institution. The average amount given of contributing households was $899, or 2.2 percent of income, for a total in 1991 of 124.77 billion. In fact, 15 percent of contributing households gave 5 percent or more of their household income in 1991.[30] Fifty-one percent of American adults volunteered in 1991. That is, 94.2 million people who volunteered an average of 4.2 hours per week. Sixty-one percent of the teenagers between twelve and eighteen volunteered an average of 3.2 hours per week.

A major 1985 survey of *The Charitable Behavior of Americans* indicated that 89 percent of Americans eighteen or older had made contributions in 1984, averaging $650. Eighty-one percent believed that it is the responsibility of people to give what they can to charities. What is equally significant is that 38 percent of those surveyed thought they should be giving more.[31]

There are approximately 190 million Americans eighteen years and older. Using these rough figures, 104.5 million voted, and a little over 169 million gave and volunteered. Giving and volunteering is 61 percent higher. On the one hand, I don't want to make too much of this comparison; there are lots of apples and oranges, subtleties and other issues to be considered. On the other hand, I find the contrast remarkable, especially given the real "cost" to giving and volunteering which is absent to a considerable extent in voting. Without question, a view of citizenship within civil society and through philanthropy is extensive and robust (by these numbers when these presentations were made). By 2018, it appears that the trends in giving and volunteering have decreased. A close analysis of how might indicate a lot about the respective health of civil society and political society.

These two different kinds of action represent one part of an ancient and consistent dichotomy in the history of political thought: the contrast between civil society and the state. Providing a concrete measurement of philanthropy within civil society, then, is a great deal more than rhetorical. It suggests a way to "measure" the vitality of civil society through the extent to which individuals give and volunteer. It also opens the discussion to how philanthropy might enhance or rebuild a civil society. There is a crucial role philanthropy must and can play to revive and maintain a civil society that is free, prosperous, and humane. The problem is to conceptualize the issue and then provide a practical way to envision it and act on it.

BRINGING CIVIL SOCIETY BACK IN

The Promise and Pitfalls of Philanthropy

When scholars and practitioners reflect upon this philanthropic sector, they are more than a bit schizophrenic about it. Henry Suhrke captures this so perfectly in the quotation used earlier in this article: living off Tocqueville for years, fearing to be independent, and ever eager to present a list of "gimme's" to government. Our field says lofty things about philanthropy and it displays great hubris (see chapters 3 and 4 of this collection) in doing so. We then retreat to cry out that philanthropy cannot rely on the very voluntary institutions and means of civil society. We always seem to believe fixing it — so much so-called voluntary failure to fix — must be done via government.

As one way to see this, consider that in 1970, a survey of charitable organizations in Chicago by the Commission on Foundations and Private Philanthropy found concerns among them that increasing government funding would subject them to political winds and government bureaucracy.[32] More recently, in 1988, the Rockefeller Institute of Government surveyed nonprofits receiving significant funding from the State of New York:

> Among those interviewed, however, there was general agreement that the "scale of interdependence" is clearly tipped toward nonprofit dependence on government... Just under half the nonprofit survey respondents shared such views. They agreed that nonprofit organizations are too dependent on government funding and that receipt of state funds has significantly changed the program priorities of voluntary agencies. Even more important, more than a third feel government financing has actually changed their mission.[33]

I have a very critical eye when looking at both the promises of philanthropy and the pitfalls and pratfalls of nonprofit practice. Over decades, however, there has been a "displacement" strategy that transfers private, philanthropic decision making to the coercive, bureaucratic, and self-interested means of government. Ironically this also becomes a displacement that reduces real accountability. This view may seem excessive to some readers, but I believe it is defensible. It likely fits reality better and more often than the questionable explanatory powers of the ideas of interdependence, voluntary failure and partnership.

Interdependence, for instance, exists and is important. But by situating philanthropy *not* as an adjunct to the welfare state or market, but as a defining characteristic of a civil society, with a history of results and promise, we develop a platform to explore civil society's and philanthropy's independence and relevance. Such a perspective raises many challenges about some of the most influential theories and models of philanthropy and opens up new avenues of inquiry about the responsibilities philanthropy carries for the health of society.

It is especially important to maintain the conceptual and factual distinction between civil society and the state (especially because doing so is rare). As Reinhard Bendix forcefully puts it: "The experience of democratic orders has demonstrated that the antithesis between the state's monopoly of power and civil society's private associations must be maintained if democracy is not to degenerate into anarchy or dictatorship."[34]

Then there is failure. While philanthropy has a commanding role to play in civil society, it is hampered by its own failures and inefficiencies. No doubt about that! They are real, and I believe there is a wealth of evidence that civil society and philanthropy has embedded within it a variety of valuable self-correcting aspects.

This is different from the failures of the theory of voluntary failure. I am thinking of the very failures that the theory of voluntary failure picks up from its inherent assumptions about the politicization of society. That in turns supports the assumption that philanthropy must be subservient to government and has not the vision or means to do more voluntarily. And finally, there is the attendant failure to develop, improve and use the voluntary means available to solve problems.

Finally, partnership is another idea that describes a lot that is good about and necessary for the voluntary sector. The problem is that it is also used to define and restrict our vision. (See, for instance, "Some Measure of Leadership?" in chapter 4 of this collection.) The level of genuine reciprocity that is presented is hardly "balanced." Partnership so often hides a preeminence of government action over the voluntary sector. The point is not to oppose or give up all government programs, but it is to question their usefulness in many cases, as well as to consider alternatives to them.

Simply put, true interdependence, voluntary failure, and partnership are rare. Using the terms as colored glasses for seeing and assessing philanthropy and civil society is very often quite biased: tending to hide and rationalize subservience, as I have also developed in many of the essays throughout this collection.

Conclusion

In a sense, it comes down to what kind of society do we want and what means will we use. It goes back to key beliefs about the dynamics of human action, the role of the state, and the nature of civil society. We are asking ourselves what kind of citizenship will be most helpful in promoting a free, democratic and diverse society?

Social life always has a strong element of being contentious. More so now than ever in this country. As David Mathews presciently wrote years ago, "The 'We the People' versus 'They the government' clash is shrill and counterproductive."[35] That is quite right. Are we talking about "we the people" as a political body (employing primarily collective, coercive, zero-sum decision making)? Or do we want "we the people" as a "commonwealth of citizenship outside the state," (employing primarily voluntary and cooperative means through a vast diversity of individuals and institutions)? It is not an either/or choice, but the implications of the balance between each is key.

This perspective or paradigm deepens our understanding of citizenship, civil society, and philanthropy. A truly civil society can exist only if philanthropy is vital *and* recognized as such. And philanthropy can be vibrant and robust *only* if we accept the potential, responsibilities, means, and constraints of being part of civil society. It takes effort, understanding, and commitment to the means of civil society. Otherwise, philanthropy may be overlooked as Bob Payton ruefully pointed out in 1988:

> The new *Britannica* overlooks philanthropy, as far as I can tell, although an earlier edition — the eleventh — dealt with it quite adequately. That's the way it goes: One day you take it for granted, and the next day it's gone.... Philanthropy in some organized form appears in all the major cultural and religious traditions, and it might be argued that *philanthropy is an essential defining characteristic of civilized society.* [36]

We can help to revive the value of civil society together with the practice and means of voluntarism and philanthropy. In seeking to do so, we must develop a robust alternative perspective to current state-centric social theory and practice where philanthropy is a handmaiden and "gone." It seems to me that the claims of philanthropic citizenship are compelling. Getting the will and the results to catch up is the challenge before us.

This article is an amalgam. In September 1993 I presented "Civil Society and Philanthropy" to the Hudson Institute's Program for Political Institutions in Indianapolis. Earlier, I published a draft research agenda titled "Citizenship and Voluntarism" which appeared in The Federalism Report, *V. 18, No. 3, Spring 1993, published by the Center for the Study of Federalism, Temple University, thanks to Director Daniel J. Elazar's enthusiasm. Finally, those efforts became parts of several book outlines I prepared for grant applications, and for a monograph to be titled "The Idea of Civil Society: An Alternative to Political Stagnation" for the CATO Institute. I had to set that aside when I took the job at the J. M. Kaplan Fund.*

---

[1] Richard Cornuelle, "New Work for Invisible Hands," *Times Literary Supplement*, April 5, 1991.

[2] Frank Prochaska, "But the Greatest of them...", *Times Literary Supplement,* January 15, 1993.

[3] David Mathews, "The Civil Opportunities of Foundations," *Foundation News*, March/April 1991, p. 33.

[4] Robert L. Payton, *Philanthropy* (New York: Macmillan Publishing Co, 1985), p. 32.

[5] *The Nonprofit Sector in New York City* (New York: Nonprofit Coordinating Committee of New York, 1992). Discussed in *The Nonprofit Times*, August 1992, p.4.

[6] Consider the comment by Librarian of Congress James Billington: "In my office the other day were thirty to forty students from Nizhnii Novgorod, the former city of Gorky. These young Russians had discovered a lot of ideas and institutions that Americans don't even think about: 4-H clubs, Rotary Clubs, things that are as American as apple pie.... But they see such institutions and think that they can do even more than they are doing in the United States." *The Idea of a Civil Society* (Research Triangle Park, NC: The National Humanities Center, 1992), p. 5.

[7] Salamon, *America's Nonprofit Sector: A Primer* (New York: Foundation Center, 1999), p. 26.

[8] See, for instance, Rob Reich, Chiara Cordelli, and Lucy Bernholz, Editors, *Philanthropy in Democratic Societies* (Chicago: The University of Chicago Press, 2016); Anand Giridharadas, *Winners Take All* (New York: Alfred A. Knopf, 2018); and Rob Reich, *Just Giving: Why Philanthropy Is Failing Democracy and How It Can Do Better* (Princeton: Princeton University Press, 2018).

[9] Henry Suhrke, "Maxims for Philanthropy: Give Us the Tools and We'll Do the Job," *Philanthropy Monthly*, May 1995, p. 5 and 6.

[10] In *The Affluent Society*, (Boston: Houghton-Mifflin, 1958), J. K. Galbraith talked only about two sectors, a public/governmental and a private/commercial. Ironically, no one noticed the omission for years. cf. Cornuelle, *op. cit.*, p. 182.

[11] James Madison, as quoted in Albert Jay Nock, *Our Enemy the State* (New York: Free Life Editions, 1973), p. 4.

[12] Ralph M. Kramer, *Voluntary Agencies in the Welfare State* (Berkeley: University of California Press, 1981), p. 292

[13] Reinhard Bendix, *Kings or People*, (Berkeley: University of California Press, 1978), p. 523.

[14] Michael Walzer, "The Idea of Civil Society," *Dissent*, Spring 1991, p. 293.

[15] Susan Ostrander, "Towards Implications for Research, Theory, and Policy on Nonprofits and Voluntarism," in Susan Ostrander, Stuart Langton, and Jon Van Til, Editors, *Shifting the Debate* (New Brunswick: Transaction Books, 1987.), p. 130.

[16] Max Weber reminds us that (this is W.G. Runciman quoting Weber "by running together his most important assertions"): "the state cannot be defined in terms of what it does. There is scarcely any task that some political association has not taken in hand... Ultimately, one can give a sociological definition of the modern state only in terms of the specific means peculiar to it, as to every political association, namely, the use of physical force." W.G. Runciman, *Social Science and Political Theory*, (Cambridge: Cambridge University Press, 1963) p. 35. Also, Runciman himself, "the criterion of the 'political' is means and not results", p. 41. Also see Franz Oppenheimer, *The State* (New York: Free Life Editions, 1975). One of the "means" that distinguishes civil society is its nature of "corrective processes" that are at work. See for instance, Chandran Kukathas' extremely fine discussion and critique of this idea — in opposition to the usual excuse of "failure" in his Chapter 3 of *Hayek and Modern Liberalism* (Oxford: Oxford University Press, 1989).

[17] Daniel J. Boorstin, *The Decline of Radicalism*, (New York: Random House, 1961), pp. 46 and 68.

[18] A.J.P. Taylor, *English History: 1914-1945* (Oxford: Oxford University Press, 1965), pp. 174-175. Contrast this emphasis with how the advance of nonprofit initiatives is being hindered in East Central Europe by the drain of activists and intellectuals from the fledgling independent organizations and nonprofits to the political arena. On one of the impacts of the political sensibility and assumption, cf. Daniel Siegel and Jenny Yancy, *The Rebirth of Civil Society* (New York: The Rockefeller Brothers Fund, 1992), p. 16.

[19] Adam Michnik, "Towards a Civil Society: Hopes for Polish Democracy," *Times Literary Supplement*, February 19-26, 1988, p.188. "The crucial problem is therefore to build a democratic society which renders totalitarianism impossible by altering the social mechanisms of power."

[20] Adam Michnik, *Letters from Prison* (Berkeley: University of California Press, 1985), p. 124.

[21] See, for instance, Michael O'Neill, *The Third America: The Emergence of the of the Nonprofit Sector in America* (San Francisco: Jossey-Bass, 1989).

[22] John Gray, *Post-Liberalism* (London: Routledge, 1993), p. 159.

[23] See, for instance, the important work of Víctor M. Pérez-Díaz, *The Return of Civil Society: The Emergence of Democratic Spain* (Cambridge: Harvard University Press,

1993); and Ernest Gellner, *Conditions of Liberty: Civil Society and its Rivals* (New York: Viking Penguin, 1994)

[24] Ralf Dahrendorf, Warden, St. Anthony's College, Oxford, speaking to the European Foundation Centre Annual General Meeting, November 8, 1992. Quoted in *The Philanthropy Monthly*, September 1992, p. 3.

[25] "The Liberty of Ancients Compared with that of the Moderns" speech given at the Athenee Royal in Paris, 1819. In *Benjamin Constant, Political Writings*, edited by Biancamaria Fontana, (Cambridge: Cambridge University Press, 1988), pp. 316, 310-11.

[26] See, for instance, Judith Shklar, *American Citizenship*, (Cambridge: Harvard University Press, 1991) and Hannah Arendt, *Between Past and Future*, (New York: Penguin Books, 1977).

[27] Raymond Wolfinger and Steven Rosenstone, *Who Votes*, (New Haven: Yale University Press, 1980), p. 8.

[28] Henry David Thoreau, *Reform Papers* (Princeton: Princeton University Press, 1973) p. 69, in the essay "resistance to Civil Government".

[29] Frank Prochaska, "But the Greatest of them…", *op. cit.*

[30] "Facts and Figures on the Independent Sector," (Washington: Independent Sector, n.d.)

[31] *The Charitable Behavior of Americans* (Washington: Independent Sector, 1985).

[32] Cf. the article "The Role of Philanthropy in a Changing Society," reprinted from the report and recommendations of the Commission on Foundations and Private Philanthropy, 1970, as reprinted in *America's Voluntary Spirit*, Brian O'Connell, Editor, (New York: The Foundation Center, 1983), especially p. 296.

[33] Sharon Dawes and Judith Saidel, *The State and the Voluntary Sector*, (New York: The Nelson A. Rockefeller Institute of Government and The Foundation Center, 1988), pp. 52-53.

[34] Reinhard Bendix, "State, Legitimation and "Civil Society", *Telos*, #86, Winter 1990-91 p.150.

[35] Mathews, *op. cit.*, p.33.

[36] Robert Payton, *Philanthropy: Voluntary Action for the Public Good* (New York: American Council on Education/Macmillan Publishing, 1988), p. 40.

SECTION TWO

THE PRACTICE OF PHILANTHROPY

A decline in voluntary activity is a measure of decay within a liberal society.... The political maturity of a country is not measured by the size or form of government. It is measured by a polity that provides the conditions of liberty conducive to civil society and by what citizens willingly do for themselves and one another. — Frank Prochaska

There is a significant tradition of state intervention built around the idea of citizenship for which there is no real equivalent to underpin voluntary activity. — Desmond King

Billions are wasted on ineffective philanthropy. Philanthropy is decades behind business in applying rigorous thinking to the use of money. — Michael Porter

CHAPTER 3

THE HUBRIS OF PHILANTHROPY

Let's focus on what keeps philanthropy from solving serious problems: the unwillingness of foundations and big donors to realize they don't have all the answers. — Pablo Eisenberg

The recognition of the insuperable limits to his knowledge ought indeed to teach the student of society a lesson in humility which should guard him against becoming an accomplice in men's fatal striving to control society — a striving which makes him not only a tyrant over his fellow, but which may well make him the destroyer of a civilization which no brain has designed but which has grown from the free efforts of millions of individuals. — F. A. Hayek

Most experts ... don't know more than the average person. They may act as though they are engaged in real science. They do studies, follow certain methods and have results. But they are really practicing what I call "cargo-cult science." ... To distinguish between what is valid information and what is cargo cult, people need use only common sense. They need only look at the effects of policies. — Richard Feynman

The only Big Plan is to discontinue the Big Plans. The only Big Answer is that there is no Big Answer. — William Easterly

The day after I became executive director of the J. M. Kaplan Fund, Kent Barwick sidled up to me and congratulated me. He said: "That is great news, Chuck. But yesterday was the last time you will ever get a bad meal, ever tell a bad joke, or ever get an honest compliment." That rather stark prediction was largely true. But the impact was less on how people would view me and more about how I and philanthropists start viewing ourselves. All meals did taste good, all jokes were hilarious, and the compliments I got simply confirmed how brilliant I was. Therein lies a story about philanthropic hubris.

As much as I respected and admired so many of my colleagues, I found the conceit and hubris all too common. True humility took constant effort. I found that listening and asking questions were good antidotes. I was careful about making suggestions since they were so often heard as requirements hidden in a grantor's pontifications.

Hubris is a common human affliction, but I found it was particularly infectious in philanthropy because there were no antidotes. The power of money brought me right back to Kent's ominous prediction: there was precious little honest feedback to be had. Each quotation on the title page of this chapter addresses this phenomenon with slightly different takes. These two chapters address the unintended presence of philanthropic hubris in our work.

Another story. Ten years after Kent's comment, The Clark Foundation and I were being honored at a United Neighborhood Houses gala. UNH was the intermediary for the settlement houses in New York City. During my time at Clark we were big funders of many of them. At the reception, the executive director and board chair of a large settlement house came up to me. I had worked with them closely and they were annual recipients of large grants. The two of them basted me with unstinting praise for what seemed like many minutes. While no doubt well deserved, my head was reeling, and my BS-detector was deep in the red zone. A moment after they left, the ED turned to the board chair and said in a whisper she didn't know carried, "Now, the dirty deal is done!"

We continued to fund their good work, by the way. And I knew they really meant that I was not so special after all. Those kinds of experiences helped keep me humble and no doubt contributed to whatever skill and effectiveness I brought to my wonderful time in philanthropy.

1. Getting Beyond Philanthropic Colonialism

Peter Buffett deserves lots of credit for his 2013 op-ed piece "The Charitable-Industrial Complex."[1] It is an invitation to participate in what he and his wife, Jennifer, are learning about philanthropy. When I met them several years earlier, they were genuinely trying to learn. Their NoVo Foundation began in 2006 with a big commitment from Peter's father, Warren. At the end of 2016 (based on the latest available 990, as of August 2018), it had an endowment of about $652 million and had given away about $100 million each of the two previous years. It had and has very ambitious goals for empowering adolescent girls and ending violence against girls and women. The responses to his *New York Times* op-ed were numerous. *The Chronicle of Philanthropy* ran an interesting piece by Phil Buchanan[2] and short excerpts from other experts.[3] Buffett also wrote a short *HuffPost Blog* entry with some comments going beyond the *Times* piece.[4]

His evident frustrations at established philanthropy were refreshing, legitimate, and heartfelt. But I found some of his assumptions and suggestions reflected other troubling aspects of what is more deeply wrong with much of philanthropy today. While I focus on his comments and occasionally refer to NoVo Foundation to look at these issues, they are simply examples of bigger problems. Getting beyond "philanthropic colonialism" is an ongoing challenge across the field.

Buffett rightly identifies the destructive and often unintended consequences of what he calls philanthropic colonialism: when "a donor [and, I would add, many a foundation program officer and executive] had the urge to 'save the day' in some fashion. People … who had very little knowledge of a particular place would think that they could solve a local problem." Most commentators on his article glossed over his specific point about local knowledge and avoided the larger one about hubris among philanthropic practitioners. Philanthropic colonialism as Buffett describes it is just a variant of the hubris that infects so much philanthropic practice of donors and professional philanthropoids. It is, alas, a warning that has often been voiced and just as often ignored.

I have been amazed how often foundation program officers and executive directors thought "I know better" about the problems and solutions to school reform, poverty alleviation, merging nonprofits, etc. — much to the horror of nonprofits on the ground and the clients they serve. Indeed, many of the writings that have come out of what we might call "the strategic philanthropy complex" encourage, unintentionally or intentionally, this unfortunate attitude among philanthropists. (See my review essay on the pitfalls of strategic philanthropy immediately following this article.[5])

Buffett goes on to identify additional damaging factors behind philanthropic colonialism. Invited inside the corridors of power, he was dismayed that as elites search for solutions, others at the same table have created the problems. That is certainly true in one sense: power corrupts! But sadly, he assumes too simple a dichotomy in most cases of those seemingly creating problems and those seemingly trying to solve them. Sadly, what he is mostly seeing is a self-justifying negative feedback loop: problems beget hubristic solutions, which in turn requires new solutions, which in turn ... *ad infinitum*. The difficult questions are how do we change out those at the table, how do we fight hubris, and do we get off that destructive feedback loop?

The impression Buffett leaves is also that the cause of these problems is capitalism and markets. This is too superficial to be helpful, and is likely harmful by being way too simplistic. Foolish political correctness has no useful role here, except as a "hobgoblin of little minds, adored by little statesmen and philosophers and divines," to borrow from Emerson. Buffett is not one of those. He rightly sees that something is wrong, but he needs to be more thoughtful about the causes and the solutions.

Of course, market, nonprofit, and government failures are all at work. However, we need to be more precise about what we mean if we are to diagnose and address causes clearly. Only then can we develop solutions that work and don't exacerbate the situation or further entrench the elite.

As a small step in that direction, I would suggest using a more focused term like "corporatism," as Nobel Laureate Edmund Phelps does in his important and moving book, *Mass Flourishing: How Grassroots Innovation Created Jobs, Challenges and Change.*[6] Those experts Buffett observed are an unholy alliance of diverse and yet entrenched interests. In government, corporations, unions, and yes, philanthropy, they happen to congregate in the corridors of power. These are institutional arrangements that contribute greatly to the mess we are in and hamper solutions. The important point is that open and candid discussion from all points of view is necessary if we are to understand clearly the complexity of what is going on. Not to do so increases the probabilities of stasis, failure, or worse. In most ways, Phelps' book would go a long way in disabusing one of such simple explanations.

As a result of his observations gleaned from the passageways of power and influence, Buffett has decided that much of donor philanthropy is simply "conscience laundering." Again, he senses a real problem. Frankly, however, I have seen that most often among a narrow elite of foundation boards, staff, and policy analysts. That is not what I have mostly seen working with many wealthy donors, who tend to be passionate and committed to their causes — as is Buffett. I think he hit a wrong note here.

Buffett also dismisses small philanthropic successes as he searches for big answers, which seems inconsistent with his earlier commitment to local knowledge. He rejects helping people "to integrate into our system of debt and repayment with interest. People will rise above making $2 a day to enter our world of goods and services so they can buy more. But doesn't all this just feed the beast?" Say that to the nearly one billion people in the developing world that have risen out of extreme poverty between 1990 and 2010.[7] Is he betraying his own elitist predilection to "save the day" by misconstruing how the efforts of the poor may relate to consumerism? As much as globalization is a *bête noir*, we simply can't ignore the genuine economic dynamism that has made such a profound difference for nearly a billion people, while the wealthy and privileged elites continue to hobnob around the table. Much, much more has to be done, of course. As I see it, we can't ignore the small steps that often make the difference between life and death, while they also open doors to hope and progress for those who need it most and need to be empowered to find their own ways. Crucially, this is how we learn from and stay in touch with those we care about.

Buffett hits another wrong note, as so many do, when he rejects these small changes. In their place he desires "to support conditions for systemic change," what he calls "new code." This reminds me of the biting irony in Jacques Barzun's wonderful essay "The Folklore of Philanthropy," where he writes, "the very passion of philanthropy which our forefathers kindled is now distorting judgment and superseding thought.... Philanthropy, in sum, is manipulation for the general good, anxiously contrived, timidly eager for approval, and therefore seeking love and publicity."[8] In this context, I often think of how apposite the term "coercive philanthropy" is, as coined by Margaret Rossiter in the 1970s.

I know that Buffett genuinely wants to get beyond the manipulation, power, and simplicity of philanthropic colonialism. But I think he is too quick to ignore the common, unintended consequences of straying too far into the stratosphere: from "just" wasting great amounts of money to making the lives and prospects of so many people much worse. Just consider Nina Munk's bracing book, *The Idealist: Jeffrey Sachs and the Quest to End Poverty*, which is a sad, cautionary tale of poignant passion, galloping presumption, and failed promises.[9] You can be damn sure that none of us reading (or writing) this article will pay for these tragedies. So, we need to know what makes for success or failure. Small changes and attention to what people really want can ground otherwise abstract and self-defeating initiatives in reality. Buffett knows this, and NoVo acknowledges this in much of its work. But his and their own pull towards philanthropic colonialism as evidenced in his *New York Times* op-ed is a cautionary reminder of the need for humility and vigilance.

By the end of the op-ed piece, Buffett's personal report card reveals a genuine desire to do philanthropy better. He sees clearly some of the serious weaknesses of philanthropy. But there is a dose of elitism there too. More troubling, it seems a call for "new code" that will lead one right back to the same philanthropic colonialism, simply dressed up in "new clothes."

Where do we go from here? I offer four essential topics to keep the conversation going.

Stay grounded. In one of his contributions to the discussion his op-ed generated, Buffett claims that "we should focus on creating the conditions for change as opposed to focusing on exactly what change should look like." That is misleading and at least half-wrong. Isn't the "change one will likely get" embedded in how we define and create the conditions for change? Diagnosis is not easy. Otherwise, it is too easy to impose the abstract rationalism of philanthropic colonialism and to ignore what other people want and need. I remember years ago supporting research that surveyed what the residents of the poorer neighborhoods of Washington, D.C., really wanted. They were initially suspicious of being lab rats. Once they realized the surveyers were listening, it turned out that residents wanted what we all do: clean streets, safety, etc. This flew in the face of the grand theories of a burgeoning anti-poverty industry.

Beware of group-think. Buffett bewails the gatherings, workshops, and affinity groups generated by philanthropy. I couldn't agree more! At the same time, the NoVo Foundation website makes much of the importance of concentrating expertise and learning through collaborations and gatherings of stakeholders. Rightly so. Too often, though, the people brought to the table — the so-called experts and "stakeholders" — seem more often self-selected and self-interested, entrenched in a group-think culture that limits everyone's vision. The challenge is to find the right group of insiders, outsiders, and critics willing to engage in an ongoing, open, and honest dialogue that really honors expertise, diversity of viewpoint, local knowledge, and criticism. We must "listen" outside the box. While none of us may find cynics, curmudgeons, and naysayers inspiring or even fun to be around, I increasingly find their counsel quite invaluable leavening.

NoVo doesn't accept outside proposals and, as Pablo Eisenberg recently pointed out, it is governed by a board of only three: "No matter how smart or experienced the Gateses and Buffetts are, they are wrong to think they will get the best ideas from such a small board. I fear it could easily become much more insular over time."[10] That appears to still be an issue. I am not one to always advocate for larger boards or to think that numbers alone will cure insularity. It is, however, an institutional problem that can have terrible impact on programs and results.

Commit to the long term. Throughout the NoVo website, and in some of Buffett's other writing, there is a clear appreciation of the long-term nature of the work to be done. That is a pleasant difference from the near fetish in modern foundations and among many donors for short-term results and an annual schedule. This doesn't show up in the *Times* piece, but it is critical to real success. He is right here. I hope philanthropic practice generally will become much more focused on the long term.

Focus on results. The NoVo website and those of the big, important initiatives it supports do have some of the hallmarks of slick marketing glitz. It is not uncommon to see foundations conflate promotion of programs with effectiveness.[11] Philanthropy also has a long history of avoiding paying for good, independent evaluations (these don't have to be super expensive). We aren't so good, either, at learning from or communicating about our successes or mistakes. Failures can easily become institutionalized in philanthropy and nonprofits (witness the ineffectiveness of DARE; see the next article). Those are understandable foibles to which I also succumbed. One hopes, however, that these candid evaluations are in the works, and that these impressive-looking sites will also become critical learning vehicles.

Conclusion

That was then; what about now? Are Buffett and NoVo avoiding most of the trappings of philanthropic colonialism? Of course, NoVo and Buffett are not the same thing, but they are testing grounds by which to assess philanthropic colonialism in action. For instance, over five years after Buffett's piece was published, there may be the beginnings of important evaluation data to share, but it isn't apparent or transparent on the NoVo website. This is important. They are also very locally focused. However, being focused locally and seeking and learning from local knowledge are very different. Which is it? They emphasize multi-year funding. That is great.

For the field, I worry that not a lot of progress has been made against philanthropic colonialism. Indeed, do we or Buffett have more to say about the ways in which the "conditions for change" and "what change looks like" may be more deeply connected than he averred in his op-ed?

Admittedly, Buffett's recent inspiring and poetic call about "The Fierce Urgency of 'How'"[12] is only a small part of the work and thinking we still need to do about the "six questions": What? Who? Where? When? How? Why? However, if thirty years in the field have taught me anything, it is that there is little really new in our field, except for fancy buzzwords, and what seems to be the permanent retreat to urgency looks more like an excuse to avoid the real work of diagnosis, critical conversations, and assessment. These important issues need ongoing discussion across the field. So, I wonder whether hubris and group-think are being continually challenged.

In fact, for all of us, the reason lesson about philanthropic colonialism is what economist John McMillan draws from his vast experience:

> To claim we are able to do something more premediated than trial and error is to exaggerate our knowledge of reform processes. Avoid hubris.[13]

Philanthropy is nothing praiseworthy if it isn't a continuing, demanding, and humble discovery process. It must be that, with the reminder to "first do no harm." Doing that well and constantly is one of the few checks on philanthropic colonialism and the related challenges expressed above.

Peter Buffett gave us in the field something thoughtful to think about, which still resonates today. How are *we* doing?

This is a much-expanded version of one of my contributions to the Smart Assets blog of Philanthropy New York. Originally published November 5, 2013, it is reprinted with permission from Philanthropy New York.

---

[1] Peter Buffett, "Charitable-Industrial Complex," *The New York Times*, July 24, 2013.

[2] Phil Buchanan, "Peter Buffett is Right to Call for Philanthropic Change," *The Chronicle of Philanthropy*, August 5, 2013.

[3] "Responding to Peter Buffett: What Philanthropy Experts Say." *The Chronicle of Philanthropy*, August 5, 2013.

[4] Peter Buffett, "Change Our Story: My 'Complex' Week." *HuffPost Blog*, August 7, 2013.

[5] Originally published as "A Hedgehog Moment: The Roles and Pitfalls of Strategic Philanthropy for Family Foundations and Donors," *The Foundation Review*, Vol. 3, Issue 4 (2011).

[6] Edmund Phelps, *Mass Flourishing: How Grassroots Innovation Created Jobs, Challenges and Change* (Princeton: Princeton University Press, 2013).

[7] "Growth or Safety Net," *The Economist*, September 21, 2013.

[8] Jacques Barzun, "The Folklore of Philanthropy," in *The House of Intellect* (New York: Harper & Brothers, 1959), pgs. 179 and 198. This fine essay should be read by all aspiring and actual philanthropists.

[9] Nina Munk, *The Idealist: Jeffrey Sachs and the Quest to End Poverty* (New York: Doubleday and Co, 2013).

[10] Pablo Eisenberg, "'Strategic Philanthropy' Shifts too Much Power to Donors," *The Chronicle of Philanthropy*, August 20, 2013.

[11] Sadly, this is often true. Consider my blog post reprinted in Chapter 4 of this volume, "Philanthropy as 'Invisible Aid'". Another example is the *Casebook for The Foundation*, by Joel Fleishman, J. Scott Kohler and Steven Schindler (New York: Public Affairs, 2007). Presented as exploring "100 of the highest-achieving foundation initiatives of all time," the case studies are generally thin on summarizing results and too often way too heavy on the self-congratulatory marketing side.

[12] Peter Buffett, "The Fierce Urgency of 'How'", *Yes! Magazine*, January 1, 2018.

[13] John McMillan, "Avoid Hubris: and Other Lessons for Reformers", *Reinventing Foreign Aid*, Edited by William Easterly (Cambridge: The MIT Press, 2008), p. 512.

2. A Hedgehog Moment:
The Roles and Pitfalls of Strategic Philanthropy for Family
Foundations and Donors

Introduction

In 1930, Frederick P. Keppel, president of the Carnegie Corporation from 1922 to 1941, published *The Foundation*, one of the earliest books on foundations. He noted that foundations were a distinctly twentieth-century phenomenon, and "only seven of any importance having carried over from the nineteenth." By 1930, he estimated that there were two hundred foundations with assets of almost a billion dollars, or about $13 billion in current dollars.[1] Since then the growth of foundations has been phenomenal. By 2014, it was estimated that there were nearly 87,000 foundations (an increase over 2010 of 14 percent), with assets of $865 billion (an increase of 53 percent), and giving of $60 billion (an increase of 30 percent).[2] Private philanthropy has continued to be much more robust than experts predicted, even in the recent economic downturn, as donors, families, and especially baby boomers make significant charitable plans. The future is uncertain, but the continued growth of philanthropy seems very likely for many reasons beyond the scope of this article.

However, the growing *quantity* of giving has not been matched by improved *quality*. This is the perennial challenge that afflicts philanthropy, what Keppel described as "the truly difficult task of properly distributing large funds."[3] The growth in the quantity of new philanthropy and the search for more effective philanthropy has produced a "significant moment in the marketization of philanthropy," as wonderfully named by Lucy Bernholz in 2008.[4] An outpouring of books by foundation officials, consultants, and academics has broadly emphasized the idea that "strategic philanthropy" in some form promises significant improvements. With these books, then, do donors, family foundations, and philanthropy generally have new usable knowledge to meet the challenge of quality grantmaking? Or are they being invited, mostly unintentionally, to embrace their inner hubris?

The Five Books Reviewed Here

The Foundation: A Great American Secret (New York: Public Affairs, 2007, 334 pages). Joel L. Fleishman is professor of law and public policy at Duke University. He previously served as president of the Atlantic Philanthropies Service Company, the U.S. program staff of Atlantic Philanthropies.

The Foundation is a strong moral and practical plea that "more should be expected from foundations" and offers ways that might be accomplished. Two chapters are good on foundation success and failure: chapter 8 on successful initiatives and chapter 12 on foundation failures, chosen "from among several hundred that were suggested to me."[5] These become useful background for chapters on strategy and achieving impact, which are straightforward and useful. *The Foundation* was not intended as a history of foundations. That is unfortunate since the other books reviewed here are limited by their lack of historical understanding and context.[6]

A companion volume — *Casebook for The Foundation*, by Joel L. Fleishman, J. Scott Kohler, and Steven Schindler (New York: Public Affairs, 2007) — contains 100 case studies of successes from wealthier foundations between 1901 and 2002. Sadly, too many cases read like marketing pieces from each foundation's communication department, an impression reinforced by my different assessment in several cases with which I am familiar. Far more valuable would be a candid, dispassionate book on failures and successes, with some discussion about why some foundations and program strategies are successes and others are failures.

Money Well Spent: A Strategic Plan for Smart Philanthropy (New York: Bloomberg Press, 2008, 280 pages). Paul Brest and Hal Harvey are, respectively, president of the William and Flora Hewlett Foundation and before that professor of law and dean of the Stanford Law School; and president of ClimateWorks Foundation.

The authors caution that strategic philanthropy is only for a small number of philanthropists, because it "takes a great deal of focus, time, energy, and consultation." This is an important caution echoed by Crutchfield and Tierney in their books. Nonetheless, the first part, "The Framework of Strategic Philanthropy," is valuable reading for any family foundation or donor. Just don't be lulled into assuming that strategic philanthropy is the major driver of philanthropic success.

The authors are thoughtful foundation executives who know that "the core activity of philanthropy is grantmaking." The two chapters exploring that crucial relationship are particularly useful. They are antidotes to the all-too-common conceit that grantees are not all that important or competent; that funders know better and are thus responsible for most philanthropic successes. These broader discussions of grantmaking, in addition to the narrower strategic advice, make this book the best general one on how "to design strategies to bring about results."[7]

The Essence of Strategic Giving: A Practical Guide for Donors and Fundraisers (Chicago: The University of Chicago Press, 2010, 171 pages). Peter Frumkin is professor of public affairs at the Lyndon B. Johnson School of

Public Affairs, and director of the RGK Center for Philanthropy and Community Service at the University of Texas at Austin.

This short book is a reworking of the author's unwieldy 435-page *Strategic Giving: The Art and Science of Philanthropy* (Chicago: The University of Chicago Press, 2006), which missed its mark as a clear roadmap for donors. The longer book discusses too many topics (for instance, an important critique of the professionalization of philanthropy). One of Frumkin's greatest contributions in both books is his emphasis on the "expressive" dimension of giving. The values, diversity, and goals that donors and families bring to philanthropy and civil society have their own legitimacy.

His idea of strategy is straightforward and similar to the other books. Donors are presented with a "universal model" to achieve coherence and alignment in their philanthropy by addressing five challenges: (1) find the public value desired; (2) define a grantmaking methodology; (3) find a giving style; (4) settle on a time frame; and (5) select the right giving vehicle.

The use of various academic models to explain the challenges involved will be mostly a distraction. What value is added by wrapping points in "resource dependency" and the "new institutionalism"? However, many of the author's examples of philanthropic success and failure are convincing, in part because they are often about donors and smaller projects. There is much to learn, for instance, in his discussion of the contrasts between the travails of the Everett Foundation with the New York City Central Park Zoo, and the successes of Aaron and Irene Diamond in seeking a cure for AIDS.

Do More Than Give: The Six Practices of Donors Who Change the World (San Francisco: Jossey-Bass, 2011, 238 pages). Leslie R. Crutchfield, John V. Kania, and Mark R. Kramer work at FSG, a "social impact" consulting firm founded in 1999, at the same time Mark Kramer and Michael Porter started the Center for Effective Philanthropy.

The authors use the "catalytic philanthropy" framework Kramer developed earlier,[8] though they avoid the claim that catalytic philanthropy is a "new" approach. The book is an infectious and informed call for social change. It is imbued with "urgency... to make faster progress."[9]

This book uses the same basic approach that Crutchfield and Heather Grant used when they wrote *Forces for Good* in 2007.[10] They identify six practices for donors interested in impacting social change: (1) advocacy; (2) tapping the power of business; (3) forging nonprofit peer networks; (4) empowering the people; (5) leading adaptively; and (6) building a learning organization through measurement and adjustments.

After a chapter on what it takes to commit to a cause, a chapter is devoted to each of these six practices. The chapters on peer networks and leading adaptively are particularly useful. However, the authors' enthusiasm and sense of urgency for social change can easily lead to precipitous action and donor hubris. That can unintentionally drown out the good sense and relevant cautions in the book. Readers could easily imbibe the bad habits that have always hampered effective philanthropy: thinking that change is simple, that one has *the* answer, and that asserting one's solution is mostly all it takes. Read carefully for the nuances, though, this is a valuable book.

Give Smart: Philanthropy That Gets Results (New York: Public Affairs, 2011, 245 pages). Thomas J. Tierney was CEO of Bain & Co. when he co-founded Bridgespan in 1999, a consulting firm helping nonprofits and philanthropy. Co-author Joel L. Fleishman is the author of *The Foundation*.

The book is well written, and individual parts will be helpful to new donors. It will be most useful for the small number of philanthropists who make the time and have a laser-like focus on an issue. They rightly summarize "philanthropy's terrible truths": that its "natural state is underperformance ... where there are no natural predators, philanthropy is inclined to persist, but not to excel ... and unless you demand outstanding performance from yourself, no one else will demand it of you."[11]

Rather than lay out a "universal model for strategic giving" as Frumkin does, the authors take a gentler approach by asking six key questions: (1) What are my values and beliefs? (2) What is "success" and how can it be achieved? (3) What am I accountable for? (4) What will it take to get the job done? (5) How do I work with grantees? and (6) Am I getting better?

Donors themselves would be well served to answer each of these good questions periodically. And yet several of the questions appear too focused on the donor, to the exclusion of a crucial engagement with grantees. That might easily encourage donor hubris and the grossly subservient relationship between grantor and grantee we all know to be easy and ineffective. Adding two additional questions might help mitigate hubris and focus on the right results — something like "who is achieving results and why?" and "what results can be and are being accomplished by grantees to meet their goals and our goals?"[12]

The authors rightly emphasize philanthropy's underperformance, and they tout many examples of strategic successes. Unfortunately, the examples and the overall discussion of philanthropic underperformance and success are too simplistic. Ultimately, the basic premise of the book, namely that "philanthropists making smarter decisions achieve better results," seems rather tautological.[13]

Strategic Philanthropy as the "Big Idea"

Isaiah Berlin famously and lightheartedly distinguished between the hedgehog and the fox, quoting Archilochus: "The fox knows many things, but the hedgehog knows one big thing."[14] We seem to be in the midst of a philanthropic "hedgehog moment," where strategic philanthropy is *the* big idea revealing the ways to philanthropic success.

On the one hand, the philanthropic "fox" traditionally sees many complex causes of philanthropic success and underperformance. Addressing a myriad of small, marginal improvements may in fact contribute most to success. These might include such things as clarity about the values and goals of giving; sensitivity to cause, effect, and unintended consequences; considering tactics, follow-through, and attending to the day-to-day challenges of administration and implementation; focusing and communicating results; balancing multiple philanthropic interests; muddling through family dynamics; and then honing the soft skills of good manners, judgment, humility and listening. Adam Gopnik's comment about the journalist's task elegantly captures this general advice for philanthropic practice as well: "If there is a fault in reporting, after all, it is not that it is too ephemeral but that it is not ephemeral *enough*, too quickly concerned with what seems big at the time to see what is small and more likely to linger."[15] Maybe these are the things that make for philanthropic success?

On the other hand, the current philanthropic "hedgehog" sees in strategic philanthropy *the* way to engage in successful, impactful philanthropy. This trend was sparked in 1999 when Michael Porter and Mark Kramer reframed the challenge of improving the quality of giving as one that "requires a real strategy." They go on to regret that "the word 'strategy' has been so overused in the foundation world that it has become almost meaningless. 'Strategic giving' now refers to almost any grant made with some purpose in mind."[16] Alas, more than simply strategic grantmaking or narrow strategic planning, they had something much grander in mind, a "strategic philanthropy" coming to embrace the whole organization and everything it does, focused on "creating value" and achieving impact.

All the books under review build on this broader idea. They have largely overlapping views of what it takes to be strategic. Basically, once a goal and values are chosen (the "expressive" element that Peter Frumkin emphasizes and that several of the books also mention, but all too briefly), strategic philanthropy develops as a flexible plan of action toward a goal with clear ways to assess whether the means are reaching that end. Make no doubt about it, thinking strategically in this way is something donors and family philanthropies *should* do, and have often done so without the use of the secret phrase. Simply wanting to "do good" and feel good about it is all too common, and that isn't good enough. If there is coherence and alignment of all the elements of one's goals and strategy, then the chances for impact do increase.

A problem is that strategic philanthropy — or "catalytic philanthropy," to use the term in Leslie Crutchfield's book — has gone from being a useful organizing principle to taking on a life of its own. It can mean everything and nothing: the terrible fate of jargon. The terminology, exuberance, and urgency in these books are trying to market something new and improved by emphasizing the dichotomy between traditional philanthropy and the new strategic philanthropy. Crutchfield, for instance, describes the "traditional mindset" as, "I pick grantees, they solve the problem, and at the end of the year they send me a final report and I feel good."[17] Well, that is just bad philanthropy; it is not traditional philanthropy.

Nor is strategic philanthropy new. The worry about ineffective philanthropy has always been with us. Keppel's concern and hope in 1930 shadows us still: "Sometimes I find it hard to justify many of the grants made by the foundation for which I am in part responsible or any of the others." And yet, "I am very hopeful that our activities are measurably moving toward a more logical basis."[18] Playing the "old versus new" card is a false dichotomy that tends to lend an unjustified Teflon veneer to strategic philanthropy as the new, obvious and assumed high-impact solution.

Thus, the buyer should beware. The humorous and barbed warning of Tony Proscio captures the problem well, that strategy has been taken up in philanthropy "with a giddiness of a soldier on leave.... [I]t has developed an aura of indispensability and universal relevance that grows wearisome even when it is not really out-of-place.... [T]he use of 'strategy' needs to be treated with the greatest distrust." [19]

The five books reviewed here (several of them supported — directly or indirectly — by foundations) provide a window into the current state of strategic philanthropy as the answer for improving philanthropy. They also cast a shadow of hubris over philanthropic practice. Donors and family foundations will learn a lot from these books. Being strategic *is* crucial for good grantmaking. At the same time, there are several common themes that suggest suspicion and caution about strategic philanthropy as "the big idea" that can resolve the problem of philanthropic underperformance. I look at four such themes briefly below.

Does Strategy Drive Success?

Tierney and the other authors are right that there is a perennial state of philanthropic underperformance. This should deeply worry donors and family foundations: that their hard-earned dollars can so easily be wasted. It should deeply worry foundations boards and practitioners, too. We know that so much giving is ineffective or venial. It is maddening, for instance, that even when DARE has been shown to be ineffective, it brought in over $6.5 million in revenue in 2009, which has jumped to $8.5 million in 2016.[20] But knowing what is effective and isn't effective is difficult and contestable.

Fleishman mentions Living Cities as a multi-foundation initiative that has been "unsuccessful on its own terms."[21] And yet *The Casebook to The Foundation* presents it as a success, as did a former staffer in a recent conversation.[22] The Annenberg Education Challenge is widely viewed as "one of the major failures in foundation history."[23] But *Give Smart* concludes that "it is hard to label the Annenberg Challenge a failure."[24] If it were not a failure, how can anything be described as a success or a failure?

In fact, it should not be lost on us that most cases of program failure (whether on the part of a donor or foundation) did have a strategy in place. As Fleishman's book and *The Casebook* make clear, a large share of foundation funding comes from the largest foundations whose focus is almost always on promoting large-scale, lasting social change. It is precisely those foundations that have the staff to presumably "do it right." Many — perhaps most — examples of wasteful and underperforming philanthropy were originally proclaimed as strategic initiatives by their donors and foundations. Strategic philanthropy appears to be no vaccine against failures.

Something is wrong, then, that isn't being addressed in these books. Recently, Paul Connolly wrote an article calling for more "humanism" and breadth in approaching effective philanthropy. This is the philanthropic fox. He noted several cases of large philanthropies that clearly thought they were pursuing their goals through strategic philanthropy, but without much success: for instance, the philanthropic arm of Google, the Northwest Area Foundation, and the California Wellness Foundation.[25] A new strategy in these and other cases is called for and rightly so. But these books usually don't help us see what makes some strategies good and others not so much.

These books mostly assume strategy does drive success. They also tend to be overly generous in their claims of philanthropic success (except Frumkin). It is largely unclear the extent to which success can be attributed to strategic philanthropy or to many other factors. This tendency for overblown attributions of success compromises the claims for strategic philanthropy and for philanthropy generally. We need to "get real" and be suspicious of such claims. From these books and the ancillary writing on strategic philanthropy, we simply don't know whether or how strategic philanthropy drives philanthropic success and impact.

As an aside, not enough is being done to identify and understand success and failure; nor are the lessons being generalized. Perhaps one of the most important services a new donor could provide for the field would be to start a foundation solely focused on publishing independent, broad-based evaluation research on philanthropic and nonprofit initiatives. There needs to be much more candid, third-party discourse on what has impact, what doesn't, and why.

Some commentators question the success of strategic philanthropy in a different way. They have decried the invasion of strategy into philanthropy as snatching the soul and heart of philanthropy. Bruce Sievers is among the most articulate.[26] He finds the intrusion of a business model under guise of strategic philanthropy as invasive and unjustified. Not only is it contrary to the goals, values, and sustenance of civil society, but it encourages hyper-rationalism and linear thinking, overly directive actions, and reliance on short-term solutions and measures. This is part of the broader concern Paul Connolly has expressed, too. Donors should worry about this; it certainly does happen. But this concern is misplaced.

Having a strategy is a necessary but not sufficient way to think about one's philanthropic values and goals, and about how to achieve objectives and results. This is crucial for philanthropy to be effective. All of the authors under review would agree that the expressive element of philanthropy is first, *and* that it can't be reached without a compelling and coherent overall strategy.

Frumkin is quite thoughtful about this need for greater breadth in thinking about philanthropic success. He is another philanthropic fox. Just before *The Essence of Strategic Giving* was published, he worried that the case for the rationalistic and technocratic nature of strategic giving (including his own case) does not actually explain much about philanthropic impact and effectiveness.[27] That has certainly been my experience over thirty-five years in philanthropy as both a philanthropoid and as a small donor. Strategy is but one element of success. Readers, then, should appreciate how a perspective on strategic philanthropy can help donors and philanthropists devise a roadmap to stay on track. They should also be skeptical, however, of the big a claims for the success of strategic philanthropy. Donors and philanthropists are best advised to approach philanthropy as foxes: humbly seeking to learn the many things that contribute to philanthropic success.

Unintended Consequences

Readers, thus, should be wary about how they read these books. Simply put: too quick a read might unduly encourage the scourge of philanthropic hubris and thus reinforce bad philanthropy. What a shame if these books introduced that to a new generation of donors and philanthropists eager to make a difference quickly.

One of the most pernicious and prevalent characteristics of modern philanthropy is hubris. *Money Well Spent* and *Give Smart* are explicitly clear about this. All the books are full of warnings and caveats about strategic philanthropy. They generally acknowledge that they are writing for a small segment of donors and philanthropists and that doing strategic philanthropy well takes a remarkable amount of time, focus, care, and commitment. But their general enthusiasm for marketing strategic philanthropy as the next big idea may be a toxic combination for readers looking for easy takeaways. Indeed, foundation trustees, executive directors, and program officers are looking for the same thing. Many readers will likely come away figuring the many caveats don't apply to their situation.

Consider the use of adaptive leadership as a key concept in *Do More Than Give*. The phrase tries to capture the idea that problems are complex and difficult to address. We rarely have full knowledge of the problem, causes, etc. Solutions must be discovered by engaging stakeholders. Thus, leadership requires being assertive but not directive. This is right, important, and difficult. Nonetheless, many careless readers will likely see in this discussion a shortcut to effectiveness.

For instance, *Do More Than Give* makes much of a distinction between "technical" and "adaptive" problems. In fact, the technical problems listed (such as funding scholarships) are not problems at all but projects or means to address a more complex problem. But, the authors claim, "technical problems are well defined. Their solutions are known and people or groups with adequate expertise and organizational capacity can solve them." Thus, "simple technical problems tend to resolve themselves quickly with the application of money and expertise."[28] New donors and established program officers may easily interpret their particular pet projects and solutions as simple-to-solve technical problems.

Several of the books also leave the impression that foundation and donor initiatives are to be preferred over close work with nonprofits. For instance, the claim that "most nonprofit organizations today aren't equipped to provide the kind of solutions this complex world requires" is often true.[29] Never mind that foundation and donor hubris and deafness are often big contributing factors. But the point could lead donors and foundations to believe that *they* have all the necessary skills and can ignore what are presumed to be ineffective nonprofit organizations and their expertise. I suspect that strong and successful entrepreneurs and newly wealthy donors could be particularly susceptible to this this unintentional encouragement that they know what is best.

My experience is that foundations are usually even less likely to be so "equipped" for success but more likely to believe they do have the answer. The call for donors "to orchestrate — subtly but persistently — the activities of key players to advance their causes" can further stoke the hubris that many philanthropists and donors may already have about whatever pet projects they like.[30] In early 2000, I asked a new nonprofit executive director what he thought was the biggest challenge to the sector. He had formerly been at the Ford Foundation and knew foundation ways well. Without hesitation, he said the biggest problem was that foundations thought they knew all the answers and rarely listened to the views and challenges facing nonprofits. In 2010, a former Gates Foundation executive tried to start a charter school network in NYC. He failed miserably and ruefully commented that he didn't know how difficult it would be: "I have a lot more sympathy for nonprofits now that I'm on their side of the table." This from someone who had helped spend nearly a billion dollars on educational reform programs for Gates![31] One educator commented that "He's flying 30,000 feet in the air but can't do it on the ground." A damning commentary on philanthropic hubris indeed.

The authors of these books don't generally intend to encourage such hubris. But the attitude of superiority of strategic philanthropy seeps through. There is a sense of certainty over questioning that comes through. All this can catch a read unawares and encourage precisely this kind of hubris. Readers should read the books with care and remember that humility is the first line of defense against ineffective and wasteful philanthropy; listen carefully and "first do no harm."

Implementation Really Matters

My experience, and that of many philanthropists, is that careful implementation may be as important as having a strategy. In so many ways it is more difficult. As the former CEO of the Robert Wood Johnson Foundation succinctly put it, "execution trumps strategy ... a preoccupation with strategy all too often causes us to gloss over the equally important decisions about the way that a goal — or an individual program — will be implemented."[32] The inclination to see a strategy through to its full implementation is difficult. It takes time and patience. One must suffer through many kinds of staff changes. It requires a variety of skills (hard and soft) that are not common. Strategic philanthropy is ideally broader and more encompassing that mere "strategy," as Porter and Kramer pointed out in 1999. But there is a natural and easy tendency for the rationalists among donors and philanthropists who are so wonderfully driven by a cause to stay in the heady stratosphere and avoid getting their hands dirty in the messiness of implementing, measuring, and reporting results. One can't successfully have one without the other.

Usable Knowledge: What Donors and Families Need

Donors, family foundations, and philanthropic practitioners need "usable" knowledge.[33] These books have this — and advocate it — if read with care. But it is also important to seek knowledge much more broadly: to be foxes.

Some donors and family philanthropies will practice their philanthropy as the big idea these books discuss, *and* with the great care needed. That will add to the effectiveness and variety of philanthropy. If these books are read with careful attention to the limitations of strategic philanthropy, any donor and all family foundations will learn more about the promises and pitfalls of philanthropy.

However, other readers will be seeking easy answers, and they will wrongly latch onto simple pointers mentioned in these books. After all, most donors and philanthropists are engaged with several causes and they have limited time to spend on philanthropy. They can easily embark upon action and initiatives thinking that simply stating a strategy or logic model is enough. They will take that lesson, untethered to very important cautions and nuances. This is not what any of the authors intend. But I have seen such limited takeaways drive philanthropic values into ineffectiveness.

Too many donors and family philanthropies, however, won't do the small things necessary for truly effective strategic philanthropy. Philanthropy is a discovery process in a world of uncertainty. Most of the authors acknowledge this. Remember that practical experience, local knowledge, and small step-wise changes are necessary for strategy to be implemented. Ignoring usable, local knowledge helps build the kind of insolated hubris that stultifies philanthropy and give it the bad name it often deserves.

This is where grantees are so important. They usually know what is going on and understand the difficulties in bringing a strategy to successful implementation. Most donors and foundations rely on grantees. They give money and work through nonprofits. It may be that doing "humble philanthropy" well, as William Schambra calls it, is especially crucial now:

> What foundations do best and most reliably is simply to make grants to worthwhile nonprofit organizations. This may not be as glitzy and sophisticated as attempting to harness and ride whirlwind social forces like masters of the universe.[34]

One of the keys to philanthropic effectiveness and the health of our civil society, then, is to learn from and work with nonprofits. That means to learn the skills associated with the difficult art of assessing potential grantees; make general operating support grants; grant multi-year support; help nonprofits and staff become better at what they do; hold them accountable; and constantly ask questions and listen carefully. This also requires not getting in their way: an affliction of many donors and foundations. We need to be clear about measures for success, assess interim benchmarks, and be flexible enough to change if the grand strategy isn't working.

Thus, the philanthropic fox will attend to strategy, in the context of a much broader perspective. Successful, impactful philanthropy is a job for foxes that are committed to knowing many things, including strategy. Of particular importance here are the difficult-to-learn "soft skills" of philanthropy. They may provide better philanthropic dividends over time than placing too much reliance on strategic philanthropy, and being seduced by some of the unintended consequences that go with betting on the "one big thing" of strategic philanthropy. They are the skills of

> judging the capacity, character, resilience, intelligence, and resourcefulness of the people who seek philanthropic funds. This is the kind of ill-defined and untheorized work that comes down to judgment and gut assessment ... and explains a lot more of the achieved social impact than anyone wants to admit.[35]

Seeing success as possible through "one big thing," though, encourages hubris and does a disservice to the complexity of philanthropy. The real solutions to philanthropic underperformance are myriad. Perhaps the most useful advice for donors, families, as well as experienced philanthropists is to include careful strategic considerations in your philanthropy *and* to attend to the many "small," incremental, and productive ways to increase performance and effectiveness that probably drives success most. Our failure is too often to focus on the big things and forget "to see what is small and more likely to linger."

Coda

The idea of strategic philanthropy did not originate with the books I reviewed in 2011. But it didreach a certain crescendo of marketing buzz. The phrase took on a life of its own, too. In 2014, authors John Nania, Mark Kramer, and Patty Russell partially recanted, acknowledging:

> Albert Einstein once said, 'Everything should be made as simple as possible, but not simpler.' In strategic philanthropy's earnest desire to become more disciplined and rigorous, there has been a tendency to demand and impose simple solutions to complex problems.... The more foundations embrace strategic philanthropy, the clearer its limitations become.[36]

The solution, however, is not to rejigger the meaning a bit and just call it emergent strategy. In fact, it brings to mind a variant of the old saw: "What is original about strategic philanthropy is not true, and what is true is not original."

There is much of value in the books reviewed above, but so much of that value is just about good grantmaking. Other things may be at play around this whole idea of strategic philanthropy that I can only hint at here.

One of my tentative hypotheses is that strategic philanthropy and the discussions about it are partly an identity crisis on the foundation/donor side of philanthropy. Several of these books and authors received support of various kinds from a number of foundations. There is a strong, hidden element of "foundations versus nonprofits" that seeps from these books. I had often thought program officers, executive directors, and foundation boards may feel that simply grantmaking is beneath them and their superior intelligence. These books unfortunately feed into the need for self-importance and justification. They may also help deflect attention from the fact that doing philanthropy well is hard work, and that the problems it can address are very complex and intractable.

There is a sense in which an implicit message of strategic philanthropy — intentionally and not — disses the world of nonprofits: their usable knowledge and on-the-ground expertise, their challenges. Maybe some of the "unintended consequences" mentioned in the section above were the struggles of foundations to enhance their own role and standing. As William Schambra has noted, strategic philanthropy "reflects and reinforces that impulse for control."[37] Darren Walker's response to the Kania article is particularly good:

> My perspective is informed by my experience ... as a grantee at Harlem's Abyssinian Development Corporation. During those days, I — and many of my colleagues — sometimes felt imprisoned by logic frameworks, theories of change, and elegant PowerPoint decks that sought to oversimplify how our neighborhood revitalization programs would affect our community. To us, social change could not be diagrammed with boxes and arrows, even though the foundation initiatives that funded our work demanded we explain it within a neatly organized "strategic framework.[38]

Hal Harvey (one of the co-authors of *Money Well Spent*, above) also wrote a particularly damming critique of two elements of "the presumption of strategy." I saw the same omniscience and suffocating process innumerable times ... and worse ones:

> [first] ... a major challenge for strategic philanthropy is that it can create delusions of omniscience in many program officers. Instead of reviewing grant proposals, querying experts, synthesizing ideas, and respecting those with years in the field, many program directors and officers become auteurs: They begin to see themselves as the origin of intelligence as well as the arbiters of money.

[second] The foundation made a big grant but also created 59 milestones for the first nine months of the grant and demanded weekly reporting on progress. As humor columnist Dave Barry says, "I am not making this up." The grantee was forced to refocus — away from his work and toward reporting, even going so far as to hire a full-time associate just to track and report when the milestones were reached. He was neutered by this sort of "strategic philanthropy."[39]

Ruth McCambridge of *The Nonprofit Quarterly* was neither surprised nor forgiving two days after Harvey's opinion piece walking back — a bit — from strategic philanthropy, "the nakedness of this autocratic and insistent emperor."[40] We are, alas, not as smart as we think; this is the perennial scourge of philanthropic hubris, whatever the chosen phrase of the moment. Could it be, after all, that the "old" view that promoted "charity" and working with nonprofits captures the best of philanthropy? So, let us move past strategic philanthropy and avoid it. I like the term coined by Margaret Rossiter in her fine book on *Women Scientists in America*: "coercive (or creative) philanthropy."[41] That is *the* tension along the range of philanthropy's soul. Going forward, ask ourselves — and especially listen to the opinions of others — about where on that line our philanthropic goals, strategies, actions, and results are is the most strategic thing we can do.

Originally published as a review of five books on strategic philanthropy, in The Foundation Review, *V. 3, No. 4, 2011. Reprinted with the permission of the Johnson Center for Philanthropy at Grand Valley State University. For this volume, I have made some revisions and added a short coda.*

---

[1] Frederick P. Keppel, *The Foundation* (New York: Macmillan Co, 1930), pgs. 17 and vi.

[2] Foundation Center, *"Foundation Stats."* Most recent estimates accessed July 23, 2018 were for 2014. Cf. data.foundationcenter.org.

[3] Keppel, *op. cit.*, p. 34.

[4] Lucy Bernholz, *Philanthropy.blogpost.com*, October 1, 2008. This was a review of *Money Well Spent*.

[5] Joel L. Fleishman, *The Foundation: A Great American Secret* (New York: Public Affairs, 2007), p. 191.

[6] One of the greatest obstacles to good philanthropy is that so few philanthropoids (a term originally used by Keppel in his 1930 book) know the history of

philanthropy and foundations. That ignorance leads us to repeat mistakes, wasting time re-discovering valuable lessons, and philistinism. There is no good, single-volume history of philanthropy and foundations to recommend, however. A good start would include Waldemar A. Nielsen's iconoclastic books: *The Big Foundations* (New York: Columbia University Press, 1972), *The Golden Donors: A New Anatomy of the Great Foundations* (New York: E. P. Dutton, 1985), and *Inside American Philanthropy* (Norman: University of Oklahoma Press, 1996). Two good edited volumes are *Philanthropic Foundations: New Scholarship, New Possibilities*, edited by Ellen Condliffe Lagemann (Bloomington: Indiana University Press, 1999), and *American Foundations: Roles and Contributions*, Edited by Helmut K. Anheier and David C. Hammack (Washington DC: Brookings Institution Press, 2010). Two recent, useful — and slanted — volumes would be: Olivier Zunz, *Philanthropy in America* (Princeton: Princeton University Press, 2012; and Karl Zinsmeister, *The Almanac of American Philanthropy* (Washington DC: The Philanthropy Roundtable, 2016). Zinsmeister's book has a good 73-page chapter on "Essential Books and Articles on Philanthropy."

[7] Paul Brest and Hal Harvey *Money Well Spent: A Strategic Plan for Smart Philanthropy* (New York: Bloomberg Press, 2008), pgs. xiv, 2, and x.

[8] Mark Kramer, "Catalytic Philanthropy," *Stanford Social Innovation Review*, Fall, 2009.

[9] Leslie R. Crutchfield, John V. Kania, and Mark R. Kramer, *Do More Than Give: The Six Practices of Donors Who Change the World* (San Francisco: Jossey-Bass, 2011), p. vii.

[10] Leslie R. Crutchfield and Heather Grant, *Forces for Good: The Six Practices of High-Impact Nonprofits* (San Francisco: Jossey-Bass, 2000).

[11] Thomas J. Tierney and Joel L. Fleishman, *Give Smart: Philanthropy That Gets Results* (New York: Public Affairs, 2011), pgs. 2, 5, and 82.

[12] Mario Morino's *Leap of Reason: Managing to Outcomes in an Era of Scarcity* (Washington DC: Venture Philanthropy Partners, 2011) is helpful in thinking about this.

[13] Thomas J. Tierney and Joel L. Fleishman, *op. cit.*, p. 200.

[14] Isaiah Berlin, *Isaiah Berlin: The Proper Study of Mankind*, Edited by Henry Hardy and Roger Hausheer (London: Chatto & Windus, 1997), p. 436.

[15] Adam Gopnik, *Paris to the Moon* (New York: Random House, 2001), p. 15.

[16] Michael E. Porter and Mark R. Kramer, "Philanthropy's New Agenda: Creating Value,", *Harvard Business Review*, November-December 1999, p. 125.

[17] Leslie R. Crutchfield, John V. Kania, and Mark R. Kramer, op. cit., p. 115.

[18] Keppel, *op. cit.*, p. 34.

[19] Tony Proscio, *In Other Words: A Plea for Plain Speaking in Foundations* (New York: The Edna McConnell Clark Foundation, 2000). pgs. 20-21. This is one of three short, humorous and painfully pertinent books published by The Edna McConnell Clark Foundation. The others are *Bad Words for Good* (2001), and *When Words Fail* (2005).

[20] The website alcoholproblemsandsolutions.org cites numerous studies that have consistently shown that DARE is ineffective, or even counterproductive in reducing the use of alcohol and drugs: including the U.S. General Accounting

Office, U.S. Surgeon General, National Academy of Sciences, and a study by the National Institutes of Health.

[21] Fleishman, *op. cit.*, p. 210.

[22] *The Casebook for* The Foundation, *op. cit.*, pgs. 217-219.

[23] Fleishman, *op. cit.*, p. 196.

[24] Tierney, *op. cit.*, p. 78.

[25] Paul Connolly, "The Best of the Humanistic and Technocratic: Why the Most Effective Work in Philanthropy Requires a Balance", *The Foundation Review*, Vol. 3, Nos. 1and 2, 2011.

[26] Bruce Sievers, "If Pigs Had Wings: The Appeals and Limits of Venture Philanthropy," Waldemar A. Nielsen Issues in Philanthropy Seminar Series, Georgetown University, November 16, 2001; and "Philanthropy's Blindspots" in *Just Money*, edited by Peter Karoff, (Boston: The Philanthropic Initiative, 2004), pgs. 129-149.

[27] Peter Frumkin, "What Drives Philanthropic Success?" Web blog post on Philanthropy Central (cspcs.sanford.duke.edu), March 9, 2010.

[28] Crutchield, *op. cit.*, pgs. 150 and 156.

[29] Ibid., p. 7.

[30] Ibid., p. 14.

[31] Anna Phillips, "Tom Vander Ark's New York-Area Charter Schools Falter," *The New York Times*, July, 14, 2011.

[32] Peter Karoff, *op. cit.*, "When Execution Trumps Strategy", by Steven A. Schroeder, p. 184.

[33] See Charles E. Lindblom and David K. Cohen, *Usable knowledge: Social Science and Social Problem Solving* (New Haven: Yale University Press, 1979.

[34] William Schambra, "It's Time for Humble Philanthropy", *The Chronicle of Philanthropy* April 2009, p. 40.

[35] Peter Frumkin, "What Drives Philanthropic Success?", *op. cit.*

[36] John Kania, Mark Kramer, and Patty Russell, "Strategic Philanthropy for a Complex World" *Stamford Social Innovation Review*, Summer 2014.

[37] William Schambra, "Is Strategic Philanthropy Yesterday's News?, *The Nonprofit Quarterly*, June, 10, 2014. Also see; and Thomas Scanlon, "Notes on the Limitations of Strategic Philanthropy", *The Nonprofit Quarterly*, Summer 2013.

[38] Darren Walker, "Response to 'Strategic Philanthropy for a Complex World' *Stamford Social Innovation Review*, Summer 2014.

[39] Hal Harvey, "Why I Regret Pushing Strategic Philanthropy," *The Chronicle of Philanthropy*, April 4, 2016.

[40] Ruth McCambridge, "The Strategic Philanthropy Crowd: Qualified Apologies-R-Us," *The Nonprofit Quarterly*, April 6, 2016.

[41] Margaret W. Rossiter, *Women Scientists in America, Volume 1: Struggles and Strategies to 1940* (Baltimore: The Johns Hopkins University Press, 1982).

CHAPTER 4

NOTES ON PHILANTHROPIC PRACTICE

But I am also frank to say I do not think the potential of philanthropy in contributing to the solution of community problems — especially urban community problems — has been more than barely realized. — Paul Ylvisaker

Nonprofit leaders believe most of their foundation funders lack a deep understanding of their intended beneficiaries' needs — and they believe this lack of understanding is reflected in foundations' funding priorities and programmatic strategies. Nonprofit leaders say the foundations that best understand their organizations' intended beneficiaries' needs actively engage with their organizations and their work; are humble, open, and collaborative in their approach; or are deeply connected to the issues or communities. — Hearing from Those We Seek to Help, Center for Effective Philanthropy

Many pitfalls and obstacles stem directly from the nature of the pursuit of good work in philanthropy. The altruism at the center of the philanthropic mission is so praiseworthy in itself that it can lead to complacency in how the gift-giving mission is pursued. Compounding this complacency, control of significant financial resources always implies a certain power that can breed arrogance and hubris. Complacency, arrogance, and hubris do not constitute a good mindset for learning: they are more likely to foster the kind of "know-nothing" stance that can lead to unexamined failure.... The field as a whole has yet to establish shared strategies — the knowledge, standards, and practices of a definitive domain — for avoiding them. — William Damon

M ost of the short pieces in this chapter were written while I was a Senior Fellow at Philanthropy New York in 2009 and 2010. I had recently resigned from The Clark Foundation, and this opportunity let me stay engaged and have some time to reflect. I can't thank President Ronna Brown enough for the opportunity.

As is obvious, this was during the Great Recession. Each of the first four pieces took up a topic relevant to the New York philanthropy community at that time. I tried to initiate conversations on topics from a broader, even historical context, urging foundation staff to be more critical about foundation practice, a major theme that appears in most of the articles in this book.

Looking back, each issue remains very relevant. I was particularly struck that the first article, "Some Measure of Leadership?" would lend itself to a look back on that theme from 2019. Having left New York City in 2014, I relied in part upon numerous long conversations with anonymous nonprofit executive and foundation program officers. Their illuminating and bracing insights helped me form my own distant observations and conclusions from today's vantage point.

I remain grateful for those in the field who did and do provide leadership. I do wish I had done more, and do appreciate how difficult it can be. However, it is sad that leadership within the overall philanthropic and nonprofit sectors remains weak. Worse, it is a very sad commentary that what leadership there is can be rather cavalierly ignored by the city administration.

The last, longer piece was published in 2016 and looked inside foundation practice. I discuss how important it is for foundations to align mission, lifespan, strategy, payout, and investment strategy. My experience had been that each issue is usually viewed as independent and siloed away from the others. This may be a natural result of how we focus on issues. It is part of the division of labor in organizations. And as I point out, it is often a result of self-interested or power-related motives.

Each article, then, tries to reflect on aspects of foundation practice. They underscore the many complex issues involved *and* urge us all to be more thoughtful about what will improve our practice and results.

1. Some Measure of Leadership?

Whose Leadership in 2009?

On April 6, 2009, Mayor Michael Bloomberg and his administration gave voice to some real leadership for the nonprofit and philanthropic sector, just as they did in 2006, when they established the Center for Economic Opportunity. The mayor made a speech at New York University, in which he announced three initiatives to help nonprofits:

1. Reduce fixed costs: through bulk purchasing, reduced energy costs, etc.
2. Improve city contracting procedures: through access to city information, reduced compliance review times, and increased bridge loan availability.
3. Strengthen nonprofit management: through technical assistance, referral with business leader partnerships and board recruitment.

The mayor said many of the right things, which in itself is rare in politics. What are we to make of all of this though? Talk is cheap. The mayor's announcement gives us an opportunity to start a candid conversation about what kind of joint leadership foundations, nonprofits, and the city (and business, too) are providing during this recession and more generally. And about what they are *not* doing. A sense of history gives one a queasy feeling, though. Things have been and are rather bad around the city's relationships to the human services sector. Brian Saber, former executive director of Hudson Guild, gave a colorful and accurate perspective in his long comment on the original blog:

> The measures being proposed, while undeniably positive, do not begin to get at the crux of the issue, which is that the government, supposedly serving as a voice for the people, has broken its contract.
>
> When the government developed many of its large social service programs, such as day care, it looked around and realized that it didn't have to recreate the wheel by building its own day care centers. In many instances organizations already existed that were providing similar programming or had staff and infrastructure in place to do so. The government believed that these agencies had value and that they could provide these services efficiently with proper funding.

But what has happened over the decades is a sea change in that relationship so that the direct service providers are no longer partners, or even conduits, but pawns. The game now is to see how often the government can cut funding and at the same time increase standards, expectations and reporting, before the providers yell "uncle." A famous Monty Python skit comes to mind.

And while the government continues to make its contracts more arduous and costlier, it continues to add layers and layers to its own bureaucracy. Perhaps this keeps the lawyers away, but it assures that virtually no service is provided efficiently any longer and that scores of government bureaucrats have repetitive, vestigial positions.

Also, at the same time, the direct service providers — the ones with the vision, passion and dedication to their communities or constituents — now spend an incredible amount of time and money trying to raise private funds to keep these same services going. And of course, this is also time not spent providing service or developing new programs and means of efficiency.

A favorite trick of government agencies is to reduce the amount of a funded contract and at the same time force the provider to maintain (or increase) its contracted units. They figure that if they can cut off both legs and both arms and the providers will still participate in the dance, then there must be other body parts still to be removed.

What Is Wrong?

Neither city administration nor most foundations seem to have a good sense of what nonprofits face and have faced for a very long time: the unnecessary time and effort spent applying for funds; the remarkably long delays between starting a city contract and getting paid; the tragic disparity between the actual costs for services rendered and funding provided; and reporting requirements that, among other things, used to require nonprofits to have different computers for reporting on different city contracts!

The city's own inefficiencies are well-known and not particular to any administration. A *Nonprofit Executive Outlook Survey* from Baruch College before these initiatives were announced showed a significant, recent uptick in disapproval of current administration policies and programs. The plans to reform city contracting procedures could make a significant difference and are welcome news. There is a promise that the Returnable Grant Fund administered by The Fund for the City of New York will increase from $8 million to $20 million over two years. There are also promises of further help through other lenders. But this admirable step is small compared to the size of the problem. They don't change the endemic problems: huge delays in public contract payments that have been a sad fixture for so many years.

Plans to expedite compliance review, standardize human services contracts, and increase openness for city contract information get closer to the nub of the issue (*n.b.*, still true in 2019). We have heard all of this before, of course. This time, in 2009, there seemed to be less politics and more of a drive for bureaucratic efficiency. Little did I think I would ever write that as a good thing, but I do think Bloomberg and many of his senior staff deserve significant credit. They may not have understood the problems. But my sense was they often wanted to find a solution, even as it eluded them. So, there was some hope that this administration would make it different this time.

The mere fact that the mayor and his staff thought to raise these issues, however, also shines a harsh light on the lack of current leadership among the philanthropic community. In some ways this is my most distressing takeaway from hearing the mayor's presentation. To be sure there were some foundation leaders who have had the ear of the city. (I would personally single out the sensitive and clear-eyed passion and intelligence the late Janice Nitolli brought to her several years "on loan" to the city from the Annie B. Casey Foundation.) But it was all behind the scenes. There was simply no urgency in the philanthropic community to speak in one voice, or, much less, to act. I don't think the city saw any need for it. The April 6 event was not a joint announcement of the city government and philanthropic institutions and nonprofits making a *coordinated* commitment. As cynical as we might be at such a media event, it could have become very meaningful. This should not have been left to the mayor alone.

Many foundations responded well financially to the challenges of this recession. The checks are bigger, but the strings remain. Nonprofits do indeed need to be more accountable, but foundations often throw unnecessary obstacles at them. For instance, the suspicion that those detailed reporting requirements favored by foundations are not read is all too often true. The endless foundation meetings called to "act in a more concerted way" or "improve your capacity" can be mind-numbing. They have produced, well, not much. Yet everyone still feels the need to show up for the next meeting tomorrow.

Nonprofits are also their own worst enemy while in the unenviable position of underappreciated supplicants who actually have a job to do serving the needy. Things like understanding of the real costs of programs and services are often rudimentary at best. I remember the surprise and horror that several nonprofit executive directors experienced when it was pointed out that taking on a program that was only partially funded actually saddled the nonprofit with a significant liability. When the executive director of United Neighborhood Houses convened a group of eight human services agency IT directors to discuss service integration, none of these directors had met before. Overall, inefficiencies and the clash of vested interests and turf constantly get in the way of nonprofit leadership blooming.

We need to do business in new, coordinated ways if the entire sector (philanthropy and nonprofits) and the city are to be strengthened and our work improved. That requires leadership of all levels: listening, conversation, real cooperation leading to concrete actions, and reportable results.

A Leadership and Coordination Black Hole?

While the mayor's proposals suggest progress is possible, they struck me and others as no more than first steps, given the importance of the sector. (In his speech, the mayor noted nonprofits make up 15 percent of the city's non-government workforce.)

In fact, it simply isn't clear how much cooperation with nonprofits and foundations is desired by city commissioners. My experience was very little and on their terms. The proposals, and the semi-secret process leading up to them, do not bode well. The administration did not consult with nonprofits or foundations. To be fair, it might have been easy for them to do a scan and conclude that few were worth consulting. That is probably unfair, but it is suggestive of the depth of the leadership problem within the sector. For example, to what extent were the initiatives for reducing costs and strengthening nonprofit management really informed by, and coordinated with, what currently exists? And how will they be implemented going forward? What about the extant nonprofits already doing good board recruitment and governance work, like the Volunteer Consulting Group? Group purchasing efforts have been tried and often proven to be inefficient; were those experiences considered? Finally, management assistance is indeed very important, but what is the added value being proposed here. How will we know if it is successful? Nonprofit executives report with anguish a surfeit of offerings — often of questionable quality or relevance to on-the-ground organizations — which are often "forced" upon them by foundations or city agencies. Perhaps we need less "more of it" and more focus on coordinated, relevant, deeper, and better technical assistance. How will that get done?

Serious questions remain, then, about how well city commissioners can play with others, and how well they actually understand — and engage with — the nonprofits and foundations of the sector. Are nonprofits merely instrumental vendors and foundations simply occasional outside funding sources?

What's Next in 2009?

These worries aside, the mayor's comments suggest that there is a commitment to strengthening the infrastructure, efficiency, and effectiveness of New York City's nonprofits, including the important web of community-based organizations. New York City's troubles and the challenges facing the poor and disadvantaged can be solved only with genuine leadership at all levels. Government really isn't very good at that. We should all run screaming from the idea of yet another photo op or group meeting untethered from real results. How, then, can we, as the philanthropic/nonprofit sector, intercede and develop broader leadership that produces real concerted action? Saying "just do it" is tempting, but I know better than that. It will require risk-taking, coordinated leadership, careful analysis, pinpoint pressure to get things done, and laser-like attention to benchmarks and impact. And leave egos at the door, thank you very much.

Reforms rarely live up to the fanfare with which they are announced; the Bloomberg administration has so far been better than most in this regard (witness school reform, out-of-school-time efforts, and a huge technology overhaul). The administration should commit to a regular "report card" to the public with specific benchmarks and a clear timeline for achieving these reforms. The real test of the mayor's initiatives will be how well the administration carries through, puts its own house in order, measures it, and reports its outcomes.

Philanthropy should also put its house in order and ask how we are helping as a field. We all have our individual lists of what that might entail. My list includes more general operating support; multi-year funding; building organizational and sector infrastructure; professional development and board capacity; improving capitalization and cash flow; and well-defined results. In addition, foundations need to listen to grantees and simplify what they do for — and to — them. Their job is not to pontificate and make work. But the key to leadership is coordinated action; that is difficult *and* necessary. Where is that?

Finally, we must put these city initiatives and what is to come in proper perspective. Action now is important (albeit slow and probably only modestly effective). But these prospective actions are sometimes presented as if they are newly discovered and important now only because of the recession. When we look at leadership from a longer-term perspective, however, what is important now is what has always been important. Most of the solutions are obvious, albeit not easy to implement. Do the actions proffered now only prove a failure of long-term leadership and results over the last five, ten, fifteen years? No doubt. Going forward, then, let us concentrate not just on the immediate and easy, but always on what makes for good grantmaking, good government, and good nonprofit management.

What do you think and why? How would you take the current measure of leadership for foundations, or nonprofits, or the city? What real partnering with real actions would strengthen the effectiveness of this funny three-legged stool of nonprofits, philanthropy, and government? (One scholar on voluntary associations, in a slightly difference context, called this "a murky *ménage a trois.*") All of us in the Philanthropy New York community hope to hear from you.

That Was Then, This Is 2019

Someone should now ask whether the initiatives announced ten years ago were implemented. Did they have a positive impact? What worked, what didn't, and why? Were they even the right goals in the first place? (I remember that last question being raised in private conversations with grantees, but there was never a public conversation about it as far as I know.) Can the city and the sector learn anything by it all? Finally, were any positive changes carried over to a new administration (which should be one indicator of success)? I don't think the Bloomberg administration, or another entity, reviewed what was being accomplished and reported on that. It would be very nice if those questions were routinely asked and answered, however. There is also the matter of accountability; shouldn't officials have their feet singed when they overpromise? The worries I expressed ten years ago sadly still ring true. That is not a good thing.

The nonprofit sector did "survive the economic downturn," as the 2009 press release promised. But stronger? It is reasonably certain that the initiatives played only a paltry role in any case. From a larger perspective, the problems encountered then largely remain, almost intractable to the delight of bureaucrats and reluctant pontificators like me. Overall, the positives were sadly offset by cuts in funding and an accompaniment of counterproductive regulations. More narrowly on the three specific initiatives announced in 2009, progress was trifling:

Reduce fixed costs: through bulk purchasing, reduced energy costs.
Not a lot of progress.

Improve city contracting procedures: through access to city information, reduced compliance review times, increased bridge loan availability.
Significant changes, though delays in getting funding and then not funding true costs are still serious problems.

Strengthen nonprofit management: through technical assistance, referral with business leader partnerships and board recruitment.
Not a lot of progress

A longtime human services consultant who had worked for decades for nonprofits and foundations simply said, "We miss Mike." This was less about great progress and more about an earnest effort made. While the Bloomberg administration loved grades, my quick and dirty sense is that C+ about covers it. Sadly, I know of no effort to do a serious assessment.

My additional sense is that many of the specific problems behind the initiatives could (should) be more fully addressed by nonprofits and foundations by displaying real albeit difficult and risky leadership, such as real cooperative partnerships with success measures; better and more focused TA; better board training and recruitment; larger capacity and effectiveness measures; and of course more sensible private funding patterns (bigger, multi-funder, multi-year grants), etc. Instead, they seem satisfied to punt the problem and complain that they need more leadership from the city.

It is not clear the extent to which any positive changes from the Bloomberg administration have been carried forward. The de Blasio administration has had its own set of priorities with attendant successes and failures. High expectations, though, have led to feelings of disappointment. Again, my sense is that the administration is a setback in ways: alternately lazy and very tone-deaf, with elemental micromanaging at agencies and political favoritism at the top clouding genuine change. Some recent hard-won victories, such as changes in the indirect rate, COLA increases, and the start of some model budgeting work, are significant. However, getting past the press release to implementation is a great big new battle with painful delays. Some of these changes do promise to be huge if not offset by various "monkey-methods" that continue to hobble nonprofits. Whatever administration is in power, the ongoing and seemingly permanent "politics of the workaround" remains demeaning to a dedicated and creative — albeit sometimes ineffective and inefficient — sector.

PHILANTHROPIC LANDSCAPES

The "City" That Never Sleeps and Barely Listens

As I look back, I see larger lessons. While city administrations, the human services sector, and foundations desperately need each other, the cooperation and synergies are — pardon the mixed metaphors — flabby and always full of too much grit and too little lubricant. As one agency executive director intoned, "Could philanthropy help align the city and the nonprofit sector, instead of, for example, funding the mayor's own initiatives?" It could, but as the ED continued, "I think no one fears our bite because we are afraid — afraid not to get the grant, afraid not to pose for a photo with the mayor because we might lose our funding." As good as many commissioners and staff often are, they have political and self-interested motivations that are too often different from those of the sector. And those motivations color their commitments to the needy. Sadly, a presumed and hyped shared concern for those in need can't take the place of solid implementation. More troubling, I have come to believe that administration commissioners and staffers too often compulsively lack an understanding of the larger role and importance of the sector. They don't listen well; they only see city government. Alas, numerous city watchers and nonprofit advocates have noted that the city only reluctantly recognizes that one of their goals should be to help make the sector better and not make it worse.

This, of course, is the nature of power. It seems to be a natural and learned trait that administrations view nonprofits and even foundations solely as a means for doing their bidding. Everything is seen through the lens of the city government. The hubris was often palpable. I remember a meeting Phoebe Boyer (then executive director of the Tiger Foundation) and I had with one of Bloomberg's more trusted, committed, and intelligent commissioners, Linda Gibbs. It was about how to ensure the quality and growth of charter schools in NYC. We made the pitch that an independent support organization could make a big difference. She advocated for an effort that must be housed within city government, and, significantly, funded through the City by private foundations. We were pretty adamant that independence was crucial for many reasons. I finally pointed out that support for charters had to be independent of transitory city administrations. I thought that longer-term perspective would be the *coup de grace* against her hesitancy. But it was clear she had no vision beyond the Bloomberg administration.

Leadership Agonistes

In my original blog, I wrote that my most distressing takeaway from hearing the mayor in 2009 was that his actions "shine a harsh light on the lack of current leadership among the philanthropic community." That still rings true to me. I hasten to add that I know that nonprofits and foundations do remarkable work under difficult constraints. But leadership should have a higher bar. It is something different that foundations must rise to. (Since my career has been on the foundation side, I emphasize them here.)

One of the reasons philanthropic leadership is wanting was captured in 1977 when Paul Ylvisaker noted

> ... the weak identity and self-image of foundations and of the third sector generally. There is little sense of presence — not as much as some of our prose would indicate. When public criticism mounts and attacks begin, we don't bark very loud, and I guess it may be because nobody fears our bite. But I think it may be even more because of public uncertainty over who we are.

It is that and more. We are awed by the power of the city. I remember the day when the new school chancellor, Joel Klein, was introduced to a gathering of foundation program officers and executive directors. We of course wanted to meet him and hear his initial thoughts. But what struck me strongly was the almost giddy sense of anticipation from the audience, as we looked forward to *his* wise leadership (an attitude I am sure made Joel cringe).

However, along with the weak self-image, the hubris of philanthropy leads us to believe we are in the right. After all, most grantees "love" us for good reason, right? And yet there is an existential struggle (forgive the phrase, but it seems right) between our conceits and our personal and institutional lack of faith in what we can do. Thus, we are up against an inability to take the risks to act and have others join us in action. Hence, foundation leadership is scarce.

Creating Philanthropic Advantage Through Intermediaries

Foundation leadership can come in many forms. For me, examples I have seen are in large part captured by a comment Paul Grogan made in his 2000 *Comeback Cities* about his own practice:

> Why foundations and other backers of the community development field have not sought to replicate the successful use of intermediaries in other fields is a mystery. The American system of local job-training programs operated by the public sector and nonprofit organizations, for instance, is largely a disgrace.... There are no organized mechanisms for large-scale private capital or employer involvement, or for elevating and

spreading the best approaches, or for driving out the purely political operations.

I had been seeking something that went beyond simply grantmaking, though I quickly came to realize how difficult just good grantmaking is. I never really trusted foisting big ideas on grantees. The idea of engaging in real partnerships of various kinds that had legs and longevity — the definition of an intermediary! — struck me as sound advice. It didn't have to weigh down the very sector we intend to help. It was clear to me that leadership wasn't just sitting around talking to stakeholders in comfy conference rooms. I wanted to do things that would facilitate successful action over time. The well-known nonprofit consultant David La Piana once described nonprofit strategy as a "coordinated set of actions toward an end to creating and sustaining a competitive advantage." This is exactly right: leadership means creating and sustaining a competitive advantage. Practically speaking, that includes

- conveying a coordinated and coordinating mission;
- involving sector and institutional inclusiveness, including other funders, nonprofits, business, the city, and clients;
- embodying the practice of humility, listening, and muddling through to useable agreement (leaving egos at the door);
- understanding that change comes in steps and adjustments (embrace that process);
- implementing and measuring/reporting;
- getting the right institutional management (executive director and board);
- empowering the right staff;
- committing to taking actions with results; and
- surviving over time (i.e. not just a flash-in-the-pan "project").

Shades of Jim Collins. Leadership is going from "good to great" not primarily as an organization, but as a sector and community of partners focused on solutions. From other colleagues in philanthropy and the nonprofit sector, I have learned that this is attainable. I can be part of such a process and know it when I see it. But providing an exegesis of the process is well beyond my purpose in this article. So, while there have been many successful and unsuccessful examples of an inclusive leadership through intermediaries, let me comment of four because I knew them.

New York City Charter School Center. Founded in 2004 by Joe and Carol Reich, the Robin Hood Foundation (Emary Aronson) and the Tiger Foundation (Phoebe Boyer). The Clark Foundation was the runt with an initial commitment of $500,000. It was the first citywide charter school strategy and support organization in the country. Long-term ED James Merriman coordinated funders, schools, teachers, the city, and consultants in a feat of herding cats. For 2017–18, 227 charter schools serve 114,000 children well. Now with a city administration hostile to charter schools, the center's independence has shown the kind of progress that could not have happened without it.

JobsFirstNYC. In early 2006, The Clark Foundation and Tiger Foundation, together with Workforce Funders and Public/Private Ventures, started JobsFirstNYC, which has carefully seeded and supported multiple partnerships with expertise to achieve better outcomes for out-of-school and out-of-work young adults. These 18- to 24-year-olds easily get lost between the cracks separating different agencies. By engaging community, sector, government, and corporate expertise and resources, JobsFirstNYC has exceeded expectations: raised awareness and knowledge through careful reports, advanced effective evidence-based practice models, and worked with partners to increase significantly the investment in workforce services. In 2017, longtime ED Lou Miceli successfully led a seamless succession.

The Workforce Funders. Workforce Funders, founded in 2000 with original support from the New York Community Trust (and the leadership of Pat Jenny), The Clark Foundation, and the Robin Hood Foundation, established a collaborative presence of more than seventy-five foundations and corporate philanthropies. With the help of longtime staff consultant Bret Halverson, it has successfully — over a very long time — increased knowledge, funding, and focus for the advancement of low-income populations to jobs in growth sectors of the New York City labor market. It has received more than $13.5 million in grants from participating funders, along with more than $32 million in aligned funding. Through its clear focus, it has played a broader role as funders emphasized workforce development in their own funding. In 2017 they overall gave $76.7 million for workforce services in New York City — up from $18.4 million in 2004.

Juvenile Justice Initiative. In 2009, Philanthropy New York brought together some twenty funders and a few individuals (a judge, for instance) to try to build a collaborative focused around the issue of juvenile justice. I was tasked to facilitate the meetings; I failed miserably. Most of the funders couldn't get beyond their own narrow interests. Or they got bollixed up proclaiming that prioritizing a few keys actions was impossible since the issue was so complex. The nitpicking and grandiosity occurred unselfconsciously and in unison. Collaborations are difficult, but it was amazing as everyone attended every meeting *and* would fight taking any actions. At the penultimate meeting I whispered to a friend next to me: "Makes me wish I were the demon barber of philanthropy street!"

A Measure of Leadership in the Future

I think it only right that philanthropy, the nonprofit sector, and city government be held to a high standard of leadership where coordinated actions are expected and measured. That is the larger purpose of this expanded article: to ask if words have led to successful action. Failures and successes always coexist, of course. The three successful cases above are not perfect, nor do they exhaust examples of philanthropic leadership. Still, leadership is rare, and it is eminently doable. As Jim Collins reminds us: "Every institution has its unique set of irrational and difficult constraints, yet some make a leap while others facing the same environmental challenges do not…. Greatness, it turns out, is largely a matter of conscious choice, and discipline." In another ten years' time, perhaps there will be fewer vacuous words, more broad cooperative leadership, and better measurable results for city nonprofits and citizens. That would be worth celebrating.

Postscript

I worked in New York City for nearly forty-seven years. It is one of the great cities. One factor that makes it so are the people who have dedicated their lives to helping others thrive and participate when the odds were against them.

On February 21, 2019, a dear friend read page proofs of this article while basking in the Sarasota sun. Over many years he has grown a youth-serving nonprofit into a large and quite successful organization. His response to the article was, "Things with the City administration are so much worse than you describe." That is deeply tragic, not for me or most of the people who will read this book. So my take-away is that progress and leadership from the City can be real but is too often ephemeral and counterproductive. But this friend is but one example of many nonprofit leaders who continue to expand the greatness of New York by giving New Yorkers an opportunity to thrive. Thanks to each and every one of you for *that* ongoing leadership.

The original version of this piece was published April 23, 2009 as one of my contributions to the Smart Assets blog of Philanthropy New York, while a Senior Fellow there. Reprinted with permission from Philanthropy New York. It has been greatly revised and expanded for this book.

2. Capacity Building Begins at Home

This title comes from the title of a *Foundation News and Commentary* article (September/October 2000) by Robert Mayer, then chair of the Nathan Cummings Foundation in New York City. He was right. At any time — and especially during an economic downturn — the question we should ask is, "What is the best use of foundation resources?" The point is a simple one: The whole independent sector would be better served if foundations invested resources more wisely in their *own* capacity to do a more effective job.

Spending time and money on capacity building and technical assistance for grantees should also be an important part of what foundations do. In fact, many nonprofits are handling the economic downturn precisely because they and their funders previously invested in their infrastructure. Too bad there wasn't more of that over the last ten years. Sadly, however, foundations have a penchant for fostering their ideas of technical assistance and capacity building on nonprofits. Responding to what nonprofits say they need is rare. It is strange to me that with endowments greatly eroded and grantmaking budgets down, foundations around the country seem compelled to offer more and more technical assistance and non-monetary help as a big response to the recession. A cynic might hypothesize that foundation staff, having less money to give away, are simply finding other ways to spend their time and interfere with grantees.

Many nonprofits have always felt that the internal capacity and effectiveness of foundations is flabby anyway. Even so, careful focus on their internal effectiveness and efficiency could be the most valuable capacity building foundations can do. Clara Miller, then president of the Nonprofit Finance Fund, put it nicely: "And while most of the sector's management improvement and capacity-building work focuses on fixing the management practices of nonprofits themselves, *much greater untapped leverage resides in improvement of funding practices...*" (emphasis added).

The first step is to identify what foundations should do to become more effective. That is easier said than done, as Tony Proscio presciently pointed out: "Often the writer who uses 'capacity' genuinely doesn't know what an organization's problem really is." Incidentally, his wonderful *In Other Words: A Plea for Plain Speaking in Foundations* (New York: The Edna McConnell Clark Foundation, 2000) should be required reading for all philanthropoids. That insight about first knowing what our capacity problem is before acting is especially true when we are talking about our own philanthropic practice. Thus, the first two steps could be:

- Survey grantees about our own performance, and then take the feedback seriously.

- Review some of the fine literature about foundation effectiveness and lack thereof. I am thinking, for instance, about the findings in the June 2008 *Drowning in Paperwork, Distracted from Purpose*, a report from Project Streamline; and the many publications of Grantmakers for Effective Organizations. There continues to be lots of such useful information, which seems only to gather dust in the minds of foundation executives.

Great advances in foundation practice can be made. Each of the following suggestions would reduce foundation costs over time and reduce the unnecessarily "costly" burden of time and money for grantees and prospective grantees. Each one needs further development, but perhaps this short list will get people thinking:

- Simplify application forms and report forms: thereby making them less expensive to prepare and more appropriate to grant size. Foundations should join together to develop something better than the milquetoast Common Application Form.
- Communicate more clearly about mission, programs, and guidelines: thereby eliminating unnecessary requests. This is an area where foundation boards should take the lead.
- Ask for what you need and will use to make decisions. At a meeting of several hundred development officers, three executive directors — including me — were asked point blank if we actually read and used the annual and often biannual reports required of them. Our embarrassed response was, "Umm…"
- Respond much more quickly and candidly to inquiries and requests: thus, encouraging honesty, eliminating uncertainty, and encouraging a better use of nonprofit staff time.
- Provide serious professional development for foundation staff (especially in the areas of governance and financial expertise): thus improving due diligence and oversight.
- Encourage all program staff to join a board (not of a grantee): thus also improving staff understanding of what nonprofits are really like. The most successful foundation staff and executives have served on boards of other nonprofits. They have served as staff members of a nonprofit organization as well. These viewpoints contribute to the ability of a program officer to understand grantees better and to provide support in a way that is grounded in a common experience.
- Invest in technology: thus reducing duplication.

- Clarify impact measures and benchmarking used: thus communicating clear outcome expectations and reporting requirements.

- Review foundation staffing requirements and expenses: foundations have often seemed overstaffed to me. That, and clarifying roles and expectations, will give foundations the appropriate, streamlined capacity (the "right people on the bus"), and they will likely have more funds to grant.

- Work much more closely with other foundations — sharing, for instance, a) common applications, b) common reports and outcome measures, and c) coordination of TA offerings: thus largely eliminating vast amounts of silly duplication and sending more unified messages to the nonprofit community.

For instance, as David LaGreca reported in a response to the original blog piece in 2009:

> As a Board Chair, I was told several years ago by the executive director of a foundation [that would be me], 'when the time comes to report on your progress in achieving the goals outlined in your proposal, send us a copy of the report that you are sending X foundation [another one of our supporters]. Don't even go through the motions of changing the foundation name on the report; just send us a photocopy of their report with a handwritten note to us.' That was the first time that has ever happened — and the last as well.

Common sense, the experience of grantees, and various studies by the Urban Institute, Center for Effective Philanthropy, and Grantmakers for Effective Organizations find that so much more can be done. These and other changes would improve foundation efficiency, reduce the cost to nonprofits of working with foundations, and thereby increase the effectiveness of both.

This is not a plea to cut back on capacity building and technical assistance for grantees, but simply a reminder that we must not ignore what can be done to make our own operations better, more impactful, etc. The recession makes it even more important that foundations look at themselves and make internal changes. Now *that* would be a great gift to our grantees.

In early 2009, during the recession, many nonprofits have written revealing and helpful letters to supporters about what they have done in response to the recession by reducing costs and improving efficiencies. A few foundations have written about what they are doing *for* their grantees.

What about writing to grantees about what a foundation has done to increase *its* efficiency, reduce *its* costs, and improve *its* funding practices? That would be an exercise in the ultimate accountability. What about — heaven forfend — asking grantees what they think foundations should do! This is an area where The Center for Effective Philanthropy continues to do some interesting work. They have surveyed the grant recipients of many of the big funders in the country. Indeed, as Kevin Bolduc of the Center for Effective Philanthropy reported in 2009:

> [A] third-party assessment of funders' actions in response to their results from CEP's survey shows that nearly 100 percent of them made changes in their operations. And many improve in subsequent surveys. It's not just navel gazing. Grantee feedback drives change in effectiveness when it's taken seriously.... Similarly, it's only by asking grantees how funder-provided technical assistance is experienced that we can provide it most effectively. In our recent research, *More than Money*, we pretty clearly painted the picture from the grantee side—most non-monetary assistance isn't provided very well by funders. It's only when funders provide intensive assistance across multiple areas that grantees say it really matters.

Nonprofits may care primarily about getting a grant and not a whit about the internal workings of foundation funders. We, however, should care about it, and be attentive to what we are doing to increase efficiency and effectiveness "at home." There has been some progress over the years. And it is a shame that this short piece is just as relevant now as it was in 2009. As Mayor Koch showed, we should continually ask, "How are we doing?"

The original version of this piece was published June 4, 2009, as one of my contributions to the Smart Assets blog of Philanthropy New York while a Senior Fellow there. Reprinted with permission from Philanthropy New York.

3. Can We Still Improve Philanthropy?

Being away from the day-to-day administration of a foundation has allowed me some time to think about how philanthropy can be improved. That is a huge topic that can't be given justice in this short piece. It is also a topic that naturally led me to *Criteria for Philanthropy at Its Best*, published in early 2009 by the National Committee for Responsive Philanthropy. The five articles that Paul Brest wrote about *Criteria* in HuffPost were quite good, but most of the other commentary and the responses from NCRP proved to be too partisan to be very useful or interesting.

Criteria offers a lot to like and think about, but I was struck that it may be remembered for falling back on two common but misleading approaches that will not improve philanthropy:

1. resorting to questionable quantitative measures that divert attention from what effective philanthropy consists of; and

2. seeing the source of foundation dollars as "partially public," which is a profoundly troubling abrogation of the value and independence of philanthropy and the nonprofit sector.

Quantitative Criteria

Criteria presents ten benchmarks that are "the most critically important issues for foundations to consider." I have long believed in and acted on many of these, others not so much. Seven benchmarks are quantitative:

1. funds benefiting lower-income communities (benchmarked as "at least 50 percent of [a foundation's] grant dollars");
2. general operating support (at least 50 percent);
3. multi-year grants (at least 50 percent);
4. funds dedicated to advocacy (at least 25 percent);
5. board size (at least five people);
6. payout ("at least 6 percent of assets annually in grants");
7. and mission-related investing ("at least 25 percent of its assets").

These seven have the feel of an incoherent hodgepodge. General operating support and multi-year grants are terribly important. I personally agree with #1, but isn't that the purview of the board and donors? There are many different mission goals that are legitimate. Number 3 depends on mission goals, too. I agree with #5 as a practical matter. Number 7 should depend on mission and return objectives, not on an untethered percentage.

And of #6, lots of data and time-series calculations show such a payout would guarantee spend-out. That is fine if that is what a foundation's board intends. Otherwise, it is silly.

To *Criteria*'s credit, they raise the issues. Each topic deserves a fuller, more objective discussion of alternative viewpoints. But the tone of much of *Criteria* suggests otherwise. It reads as "the truth discovered." Finally, as any of us in the field knows, there are way too many poor and wasteful grants that would nonetheless meet these benchmarks. These percentages do not define effectiveness, and foundations aren't more effective by simply meeting these numbers.

In fact, the subtle, lasting effect of such quantitative quotas may well be that they become the sole measures for deciding whether foundations are effective or not (in the same way that simple benchmarks for administrative expenses have misconstrued nonprofit effectiveness). This will distract foundation staff and boards, policymakers, researchers, and legislators from the much more important and difficult issue of determining — and communicating — what effective grantmaking is.

One good example of this last point is the dearth of any attention to board governance. This is a big topic. Clearly philanthropy at its best depends on quality governance. That is rarely captured with the quantitative points made in *Criteria*.

Keeping the Sector Independent

Many writers have claimed that philanthropy's public trust rests on the idea that foundation dollars are at least "partially public." *Criteria* uses this idea rather uncritically as an organizing principle. I believe that position contains a profoundly troubling and unintended attack on the value and self-determination of the entire independent sector. There are legal, economic, and political aspects of this idea that need a full discussion. And, I would argue, there are far better rationales for the serious and real public obligations philanthropy and the entire independent sector have. I can only raise a few points here.

If "generous tax subsidies provided to donors and to foundations make the government and the public partners with philanthropists in pursuit of the public good," then this concept must apply to the entire third, nonprofit, or independent sector because of their "subsidies." Is all or most money in philanthropy, and given by donors, actually the property of the state? This may seem absurd. But there is a long history of efforts to politicize philanthropy along those lines. It is no doubt a tempting siren song, since we all want to be around power. This is a crucial issue that can't just be assumed away. It deserves full and careful discussions from many points of view — impossible here.

Wouldn't this view of tax subsidies apply to the mortgage deduction and tax breaks of any kind? Does "partially public" mean foundation distributions should be allocated by a government bureaucracy? At one point, *Criteria* posits "at least 45 percent" that is "public." What does that mean? Practically speaking, could the state be within its rights to restrict the use of foundation giving depending, for instance, on whether people have voted for or against such divisive issues as gay marriage? When the Bush administration banned federal funding of stem cell research, would this public assumption have given the administration an excuse to ban 45 percent of foundation funding for the same? Not only is this logically absurd, the democratic diversity and independence of the sector would be destroyed. There are those who will eagerly use similar excuses for their purposes, whether on the left or right. Consider *Philanthropy in Democratic Societies,* edited by Rob Reich, Chiara Cordelli, and Lucy Bernholz (Chicago: The University of Chicago Press, 2016). While an important book, many of its points would put philanthropy further under the thumb of the state.

How have we so quickly forgotten about the theory and practice of civil society theorists and advocates against totalitarian countries and restrictive governments that have partially defined history, especially in the last several decades! Warnings of several generations of philanthropy watchers have been lost from this discussion.

As an aside, we really must remind ourselves of the importance of the ideas and practice of civil society. One could usefully start by perusing *Civil Society: The Underpinnings of American Democracy*, by Brian O'Connell (Hanover, NH: University Press of New England, 1999); *The Return of Civil Society* by Víctor Pérez-Díaz (Cambridge: Harvard University Press, 1993); and *The Essential Civil Society Reader*, Don Eberly, editor (Lanham, MD: Roman and Littlefield, 2000). And there are many others. Ideas do matter. These perspectives are in stark contrast to the statist — dare I say proto-authoritarian — underpinnings inherent in *Criteria*.

Brian O'Connell, the founding president and president emeritus of Independent Sector, makes the same point. He rightly warned us years ago that "the very hint that tax exemption should depend on the political popularity of ideas under examination is a fateful step down the totalitarian road." Consider, for instance, the comments in David Carr's *New York Times* column on "Separation of Press and State" on May 10, 2009. The author warned: "Government bailouts, including special tax status, seem likely to kill independent journalism, not save it. A free press that serves at the pleasure of its government is a diminution of the intent of the founders and not, by the way, a free press." Similarly, there is simply no such thing as an independent nonprofit sector, nor an independent philanthropic sector, nor even free choice for donors in a worldview based on the concept of "partially public" dollars. There would simply be no "room of one's own" for the independent sector. And yet, *Criteria* takes us well down that path, whether the "crossing guard" is from the left or right.

Paul Ylvisaker was a complex and endlessly probing thinker on philanthropy. In *Conscious and Community* (New York: Peter Lang, 1999, pgs. 309 and 312) he makes a similar point:

> We have clearly moved from business dominance over philanthropy to what is emerging as governmental dominance over philanthropy.... The radical question that I would have to ask in this context is, has philanthropy gained more or lost more by being associated with tax advantage, which has brought us into being but may well compromise our future? It is an excuse [for] regulation, it is an excuse for harassment, and more than that (as I have argued elsewhere) it has kept the third sector from having the full range of free speech.

Tax advantages for the entire sector should be reexamined, by all means; maybe they aren't good public policy. It is clear to me, though, that using "partially public" dollars as an underpinning for improving philanthropy and discussing its public obligations is disastrous. It will be used by different and opposing political interests for regulation, harassment, prohibitions. There is no independent sector in that scenario.

The philanthropic sector and the entire independent sector do immense good and are also fraught with serious problems. We need to ask the right questions; highlight what works; candidly address the real problems (e.g., philanthropic hubris, wasted grants, and little sense of results); and maintain the special place voluntary philanthropy and institutions should have. Philanthropy's public trust and obligation have been frayed and need to be reasserted and improved.

Shackling the complex challenges of improving philanthropy with simple quantitative benchmarks within a "partially public dollars" framework encourages the wrong discussions and trivializes the independence of the sectors. Real effectiveness and authentic independence are two of the keys for getting philanthropy to its best. Alas, *Criteria* sadly contributes only a little to that job.

The original version of this piece was published July 17, 2009, as one of my contributions to the Smart Assets blog of Philanthropy New York while a Senior Fellow there. Reprinted with permission from Philanthropy New York.

4. Philanthropy as "Invisible Aid"

Philanthropy was once described as "invisible aid." Whatever Walter Gifford meant at the time (he was president of AT&T and chair of the Organization on Unemployment Relief in the early 1930s), foundations and their work remain too "invisible." If we don't redress what makes philanthropy invisible, we cannot address accountability, protect its unique role, or legitimately participate in the public discourse about the challenges in this society.

I thought of this recently when I decided to read the thirty-two profiles posted in the "30 Grants in 30 Days" section of Philanthropy New York's website. This was an effort to communicate and highlight self-proclaimed "exemplary philanthropic initiatives" — to make philanthropy more "visible". I decided not to name names, because I am interested in themes. However, I would single out the New York Foundation and the Rauch Foundation as among the best.

The Value of Invisibility

Let me start first by suggesting that there are several senses in which philanthropy and foundations arguably should be invisible aid:

Grantees matter most. The main work of philanthropy is usually best reflected in the work of its grant recipients. Surprisingly, few of the profiles emphasized the crucial role of nonprofit partners, and almost nothing was said about strengthening the sector's infrastructure. Philanthropy would benefit greatly by highlighting its nonprofit partners more.

Being under the radar can be important. Transparency is important. I nonetheless appreciate that foundation work requires decisions to be made and risks to be taken. It can't always be a group decision of all the stakeholders that would clamber for a say. Decisions may need to be made out of the limelight if they are to be effective, even if that means that some decisions will defy the multitudinous "influence peddlers" that can make decisions impossible. Nothing explicit on this issue came up in the profiles — that is not surprising — but it seemed clear that many of the initiatives could only have succeeded through the independence and private focus of foundations and their grantees.

What Does Philanthropy Have to Hide?

Sadly, philanthropy is also invisible in negative ways that reflect the sector's inadequacies, weaknesses, and inabilities to communicate well.

No useful knowledge to impart. All too often in this field, a particular grant or initiative is inadequately thought-through and poorly articulated. Some profiles did show foundations supporting research and basing their work on the results of research. In other profiles, they seemed driven simply by the desire to do good work and support good causes, without reference to the rationale and evidence. Whether that is true or just a failure of communication doesn't matter. Future profiles could be more explicit about the thought and evidence behind initiatives. Otherwise, one is left with the uneasy feeling that whim rules. I, for instance, vividly remember a senior program officer remarking that he was concluding funding for an organization he admitted had good results, because... wait for it... he was "bored with it!"

Foundations can also exhibit an astonishing hubris, thinking they know everything and refusing to examine alternatives. Gene Steuerle made the same general point in his August 13, 2009 *Smart Assets* post: "Why Are Foundations Often Absent from Major Policy Shifts?" There were hints of that hubris in some of the profiles as well.

Let us not also forget hubris and whim *are* prevalent traits in philanthropy that have "no natural predators and so can multiply at will," in the ever-so-neat phrase Tony Proscio used in a different context in *In Other Words*. In cases of whim and hubris, being invisible hides laziness or incompetence. Indeed, perhaps philanthropy deserves to be ignored when foundations have neither useful information to impart nor an openness to genuine inquiry that would add to the public discourse.

No results to show. While foundations are getting better about this, they too often don't know — and seemingly don't want to know — whether their work has had the intended outcome, or any outcome for that matter. Lisbeth Schorr's article in *The Chronicle of Philanthropy* is just one very good piece on this topic: "To Judge What Will Best Help Society's Neediest, Let's Use a Broad Array of Evaluation Techniques," (August 20, 2009). She has cautionary words about the holy grail of evaluation while emphasizing we must talk about results. Sadly, few of the profiles revealed anything about results. Some may have good results, but success or failure is not communicated. Thus, the work remains largely untethered to results and invisible as far as usefulness goes.

It is true that many foundations have gotten much better about communicating when they have failed and what they have learned. That is so important. It would have been refreshing to see profiles that acknowledged a failure and how they changed to address it with success.

No *"stick-to-it-ive-ness."* Too often, philanthropy retains the same short-term horizon that afflicts business. Building impact and influence takes time. But ever-changing programs and fickle priorities limit success and encourage the public to dismiss foundation efforts as so many flashes in the pan. Here the profiles were largely exemplary. The most successful programs featured long-term philanthropic commitments that also built collaborations with other funders, nonprofits, the business world, and/or government.

The Right Kind of Communication

On the one hand, foundations are most often invisible because they and the philanthropic field have not done a good job of communicating and marketing. Years ago, the Council on Foundations conducted several studies and discovered that the general public, opinion leaders, and political leaders didn't understand what philanthropy *is*, what foundations *do*, and what they have *accomplished*. For instance, more than half of "engaged Americans" could not name a foundation and only 15 percent could give an example of a foundation's impact. I suspect nothing has changed since those surveys were done. We still need to be much smarter about how we communicate and more open about it.

On the other hand, let us be honest about what we communicate. Indeed, too many of the profiles seemed to represent "marketing" in the worst sense of the term. Many of the brief profiles probably came from existing materials or were rather quickly written. They came across as self-congratulatory and left a very strong aftertaste of "buyer beware."

I saw this problem even more starkly when reading the companion volume to Joel Fleishman's fine *The Foundation* (New York: Public Affairs, 2007). The *Casebook for The Foundation*, was hyped as "100 of the highest-achieving foundation initiative of all time." Here the cases were not submitted by foundations but separately chosen and independently written. And yet. Admittedly, each case was limited to about two pages. That doesn't excuse such a pervading heavy uncritical tone to them all. In about a dozen of the cases with which I had some familiarity, I thought the cases were quite off-base, mostly uncritical, and unduly positive. Admittedly, this is a difficult task. Foundations themselves, and the scholars and commentators on them, have to do a better job.

We simply need to do a better job of communicating our stories and impact. The profiles were incredibly diverse. They were often inspiring, and suggested philanthropy does indeed have something remarkable to communicate. This effort should be widely — and thoughtfully — expanded. To increase visibility *and* believability, it might be useful if future contributions include brief answers to key questions, such as:

- What is the issue addressed and how does it fit the mission?
- How was the particular approach and strategy determined?
- What partnerships with nonprofits were built and funded?
- What results were expected and what does the evidence suggest?
- What has been learned that can be applied elsewhere?

As seems clear, the public and government leaders still do not fully understand the role philanthropy and foundations play in American society. It can't surprise us that philanthropy is not understood; its impact is not known; and its knowledge and commitment appear so limited. It is our own damn fault philanthropy is invisible. It then becomes an easy target for misinterpretations and attacks.

It must be an increasing part of our job to communicate *well* and *candidly* what we know and what we accomplish, without grandstanding and with our failures acknowledged. At that point philanthropy will be truly visible to all. We can then more fully contribute — and will be asked to contribute — to the public discourse about the challenges in this society.

This piece was originally published August 31, 2009, as one of my contributions to the Smart Assets blog of Philanthropy New York while a Senior Fellow there. Reprinted with permission from Philanthropy New York.

5. How Family Foundation Boards Can Align Payout With Mission, Lifespan, and Investment Policy

Introduction

The last decade has been a bracing reminder of both the volatility (highs and lows) and uncertainty (evident risks and varying prognoses) facing foundation financial strategy. Indeed, slow overall economic growth was the expected near future when this article was originally published,[1] and yet that has not proven to be the case in the short run, given the remarkable 2017 total return of the Dow of 27 percent. The Dow is up over 11 percent year-to-date from late February 2019. The point is simply that we live with constant change and uncertainty both up *and* down. We must make plans and decisions that take that reality into consideration. This makes it even more important for boards, donors, and foundation executives to take a careful look at what they are doing and how it all fits together. This article focuses on how the alignment of four key leading indicators, listed below, is the lynchpin for foundation success:

- Clarity of mission;
- Intentions about intended lifespan —longevity or spend down;
- Appropriate payout rates; and
- An investment policy reflecting these factors.

By making sure these issues are in alignment, foundation boards and managers can avoid surprises and manage the risks and opportunities they inevitably face as they strive for impact for the public good. This kind of coordinated decision making is not easy or particularly "natural" for foundations. Each issue is habitually thought about separately. Some might even complain that boards already spend too much time on financial matters. I would suggest, however, that too much time is too often rather poorly spent on financial matters. Of course, there is much more to effective and efficient foundation management. The co-equal challenges are to develop operational and grant-making strategies, ensure good governance, and establish meaningful ways to diagnose problems and assess results. These are topics for a companion article.

Spending the time to make sure that these four key factors are in alignment does several important things. It protects and deploys assets better. It integrates finance and investment more fully into the life and goals of a foundation. And it mitigates some of the potential unintended financial consequences of ill-considered actions that can cripple mission success.

In this sense, these factors are truly leading indicators that will improve philanthropic impact, effectiveness, and satisfaction. This article focuses on each of the leading indicators in turn.

What Is Our Mission?

It all starts here, but one survey showed that less than three quarters of reporting foundations have a vision/mission statement.[2] For too many foundations, the mission may simply be the generic purposes common in trust or corporate legal documents. For others, the mission is merely implicit or is subject to the disparate whims of board members and the exigencies of the moment. Many are old and rarely reconsidered or revised. That is not enough to be effective.

A written mission statement is essential. The finished document should grow out of discussions about the values and vision, specific interests, and goals that the board sets for itself. It may focus on a single issue or small group of issues; emphasize a geographic area; or support research, immediate relief or long-term approaches. Family foundations often include the founder's intent and desired family legacy. Finally, a mission statement serves as an initial test of whether a foundation is achieving its goals and meeting the values it has identified.

I have seen great mission statements written on the back of an envelope, and others that run to many pages. I know of one such document that runs 143 printed pages. There is no one ideal format, and a mission statement needn't be — indeed cannot be — "perfect." Over time, it will change and become more focused as the world and the board evolves. Getting started can appear daunting, but there are many helpful resources.[3]

Only the board can get the mission right. It reflects the soul of the foundation and provides focus and benchmarks for aligning both financial operations and grantmaking goals. As Kelin Gersick has noted, "clarifying mission pays off not only in survival, but in performance."[4] The other three leading indicators for foundation success support and inform the mission. They must do its bidding.

What Is Our Future — A Finite Term or Existing in Perpetuity?

When family foundations were most recently surveyed regarding the intended lifespan of the foundation, in 2008, 63 percent envisioned perpetuity, 12 percent planned spend-down, and 25 percent were undecided.[5] Most legal documents forming foundations assume perpetuity, and most foundations operate that way simply by default. Some foundations may assume perpetuity but choose to spend at an unsustainably high payout rate that will inevitably lead to spend-down. That is fine if the decision to do so is explicit. Others assume spend-down and even reflect it in the payout rate. That too is fine. There are those cases, however, when spend-out decisions are clearly contrary to the mission statement and unrelated to the actual investment strategy. In these cases, clarity and alignment of the leading indicators are missing. Good works can still be accomplished, but the likelihood of a larger success, focus, and effectiveness are compromised. Being clear about a foundation's expected lifespan is an important discussion for any board to have.

There is strong support for both perpetuity and spend-down.[6] Each side seems to cherry-pick the pros and cons supporting their positions. Either decision can be good and appropriate, as long as it is part of a larger examination of goals. When Francie Ostrower interviewed executives and trustees of foundations planning to spend-down, she found that to be true:

> [S]unsetting was not typically selected for philanthropic strategy or experienced as having a substantial impact.... It is not lifespan *per se*, but how foundation leaders approached and used that lifespan that, in the end, led sunsetting to impact not only the way their foundations ended, but how they lived.[7]

The same point should apply to *all* foundations, when the lifespan decision is being made. This is not an easy conversation for boards. The values and motivations of decision makers can be complex. What are trustees and donors to do? Three considerations stand out.

Family Values

A choice about lifespan is clearly influenced by the mission statement and the values embedded in it. Did donors express an opinion about perpetuity? The desire to maintain a charitable legacy across generations and use it as an intergenerational learning experience can be key for some donors and families. There can be a delicate balance here between commitments to philanthropy generally or to specific current causes. Maintaining a commitment to specific causes can be one factor suggesting a limited lifespan; passing on a legacy of philanthropy may suggest a longer lifespan, with the flexibility to change missions as successive generations make their own decisions. For example, I know two donors who chose to start a small family foundation in perpetuity over 25 years ago as their "ethical legacy" to their young children. After 10 years, they realized that philanthropic values had been deeply instilled in their children. The donors decided to focus more on specific issues that most moved them personally and spend down in a decade or so. And yet, in 2017, one of the sons touchingly told his parents that he wanted the foundation to continue: better, he said, to leave most of any small estate to the foundation and not to him! One child and his wife have now taken a lead in the foundation and want to continue this philanthropic family legacy as their own.

Importance and Pitfalls of Enduring Institutions

In an "exit interview" published in *The Chronicle of Philanthropy* before she left the Ford Foundation, Susan Berresford talked passionately about the importance of long-term institutions: "Our society values enduring institutions… We treasure them because they express and reinforce our values."[8] A foundation that has a long history, existing culture, experience, and both financial and human capital may be a valuable "teaching" institution as well as a "countervailing" institution separate from governmental, corporate/commercial, and other special interests. History should remind us that if one is going to talk about the "public good," surely long-lived foundations should be one value to consider.

The goals and causes one wishes to address affect lifespan expectations. Many of the most troubling social issues cannot be solved in a lifetime. Long-term commitments to those causes can be critically important, bringing to bear continuing commitments and financial resources, on-going assessment and advice, as well as the human capital needed to address such issues with success. The Clark Foundation in New York City, for instance, has supported many of the same organizations for decades, with annual reviews and assessments. Rather than encouraging dependence, I would argue that many nonprofit stalwarts in New York are much stronger and more successful because of that long-term support.

There are, of course, some less attractive reasons for perpetuity. It can be the unthinking, default position for far too many foundations and donors. Sometimes a false belief in donor immortality, and the urge for control from the grave, are at play. And perhaps perpetuity dampens the sense of urgency for results and can lead board and staff to bask in a sinecure for professional philanthropoids. I have seen that more often than I care to admit. These factors may or may not be at play, but it behooves boards to beware of these hidden and less-then-honorable motivations.

Advantages and Disadvantages of Spending Down

Over the last decade, spending down has become such a popular position among some commentators, regardless of political outlook, that it seems to be the new default position — promoted as a strong "should" or even advocated as a legal requirement. There are good reasons to consider spending down. Some donors or boards desire it as an antidote for mission-creep. There are indeed goals, projects, and technical issues that may be best addressed by a short-term focus. The passion, planning, innovation, and larger payout possible can have a powerful and immediate impact.

Francie Ostrower, among others, has written eloquent case studies about how well several foundations planned a spend-down strategy and then implemented it.[9] Interestingly, having clear and urgent goals and strategies not only focused the foundations' passion and largesse, it encouraged a greater commitment and sensitivity to grantees and their longer-term health. Sunsetting can also avoid the institutionalization and bureaucracy of the operations, and the "warehousing of wealth" that can infect longer-lived foundations.

That positive result in some cases, however, should be balanced by the possibility that going for short-term success may be misplaced in other cases. Can we, for instance, eliminate poverty or cure cancer in (pick a number) 5, 10, or 20 years? Years ago, a Chicago-based foundation started a small grants program of less than $20,000 a year, to address the serious high school drop-out problem. When it didn't see success after only three years, it stopped funding. Yet school drop-out is hardly a problem amenable to short-term solutions. There should always be benchmarking and assessment of results no matter what, of course. But a short-term funding time horizon in cases like this can be counterproductive.

As spending down comes up for discussion, there can be other motivations. It can be in the self-interest of foundation staff and boards, because it seems to increase their short-term "giving power," impact, and personal power. Some board members, foundation staff, and donors favor spending down because they believe only they can make the best decisions; they tremble at the idea of passing control to others. Or they are flummoxed by how to negotiate the genuinely challenging generational transfer of governance and intent. Some outsiders and policy people may emphasize the advantages of spending down because they fear and distrust the independence of foundations, or because they want more money given to nonprofits now rather than have it "sit" in foundation coffers.

Whether it is to make an enduring institution successful or a spending down strategy effective, these questions and motivations need to be considered. Perhaps not all will be relevant in each situation. Having candid discussions about lifespan will make perpetuity decisions clearer, which can then be aligned with the other leading indicators.

What Is Our Spending Policy/Payout Rate?

Payout rates loom large because they determine lifespan.[10] That connection is not well understood. There can be very wide and perfectly appropriate differences in the spending policy and payout rates different foundations choose, beyond the federally required 5 percent minimum payout. Yet, according to one report, only 48 percent of reporting foundations had a formal spending policy.[11] This suggests that far too many boards do not discuss this issue and are simply falling back on the minimum 5 percent rate as the maximum by default. Or they spend over the minimum without knowing the implications of doing so.

Unthinkingly maintaining the minimum payout without regard to mission and lifespan considerations can hobble effectiveness. Ignoring payout can also unintentionally lead to spending out. One needs to understand the complex factors around payout decisions so that a spending policy is in alignment with the leading indicators that help foundations succeed. Discussion of the four subsequent questions will help reach alignment.

Is there a proper payout rate?

When it comes to grants, we all want to spend more. Indeed, grantmakers have that choice, but it is important to be realistic about the consequences and opportunity costs of doing so. Recently, a foundation board heard from their accountants after they completed the audit: "It looks like you are spending down." This came as a complete surprise to a board that explicitly did not want to spend down. Board members hadn't made the connection between payout rate and the ability to maintain the endowment.

There is often an assumption that a greater payout now is simply better than grants made over a longer period — and that doing so is largely "costless." One publication favored increasing the 5 percent minimum because it "reaffirms some of the basic principles of effective grantmaking, such as mission clarity, focus and impact."[12] It does no such thing of course. Payout does not determine mission, effectiveness, or social benefit. It should be the other way around. As Michael Klausner has written, "there is no valid reason to conclude that future charity is necessarily worth less than current charity."[13] Or vice versa, for that matter. When these factors are in sync, then a foundation can do what it intends to do. What is required are conscious, consistent choices that align with each other.

What Is Your Total Philanthropic Value?

Payout decisions affect what some have termed "total philanthropic value" in surprising ways.[14] Higher payout rates intended to increase the money being granted may actually decrease total grantmaking over time while also setting a foundation on the path toward spend down. One can, for instance, calculate (1) the annual total of a foundation's cumulative grantmaking over time, and (2) the foundation's remaining assets in the endowment at the end of that time. The combination is the dollar value that a foundation represents over time: total philanthropic value. A lower spending rate can often result in a *higher* total philanthropic dollar value of those two elements, because the endowment grows. Higher payout can reduce the endowment size each year, thereby reducing the total dollars given at even a larger payout percentage. In addition, some of the advantages of market growth and compounding are foregone.

For example, I remember that the J. M. Kaplan Fund in New York City was regularly paying out 8-10 percent in grants and charitable administrative expenses in the early 1990s. While doing so could be a perfectly fine choice, it was being done without board members understanding what their decision meant. I presented a simple analysis of spending over time at both 8-10 percent and 5-6 percent. At the higher rate, two things were clear: (1) the higher payout was depleting the endowment; and (2) as a result, over about a 15-year period the higher payout actually provided less total grant money than a lower rate based on a growing, larger endowment. If the foundation's payout were kept at 5-6 percent during the same period, the growing endowment would have very likely allowed the foundation to distribute *more* money to grantees in total — *and* to grow its endowment base (providing a cushion to weather periodic market downturns or to respond to crises or opportunities).

Because of this analysis, the board brought its annual spending down to the 5-6 percent range as a better way to manage the dual goals of larger grant budgets over time and existing in perpetuity. Not every foundation will want to make the same decision. Missions and goals differ. The particular economic environment can change the analysis. But boards should routinely discuss the varying implications of different payouts.

Most empirical research has shown that a payout rate of 5 percent is actually the *maximum* that will give foundations a decent chance of existing in perpetuity, taking into consideration market cycles, administrative expenses, excise taxes, and inflation.[15] A J. P. Morgan Asset Management report looked at 20-year time frames from January 1926 through August 2002 and concluded that "a 5 percent spending rate is very risky and can be sustained only if markets are strong.... Over a long horizon, even a 5 percent distribution rate will very likely erode the corpus substantially."

They concluded that an aggressive asset allocation of 80 percent equity and 20 percent bonds would only "support a spending rate of approximately 4 percent without damaging the long-term real value of the portfolio."[16] A more recent 2013 analysis has further strengthened the point in an understated conclusion: "Updated simulations using hypothetical portfolio data from 1969-2010 confirm that a 5 percent payout rate makes the goal of maintaining purchasing power in perpetuity somewhat challenging."[17]

There is no one proper payout rate. Indeed, nearly 15 years ago, several scholars suggested that eliminating any and all mandated payout rates would be a positive thing; it "would clearly encourage foundations to adopt a payout rate that strategically links mission and payout decisions within foundations."[18] I agree. That is hardly a realistic policy prescription, though it did cause minor apoplexy among some policy wonks and philanthropoids! But their paper does reinforce the importance of having payout decisions integrated with the other leading indicators.

Are There Unintended Consequences of Higher Payout?

Whatever the chosen payout rate, attention to possible unintended consequences is crucial. It has been suggested that any endowment loss and any foundation closures because of higher payout will be offset by the creation of new foundations. Perhaps. Foundation formation, even in recent years, remains quite strong as a result of such factors as economic growth, the intergenerational transfer of wealth to heirs, new philanthropy that baby boomers are now undertaking, the financial dividends of innovation, and the success of efforts such as the Giving Pledge. That all renews philanthropic coffers for the public good. However, a mandated higher payout rate will likely lead foundations to spend down over time. That could easily in turn decrease the attractiveness of foundation formation to donors for whom perpetuity and family legacy are important. Alternatives — such as current consumption, private investment, larger legacies for children and favorite charities, or other philanthropic vehicles — will become proportionately more attractive. That could significantly reduce the growth of philanthropy and the role of foundations as independent and creative institutions of civil society.

Others have urged eliminating charitable administrative expenses from the 5 percent minimum. This would increase the amount of grantmaking necessary to meet the minimum. That means actual foundation expenses including grantmaking and administrative will rise and pull overall actual payout well above 5 percent. In a surreptitious way, that will push many, if not most, foundations into spend-down mode.

Such a maneuver would also be self-defeating by reducing overall foundation effectiveness. Foundations are finally beginning to understand that the administrative expenses of grantees are often integral to their organizational health and program effectiveness. The same is true for foundation charitable expenses. Eliminating administrative expenses from qualifying distributions would likely put pressure on foundations to decrease the amount spent on due diligence, public policy, advocacy, assessment, communication, and technical assistance by, in effect, increasing their cost in comparison to grants. While this surely will eliminate some administrative "fat" at some foundations, it also will likely decrease the effectiveness of grantmaking programs.

In good times, endowments may indeed grow, leading some, rightly, to raise the "warehousing of wealth" alarm. We might also ask: Aren't foundations simply being fiscally prudent by saving for a rainy day? Over time, markets go up and down, wreaking havoc on endowments and the nonprofit sector in general (consider, e.g., the 1970s, 1987, 2002, and the Great Recession). The Ford Foundation, for example, lost a third of its value in the 1973 recession — $1 billion — leading to nearly 50 percent cuts in staff and grants. If foundations protect their missions, grant-making programs, and their future (whether short- or long-term) by maintaining and potentially growing endowments, they have better chances to respond to crises or make innovative and big bets when opportunities or new pressing needs arise? You decide and choose accordingly.

Does Increasing Payout Improve Results?

The calls for greater payout derive in part from a desire to get more funds into the hands of nonprofit organizations for their programs, clients, and causes. That can be a very good thing. There are many times when making a grant, or a larger grant, now rather than later is critically important. Research cited above does show that some foundations that spend down are particularly responsive to impact and grantees. Perhaps, however, spending more now is simply a temporal illusion — the philanthropic version of the shortsighted, short-term strategic thinking that plagues American corporations in search of short-term profit.

Assessing the merits of greater payout must be made within the larger context of a foundation's philanthropic goals and mission and the respective results obtained. There may be self-interest in these calls as well, since nonprofits want access to more funds too. But there is an unspoken assumption here that simply getting more money out the door will ipso facto improve results. That may or may not be true, but this assumption provides a moral patina that simply hides a deeper truth about the need to assess what the results are.

There is no necessary correlation between greater payout, more grantmaking dollars flowing out, and greater philanthropic and nonprofit impact. For example, about 15 years ago I heard the same lament from five executive directors and senior program officers. Each person complained that there simply were "not enough good organizations and programs" to fund. I would add that I occasionally faced the same quandary. There are times when meeting the budgeted 5 percent payout meant that less effective organizations were funded. In addition, since the mid-1980s, when recessions or significant economic downturns showed up in reduced grant making budgets at many foundations, some staff candidly admitted that this was an opportunity to cull their grantee lists of those organizations they considered less effective.

Not finding enough good organizations is surely partially the fault of the foundations. They sometimes have extremely narrow missions and imaginations; they may have theories of change or grant agendas that narrow the list of potential grantees. And foundations certainly can get in the way of nonprofits becoming more effective organizations (because of hubristic and restrictive funding and overlooking or interfering with nonprofit management). The point remains: the call for greater payout and thus greater amounts of money flowing to nonprofits does not necessarily increase social benefit in and of itself. It may even lead to support of a layer of less effective organizations and programs that are societally suspect and wasteful.

In sum, a mandated 5 percent payout rate may be the most practical choice precisely because it allows for the kind of diversity and choices of lifespan, mission, and strategy that makes philanthropy a vibrant part of civil society. But that should *never* be the default decision. The four issues raised above are intended to begin a discussion by pointing out the complex issues, varying motivations, and unintended consequences that can shroud what goes into a payout decision. My intent is not to advocate for either a minimum or a higher payout rate. Donors, boards, and foundation staff should engage in a robust discussion of what payout fits best with their mission and lifespan expectations.

Does Our Investment Policy Support Mission, Lifespan, Spending Goals?

The right payout for a foundation is also affected and constrained by market performance. The final leading indicator is the investment policy statement (IPS), which tries to make the best decisions to align markets and the other leading indicators. Developing and implementing the right financial strategy requires a carefully thought through IPS. It provides a set of strategic goals and general guidelines for the "care and feeding" of the endowment and usable income. It can be short and general or long and quite detailed. It also provides targets and benchmarks by which the performance of the investment managers and investment committee can be evaluated. However, many foundations have not attended to this critical issue. For instance, Exponent Philanthropy found that only about 76 percent of their reporting foundations had an investment policy statement, and only 48 percent had a spending policy (although many spending policies are part of an IPS).[19]

Prudent financial care is one of the foremost legal responsibilities a board must shoulder. The endowment and its earning power represent the means by which a foundation achieves its mission and has impact. Yet one often hears criticism about how foundation boards spend too much time on dry investments and not enough on other issues such as grantmaking. That is because many foundation boards are probably thinking about investments in the *wrong* way. If what seem to be perfectly rational investment policies are untethered from considerations of mission, lifespan, and payout, then performance and impact will suffer. Once again alignment of these leading indicators is essential.

Many boards don't have the financial expertise to develop a sophisticated investment plan on their own. Investment advisors, managers, consultants and accountants should be involved to provide the details and facts needed to craft a reasonable statement. Unfortunately, outside financial managers are often tasked with the development of the *entire* IPS. *Don't let that happen.* Only the board has the knowledge to make sure an IPS is aligned with foundation goals. That must come first and then the appropriate investment goals and policies can be chosen. Board members must ask questions of themselves and their advisors. Then they should review the IPS at least annually, to assess performance, and to reassess the IPS's relevance in light of changing economic and foundation realities.

Several things make an IPS and its alignment with the other leading indicators particularly important in the current environment. First, we are in what may be an extended period of low interest rates, slow overall economic growth, and high volatility and uncertainty. As if to underscore the role of uncertainty, note this article was originally written in 2016. In 2018, economic growth is approaching 4 percent. Who knew? This is exactly the point. These factors may mean average investment returns vary considerably. Second, achieving both income goals and maintaining or growing the endowment in perpetuity will be quite challenging roller coaster rides. Third, in this environment, foundations will likely be taking greater investment risks as they try to enhance returns and protect their endowment. All these factors increase the chances that mission objectives and actual investment performance may be mismatched.

The Role and Challenges of Impact Investing

The idea of using every dollar in an endowment for social impact is an old concept now reimagined as "impact investing" by advocates and Wall Street alike. For all its hype, though, mission investing has not exactly taken off. In a recent *Chronicle of Philanthropy* endowment survey only 15 percent of respondents reported using social investing (36 of 238 respondents). An earlier survey of large foundations saw 26 of 64 responding foundations engaged in social investing but devoted only a median of 2 percent of endowment assets in that way.[20] However, the idea is both compelling and oversold: and will continue to be. As with all investment decisions, careful analysis — not simply having a "good feeling about it" — is imperative if foundations want to make impact investing a legitimate asset class for participation.

"Impact" investments are sometimes viewed as an asset class because of their common mission-related focus. But the vehicles can run the gamut from program-related investments, which count as charitable spending; to common types of investments such as loan guarantees for nonprofit borrowers; investment screens and impact investment mutual funds; to private or public equity stakes. And new IRS rulings have now relaxed foundation concerns about jeopardizing investment penalties for social investments.[21] Impact investment vehicles thus provide (1) a social benefit and (2) some rate of return that can vary from extremely low to a market rate. Indeed, some advocates and Wall Street commentators think that there is a quite large social-investing market that can provide market returns. Nonetheless, there is concern that getting market rate returns is difficult and carries with it increased risks and illiquidity. Without proper due diligence, expectations can outstrip risks and reality. As an asset class, some types of impact investments can make a lot of sense if the time horizon, overall return targets, and opportunity costs compared to other asset classes are analyzed. Overall alignment is always important to consider.

Social investing also adds challenges of definition and measurement. The methods and historical data necessary to determine viability and success are getting better, but this kind of social analysis is still in its infancy. It is too easy to feel good about the idea and simply assume real benefits that may not be there. That applies to individual investments (which, like private equity, have long lockups and carry both high risks and potential rewards) as well as to the entire asset class. As Paul Brest and Kelly Born have cautioned:

Estimating the expected financial return from an investment is a difficult but familiar exercise. Estimating social return is intrinsically much harder because of the complexities of placing values on social and environmental outcomes and predicting what outcomes an organization is likely to achieve.[22]

Special care must be taken to ensure that adding impact investments fits with the foundation's overall investment return targets and doesn't unintentionally jeopardize grantmaking budgets or lifespan considerations. For instance, the Kresge Foundation is a leader in impact investing. As their chief investment officer put it, "We don't have the capacity to take below-market returns in an environment where we think it's going to be difficult enough to meet our base hurdle [of a 7.5 percent rate of return to cover grantmaking, expenses and inflation]."[23]

Nonetheless, discussing and carefully analyzing impact investments re-affirm the critical role of aligning the leading indicators. A foundation's mission, lifespan expectations, payout, and IPS need to be in sync to achieve the greatest success and impact. In many cases, that will include some exposure to impact investments; in a few cases impact investments might make up the vast majority of assets. At the same time, "traditional" market investment also meet mission by delivering the growth and income needed to meet a foundation's grantmaking purposes and lifespan priorities. A well-diversified portfolio that includes exposure across all of these asset classes will most likely provide the most overall impact.

Investment Policy Statement Discussion Checklist

An IPS provides an opportunity for clarity. Boards not only have different answers about how the leading indicators interact, they also have varying investment expertise, goals, and tolerances. There is no single template for an investment policy statement.[24] Below, however, is a general outline of some of the topics that an IPS (and spending policy) might include. It can serve as a discussion guide to be adapted by each foundation:

Foundation Mission: A summary of the mission statement includes the passion, purpose, and interests that motivate the foundation as well as insights into whether it currently intends to exist in perpetuity or spend down over a specified number of years.

Grantmaking: An annual summary helps assure the grantmaking strategies — such as long-term and multi-year funding, big grants, or desire to be quick in responding to opportunistic opportunities or tragedies — are supported by the financial plan.

Division of Responsibilities: The ultimate fiduciary responsibility to manage the foundation's investments lies with the board in accordance with all laws and especially with the Uniform Management of Institutional Funds Act (UPMIFA).[25]

Investment Committee: Investment duties and responsibilities are typically delegated to an investment committee of board members and sometimes outside experts. The size, job description, number of meetings per year, reporting requirements to the full board, etc. are set forth. The investment committee is usually empowered to appoint external investment advisors or managers to work with the foundation. (A separate agreement with outside managers/advisors describes the responsibilities, reporting expectations, and areas of discretion delegated to them.) Members of the investment committee should not also be outside investment managers.

Investment Objectives: This covers overall guidelines for such things as the preservation of capital, income and liquidity targets, and investment time horizon, as well as any situations unique to the foundation. Measurements and ranges of acceptable risk and volatility are commonly outlined, here or in a separate section.

Spending Policy: A payout rate target should be established that is consistent with mission, lifespan, and grantmaking goals. Many foundations calculate spending policy on a three- to five-year rolling average to smooth the payout level. A spending policy may also be a separate document, but that seems unnecessary and can introduce inconsistencies between spending and the IPS.

Risk and Volatility: In many ways, the level of tolerable variability and risk embedded in an investment portfolio is as important as income. It is important to set short- and longer-term goals/targets/benchmarks.

Liquidity: What are the specific annual and medium-term cash or liquidity needs for the foundation's operations and grantmaking? What assets are included as liquid assets? What cash reserves should be planned for?

Asset Allocation Targets and Diversification: The heart of an IPS is asset allocation and diversification because they are major contributors to both investment returns and the management of risk and volatility. Recommended asset class targets, expected range, and the neutral weighting for the various accepted asset classes are outlined. Sophisticated investment policy statements will often include allocations for hedge funds, alternative investments and mission-related investments.

Permissible Investments: What types of investments are permissible within each asset class? An IPS may be quite broad here, giving managers wide discretion. Others may restrict international equities, lower-rated fixed income instruments, or real estate, etc. Social investing goals also can be discussed here that require social screens and other vehicles, program-related investment goals, etc.

Limitations on Investments: There are legal restrictions and limitations relating to types of investments, particularly relating to high-risk ones. It is important to recognize, limit or prohibit such investments — e.g., vehicles governed by jeopardizing investment rules, excess business holdings, self-dealing, UBIT — depending on the sophistication of the board.

Rebalancing: Market fluctuations and investment decisions change asset allocations from their targets over time. The best investment strategy is to consider rebalancing the portfolio in accordance with the target allocations. Address how often this should be done, and by whom. It is recommended that this be done at least annually, though investment managers are often given some discretion here.

Manage the Excise Tax: Foundations are still subject to an annual 2 percent excise tax on their net investment income. The tax can be reduced to 1 percent based on a formula of increasing annual levels of grantmaking. That can save considerable money. (There have been efforts for years to change the law and set a single rate, but to date, nothing has been done.) Many foundations explicitly plan to maintain a 1 percent rate. But an annually increasing level of charitable distributions can conflict with established payout goals, lifespan goals, and endowment growth targets. Many foundations also manage excise tax payments by reverting to the 2 percent rate every three to seven years to "rebalance" the level of charitable giving. The subsequent year they revert to paying the 1 percent.

Proxy Voting: Voting proxies used to be delegated to outside investment managers with little input or interest from the board. Today, casting proxy votes is seen as a method of increasing a foundation's mission impact. While many boards don't want to be bothered by deciding every case, they do give their managers specific mission-related guidelines or even hire outside consultants to advise them about these matters.

Performance Benchmarks: The changing economic environment demands ongoing assessment quarterly, annually, and, most helpfully, over a five-or-more-year rolling average. There are many approaches to assessing an investment portfolio's performance as well as the performance of outside managers and the investment committee. The IPS sets the relevant benchmarks, which usually include comparative market indices for return, volatility, and risk. Outside investment managers usually recommend market comparatives and the investment committee should be sure they make sense. Sometimes, independent firms are hired to perform such a review. Over a reasonable period (usually three to five years) the overall portfolio — as well as each individual asset class — should meet or surpass the comparable market indices.

Monitoring and Review: How often does the investment committee review results (often quarterly)? How often do outside managers meet with the investment committee and/or the entire board (at least annually and often biannually)? Finally, every five years or so outside managers should be assessed, with an eye towards renewing the engagement or seeking other managers.

Ongoing Review and Approval: An IPS is a living document and must be reviewed every three to five years to take into account any changes in the markets, mission, and in investment managers. As this is done, the new IPS should be dated, so there is no confusion about which provisions are current.

Conclusion: What Is a Foundation to Do?

Being engaged in foundation work can be immensely satisfying. That may be especially true when you are part of a family foundation. But satisfaction does not necessarily translate into effectiveness and impact. You are not embarking upon a "feel good" activity. The four key alignment factors above can be helpful guideposts on the way to foundation success.

When trustees sit down and discuss the four leading indicators presented, and how they interact for their foundation, alignment is possible, perhaps even likely. After all, some common impetus brings trustees together. With alignment comes a renewed understanding about what makes a foundation successful. When these factors are not discussed and not in sync, a trustee's labors and a foundation's efforts can be pulled in conflicting directions. Impact becomes elusive at best.

This is a reminder to have these discussions. Don't proceed on unexamined assumptions. The observations and questions posed here are intended to get the conversation going by pointing out some of the complex issues, varying motivations, and unintended consequences involved. In my experience, the process is neither onerous nor unduly time-consuming. Once these discussions begin, alignment can become almost a natural, iterative process that influences every board meeting. This process has a larger impact that will deeply influence the grantmaking strategies and help ensure the positive impact we all seek for our philanthropy.

This article originally appeared in Family Foundation Advisor, *Vol. 15, No. 6 (September/October 2016) and is reprinted here with permission. All other reproduction or distribution, in print or electronically, is prohibited. It is a bimonthly devoted to helping foundation administrators and professional advisors preserve foundation assets, avoid legal pitfalls, and ensure that the foundation has a positive impact on the community it serves. For more information, write Civic Research Institute, 4478 U.S. Route 27, P.O. Box 585, Kingston, NJ 08528, 609-683-4450. Web: http://www.civicresearchinstitute.com. Copyright © 2016 Civic Research Institute, Inc.*

---

[1] The Council on Foundations/Commonfund *2015 Study of Investment of Endowments for Private and Community Foundations* found an average return of 0.0 percent in 2015. The CIO of Commonfund, Mark Anson, warned "it could be a bumpy road ahead." In Megan O'Neill, "Foundation Investment Returns Fall, But Spending Rate Remains Steady," *The Chronicle of Philanthropy*, August 23, 2016.

[2] According to Exponent Philanthropy, only 71 percent. *2016 Foundation Operations and Management Report* (Washington, DC: Exponent Philanthropy, 2016), p. 11.

[3] See, e.g., Mark E. Neithercut, "Have a Mission to Preserve a Vision," *Family Foundation Advisor* Vol. 13, no. 6, Sept./Oct. 2014, p. 1; and Council on Foundations, "The Development of Mission and Values Statements for Family Foundations," Family Foundation Webinar, January 13, 2009. Organizations such as the National Center for Family Philanthropy, Exponent Philanthropy, and BoardSource also provide examples of focused and inspiring mission statements, as well as templates and outlines that might be useful.

[4] Kelin Gersick, *Generations of Giving* (Lanham, MD: Lexington Books, 2004), p 187.

[5] Loren Renz and David Wolcheck, *Perpetuity or Limited Lifespan: How do Family Foundations Decide?* (New York: Foundation Center, 2009), p. 1.

[6] Cf, for instance, Ray D. Madoff and Rob Reich, "Now or Forever: Rethinking Foundation Life Spans," *The Chronicle of Philanthropy*, March 30, 2016; and Emmett Carson, "Limits on the Life Spans of Foundation Endowments Make No Sense," *The Chronicle of Philanthropy*, April 28, 2016.

[7] Francie Ostrower, "Perpetuity or Spend-Down: Does the Notion of Lifespan Matter in Organized Philanthropy?" *The Nonprofit Quarterly*, March 31, 2016.

[8] Ian Wilhelm, "Philanthropy's Challenge: Communicating Its Value to Society." *The Chronicle of Philanthropy*, December 13, 2007.

[9] See for instance, Ostrower, *op. cit.*; and *Giving While Living: The Beldon Fund Spend-Out Story.* The Beldon Fund, 2009.

[10] While payout is often used to refer solely to grants, it is actually a complex calculation of the net investment assets of the previous year, including grants as well as administrative expenses related to charitable activities. It doesn't include investment related expenses. This article assumes payout includes grants and charitable administrative expenses.

[11] Exponent Philanthropy, *op. cit.*

[12] Heidi Waleson, *Beyond Five Percent: The New Foundation Payout Menu* (New York Regional Association of Grantmakers, Nd), p. 32.

[13] Michael Klausner, "When Time Isn't Money," *Stanford Social Innovation Review,* Spring, 2003, p. 58.

[14] See, for instance, *Smarter Giving for Private Foundations.* (New York: AllianceBernstein, 2010).

[15] See, for instance, Cambridge Associates, Inc., *Sustainable Payout for Foundations* (Grand Haven, MI: Council of Michigan Foundations, 2000); DeMarche Associates, *Spending Policies and Investment Planning for Foundations*, originally prepared by Donald W. Trotter in 1990, updated in 1995, and updated again by Carter R. Harrison in 1999. (Washington, DC: Council on Foundations. 1999).

[16] Stanley Kogelman, *Wealth Preservation: The Spending Rate Matters More Than Asset Allocation.* (New York: J.P. Morgan Private Bank, 2002), p. 2 of the Summary and p. 18.

[17] Petra Bignami, *Sustainable Payout for Foundations: 2013 Update Study.* (Cambridge: Cambridge Associates, 2013), p. 2.

[18] Deep, Akash and Peter Frumkin, "The Foundation Payout Puzzle", in *Taking Philanthropy Seriously*, edited by William Damon and Susan Verducci. (Bloomington, IN: Indiana University Press, 2006). Pages 189–204.

[19] Exponent Philanthropy, *op. cit.* p. 1.

[20] Ben Gose, "Foundations are Cautious on Impact Investing." *The Chronicle of Philanthropy*, December 1, 2015. For more general discussions of social-impact investing, see Matt Alsted, Charles Lowenhaupt, and Don Trone, "A Ripe Time to Align Principles With Purpose and Process," *Family Foundation Advisor*, Vol. 11, No. 2, Jan./Feb. 2012; Jeffrey A. Zaluda, Brian H. Axelrad and Chelsey E. Ziegler, "Tax Considerations of Double Bottom Line Investing, Part I," *Journal of Taxation of Investments*, Vol. 32, No. 1, Fall 2014; Jeffrey A. Zaluda, Brian H. Axelrad and Chelsey E. Ziegler, "Tax Considerations of Double Bottom Line Investing, Part II," *Journal of Taxation of Investments*, Vol. 33, No. 1, Fall 2015.

[21] See Katherine E. David, "Recent IRS Guidance Affirms 'Mission-Related' Investing," *Family Foundation Advisor*, Vol. 15, No. 1, (Nov./Dec. 2015).

[22] Paul Brest and Kelly Born, "When Can Impact Investing Create Real Impact?" *Stanford Social Innovation Review*, Fall 2013. Also see this interesting attempt to bring performance measurement to bear: *Introducing the Impact Investing Benchmark* (Cambridge: Cambridge Associates/Global Impact Investing Network, 2015).

[23] Ben Gose, "Investment Returns: Time to Lower Expectations," *The Chronicle of Philanthropy*, December 1, 2015.

[24] See "Investment Policy Statements for Nonprofit Organizations." (New York: Greystone Consulting/Morgan Stanley Smith Barney, 2013). There are many other web resources, templates and samples available from organizations such as Exponent Philanthropy and the National Center for Family Philanthropy.

[25] Information about UPMIFA and State enactment status is available from the Uniform Law Commission, at uniformlaws.org (search "Prudent Management of Institutional Funds Act).

CHAPTER 5

THE INTERGENERATIONAL TRANSFER OF
WEALTH AND GIVING

What difference can individual and organized philanthropy make? The answer requires both an estimate of the capacity of individuals and organized philanthropy to fill any gap and also a sense of strategy about how organized philanthropy might use its funds and influence to address the issue.... The future will have to be pieced together from disparate sources, but the capacity is there. What is needed is leadership, will, and the incentives to produce such changes. — William Diaz, et al.

... at the root of much of the interest in the measurement of giving: improving the reliability and rigor of charitable statistics could help in the effort to encourage Americans to give more, and to give more efficiently. At the same time, the research would help to delineate the limits of the sector in the face of the exaggerated notions of what voluntarism could accomplish.... we may be witnessing a new wave of interest in charitable statistics. If so, this is an important opportunity to think carefully about why, what, and how we are counting.... The insights that we glean ... can help ensure that when we assess American generosity, we are measuring the things that matter most to us. As Nobel laureate economist Joseph Stiglitz — who knows a thing or two about the value and perils of quantitative indicators — reminded us in 2009, "What you measure affects what you do. If you don't measure the right thing, you don't do the right thing." — Benjamin Soskis

T he prospect of a huge intergenerational transfer of wealth becomes news every few years, especially about portions that might go into philanthropy. (Remember that I use the term to include the entire nonprofit sector.) Phrases like "a golden age of philanthropy is dawning" and "the windfall years" are common. There is a lot of truth in this, never mind that transfers are a continuous feature of life and death. But "we" 79 million baby boomers are in 2019 entering the "busiest era for estates closing." Lucky us!

The outlook is a siren song and easy sound bite. The number are huge. For the ten-year period 2018–2027, the estimated wealth transfer is $8.5 trillion with $424 billion potentially going to philanthropy. For the fifty-year period 2017–2067, the numbers are $89.7 trillion, with $4.5 trillion potentially going to philanthropy. These projections are contingent upon many assumptions, such as the actual giving by the wealthy; the status of the economy; and the ability of the sector to make the case that donations will meet a donor's values and have impact.

It has always struck me that this phenomenon is reported as if it (1) appears *ex nihilo*, out of nothing, and (2) may arrive in foundation and nonprofit checking accounts with a minimum of fuss and effort. It is as if the money is just sitting there, waiting for people to die. Then it can be harvested from donors for heirs and philanthropy. Nothing could be further from the truth. The prospect of a windfall too easily drowns out a fuller understanding of the contingencies that will affect size and allocation of such a vast intergenerational transfer of wealth.

The first article in this chapter was written for this volume. It gives a brief history of this intergenerational transfer idea and brings it up to date. In doing so, I take very seriously the cautionary remarks of both William Diaz and Bill Soskis, quoted at the beginning of this chapter. And this brief history is also penned in appreciation of the work of Paul Schervish and John Havens. They produced much of the data underlying the idea and size of an intergenerational transfer. Easily as important, they also (Paul especially) did so much to emphasize the values and culture of care behind philanthropy, family giving, and the numbers. Neither aspect of their work is the last word on complex subjects. But without appreciating and "operationalizing" Paul's words on the spirituality of giving and the culture of care, the full capacity of this transfer phenomenon will not happen.

The second article combines three articles. It gives my perspective from the mid-1990s. In 1994, 1995, and 1996 I wrote three outlooks on the transfer. One was written for donors, a second for the nonprofit sector, and the third was a keynote address to fundraising professionals.

1. The Making of the Intergenerational Transfer

One early notice of an intergenerational transfer came from two respected tax specialists in 1987. While the relationship of wealth and giving wasn't well researched back then, authors Gerald Auten and Eugene Steuerle predicted a significant increase in the rate of giving:

> The American people have always been extraordinarily generous in their charitable endeavors. A number of factors, however, combine to make us believe that this past generosity may even be surpassed and that the near future could see an increase in the rate of giving or, more formally, in the percent of national income devoted to charitable causes.[1]

Much has happened — and much has been forgotten — since then. This new article takes a summary look at some of the hoopla about an intergenerational transfer over the last thirty years, until now, when those peak transfer years are starting for baby boomers. Then I highlight some of the key features, risks, and possibilities. This cannot be the last word on the topic and I hope these issues will be more robustly discussed and some significant actions taken to encourage the hoped-for result. Only in that way will this intergenerational transfer not only come to fruition for philanthropy but will do so productively for donors, the field and civil society.

New Life for the Voluntary Sector?

The early talk about an intergenerational transfer of wealth that would accrue in some significant way to the nonprofit sector came at just the right time. The sector has always been seen in schizophrenic ways: as both crucial and invisible. The decades after World War II saw an increasing sense that *if* the sector could develop in healthy and vital ways, there would be new and robust opportunities to address the myriad of problems of a complex civil society. There was a huge increase in the number of nonprofits. There was, as well, an enormous increase in government and use of the sector by government, which was blurring the lines between voluntary institutions and the government. While real partnerships were important, Peter Drucker and others voiced the urgent need for a realignment and a "new social priority," if the problems and challenges of American society are to be met:

> Government has proved incompetent at solving social problems. Virtually every success we have scored has been achieved by non-

profits.... "Nonprofitization" may for modern societies be the way out of mismanagement by welfare bureaucracies.[2]

In late 1989, at a meeting of major foundation executives, Peter Goldmark, then president of the Rockefeller Foundation, was reported as saying, "Whether you are liberal or conservative, there's a sense now that private initiative is preferable to state.... What's better for the country? Does this money belong in government's pocket? Or should it go to those *thousand points of light?*"

One of the sticking points of course is, where are the funds? Goldmark had addressed that issue too, when he said, "We have the wherewithal. It is supply driven: I personally know five donors who each could create Ford Foundation-size foundations tomorrow."[3] It almost seemed that the supply side could take care of itself, thanks to a changing ethos of inheritance, the size of the baby-boom generation, economic growth, and a resultant huge transfer of wealth. From the 1980s, a golden age of philanthropy seemed increasingly likely. As William Diaz and associated authors noted in 1996:

> What difference can individual and organized philanthropy make? The answer requires both an estimate of the capacity of individuals and organized philanthropy to fill any gap and also a sense of strategy about how organized philanthropy might use its funds and influence to address the issue.... The future will have to be pieced together from disparate sources, but the capacity is there. What is needed is leadership, will, and the incentives to produce such changes.[4]

However, most of the time, the idea that philanthropy had the capacity was quickly dismissed with a curt sound bite. A fuller discussion and research hardly seemed necessary. Key contingencies didn't get much attention. Even in those early years, this transfer was couched as a possibility. Consider what else Auten and Steuerle wrote in 1987:

> These results are not inevitable, however. Potential donors need to be convinced of the unique value other charitable dollars have when effectively and productively spent. Individuals appear to be influenced by the nature of the appeals and requests made of them. An increase in the future supply of giving, therefore, will be determined partly by the way in which the charitable sector puts forward the "demand" for giving.[5]

They warned that the supply of wealth *for* philanthropy faced two especially important hurdles from that the demand side. First, there was the cogency of the "ask," the demand for contributions coming from the philanthropic sector. This is a crucial point and goes well beyond the mere professionalism and practical messaging of fundraising and development. It speaks to the effectiveness and efficiency of the sector generally and to how well specific organizations are meeting needs and mission. The implication was — and is — that nonprofits must do a much better job of attaining and documenting results and then communicating them if they are to attract and keep donors for whom values and results matter. There is still time.

There is a second part of the demand side: the values and motivations of the donors themselves and the different choices they can make with their funds. I remember attending one of the early Indiana University Center on Philanthropy *Taking Fundraising Seriously* symposia in the early 1990s. During a session, a director of fundraising for a mid-sized college turned to me and noted in admiration, "This is the first time I have attended a fundraising session where listening to donors and taking their values and perspective is taken so seriously." As Paul Schervish and John Havens have often pointed out: "the meaning and practice of wealth transfer among the very wealthy need to be understood in a new way and that to do so reveals why so many current research findings involving the very wealthy are at best ambiguous and at worst mistaken."[6] Misunderstandings about what drives the behavior of the wealthy — as well at the not-so-wealthy — remains a deeply embedded part of the *weltanschauung* of the sector. Better research about the varieties of data sources used also remain confusing and very incomplete.[7]

While Schervish and Havens are best known for their estimates of the size of the possible transfer, by far the most important part of their work (and especially Paul's) has been researching and thinking about:

> how the wealthy actually come to obtain a philanthropic identity.... Defining philanthropy as a social relation of *caritas* suggests that efforts to improve the quality of philanthropy among the wealthy, including increasing their generosity, entails a two-fold attention to the issues of self-identity.... We must see philanthropy as a matter of self-development among donors.... It means expanding the horizons of care within which donors experience an obligation of identification, a vocation of communion, with other human beings as radical ends.[8]

This is not a new insight particular to Schervish. But the point is still imperfectly understood and even less perfectly implemented in fundraising. When values and impact don't drive philanthropy and donors, they are often beneath the surface. And being more explicit about it may be a firmer basis for the growth of philanthropy in the future. We need to keep trying![9] Much of Schervish's writings and those of others are very useful and provocative here. Schervish has often explored what he calls the "moral biography of wealth" and the many "vectors" of a "new physics of philanthropy" that motivates the wealthy. They are not as well-known as they should be. They are philosophically, sociologically and practically important. Going into detail is beyond the scope of this article, but it strikes me that his work and that of others on this topic are an extremely important part of understanding how and why an intergenerational transfer of wealth can lead to such an outpouring of charitable feelings *and* funds.[10]

The key point is that, rather than focus on the sheer potential size of a generational transfer — $10, $41, $59 or $90 trillion — policy wonks, commentators, and the sector itself should shift attention to what many wealth holders are already doing, and help them to do it better:

> To the extent wealth holders begin to complement an orientation based on accumulating wealth, with one based on disposing of that wealth in accordance with their values and goals, they will be the progenitors of a golden age of philanthropy.[11]

The Intergenerational Transfer of Wealth: Then and Now

For all of that, size does matter. Since the three articles that follow this one were written in the mid-1990s, the remarkable work of Paul Schervish and John Havens beginning in 1998 gave the intergenerational transfer of wealth idea serious intellectual heft. For a very long time, the thought of $41 trillion being transferred — with $6 trillion potentially going to charity — between 1998 and 2052 was mesmerizing.[12] There were always various assumptions, scenarios, and caveats, of course. They provoked controversies and disagreements and that is a good thing. In 2003, Schervish and Havens reevaluated and stuck to those numbers.[13]

Then, in 2014, Havens and Schervish released their final report based on 2011 numbers. This report took into consideration the devastation of the Great Recession, but still, "wealth transfer adjusted for the recession … exceeds our 1999 estimates…. 12 percent greater than our original estimate."

Assuming 2 percent growth and a subsequent increase in the estate tax exemption to $5 million, these 2014 transfer estimates (in 2007 dollars) are large (all very conservative assumptions):

For the 20-year period 2007–2026:
- estimated wealth transfer of $15.55 trillion
- charitable potential of $6.4 trillion

For the 55-year period 2007–2061:

- estimated wealth transfer of $59 trillion
- charitable potential of nearly $26.9 trillion

These were only estimates, though for many they took on a life of their own. This was complex work they did and there are many caveats, scenarios, and assumptions.[14] *Giving USA* and the Retirement Institute suggested different estimates and many scholars and practitioners thought the estimates unrealistically high or, as fundraising consultant Robert Sharpe put it, "These projections set a very low bar."[15] On the charitable side, Havens and Schervish noted two key factors that would determine the actual transfer amount and allocation. First, "Americans at every income and wealth level tend to identify with the needs of others in society and try to help in ways that are appropriate to their circumstances." Second, if fundraisers and charitable causes become more effective in their approach to fundraising — and I would strongly add, in their organizational efficiency and effectiveness — "they have an opportunity to increase the amount that goes to charity well above our estimate."[16]

Schervish and Havens retired in 2015 and the Center on Wealth and Philanthropy closed its doors. The wealth transfer baton — largely following the methodologies Schervish and Havens used — has been carried forward in 2018 by a partnership between LOCUS Impact Investing and the Center for Rural Entrepreneurship. They presented new, eye-popping indeed, estimates of the transfer potential. They mostly focused on a shorter, ten-year time span, 2018–2027. At their low growth assumption of 2 percent and with a 5 percent plug for charity, they estimated:[17]

For the 10-year period 2018–2027:
- estimated wealth transfer of $8.5 trillion
- charitable potential of $424 billion

For the 50-year period 2017–2067:
- estimated wealth transfer of $89.7 trillion
- charitable potential of nearly $4.5 trillion

The Future and Its Uncertain Possibilities

So how is it turning out, this intergenerational transfer of such wealth? We still don't know how donors and families will behave over the long haul; we don't know how the economy will perform; and we don't know how philanthropy and advisors will improve their ask and results. The impact of the 2017 tax bill has brought with it contrasting predictions of more giving or considerably less giving. No doubt new tax machinations will wash over us all. We don't yet know what short-term and especially longer-term effects there will be, as individual behavior changes and adjusts. *Giving USA* reported in 2018 that the last three years have seen record charitable giving. Giving in 2017 grew to $410 billion, 3 percent up from 2016.[18] But the number of individuals giving is declining. It is not clear why, but that is a troubling trend. A recent article reports that "the *Chronicle's* reporting over the past year suggests that the future of philanthropy might be shaky."[19] There are indeed troubling signs, though the six "worrisome trends" listed in the article seemed, well, confusing, contradictory, or mostly irrelevant.

These trends, however, refer mostly to giving from income. The big transfers from the wealthy come from a different angle. As many have noted, giving from net worth wealth is different from giving from income. For instance, the positive effect of the charitable deduction on the amount of *income* given by individuals may be different from what drives the amount of net *wealth* going to philanthropy.[20] The tendency to give more when thinking in terms of wealth — especially in an estate planning context — occurs most often among the very wealthy.

Families with significant wealth also act differently. Beginning in 2018, notes this baby boomer ruefully, we are entering the busiest time for baby-boomer deaths and estate giving. It appears that there is a trend of more going to philanthropy. Schervish noted this in 2000: "there appears to be a growing preference among the very wealthiest estates for charitable bequests … there must be some additional positive disposition coming into play that accounts for the upswing in the proportions of large estates going to charity beyond taxes."[21] My sense is that this tendency is still very much in play. As individuals adjust to changes in the tax law, I hypothesize giving will increase significantly. One gigantic caveat is that the constant seesaw of changes in tax regulations introduce tremendous uncertainty and that will upset charitable planning. We just need to know more and follow the trends. We need to make sure charitable intent and giving are encouraged, and that they are free of intended or unintended consequences that will dampen such a robust aspect of civil society.

What follows are brief discussions of some of the key factors that can make or break that giving phenomenon: helping to determine the size and impact of this potential golden age of philanthropy. In doing so, I will use the structure I used above: first, address some key issues about the "supply," second, address the "demand" side from the donor's perspective, and finally look at the demand side from the nonprofit arena and what needs to be done to encourage philanthropy in this time. (My use of the terms *supply* and *demand* differ from how Schervish uses them. For me, *supply* refers to the amount that might be transferred and is most affected by exogenous factors like economic growth and taxes. I take the demand side to include the demand from donors to give and the demand and need from nonprofits.)

The Supply Side: Promoting Economic Growth and the Costs of Recession

Philanthropy is a derivative phenomenon; money is given for that purpose. The questions are how much, and what factors, intentionally and unintentionally, help determine scale. In his brief monograph written many years ago, economist Richard McKenzie wrote:

> Little has been written on how the flow of philanthropic contributions is linked to the institutional setting — that is, the economic and political systems — within which these contributions must emerge.... philanthropy is fundamentally tied to economic success, and economic success is, no doubt, tied inextricably to institutions — in particular, markets. [22]

The failure to connect economic success with philanthropic wherewithal and success does continue. Recently, Nobelist Edmund Phelps makes the very important point that "the modern economy answered a widespread desire for the good life":

> Far from being a system of materialism, coarseness, Babbitry, Philistinism, and greed that stands in the way of the good life, the modern economy answered a widespread desire for the good life.[23]

That is true, and that dynamism also accrues to philanthropy. However, the connection between economic success and philanthropy is nearly entirely missing in this fine scholarly and inspiring book. Indeed, Phelps seems to relegate nonprofits, foundations, churches, and the home to being sanctuaries for "finding traditional values" of community, the state, and a safety net. That is hardly the liberal tradition of civil society, in such a valuable, genuinely liberal book. In two places, Phelps does note Tocqueville's appreciation of the dynamism possible in the voluntary sector. Many other economists see the connection. Overall, however, Phelps seems to miss most of the connection between economic dynamism and the dynamism in philanthropy and civil society. Too many commentators from the philanthropic side also ignore the key role of economic success in philanthropy.

It would not be out of place to ask in what ways might philanthropy aid or hinder a golden age of philanthropy. We need that kind of discussion to ensure that more funds flow to philanthropy. That "more" is possible because of a dynamic and growing economy. As Schervish and Havens noted: "anyone who wants to boost lifetime giving must also attend to what is required to promote strong and steady growth in the economy.... a growing and vibrant economy that fulfills the desires for family well-being is an indispensable ally of philanthropy."[24] Indeed, purely on a self-interested scale, promoting economic growth would be a bigger win for philanthropy than advocating, for instance, steep estate taxes and bigger philanthropic deductions. Attending to economic growth may be the most important way to ensure a golden age of philanthropy. Let us briefly consider three aspects of this.

Economic Growth

The most recent transfer projections from LOCUS assume an average real rate of growth in household wealth at 3 percent. Their projected spread between low growth of 2 percent and high growth of 4 percent is very telling for the generational transfer projections that might go to philanthropy. It starkly shows the impact of economic growth on philanthropic "supply" and "income." From their estimates:

Over the next decade:

- At 2 percent growth, philanthropy is projected to get $424 billion.
- At 4 percent it is $459 billion, a difference of $35 billion or 8.25 percent.

Over the next 50 years:

- At 2 percent growth, philanthropy is projected to get $4.49 trillion.
- At 4 percent it is $6.01 trillion. That is a difference of $1.52 trillion or 34 percent.

The size of this impact could be greater. The noticeable trend among high net worth families is to allocate more wealth to philanthropy in lifetime and in estates, and away from heirs. The current 2018 federal estate and gift tax exemption is $11,180,000 per person. While estate taxes may encourage some charitable gifts to avoid estate taxes, the large exemption can also mean that a lot more funds of the very wealthy might not go to taxes and thus be available for charitable purposes. How important that is needs more research to determine, but very suggestive answers are mentioned briefly below.

The Great Recession

We should be chastened, however, by the knowledge that economic growth rises and falls. The current strong economic years will not continue indefinitely. President Trump's trade tariffs and other economic craziness make the end of the boom more likely and the fall likely more precipitous, if history and simple economic theory are any guide. We will see.

The economic loss occasioned by the Great Recession (end of 2007 to June 2009) shows the "cost" to philanthropy of greatly reduced economic dynamism and growth. As a static point in time, the fourth quarter of 2008 GDP growth was a remarkable negative 8.2 percent.[25] That represents a significant loss to the economy, jobs, families, etc. As Schervish and Havens noted in their 2014 report: "[H]ousehold wealth (as measured by net worth) declined by about 25 percent both on average and in aggregate during the recession. Moreover, the loss of wealth was pervasive…. It's worth repeating this important finding: half the households in the country lost more than 80 percent of their aggregate wealth during the recession." That all had a major impact on the ability of households generally to make donations. For wealthy families, the impact was still real but "the recession's impact on wealth transfer and charitable giving was somewhat attenuated."[26]

Schervish and Havens estimated that about $350 billion would have gone to charity if the Great Recession had not occurred. Even if high, that suggests an extraordinary cost to philanthropy.[27]

Whatever combination of government and market failures conspired to bring on the Great Recession, the impact on philanthropic dollars likely available to civil society is huge, but rarely a topic of notice. While there is disagreement on such a complex topic, there is considerable evidence that numerous government and regulatory failures were among the precipitating causes for such an economically painful time. This is a sobering reminder of how policy can affect economic stability, dynamism and growth, with massive unanticipated consequences and costs to philanthropy and civil society. The point here is simply that philanthropy has a big stake in economic growth.

Scholars, practitioners, and philanthropic leaders need to be more knowledgeable about these effects. We don't need to be uncritical of some of the results of economic growth and dynamism. But we do need to note with appreciation the power of growth and of its supply of funds for the philanthropic sector. It deserves significant, nuanced support. The dynamism of the economy was on show in the post-recession period that recouped the losses from the Great Recession. Schervish and Havens raised their new, post-recession projections from their early 1999 projections.

With almost evangelical fervor, they intoned: "a golden age of philanthropy still beckons as a shining beacon at the end of this long recession."[28]

The Taxing Question

The issue of the estate tax and its exclusion has been a perennial controversy. It is complex and there have been many and changing perspectives on it. The usual assumption had been that estate taxes positively affect the amount of wealth transfer going to philanthropy by "pushing" funds to charity in order to minimize estate taxes. That appears to have been true, but its continuing relevance over time is in question. For one thing, the estate tax also decreases the dollars available for charitable bequests. There has been evidence for that. A 2000 Bankers Trust survey found that reducing the estate tax would likely produce a significant increase in the amount going to charity (i.e., a 76 percent reduction in taxes would result in a 63 percent increase in bequests to charity).[29] In addition, a variety of estimates have shown that a greatly reduced estate tax burden had other positive externalities. A reduction in the unproductive economic activity devoted to tax avoidance and estate tax minimization would increase the amount of funds going for productive uses in the economy (jobs, etc.). As a result, some models have shown that the rate of economic growth could grow meaningfully — thereby further increasing the amount available to philanthropy.

Even so, the large estates had presumably always been greatly influenced to make charitable bequests by the size of the bite of the estate tax and the size of the exemption. Schervish and Havens, for instance, had held that view. By 2001, their extensive data research and many surveys of wealthy individuals led them to reevaluate that view: "wealth holders are already shifting bequests from heirs to charity." [30]

They found that other factors were more important in influencing giving. The estate tax actually dampened charitable giving: "that wealth-holders do not look to taxes as the sole or even primary factor in allocating their final or lifetime giving. The question is not just one of quantity: how much for me or for the government? It is more a question of quality: quality of life for me, my family and my community."[31] This is a very important issue that rings true from my limited experience. It needs more survey data and research. In any case, the current very large estate tax exemption is partially a recognition of the estate tax's ineffectiveness on multiple levels. (See, for instance, my piece in Chapter 8 for a brief look at is ineffectiveness.) As Schervish summarizes both the supply and demand side:

If the repeal of the estate tax leads to greater national and personal economic growth and unleashes the compelling motivations of voluntary choice and care for others, then there is reason to believe that the trends I cite [the data showing "there appears to be a growing preference among the very wealthiest estates for charitable bequests"] will continue, perhaps even flourish, as tax considerations fade. [32]

> ... tax incentives may in fact be fading in importance as a motivation for charitable giving... the introduction of the supply-side approach as integral to fund raising and to financial planning strategies increases the probability that charitable giving will be pursued as a personally fulfilling and socially productive decision, independent of tax benefits.... the customary relation, or conventionally conceived relation, between estate taxes and charitable giving may no longer obtain. [33]

It certainly appears that estate tax considerations are diminishing in a donor's hierarchy of motivations. Perhaps charitable giving can be and will be pursued more often because of the values it expresses for donors, its family legacy, and it socially conscious impact. It is incumbent upon scholars to research this apparent shift. And policy makers need to factor in these value complexities as they think about both how to encourage philanthropy and determine what role an estate or other tax regime should have.

Most important, it suggests that the "ask" and the case made for philanthropy have to become more value-based and less reliant upon external, tax minimization strategies. What would have seemed incongruous at one point may now more likely fuel the demand side of the intergenerational transfer of wealth:

> ... a repeal of the estate tax may be the basis for a new era of spiritual depth in philanthropy — revolving in part around making the voluntary act of charity truly voluntary, rather than a financial strategy.[34]

The Demand Side: Donor Motivations and Philanthropy's Case

I divide the demand side of the generational transfer phenomenon into two parts. One part considers the changing motivations for, and the use of, inheritance and giving that individuals and families consider when they decide how to allocate their wealth. And then there is the case that philanthropy and nonprofits — as well as financial and legal advisors —

make in their solicitations for funding. They need to attend to the interests and values of donors and families. They need to be compelling and persuasive. Both elements will have a significant impact on the extent to which the transfer of wealth flourishes (and indirectly upon the success and impact of that support).

As more donors seem to rely on values, personal passions, and choices within a larger family context, advisors and nonprofits will have to be more sensitive to those motivations regarding the charitable use of those funds. Lack of sensitivity by preferencing tax and financial consideration might mean squandering this amazing opportunity.

The Changing Ethos of Inheritance

Individuals facing estate questions usually consider family first. What kind of inheritance is possible and what will make sense on all sorts of levels? Back in 1988, John Langbein published an article that proved to be quite prescient. "The Twentieth Century Revolution in Wealth Transmission" discussed significant changes in the "ethos of inheritance" as he called it.[35] First, there was, he saw, a shift to *inter vivos* transfers — i.e., while living — instead of solely depending on bequests. Among other things, this often meant using money on human capital development for heirs instead of holding it back until death. Passing on an "ethical will," both explicitly and through example, to heirs is part of this too. When Schervish and Havens looked at 2004 data, they concluded that: "this analysis suggests that in addition to income and wealth, inheritance status has a positive effect on charitable giving."[36] There continues to be ample anecdotal evidence to suggest so.

Second, along with *inter vivos* transfers, there was a tendency to limit the amount of inheritance going to heirs. The very wealthy often fret about spoiling their kids or giving them too much. This worry is more prevalent now for a variety of reasons. For example, as wealth increases, the percentage that is "needed" to get children started or to provide a safety net decreases. A vibrant, growing economy reduces the perceived need to leave a safety net — our children will be just fine. Patriarchs and matriarchs are also learning that "modeling" charitable behavior, instilling such values, and even leaving charitable dollars for heirs to steward, are all increasingly valuable inheritances in and of themselves.

It seems that Langbein's perceptions have turned out to be largely correct. This is certainly a topic that deserves greater exploration. But wealthy donors are changing the way they look at and integrate philanthropy into their lives and plans.

THE INTERGENERATIONAL TRANSFER

Donor Motivations and Values

Different motivations and values are beginning to drive the nature and limiting factors about inheritance. The dollar sizes of potential inheritances and the worries about encouraging lazy heirs are there. But something else important is afoot. The motivations around both inheritance and giving seem to be changing: expression of values, quality of life, human capital development, and the meaning of life may be more prominent in the hierarchy of values of the very wealthy. I believe that some anecdotal evidence shows this. The available "supply" of funds swelling the transfer possibilities is thus often being driven by the "demand" of donors and families to express their larger philanthropic values for heirs and nonprofits. The Giving Pledge is an example, but the point often applies at lesser levels of wealth. There is this sense of wanting to leave a broad "legacy of care." Again, as Schervish and Havens noted in 2006:

> ... a legacy of care, both for their heirs' well-being and for charity, prompts wealth-holders to limit inheritances and to allocate more to charity. ... the critical factor for wealth-holders who are allocating a large estate is their concern for a legacy of care... In sum, the wealthiest Americans do not appear to be trying to maximize the transfer of wealth to their heirs. It seems instead that once wealth-holders recognize their families are financially secure, they tend to look for deeper purposes for their material means.[37]

This ongoing search for values and motivations beyond self is key. It helps donors and families to apply different motivations to their financial allocations of estates. These values will turn what is only a statistical possibility of a huge intergenerational transfer for philanthropy into reality. More research and analysis are needed to confirm both trends on the donor/family side in the waning years of the baby boomers. In fact, while not appreciated or given the attention that the bare numbers have gotten, Schervish and Haven always emphasized the crucial importance of a growing sense of a creative moral purpose to the growth of philanthropic capacity. In their original monograph in 1999, they identified an "array of cultural trends and new estate planning approaches" that would add a

> ... further positive shift in charitable inclination and away from heirs. Even more significant is that we do not project any additional positive shift toward charity and away from taxes — something the entire financial and charitable industries are now

counting on and encouraging, and something wealth holders are inclined to do.... [38]

This is one of the reasons I have relied so much on the work of Schervish and Havens. From the beginning they emphasized the importance of a shift to a more robust sense of creative moral purpose, a more vivid values-based case for philanthropy, and the attending to the possibilities of a donor and family's moral biography of wealth. Sometimes it was not entirely clear how much of their emphasis was normative and how much a positive description of what exists. But I think that ambiguity captures the complex interaction of the actual and the possible that is, after all, the nature of social life. They both are important as trends capable of "presaging a golden age of philanthropy."

Yet, twenty years later, emphasizing the value-based motivations for growing philanthropy continues to be crowded out by the mesmerizing raw numbers. As baby boomers face the "prime" years for the transfer, one should *accentuate* the: (1) values of philanthropy to donors and families and (2) the effectiveness and efficiency of nonprofits as the other reason to give.

Nonprofits Making the Case for Philanthropy

Twenty-five years after my initial articles, it is telling that the editor of *The Chronicle of Philanthropy* introduced the new transfer estimates in 2018 with "Get Ready for the Golden Age." But she also laid out a clear admonition:

> If nonprofits take smart steps now, by 2027 we could see the dollar equivalent of 10 Gates Foundations pour into philanthropy.... [These estimates] should serve as a call to action for organizations to get more serious about asking their most loyal supporters to make philanthropy part of their legacy."[39]

I read this caution in part as a too gentle acknowledgment of the failure of nonprofits to connect with donors on the levels of values and compelling results. This is not the place to speculate on why it is that philanthropy and the nonprofit sector have too often been tone-deaf to donors, often mediocre on results, and meek on their responsibilities to society. Don Macke of the Center for Rural Entrepreneurship that helped develop the latest transfer estimates, urged on nonprofits: "Now it's up to you to go out and capture some of that."[40] The opportunity is there and has been lingering under the numbers since presentation of the idea of an intergenerational transfer of wealth become a sound-bite. Nonprofits must do much, much better on two fronts. We will see.

One practical need is for financial and legal advisors, as well at the leadership and development people in the sector, to engage donors and families at these levels of values and results. They need to support this inclination for donors and heirs to reflection and make wise donor decisions and wise philanthropic choices. This isn't just a matter of communicating differently. It means listening to and engaging donors.

It also means the sector needs to make its case based on organizational and program efficiency and effectiveness (not just talk a good game about it). They need to prove they have real, valuable results to show for the support they seek. This is an area, I am afraid, where philanthropic leaders and development people, as well as, financial and legal advisors have been less than forthcoming. They seem eager to deflect such thorny questions. Here again, I think Schervish raises a challenge that is as true today as it was then. Instead of focusing on tax incentives, for instance:

> ... charities and fund raisers might do better to contemplate how to become effective in a new environment, one in which contributions can flow to them — via a far less circuitous and expensive rout — from donors with deeper pockets and fuller hearts."[41]

This will take time. Increases in giving are not automatic and require changes in the case made to give. Throughout this brief look at the idea of the intergenerational transfer, it seems the sector has generally been unprepared to take advantage of and make real what remains a truly huge "supply," which remains forever potential until nonprofits can make a more effective case.

Conclusion

My experience with donors and development professionals spans thirty years. While admittedly anecdotal and by no means universal, I found donors and families struggling with the values and legacies they wanted to impart. While not uppermost in their minds, the effectiveness of the organizations they gave to was very important. And yet, both financial advisors and fund raisers tended to rely on tax minimization as the presumed motivator for charity. I was astonished how little development people knew about programs and their impact. I would watch as a spiel for support was vague. Prospective donors would zone out even as they wanted to support the cause. The values and mission of the organization as well as knowledge about the programs and results were too often glossed over. I rarely saw donors asked questions about their values. They tended to be talked "at" rather than listened "to."

Yet the "tax deductibility angle" was usually not number one in the hierarchy of reasons donors had for giving. Practically speaking, talking values, causes, etc., *is* uncomfortable to many professionals; it is seemingly outside their bailiwick and comfort zone. Perhaps it was viewed as an intrusion upon the donor.

I always felt donors wanted and deserved a more value-based engagement about their financial and family legacy planning. That is happening more, but still not enough. Nonprofits are still hesitant about promoting their results, for whatever reason. That failure doesn't do justice to their mission or it hides lack of results. In any case, nonprofits and donors owe it to themselves and to the "partnership" between them, to adjust the terms of their discussions and to acknowledge that values and results matter.

This article started as an exploration and history of the idea of the intergenerational transfer of wealth for philanthropy that has garnered so much press and anticipation over the last several decades. The prospect is a heady one indeed, not just for the nonprofit organizations that may benefit financially. It also suggests something positive and hopeful about the vitality of the American economy, civil society and the "character" of its people. Donors and families know they have a stake in the values of philanthropy and can have a very large impact. So, behind the excitement of stale projections of very big dollars, there does indeed remain the possibility of a "golden age of philanthropy," if only…

Perhaps it is fitting, then, to leave the last word to Paul Schervish in his 2008 article "Why the Wealthy Give" (and I would argue that his comments often apply to the not-so-wealthy, too):

> Increasing numbers of wealth holders and at an earlier age are seeking to understand the creative moral purpose and not just the quantitative prospects of their wealth. In essence, they are capable of asking and seeing answers about how to deploy their wealth as a tool to achieve the deeper purposes of life when achieving a higher standard of living or acquiring more wealth ceases to be of high importance. They face the question about how to live and impart to their children a moral biography of wealth while, at the same time, expanding the quality and quantity of care for the moral biography of others. Clarifying and drawing on the motivations that mobilized the allocation of wealth for philanthropy will help individuals make care simultaneously for neighbor and self a path to greater happiness, which I define as the confluence of effectiveness and significance.[42]

This article was written expressly for this volume, to provide a current summary about the intergenerational phenomena. It is also meant to acknowledge the very important continuing relevance of the broad thinking of Paul Schervish and John Havens. I and the field are deeply indebted to them.

---

[1] Gerald Auten and Eugene Steuerle, "The Coming Boom Years for Charitable Giving," *Philanthropy,* Winter 1987-88.

[2] Peter F. Drucker, "It Profits Us to Strengthen Nonprofits," *The Wall Street Journal,* December 19, 1991.

[3] Goldmark quoted in Alan Farnham, "The Windfall Awaiting the New Inheritors," *Fortune,* May 7, 1990, p. 77.

[4] William A. Diaz, Dwight F. Burlingame, Warren F. Ilchman, David A. Kaufmann, Shawn D. Kimmel, "Welfare Reform and the Capacity of Private Philanthropy," *Capacity for Change? The Nonprofit World in the Age of Devolution* (Indianapolis: Indiana University Center on Philanthropy, 1996), pp. 129 and 145.

[5] Cf. Gerald Auten and Eugene Steuerle, op cit.

[6] Paul Schervish and John Havens, "How do People Leave Bequests: Family or Philanthropic Organizations?" in *Death and Dollars,* edited by Alicia Munnell and Annika Sunden, (Washington, DC: Brookings Press, 2003).

[7] Benjamin Soskis, "Giving Numbers: Reflections on Why, What and How We are Counting," *Nonprofit Quarterly,* Fall, 2017.

[8] Patricia Dean, editor, *Taking Giving Seriously* (Indianapolis: Indiana University Center on Philanthropy, 1993), articles by Schervish, "Taking Giving Seriously," and "Philanthropy as a Moral Identity of Caritas," pp. 32 and 99.

[9] Ruth McCambridge, "Changes in Giving Patterns: Understanding the Dialectics," *Nonprofit Quarterly,* Fall, 2017.

[10] Several examples of this work would include: Schervish and Havens, "The New Physics of Philanthropy": Part 1: "The Supply-Side Vectors of Charitable Giving," Nov. 2001; and Part 2: "The Spiritual Side of the Supply Side," March 2002, in *The CASE International Journal of Educational Advancement*; Schervish, "The Sense and Sensibility of Philanthropy as a Moral Citizenship of Care," *Good Intentions: Moral Obstacles and Opportunities,* David H. Smith, editor (Indianapolis: Indiana University Press, 2005); and Schervish, *Receiving and Giving as Spiritual Exercise* (Indianapolis: The Center on Philanthropy, 2008); Schervish, "The Moral Biography of Wealth: Philosophical Reflections on the Foundation of Philanthropy" (Boston: Center on Wealth and Philanthropy, Boston College, 2005). They speak to the changing nature of philanthropy and its motivating forces for donors. Much of Paul's research is about the very wealthy. For instance, see his important *Gospels of Wealth: How the Rich Portray Their Lives,* written with Platon Coutsoukis and Ethan Lewis (Westport, CT: Praeger, 1994). Many of his insights and points may well apply in different ways to donors more generally.

[11] Schervish and Havens, "The New Physics of Philanthropy": "Part 2: The Spiritual Side of the Supply Side," *The CASE International Journal of Educational Advancement*, March 2002, p. 239.

[12] Schervish and Havens, "Millionaires and the Millennium: New Estimates for the Forthcoming Wealth Transfer and the Prospects for a Golden Age of Philanthropy" (Boston: Social Welfare Research Institute, Boston College, 1999).

[13] Schervish and Havens, "Why The $41 Trillion Wealth Transfer Estimate Is Still Valid: A Review of Challenges and Questions," *The Journal of Gift Planning*, V. 7, N. 1, January 2003.

[14] Havens and Schervish, "A Golden Age of Philanthropy Still Beckons: National Wealth Transfer and Potential for Philanthropy, Technical Report" (Boston: Center on Wealth and Philanthropy, Boston College, May 28, 2014), see Table 4 and 5.

[15] Holly Hall, "Experts Question $58-Trillion Wealth-Transfer Estimate," *The Chronicle of Philanthropy*, June 5, 2014.

[16] "A Golden Age of Philanthropy Still Beckons: National Wealth Transfer and Potential for Philanthropy, Technical Report," op. cit., p. 6.

[17] See "Understanding Transfer of Wealth: 2017 National Analysis," LOCUS, April, 2018; and "$9 Trillion and Counting: How Charities Can Tap into the Transfer of Wealth," *The Chronicle of Philanthropy*, April, 2018.

[18] *Giving USA, 2018*, Giving USA Foundation.

[19] Drew Lindsay, "6 Signs of Trouble Ahead in Charitable Giving," *The Chronicle of Philanthropy*, July 6, 2018.

[20] See, for instance, Claude Rosenberg, Jr., *Wealthy and Wise*, (Boston: Little, Brown and Co., 1994); and Schervish and Havens, "The New Physics of Philanthropy": "Part 2: The Spiritual Side of the Supply Side," *The CASE International Journal of Educational Advancement*, March 2002, p. 229.

[21] Letter to the Editor: "Estate Tax Repeal: What Would it Mean for Philanthropy?" *The Chronicle of Philanthropy*, August 24, 2000.

[22] Richard McKenzie, *The Market Foundations of Philanthropy* (Indianapolis: The Philanthropy Roundtable, 1994), pp. 5 and 11. Also see his more extensive occasional paper for the Center for the Study of American Business at Washington University, St. Louis, *Was the Decade of the 1980s a Decade of Greed?*

[23] Edmund Phelps, *Mass Flourishing: How Grassroots Innovation Created Jobs, Challenge, and Change* (Princeton University Press, 2013), p. 307.

[24] Schervish, Havens and Whitaker, "Philanthropy's Indispensable Ally," *Philanthropy*, May/June 2005, pp. 8 and 9.

[25] Jason Furman, "The Economy is Growing Faster than The Government Says," *The Wall Street Journal*, July 10, 2018.

[26] "A Golden Age of Philanthropy Still Beckons: National Wealth Transfer and Potential for Philanthropy, Technical Report," op. cit., pp. 3-4.

[27] Holly Hall, "Experts Question $58-Trillion Wealth-Transfer Estimate," op. cit.

[28] *Ibid.*

[29] Bankers Trust Private Bank, *Wealth with Responsibility Study*, 2000, p. 15.

[30] Schervish and Havens, "The New Physics of Philanthropy": "Part 2: The Spiritual Side of the Supply Side," op. cit. p. 235.

[31] Schervish, Havens and Albert Whitaker, "Recent Trends in the Timing and Allocation of Charitable Giving," *Philanthropy*, October 1, 2007.

[32] "Estate Tax Repeal: What Would it Mean for Philanthropy?" op. cit.

[33] Schervish and Havens, "The New Physics of Philanthropy": "Part 2: The Spiritual Side of the Supply Side," op. cit. pp. 229 and 234.

[34] *Ibid*, p. 236.

[35] John Langbein, "The Twentieth Century Revolution in Wealth Transmission," *Michigan Law Review*,1988, p. 84.

[36] Schervish, Havens and Whitaker, "It Is Better to Receive and to Give," *Philanthropy*, July/August 2006, p. 12.

[37] Schervish, Havens and Whitaker, "Leaving a Legacy of Care," *Philanthropy*, January/February, 2006, p. 13.

[38] Schervish and Havens, "Millionaires and the Millennium: New Estimates for the Forthcoming Wealth Transfer and the Prospects for a Golden Age of Philanthropy," op. cit., pp. 17 and 19.

[39] "$9 Trillion and Counting: How Charities Can Tap into the Transfer of Wealth," op. cit.

[40] *Ibid*.

[41] Schervish and Havens, "The New Physics of Philanthropy: Part 2: The Spiritual Side of the Supply Side," op. cit. p. 237.

[42] Paul Schervish, "Why the Wealthy Give," Adrian Sargeant and Walter Wymer, editors, *The Routledge Companion to Nonprofit Marketing* (London: Routledge: 2008), p. 179.

2. The Coming Boom in Philanthropy?

The Coming Boom in Giving

As seen from the 1990s, a dramatic expansion of American philanthropy is in the making. Dubbed the "intergenerational transfer of wealth," some people have predicted a "decade of altruism." (This article was written in the 1990s. The first article in this chapter presents the history, prospect and challenges of the intergenerational transfer as seen from 2019.) This is no trivial matter. Our charitable tradition is one of the unique characteristics of American life. It is a powerful engine for change. In 1991, for instance, Americans contributed nearly $125 billion. Seventy-two percent of American households gave an average of $899. Well over 50 percent of Americans twelve and over volunteered an average of more than three hours per week.

Whatever influences the vitality of this tradition is noteworthy. Five particular ones will make and shape this potential expansion of giving:

Economic growth: Economic growth goes hand-in-hand with the health of philanthropy. Wealth creation blossomed since World War II and through the 1980s. It sets the stage for increases in giving. That trend will be more important in the future (and has been through 2018).

Intergenerational transfer: A huge intergenerational transfer as large as $10.5 trillion will occur over the next several decades. A very large amount will likely fall to nonprofits and foundations. (As the first article in this chapter shows, by 2018 the estimate is much larger.)

Demographic bubble: The baby boom generation is a bubble of over 70 million. They are giving now but will reach peak giving years around 2020. They will have more to give and will give more. They will likely also give in different, even peculiar, ways.

Can donors afford it?: Potential donors often hesitate and ask, "Can I afford to give more?" A wider dispersion of wealth will make that easier for many. And an interesting book suggests new ways to think about and analyze what one can afford while living, with quite remarkable results for the potential boom in giving.

Philanthropy's case and impact: All of these factors make for a large – but only potential – philanthropic windfall. It is here that donors matter in new and important ways. Nonprofits and philanthropic organizations must listen to donors, make a compelling case, and then deliver with efficiency and effectiveness.

These factors affect all aspects of philanthropy. The increasing number and size of new foundations and donor-advised funds should be particularly noticeable — some with massive endowments in the offing. Many new and large nonprofits will arise, too.

Such an outpouring of philanthropic intent is not inevitable, however. Charitable giving could be impeded by poor planning on the part of individuals, as well as by wrongheaded policies and negative unanticipated consequences from Washington. Perhaps more important, nonprofits will need the vision and leadership to make the right pitches to elicit support: a case that moves emotions and proves impact.

But if it can develop in healthy and vital ways, there will be opportunities to address the myriad of problems confronting a complex civil society. Peter Drucker, Waldemar Nielsen, and Richard Cornuelle are just a few who emphasize the necessity for a strong voluntary sector. Drucker, for instance, wrote about an urgent need for a "new social priority" in *The Wall Street Journal* (December 19, 1991):

> Government has proved incompetent at solving social problems. Virtually every success we have scored has been achieved by non-profits…. "Nonprofitization" may for modern societies be the way out of mismanagement by welfare bureaucracies.

This is a tall order. A boom in giving could provide the resources.

The Economic Success in the 1980s

Every year my wife and I read Charles Dickens's *A Christmas Carol* to our two boys. Several years ago, our now eleven-year-old first grasped the story and loved it until the very end. After the three ghosts of yesterday, today and what is yet to be had visited, Scrooge began giving his money away. Our son expressed deep dismay. He plaintively asked, "What if Scrooge runs out of money?" We were initially horrified, but like any good parent, I see brilliance in our son's insight. He was reminding us that, in ways Dickens did not see, the marketplace makes giving possible. In fact, its own job creating, wealth creating, and humanizing effects are a great boon to humanity – a great charitable force in itself, if you will. We can see it in the remarkable ability of trade to raise hundreds of millions from poverty. Unfortunately, too many in philanthropy lack understanding of the impact of free markets, just as too many who appreciate markets ignore the attendant problems. They commonly fail to understand the nature of philanthropy as "voluntary action for the public good."

Many factors influence giving, but the link between economic health and giving is easy to see. In many ways, the 1980s was a decade of unusual economic success in America. Productivity, wealth-creation, job-creation, and many other indicia of economic growth were evident, if not universal. While some commentators have labelled the 1980s a decade of greed, in truth it was a decade of surprisingly strong growth in the charitable impulse as well. Between 1955 and 1980, total giving by individuals, corporations, foundations, and through bequests grew from $34.5 billion to $77.5 billion. By contrast, in the ten years between 1980 and 1989 alone, giving increased 56 percent, from $77.5 billion to $121 billion. This is a growth of 5.1 percent between 1980 and 1989 (compounded annually) compared to 3.3 percent for the earlier period of 1955 to 1980. Adjusting for inflation and population growth, economist Richard B. McKenzie has written in his *Was the Decade of the 1980s a Decade of Greed?* that: "Total annual giving in constant dollars was, on average, more than $14 billion and 16 percent higher during the 1980s than would have been predicted from the giving patterns of the 1950s, 1960s, and 1970s. In 1989, actual total giving exceeded predicted total giving by more than $28 billion, or by 30 percent."

My points here are twofold. First, economic health is crucial for philanthropy. We have a philanthropic stake in supporting economic growth and free markets. Second, the 1980s suggest that there is more untapped giving potential than most people expect. The capacity is there.

The Effect of Taxes

Not only is giving related to income and wealth, but to government policies as well. These policies have a powerful effect on the charitable impulse. The relationship is complex, with different, often contradictory pressures involved. There is more agreement today that government has neither the resources nor the competence to solve society's intractable problems. As taxes become more onerous, productivity decreases generally. Everyone is left worse off than before. The crowding-out effects — of government programs, inflation, income and estate in particular — on charitable contributions will be one of the most important economic and psychological factors in limiting the success and growth of philanthropy.

In their quest for funds, state and federal governments are always looking carefully at both tax rates in general and inheritance taxes specifically. Taxes at death are a potentially inviting pot of gold. After all, the dead are not a very vocal interest group. The moral issue — if individuals have a right to use their wealth during their lives, why can't they make distribution decisions at death — seems easily ignored.

Tax interference with donors' charitable wishes tends not to be good for philanthropy, much less society. As a study produced jointly by the Institute for Research on the Economics of Taxation and the Center for the Study of Taxation concludes: "Transfer taxes reduce the total amount of wealth created in the first place, thus limiting the amount that can be left to both individuals and charity. Once [the] impact of transfer taxes is taken into account, it is likely that transfer taxes discourage private charitable giving."

Intergenerational Transfer of Wealth

We now come to the second factor influencing philanthropy's potential. One particularly striking aspect of this earlier economic success is the huge legacy the older generation will be leaving in the form of bequests. Cornell University economist Robert B. Avery and associates have made the best estimates. They estimate that people over fifty will make bequests totaling nearly $10 trillion (in 1989 dollars). This large intergenerational transfer of wealth will come in nearly 115 million bequests over the next several decades. It is hard to comprehend this number. To give you an idea of what we are talking about, that number is 62 percent of the total 1989 US household wealth of $16.7 trillion.

This generation of seniors will pass its wealth on to new beneficiaries. A significant portion of this amount will, of course, go to children and other family members. But it will be different in many ways. Interestingly, inheritances will descend upon family members often older than during earlier transfers. Many will be financially successful in their own right. They won't "need" inheritances in quite that same way if they received it at a younger age. In other cases, there will also be more transfers while living (as "human capital" investments in the education and livelihood of children and grandchildren).

Philanthropy will no doubt also be a major beneficiary as estates settle. Some very big gifts have already been given. For instance, of the nine largest known gifts to institutions of higher learning (totaling $885 million), one was made in 1979, three in the 1980s, and five (totaling $528 million) have so far been given in this decade (i.e., the 1990s).

The institutional forms this charitable giving will take will vary. Much of it will go into existing and new foundations. Approximately 10,000 of the more than 30,000 private foundations in the US are less than ten years old, and typically there is a ten-year lag between a foundation's creation and full funding. Several of these foundations promise to be very large. Peter Goldmark, president of the Rockefeller Foundation, was quoted in the May 7, 1990 *Fortune* saying that, "We have the wherewithal. It's supply driven: I personally know five donors who each could create Ford Foundation-size foundations tomorrow. And, whether you are liberal or conservative, there's a sense now that private initiative is preferable to state."

But it is bigger than that. There has been an explosion of small independent or family foundations. This includes some of the approximately 200,000 individuals with fortunes of $10 million or more. The explosive growth of donor-advised funds will no doubt replace much small foundation growth while dramatically expanding – democratizing – giving generally. A recent survey by Kidder, Peabody & Co. showed wealthy donors were increasingly interested in starting foundations.

Giving is thus becoming more complex. What might once have been a single no-strings-attached gift from individuals to one charitable organization may now be a series of smaller gifts renewed over time and administered by an intermediary organization like a community foundation, private foundation, or donor-advised fund. We may even begin to see consortia of small private foundations establishing themselves with clear goals to concentrate their joint grantmaking. And a number of additional elements may be embedded in the intergenerational phenomenon:

- These are more liquid assets now than when inheritances were traditionally bound up in family businesses, farms, homes, and other tangible assets.

- Some may argue that the values of the baby boomers make this an interesting experiment: more donations and more engagement?

- There will be some amount of dispersal of this transfer (due to divorce, stepchildren, numbers of children, bequests to friends, etc.). The distribution will still be heavily skewed, of course, with vast amounts tending to go to few individuals.

- No doubt the needs and opportunities facing our society today make the dynamics of this transfer important to watch.

- Finally, this is the only transfer we've got. It is upon us now. It can be huge if we attend to its nature.

The Baby Boom Generation

Let us now look at the third factor: the baby boom generation. These intergenerational transfers will be driven by the baby boomer beneficiaries. They show philanthropic promise with their own wealth and proclivities.

The baby boom generation is over 70 million Americans, or about 30 percent of the population. They are now reaching the age (mid-forties) when people traditionally start to devote more time and money to philanthropic activities. Earlier inheritances will also significantly increase the wealth of many baby boomers. Thus, some of these dollars will find their way into the needy coffers of philanthropy. Whether they can or will be generous is subject to different interpretations. There will be continued tension between the fabled selfishness of baby boomers and their earlier idealism. I am quite sure they will reconcile both, as they age and give more.

Baby boomers are, on the one hand, "the squeeze generation," as Peter Franceses, president of American Demographics Inc., describes them in the January 9, 1990 *Chronicle of Philanthropy*. Their wealth is circumscribed by higher costs and expectations related to children, education, health care, parents, lifestyle choices, inflation, savings rate, etc. Nevertheless, a 1993 study from the Congressional Budget Office contends that in general baby boomers are significantly better off compared to their parents at the same age. This is due in part to changes in living patterns, including later marriages and fewer children. While their giving potential is quite high just as they reach their peak giving years, the influence of economic and political events makes it difficult to predict any clear trend over many years.

It is a good sign that some baby boomers are beginning their philanthropic activities earlier than usual. And they are doing so with more dedication. They are doing exactly what Andrew Carnegie urged over a hundred years ago: engage in philanthropy while living. As one example, there is an increasing number of entrepreneurs turned entrepreneurial philanthropists, like Peter Lynch, Ben Cohen, and Michael Milken, as well as many less well-known individuals. Apple, Google and the tech industry have spewed forth many newly minted multi-millionaires. Years of honing their entrepreneurial skills and applying them to their philanthropic interests should result in much clearer expressions of donor intent for the bequests or institutions they will leave in the future.

All in all then, we are still trying to determine how baby boomers may give in their prime giving years. Will some of these above traits predominate or will age itself determine giving in ways very similar to the older donors of past generations? In truth, it will probably be both, despite the eagerness of many commentators to make baby boomers fit various grandiose predictions of behavior. Whatever works, it is clear that the size of the baby boom generation together with their earned and inherited wealth makes them *the* potent force in philanthropy over the next thirty-plus years.

Indeed, recent surveys by the Gallup organization show rather dramatic increases in the amount of time and money being donated by the baby boom generation now. Brian O'Connell of Independent Sector was quoted in the November 1990 *NonProfit Times* as saying that this "is good news for today and may suggest even better news for the future as this very large population group assumes community responsibility"

The Capacity to Give

This brings us briefly to a fourth factor influencing the potential for a boom in giving: showing that individuals can give more, especially while living. There are many aspects of this, but one seems particularly interesting.

One of the most common statements a fundraiser hears is, "I can't afford to give more." A recent book suggests new ways of looking at wealth and giving that could release, in his view, $100 billion a year in new giving "without sacrifice or financial risk," and without employing any questionable financial techniques. Claude Rosenberg's 1994 book *Wealthy and Wise: How You and America Can Get the Most Out of Your Giving* is admittedly a quirky and controversial book. But it also has a strong ring of truth to it. It is well worth considering. He claims that people just don't know how to assess their financial condition. Wealthier Americans in particular rather systematically underestimate it.

Rosenberg's discussion of, and worksheets on, assessing one's financial condition has a special emphasis on including net worth even when making current giving plans instead of focusing only on income. Emphasizing net worth in addition to income is immediately relevant to my topic. The intergenerational transfer will dramatically affect the net worth of many baby boomers. Rosenberg's approach could help potential donors understand their true capability to give now and at death; a capability that could be very large.

Listening to Donors

Charitable organizations and the philanthropic community in general are eager to make this giving potential real. If this is to happen, we need to appreciate some of the changing ways baby boomers may be giving. Then there can be more effective methods of raising funds and more relevant messaging. This is my fifth topic. There are three trends that may especially affect the release of this boom in giving. First, the donor will become increasing important in a philanthropic transaction that previously focused more on the donee organization. Second, baby boomers may give in different ways. And, finally, nonprofits and the philanthropic sector generally have to do a better job of communicating their message, values, and results. Let me briefly discuss each in turn.

Giving begins with the donor. The next generation of philanthropists will be successful to the extent that their giving plans — whether to charitable organizations, community foundations, or foundations of their own creation — are imbued with clear intent, aligned values, and impact. The ultimate responsibility rests with the donor.

These donors may also seem more fickle, at least by traditional standards. Baby boomers will probably exhibit their stronger charitable impulse differently from past generations. To begin with, they will give more while living. They and their foundations will certainly want more involvement and control than just giving some of "their" dollars. That is mostly a good thing for those organizations that can adjust. That level of engagement can be good and encourage even deeper commitments, or it can be bad when donors exhibit a know-it-all hubris. The difference requires careful management on the part of the nonprofit. And volunteering and engagement are the strongest predictor of giving in general and to particular organizations. Those organizations that can provide meaningful involvement will reap the benefits.

Donors will likely be more restrictive in their giving, and more critical of management, mission, and results. There may also be a tendency for their giving to be more diverse, more political, and therefore less readily channeled to traditional charitable organizations and areas. There may also be less long-term giving and continuity. Instead, giving could be less focused on long-standing intractable problems and be more fragmented. One might expect more short-term fads. Indeed, donor fascination with the "one big idea" and the conceit of hubris is a significant danger that may impede effectiveness. Donor fatigue will certainly become more prevalent. And finally, many donors will want to involve family members in what can be an ongoing philanthropic legacy.

This all means that the success of nonprofit organizations in the next decades will depend on the extent to which they make their mission clear and show their impact to donors. They will have to carry out their goals and objectives more effectively and efficiently. From that base, they must develop innovative ways to attract, develop, and involve donors. And then they must keep them involved and giving over time.

One of the major challenges for nonprofit executives and fundraisers will be to listen – really listen—more closely to the goals and needs of donors. Rather than viewing donors' wishes as obstacles to the use of "their" funds, fundraisers and nonprofits will in the future have to integrate more fully the donor's intent with the needs and mission of their own organizations.

As significant as larger gifts are, the potential for broadening the base of giving is evident as well. There are many thousands of individuals who could make important sustaining gifts to the multitude of nonprofit organizations that work for the public good. In all of these cases, outright bequests, charitable remainder trusts, the use of community foundations, and other charitable vehicles like the Fidelity Charitable Gift Fund will become more common. For instance, Renaissance Inc., a leading charitable gift planner and administrator, reports that 30 percent of the charitable remainder trusts they have helped establish are under $50,000 (16 percent are under $10,000). While large-scale philanthropy on the part of very wealthy individuals gets the lion's share of the publicity, it is the potential for hundreds of thousands of small philanthropists that is truly exciting. There is, in short, a possibility, not previously conceived, for a democratization of philanthropy and giving of an unprecedented scale.

The success of nonprofit organizations in the next decade will depend on the extent to which they make *their* mission clear. They will have to carry out their goals and objectives more effectively and efficiently. From that base, they can develop candid, long term partnerships with donors. They must develop innovative ways to attract, develop, and involve donors, and then keep them involved and giving over time. Donors are not unpleasant obstacles to a nonprofit's mission but an integral part of a mutual activity. Well, mostly they aren't, which means nonprofits may occasionally have to sever toxic relationships with donors: a very difficult thing to do.

Forms of Giving for Donors

Giving is thus becoming more complex. What might once have been a single no-strings-attached gift from individuals may now be a series of smaller gifts. They may be renewed and reviewed over time and administered by an intermediary organization like a community or private foundation. Community foundations are now coming into their own throughout the country. We may even begin to see consortia of small private foundations with common goals joining together to concentrate their grantmaking. In all of these cases, we may find greater family control and cohesion in giving, particularly through private foundations.

Especially interesting to me is the possibility of an explosion of family giving, through family foundations as well as donor-advised funds. Many donors want to start a serious giving program *now*. Baby boomers want to maintain greater control over the use of their funds. They want to include family members (both siblings and especially children) in what can be an ongoing philanthropic endeavor and legacy.

In any case, setting up foundations or donor-advised funds will be much more common. Doing so should require careful consideration. It requires articulating a clear mission, finding competent staff and advisors, and developing an enduring structure. Unfortunately, establishing a philanthropic organization is too easily a haphazard part of overall estate planning. It shouldn't be, given how important these issues are for its success. Values and intent can simply be crowded out by the fine points of secondary tax and legal considerations.

Two caveats should be noted, however. First, meddling and fickle donors may try to make too many inappropriate restrictions for their donations: even pressuring nonprofits to change missions. And second, eager nonprofits may be overzealous as they try to "tap" this potential intergenerational transfer. Nonprofits may over-promise and then ignore the promises once the money has been received. These things happen more than any of us would like to admit. The old adage "Buyer Beware" certainly applies to *both* donors and nonprofits as well.

Some observers of the philanthropic scene are not too sanguine about the outcome of this potential outpouring of philanthropic intent. As Waldemar Nielsen recently commented:

> As of now they have available only the legal advice of their lawyers, the financial advice of their financial advisors, and the mushy inspirational stuff of the standard establishment sources. As a result, they are going to make as many dumb mistakes and experience as many bitter disappointments as their predecessors. For their sake, and for the country's, we need to give them some practical, honest, relevant guidance. Without being too starry-eyed about it, this could avoid the wastage of tens, maybe hundreds, of billions of charitable dollars in the coming decades.

If the potential is to be reached and the major pitfalls avoided, we in the field must offer honest and careful encouragement as well as understand and counteract the factors that could impede it. It remains to be seen if philanthropy will reach its fullest fruition in the decades ahead.

Conclusion

A very large intergenerational transfer of wealth over the next decades is coming. A great deal of that transfer will go to philanthropy. But its size and success are not guaranteed. Realizing that potential has two prongs. First, it will require closer attention from donors because giving money away and doing it well are, emphatically, *not* the same thing. This newer generation of donors is interested and even eager to give more, but they will be successful to the extent that their giving — whether to charitable organizations, community foundations, or foundations of their own creation — is imbued with clear intent, humility, and a focus on results.

Second, the success of nonprofit organizations in the next decades will depend on mission, results, and their ability to communicate honestly. They will have to carry out their goals and objectives more effectively and efficiently. And, frankly, they need to stop whining and believe that they must do better. They are in fact uniquely able to have a much greater impact than most people, even in philanthropy, believe.

Finally, the key to successfully unleashing this prospective giving will come from *the real partnerships* that must be developed between funders and nonprofits. More open and candid partnerships will be important if this boom is to materialize fully and benefit our civil society.

This article is a combination drawn from three pieces I wrote on the intergenerational transfer of wealth as seen from the early 1990s:

- *"The Coming Boom in Philanthropy,"* Philanthropy, *V. 7, No. 3 (Summer 1993). It was published in advance of the Philanthropy Roundtable's November 1993 Annual Meeting on "The Future of Philanthropy: Boom or Bust?"*
- *"The Coming Boom in Giving: How Nonprofits Can Benefit,"* Nonprofit World, *V. 12, No. 3, May/June 1994, by the Society for Nonprofit Organizations.*
- *"Current Trends in Philanthropy: Is There a Coming Boom in Giving and What Can We Make of It," the keynote address at the annual Disciples Development Conference January, 20-22, 1995.*

Thanks to the publishers for permission to use portions of these works in this article.

CHAPTER 6

THE PAYOUT QUESTION

I am not in sympathy with this policy of perpetuating endowments and believe that more good can be accomplished by expending funds as trustees find opportunities for constructive work than by storing up large sums of money for long periods of time.... Coming generations can be relied upon to provide for their own needs as they arise. — Julius Rosenwald

... the one major trend about whose wisdom I have serious doubts: the dramatic shift of donor preference away from accumulating wealth in presumably perpetual institutions. ... It is no exaggeration to think of perpetual foundations as constituting America's social sector investment banks. You do not want to have to create such a bank when an unexpected social problem arises; you want these institutions to be in existence to be drawn upon when needed. — Joel Fleishman

A t first blush, foundation payout and finding the "appropriate" rate seem straightforward. As I note in the articles below, the issue can be approached as a "public policy" or as a "private policy" decision. The implications of a legally mandated rate are huge. It determines whether foundations are necessarily in spend-out mode or whether foundations can exist for a very long time for the many different reasons a donor or board may value. Most financial data and projections shows that even the current mandated rate of 5 percent limits a foundation's long-term existence. Thus, payout rates can deeply compromise the importance and flexibility of philanthropy. It can further weaken civil society and further politicize philanthropy.

The motivations behind payout talk are numerous — sometimes good and other times unattractively self-interested. Choosing the "right" rate is not like throwing darts at a dartboard full of Post-it notes with different percentages written in. There can be significant unintended consequences from the choice. What seems humdrum is a complex decision.

Sometimes a higher payout is proffered as a solution to problems in foundation behavior. Or it is advocated as a way to make philanthropy more effective. I have seen more than enough problems and inefficiencies in foundation behavior firsthand. What to do about them does need to be addressed. They can be resolved in different ways. Thinking outside the spend-out versus perpetuity dichotomy suggests interesting alternatives, as I suggest in "The Spend-Out/Perpetuity Distraction and the Merger Option" later in this chapter. Payout rates, however, are not solutions to what ails philanthropy or the sector generally. They introduce problems of their own.

As a matter of private policy, I believe foundation boards should choose the rate that most effectively helps them meet their mission and longevity plans. As a matter of public policy, I believe less interference in foundation choices produces better foundation decisions, a stronger nonprofit sector, and honors the vitality of crucial enduring institutions of civil society.

Thus, when discussions turns to payout rates, one value to factor in is philanthropy's role as a set of enduring, independent institutions, within the complex workings of society, government, and markets.

The point of these articles is to encourage thought, knowledge, and transparency. Don't simply assume the right decision for private policy or for public policy is perpetuity, or a payout of X percent, or spend-out. Think about it and explore the implications of various decisions.

1. Payout Mix-ups

In recent years, much has been made of payout rates. On the one hand, many writers have favored increasing the 5 percent minimum required of foundations because it "reaffirms some of the basic principles of effective grantmaking, such as mission clarity, focus and impact".[1] But it does no such thing; payout does not determine mission or effectiveness. Calling for higher payout requirements seems more related to political agendas or the unquestioned conceit that giving now is always better than later. On the other hand, much of the statistical research clusters around 4-5 percent as the minimum that allows foundations to be enduring institutions if that is their choice: taking into consideration market cycles, expenses, excise taxes, and inflation. The minimum, however, has become the unquestioned ceiling for most foundations because foundation officials and boards are cautious (or lazy) and fail to align budget and mission. This may be a good time to revisit the payout question.

The 5 percent rate is a proper, balanced minimum rate allowing longevity and potential endowment (and grantmaking) growth for times of crisis or opportunities that arise. But any mandated rate should always be tied to the goals, strategies, and lifespan decisions needed to meet mission. But in times of recession like these, foundations should temporarily spend above 5 percent to at least keep spending level — with the explicit understanding that doing so risks spend-out if payout isn't rebalanced to allow perpetuity and asset growth, if that is a foundation's goal.

Whatever the payout rate, foundations should approach it in two ways. First, it should be the result of explicit decisions aligning budget, mission, strategy, and impact. A single regulated rate does not fit all foundations or all situations. Several intrepid researchers have even suggested that "nothing other than the elimination [of] any and all mandated payout rates" will "clearly encourage foundations to adopt a payout rate that strategically links mission and payout decisions within foundations".[2] The mere thought caused arrhythmia among policy wonks and was so politically radical that the idea was quickly put back into the bottle! I suspect they are right.

Second, foundations should understand the implications of their payout decisions. For instance, the cost of higher payouts became clear to me when I was told the story of a foundation in the 1970s that heeded President Nixon's call for private charity to do more. They increased their giving for ten years or so; it took decades to recover their endowment. Another foundation was regularly paying out over 7 percent. That is a perfectly fine choice for a board to make, but I thought they should understand what their decision meant. An analysis of spending over time showed that the higher payout resulted in less total money being given to grantees. The board decided to cut back current funding to protect longevity and to have more money to grant over time.

In both cases, the added endowment draw was unsustainable, leading towards spend-out. It meant less total money was available to be spent over time (even at a higher payout rate) on those issues and grantees each foundation cared about. A higher payout not only eliminates assets from net worth, but it also eliminates the power of economic growth and compound interest that those assets would earn.

Attention to unintended consequences is also crucial. A mandated payout rate in excess of 5 percent almost guarantees foundations will eventually run out of money and close. It has been suggested, however, that this will be offset by new foundations. But a higher rate that forces spend-out will decrease the attractiveness of foundation formation and increase the attractiveness of other estate decisions (for current consumption, children, or favorite charities). It could further decimate philanthropy.

Some have urged an indirect approach to increase payout: eliminating foundation administrative expenses from the 5 percent minimum (currently, administrative expenses related to charitable activity can be included in the 5 percent calculation). This is an ironic and self-defeating idea, just as foundations finally begin to understand that administrative expenses are integral to the organizational health and program effectiveness of their grantees — which is the case for them as well. Eliminating administrative expenses from qualifying distributions would decrease the due diligence, public policy, advocacy, communication, and technical assistance direct expenditures of foundations by effectively increasing their "cost" in comparison to grants.

None of this, though, means that 5 percent is the proper ceiling! What is a sensible foundation to do? It depends, and that is the beauty of a diverse and independent philanthropic sector. Foundations should make sure they meet the 5 percent minimum but otherwise ignore it. Thoughtful consideration of mission and strategy will determine whether more than 5 percent is a proper payout. One writer has suggested that foundation boards develop a written payout strategy. Perhaps this could address the inevitable ups and downs of market cycles and suggest the approach to take for crisis periods or unusual opportunities.

Since most foundations report they intend to be enduring institutions, maintaining fiduciary care and being concerned about future impact are important. In good times, endowments may grow, leading some to raise the "warehousing of wealth" alarm. Assuming, however, that asset growth is permanent is to ignore the risk of market cycles. Over time, markets also go down and wreak havoc on endowments and the nonprofit sector in general (see the terrible impact of the 1970s, 1987, 2003, and the Great Recession). If foundations are careful about their assets (and asset growth), they can respond to those inevitable rainy days, crises, or unique opportunities without jeopardizing the foundation's future. If only they would do so.

Treating the payout minimum as a ceiling has meant that giving runs cyclically with economic growth: as the economy and endowments grow, so does giving. And as the economy sours and endowments take a beating, giving goes down. Thus, many foundations reduce grantmaking budgets precisely at a time of greatest need, adding turmoil to the nonprofits they are supporting. Those reductions will continue for several years to come as the economy slowly rebounds. (And yet it should be noted that many foundation staff members I've talked to have admitted that smaller grantmaking budgets have been a welcome opportunity to cull less effective grantees. Do we really need a recession to do that?) It would generally better serve grantee health if grantmaking ran countercyclically with the market. By keeping payout at the minimum during strong growth, foundations could dip into their endowments for short-term increases in spending without bringing their own existence into question or decimating their ability to respond to grantees in the future.

In summary, then, *a minimum rate of 5 percent seems to make sense and allows for the kind of diversity and choices of lifespan, mission, and strategy that makes philanthropy a vibrant part of civil society. And it builds an endowment nest egg for helping during the next recession.*

I would feel a tad better about that sentence if I really believed most foundations were deliberate in their decision making around this issue. We need more discussion, openness, and questioning about this issue, without a lot of baggage. We need foundations to become less complacent. At the end of the day, though, I trust the imperfect results of publicity and press — as well as the often-maddening diversity among thousands of foundations — more than tinkering to get a new one-size-fits-all mandated rate and basing that tinkering on all sorts of political agendas while ignoring the unfortunate, unintended consequences embedded in them.

This article, originally titled "Payout Redux," was published in my April 9, 2010, contribution to the Smart Assets blog of Philanthropy New York while I was a Senior Fellow. It is reprinted with the permission of Philanthropy New York.

---

[1] Waleson, Heidi. 2007. *Beyond Five Percent: The New Foundation Payout Menu.* (San Francisco, CA and New York, NY: Northern California Grantmakers and New York Regional Association of Grantmakers, n.d.)

[2] Deep, Akash, and Peter Frumkin. *The Foundation Payout Puzzle.* Working Paper #9, The Hauser Center for Nonprofit Organizations, John F. Kennedy School of Government, Harvard University. 2001.

2. Payout Redux

In the next decade we need more thoughtful discussion — and a deeper understanding — of the issues and implications surrounding foundation payout decisions. For instance, foundation boards and donors should discuss two questions about foundation practice, and they should be regularly revisited. Based on the mission and the intended strategy of a foundation: (1) is the intent that the foundation exist in perpetuity or spend out over x number of years? and (2) what is the best desired spending rate to meet the mission and the longevity desired?

Sadly, both questions get more attention from policy wonks and advocates than from donors and boards. About three-quarters of foundations are formed to exist in perpetuity, and they operate that way by default. Most foundations don't have a formal spending policy. They simply give away the 5 percent minimum required by the federal government. Based on predilection, mission, and strategy, foundations may decide that spending out or perpetuity is the correct decision. They may decide a 5 percent payout is where they should be, or 7 percent, or 10 percent. In any of those cases, those decisions are fine, and should be made by the donors and boards. I have no specific preference or standing regarding them.

However, my experience has been that many foundations that do give more than the 5 percent don't understand the implications for (a) their assets, (b) their ability to exist in perpetuity, and (c) the size of the foundation's combined philanthropic value over time. These implications are not well understood, to the potential detriment of particular foundations. There are also underappreciated implications for the growth and well-being of the philanthropic sector. There are important values to enduring institutions in civil society which are not given sufficient voice.

We are still affected by the dramatic economic downturn in 2008 and the lingering volatility and malaise of financial markets. Foundation assets fell a record 17.2 percent in 2008 and have started to rebound since 2009. Interestingly, the Foundation Center originally estimated in April 2010 that foundation giving in 2009 had declined 8.4 percent from 2008. This was later revised when final figures for 2009 came in; actual giving for 2009 was down just 2.1 percent. The small decrease no doubt reflects the impact of lag and smoothing, as many foundations tend to base spending on three- or five-year averages. Administrative cutbacks were also an influence. Most important, it appears that foundation percentage draws on their endowments dramatically increased. As the Foundation Center reported, "the 8.1 percent ratio of 2009 giving to 2008 assets — a rough proxy for foundation payout — was the highest level recorded by the Foundation Center since 1985."[1]

Some have — perhaps overly dramatically — described recent strains on both the financial system and the foundation world as resulting in a "new normal." Perhaps it is more accurate to say that the last few years have been a reset button for how we should think about longevity, payout, and spending. Whatever our views on these matters, donors and boards as well as foundation watchers and policy analysts should be less complacent about these issues and think more carefully about what foundations are doing and why. Interestingly, on these topics "left" and "right" are not on clearly delineated opposite sides. One would hope that this will encourage a candid discussion. Perhaps it is now a good time to revisit questions of longevity and payout through the lens of payout: a sort of payout redux.

Payout and the "New Traditional" View

Before the Great Recession, much was being made, once again, of raising payout rates for foundations. Some commentators advocated individual foundations adopt an increase voluntarily. Others wanted an increase mandated. There tends to be a bias among "philanthropoids" and in policy circles for spending policies that would accomplish spend-out over time. It has become the reigning viewpoint — it is actually the "new traditional" view right now. For instance, philanthropic adviser and teacher Richard Marker noted, "I view myself as neutral either way on the question of spend-down or perpetuity. Yet readers of my book tell me that they perceive a leaning toward long-term/perpetuity. Some of that, I suspect, is because the current fashion is to downplay the value of perpetuity in favor of spend-down."[2]

When the National Committee for Responsive Philanthropy released *Criteria for Philanthropy at Its Best*, it was a strong voice in that "new traditional" direction advocating spend-out policies: "warehousing of tax-exempt dollars does not serve the public interest; it shortchanges the social benefit of philanthropy."[3] Other publications favored increasing the 5 percent minimum annual payout required of foundations because it "reaffirms some of the basic principles of effective grantmaking, such as mission clarity, focus and impact."[4] It does no such thing of course: payout does not determine mission, effectiveness, or social benefit. Calling for higher payout requirements seems more related to other agendas, such as the unquestioned conceit that giving now is always better than giving later. There is a failure to understand the role of saving during good times.

Some outsiders and policy people may emphasize the advantages of spending out because they fear the independence of foundations, don't trust staff and boards to do the perfect thing, or want to get the money out of foundation coffers now. For foundation staff and boards, spending out may be in their self-interest, because it increases their giving "power." Some board members, foundation staff, and donors favor spending out because they believe only they can make the best decisions. They hate the idea of passing control to others. Or they are flummoxed by how to negotiate the generational transfer of intent and governance. Spending more funds on particular issues now may indeed result in greater immediate impact. For many of the problems foundations address, however, spending more now may be a temporal illusion — the philanthropic version of the shortsighted, short-term thinking that plagues American corporations in search of short-term profit. As Michael Klausner has written, "there is no valid reason to conclude that future charity is necessarily worth less than current charity."[5]

There are, of course, less attractive reasons for perpetuity as well. It is, for instance, the unthinking, default position for far too many foundations and donors. Sometimes a false belief in donor immortality and the urge for control from the grave are at play. In any case, all motivations, good and bad, should be discussed before deciding whether spending out or a longer lifespan will best serve a foundation's mission and effectiveness.

Is There a "Proper" Payout Rate?

Most of the past empirical research clusters around a 5 percent payout as the likely maximum that allows foundations the choice to be enduring institutions. It takes into consideration market cycles, administrative expenses, excise taxes, and inflation. These are practical topics on making the giving and asset allocation of an endowment congruent. Investment strategy must follow from a giving strategy. And then it should be managed according to appropriate risk and reward parameters.

We need longer, updated time series data on appropriate payout rates. Given the recent recession and continuing volatility of financial markets, this new research would surely reaffirm the previous studies done, for instance, by Cambridge Associates for the Council of Michigan Foundations in 2000 and the three studies done by DeMarche Associates for the Council on Foundations in 1990, 1995, and 1999.[6] For example, J.P. Morgan Asset Management recently published a report that used the firm's forward capital market assumptions to estimate a sustainable payout level. Their conclusion was that an aggressive asset allocation of 80 percent equity and 20 percent bonds would only "support a spending rate of approximately 4 percent without damaging the long-term real value of the portfolio."[7]

It seems pretty clear that *if* there is to be a mandated payout rate, 5 percent is very close to a minimum rate allowing potential endowment (and grantmaking) growth for those crisis times, special needs, or opportunities that always occur and need a response. The Foundation Center's revision (referred to above) of the decline of giving in 2009 from 8.4 percent to 2.1 percent shows that the 5 percent rate works. It allowed asset growth in good times, so that an increased payout or small decrease in bad times could smooth giving. A rate above 5 percent will likely erode the endowment over time and result in the foundation spending out.

Thus, as a matter of public policy any mandated payout rate should allow wide choice of the goals, strategies, and lifespan decisions donors and boards can make to meet mission. Then the "private policy" decisions that individual donors and boards make for their foundation can be based on their values, missions, and strategies, whether that is a payout rate of 5 percent or greater. Several intrepid researchers have even suggested that "nothing other than the elimination [of] any and all mandated payout rates" will "clearly encourage foundations to adopt a payout rate that strategically links mission and payout decisions within foundations."[8] The mere suggestion of no mandated payout rate caused arrhythmia among policy wonks and foundation watchers. It was such a radical policy thought that the idea was quickly put back into the bottle. Although politically unpalatable, it may well be the most sensible prescription.

The Implications of Payout Decisions on Grantmaking Dollars

In any case, foundations should understand the implications of their payout decisions. A chosen or mandated payout rate more than 5 percent greatly increases the probability that a foundation will eventually run out of money and close. That is because annual returns have to cover not only payout but also noncharitable expenses, inflation, and excise taxes. Even a 10 percent annual return (which is not the long-term average of the market or of most portfolios) would likely result in a flat endowment at best.

There is an even more important — indeed stunning — implication of such decisions. One can calculate, over a set period, the combination of (1) the annual total of a foundation's cumulative grantmaking adjusted for inflation and (2) the foundation's remaining assets in the endowment after x years. The sum of that spending and those endowment assets is the dollar value that a foundation represents over time. This has been dubbed by some as the Total Philanthropic Value. Not surprisingly, a lower spending rate can very often result in a *higher* total foundation dollar value of those two elements over a period: a larger combined total philanthropic value, as it were. This is because a higher payout reduces the size of the endowment by eliminating market growth and the power of compound interest. Thus, the total dollars paid out over a period of years can actually be reduced by a higher annual payout because the endowment size erodes: for example, 5 percent of a $100 million endowment is more than 7 percent of a $70 million endowment.

The potential costs of higher payouts became clear to me years ago through two examples. I was told the story of a foundation in the 1970s that heeded President Nixon's call for private charity to do more. It increased its grantmaking payout rate significantly over ten years or so. That is a fine decision to make. However, there was a cost involved. It took the foundation decades to recover its endowment and rebuild its grantmaking budget. Another foundation, one for which I worked, was regularly paying out between 8-10 percent in the early 1990s. That, too, is a perfectly fine choice for a board to make, and I thought they should understand what their decision meant. I ran a simple analysis of spending over time at both the current percent payout rate and the 5 percent minimum. The report clearly showed that the higher payout resulted in an erosion of the endowment, and over about a fifteen-year period, less total money was given to grantees because the lower asset base in the endowment resulted in a lower annual-dollar grantmaking budget even at the higher percentage. If the foundation had kept payout at 5 percent, the growing endowment would have allowed the foundation to distribute more in total and still have a larger endowment.

Admittedly, there are times when a grant made now is more important and valuable than amounts given later. That assessment must be made within the larger context of philanthropic goals, mission, and the flux of external events. In this last example, however, because of that analysis, the foundation's board brought its annual spending down to the 5-6 percent range as a better way to meet its goals and mission.

Unintended Consequences of Higher Payout

Whatever the payout rate, attention to unintended consequences is also crucial. Two examples will suffice.

It has been suggested that any endowment loss and any foundation closures as a result of higher payout will be offset by the creation of new foundations. Perhaps. The increases in foundation formation in recent years suggest that foundation formation will likely remain robust (because of the intergenerational transfer of wealth to heirs and as well as the success of efforts such as the Giving Pledge). However, a higher payout rate that effectively forces foundations to spend-out over time will very likely significantly decrease the attractiveness of foundation formation to donors for whom perpetuity and family legacy are important. Other alternatives will become proportionately more attractive — such as current consumption, private investment, larger legacies for children and favorite charities, or other philanthropic vehicles. That could further decimate the growth and role of foundations as independent, creative, and enduring institutions of civil society.

Others have urged an indirect approach to increase payout: by eliminating foundation administrative expenses from the 5 percent minimum (currently, administrative expenses related to charitable activity can be included in the 5 percent calculation). This is an ironic and self-defeating idea. Foundations are finally beginning to understand that the administrative expenses of grantees are often quite integral to their grantees' organizational health and program effectiveness. That is also the case for foundations. Eliminating administrative expenses from qualifying distributions will decrease the amount foundations would spend on due diligence, public policy, advocacy, assessment, communication, and technical assistance by, in effect, increasing their cost in comparison to grants. Even with fat in those expenses, this will not increase the efficiency and effectiveness of foundations.

Does Increasing Payout Improve Results?

One can understand and appreciate the call for greater payout, because it derives in part from a desire to get more funds into the hands of nonprofit organizations for their programs, clients, and causes. (A topic for further investigation is the many ways philanthropic giving should be greater, can be greater, and can be much more effective.) There may be self-interest in these calls, since nonprofits want access to more funds too. However, in all these calls for increased payout, there is an unspoken assumption that simply giving out more money will increase results and impact. This assumption provides the calls for greater payout a moral patina that is rather misleading.

There is simply no relationship between greater payout, more grantmaking dollars flowing out, and greater philanthropic and nonprofit impact. Two anecdotes may illustrate this. First, about fifteen years ago I had the strange experience of hearing, unbidden, the same story from the executive director or senior program officers of five significant New York City foundations. Each person complained that there were simply "not enough good organizations and programs" to fund. I would add that I occasionally faced the same quandary. There are times when meeting the budgeted 5 percent payout meant that less effective organizations were funded. Second, when the recessions of 1990, 2001, and 2008 started to show up in reduced budgets for many foundations, many executive directors and program officers quite explicitly saw in this an opportunity to cull their grantee list of those organizations they considered less effective.

There is no question that not finding enough good organizations is partially the fault of the foundations too. Foundations can have extremely narrow missions; they may have theories of change or agendas that narrow the list of potential grantees. And foundations are certainly partially to blame for not helping nonprofits become effective organizations, because of ways they restrict their funding or the ways they can ignore or interfere with nonprofit management. (These points also deserve their own article.) The point remains: the call for greater payout and thus greater amounts of money out the door and to nonprofits does nothing to increase social benefit in and of itself. It may even lead to support of a layer of less effective organizations and programs, which can be socially detrimental and certainly not the best use of funds.

What Is a Foundation to Do?

None of this, though, means that 5 percent is the proper ceiling for all foundations. What is a sensible foundation to do? It depends, and that is the beauty of a diverse and independent philanthropic sector. Foundations should simply make sure they meet the 5 percent minimum but otherwise ignore it. Thoughtful consideration of mission and strategy should determine whether more than 5 percent is a proper payout. Very sophisticated considerations of asset allocation, risk, and diversification, etc. become important in ensuring that a foundation's assets are appropriately invested. Certainly, foundations should have an investment policy statement (only about 69 percent do) and a formal spending policy (only about 42 percent do) that they revisit regularly.[9]

Most foundations report that they intend to be enduring institutions, so maintaining fiduciary care and being concerned about future impact are important. In good times, endowments may grow, leading some to raise the "warehousing of wealth" alarm. But we might reframe the issue with the following questions. Aren't foundations simply being fiscally prudent by saving for a rainy day? Aren't foundations providing social benefit and protecting their missions by growing endowments that will allow greater funding during economic downturns? Don't growing endowments provide more chances to make innovative and big bets when opportunities arise?

Assuming that asset growth is a permanent state (as many who advocate increasing the payout rate seem to) means ignoring the risks and reality of market cycles. Over time, markets go up, and they also go down, wreaking havoc on endowments and the nonprofit sector in general (see the 1970s, 1987, 2002, and the Great Recession). The 1973 recession, for example, resulted in the Ford Foundation losing a third of its value, $1 billion, resulting in nearly 50 percent cuts in staff and grants. If foundations are careful about their assets (and asset growth), they can respond to those inevitable rainy days, crises, or unique opportunities without jeopardizing the foundation's future, its mission, or their grantees' programs.

This appears to have been the case with 2009 giving as reported above by the 2011 numbers from the Foundation Center, cited earlier. Foundations could dip into their endowments for short periods without bringing their own existence into question or decimating their ability to respond to grantees in the future, *if* their earlier payout rates allowed them to "save" and build their endowments. There can thus be important social benefits to foundation thrift, and conversely, there can be real social costs to higher payouts (mandated or chosen) beyond the impact on a particular foundation's longevity, mission, and grantees, because of lower grantmaking in subsequent years or spending out.

My conclusion is that a minimum rate of 5 percent seems to make sense and allows for the kind of diversity and choices of lifespan, mission, and strategy that make philanthropy a vibrant part of civil society. I would feel a tad better about that sentence if I really believed most foundations were deliberate in their decision making about payout, spending, and perpetuity. We know this is not true. Thus, we need more careful discussion, openness, and questioning about these issues, without a lot of politically imbued or self-interested baggage. We need donors and foundation staff and boards to question both the default decisions about paying out at 5 percent and the simplistic calls for greater payout in and of itself. At the end of the day, though, I trust the imperfect results of open discussion, publicity, and the press — as well as the often-maddening diversity among thousands of foundations — more than tinkering with a one-size-fits-all mandated rate. Tinkering on all sorts of agendas from both the left and right while ignoring the unfortunate unintended consequences embedded in them serves no public benefit.

The Importance of Enduring Institutions

In an "exit interview" published in *The Chronicle of Philanthropy* before she left the Ford Foundation, Susan Berresford talked passionately about the importance of long-term institutions: "Our society values enduring institutions.... We treasure them because they express and reinforce our values."[10] Strong, diverse, and long-lasting institutions are a vital part of a sustained civil society. New foundations and other philanthropic formations constantly help to renew civil society, and that is a good thing. At the same time, foundations that have long histories, existing cultures, experience, working capital, and human capital are immensely valuable as well. As enduring institutions, foundations can be significant, independent organizations within civil society. They are "countervailing" institutions, to use a phrase now out of fashion. They can reveal and respond to failures of both government and market. They can stand separate from governmental, corporate/commercial, and other special interests. Both centuries of history and events in recent decades — in the United States and internationally — should remind us just how important enduring and independent institutions can be to society. If one is going to talk about public goods, surely having long-lived foundations should be one such public good.

I wrote "should be" because one of the challenges for us is how to ensure that long-lived foundations don't become calcified dinosaur bones. How can they remain an independent voice? How can they remain vital, risk-taking, and renewed organizations so they can use their history, knowledge, and cultures to enrich civil society and the causes for which they care? These broad questions and the very history of philanthropy deserve a great deal more discussion than they generally receive in the field and in the boardroom.

We need foundations with long-lasting commitments to issues that require long-term attention. All too often the short-term belief that we can, for instance, eliminate poverty or cure cancer in ten years is supremely presumptuous and wasteful. Indeed, there are some "technical" issues or projects that can be addressed by foundations easily and directly. But very few troubling social issues can be so easily solved in a lifetime. Although that is certainly due in part to foundation ineffectiveness, many problems philanthropy seeks to address are immensely complex, some must be addressed over many generations, and some may simply be part of the human condition. Foundations represent not only a workshop for immediate passion and innovation, as many have remarked. They also represent the financial, temporal, and human capital needed to address issues with a longer-term perspective.

Discussing the social value of having enduring, sustainable and independent philanthropic institutions should be an explicit part of what individual donors and foundation boards think about, though I am sure they rarely do think that way. Perhaps one needs to look beyond mission, impact, payout, and longevity. How about including consideration of a foundation's role as an enduring, vital, and independent institution; as a long-term, committed philanthropic citizen; and as a countervailing power within the complex workings of modern civil society? Having regular discussions about mission and effectiveness in that larger social context would, no doubt, be fruitful.

Assuming perpetuity and a simple 5 percent payout rate as the default, or presuming that larger payouts and spending out is the better choice, are both mistakes. Either spending out or enduring can be a legitimate strategy if it helps meet a particular foundation's mission and is the choice of the donor and/or board. Setting a payout rate, then, is properly, I believe, a complex "private policy" decision. It is not, then, a good idea to subject it to a single "public policy" prescription as many advocates have promoted in the past. Doing so not only restricts the diversity, and wide choice of the goals, strategies, and lifespan decisions donors and boards should have, but it also ignores many important implications and unintended consequences of a higher rate.

I hope that this article will help serve as a reset button for thinking more broadly and deeply about payout, longevity, spending, and the value of enduring, independent institutions in civil society.

This article was presented at the colloquium on Civility, Responsibility and Philanthropy, July 8–11, 2010, sponsored The Philanthropic Enterprise. It was subsequently published in Conversations on Philanthropy, Philanthropic Reflections, *V. 8, 2011.*

---

[1] Foundation Center, *Foundation Growth and Giving Estimates, 2011 Edition*, (New York, Foundation Center, 2011), p. 11.

[2] Richard Marker, *Smart Assets Blog*, Philanthropy New York, February 28, 2009.

[3] Jagpal, Niki. *Criteria for Philanthropy at Its Best.* (Washington, DC: National Committee for Responsive Philanthropy, 2009), p. 99.

[4] Waleson, Heidi. *Beyond Five Percent: The New Foundation Payout Menu.* (San Francisco, CA and New York, NY: Northern California Grantmakers and New York Regional Association of Grantmakers, 2007), p. 32.

[5] Michael Klausner, "When Time Isn't Money," *Stanford Social Innovation Review,* Spring 2003, p. 58.

[6] Cambridge Associates, Inc. *Sustainable Payout for Foundations.* (Grand Haven, MI: Council of Michigan Foundations, 2000). DeMarche Associates. *Spending Policies and Investment Planning for Foundations.* (Washington, DC: Council on Foundations, 1999). This last publication was originally prepared by Donald W. Trotter in 1990, updated in 1995, and updated again by Carter R. Harrison in 1999.

[7] J. P. Morgan Asset Management. *Investment Policy Statements for the Current Environment.* (New York, NY: J. P. Morgan Asset Management, 2011), p. 5.

[8] Deep, Akash, and Peter Frumkin. *The Foundation Payout Puzzle.* Working Paper #9, The Hauser Center for Nonprofit Organizations, John F. Kennedy School of Government, Harvard University, 2001.

[9] These percentages come from the 2011 *Foundation Operations and Management Report*, published by the Association for Small Foundations. Since the report focuses on smaller foundations, the percentages are probably higher for the entire population of private foundations.

[10] Wilhelm, Ian. "Philanthropy's Challenge: Communicating Its Value to Society," *The Chronicle of Philanthropy*, December 13, 2007.

3. The Spend-Out/Perpetuity Distraction and the Merger Option

There is always interest in the issue of lifespan for foundations (spend-out versus perpetuity). The topic was being much discussed in the halls of Congress and in individual foundation board rooms when these blog pieces were first published. The economic downturn at the time certainly influenced this discussion. The issue remains important today.

In most cases, however, these discussions seem like a distraction to me, for several reasons.

- Perpetuity is portrayed by supporters and detractors alike as simply "the way it has always been." That is true, but it isn't a good reason.
- Spending down is often portrayed as the right thing to do. That is way too simplistic.
- The case for spending down seems like a conflict about who controls and spends the money. That is an important issue.
- The perpetuity versus spend-out debate isn't relevant by itself and often distracts from more important and more complex questions of mission and impact.
- And more to the point of this piece, arguing about perpetuity or spend-down diverts us from looking at other, innovative organizational options for foundations.

There are, of course, good reasons to spend out, just as there are good reasons for foundations to continue in existence. These are usually decisions that are properly "private policy" as it were, and not matters for public policy. In August 2009, Anita Nager contributed a blog post on the Beldon Fund's decision to spend out.[1] More recently, Jane Schwartz discussed the Paul Rapoport Foundation's decision to do the same.[2] Both decisions were carefully and sensibly made as the best means to accomplish mission and followed the donor's explicit intent. Those were model decisions implemented well. Those foundations that explicitly decide not to spend out should lay out their respective decisions and strategies with the same openness and care. Too many foundations don't have these discussions.

The Foundation Center and Council on Foundations had previously released *Perpetuity or Limited Lifespan: How Do Family Foundations Decide?*, which discussed the factors involved with various family foundation choices to spend down or to exist in perpetuity.[3] The Aspen Institute published *Time Is of the Essence: Foundations and the Policies of Limited Life and Endowment Spend-Down*. Their historical and contemporary cases studies of five foundations is valuable. The implied presumption that spend-out is the right decision is incorrect. By focusing on spending down, the case is not being made for that one route over the other. It is a case for balance and care:

> The crucial point is that increased and persistent information about the limited life foundation option is imperative if one wishes to deter the nonprofit sector from calcifying into a single, dominant model. Ignorance of the endowment spend down tradition and effectiveness may have caused it to be under-utilized in the past — and present.... The reminder is that endowment spend down and term limitations are not inherently good — or bad. These structural conditions will be appropriate and effective only if implemented wisely. [4]

These and other works have valuable things to say. But the Foundation Center survey of family foundations makes it clear that perpetuity versus spend-out simply isn't a pressing matter. Indeed, most foundation boards and staff and most donors are rightly more concerned about mission, values, effectiveness, and impact; as well as about family issues, control, concerns about "immortality," etc. Decisions on those issues may then lead to strategies that would result in spending out or continuing into the future. We don't generally discuss perpetuity versus closing when discussing settlement houses or commercial equipment manufacturers or community foundations, for instance; why should we with private foundations? Let us stick to the important questions. Let us avoid that first, untethered distraction.

The second distraction is more unfortunate. Perpetuity versus spend out is not the overriding, either/or choice facing foundation boards. A focus on perpetuity versus spend-out impoverishes our thinking about the future of foundations and the varieties of their "existence." What other organizational options can promote mission, values, impact, and effectiveness? What about, for instance, the possibilities of foundations merging, rather than disappearing or doing the same old, staid things?

There are great examples of foundation collaborations, donor collaborations, pooled funds, funders' groups, etc. (as well as some very poor examples). Such collaborations are not easy to accomplish, but they can be innovative and effective. There is a lot of useful and cautionary literature on these. But I am limiting my focus here to different variations that are closer to a merger, that may provide new ways to achieve mission, impact, and other values as well. Many of the issues that animate discussions about spend-out and/or staying in business can be seen in a new light by asking about different possibilities, including merging. The question is relevant not only for family foundations and small foundations, but for larger, more established philanthropic institutions.

I was involved in one collaborative variation that might be a useful model. A family decided to distribute its philanthropic assets and values to five children by setting up five different donor-advised funds. Doing so honored the individual interests of the children and was also done to mitigate the common sibling warfare and logrolling that a single foundation with the five children as trustees might have encouraged. Each family member was happy with this and each went on to approach their giving in different ways.

But they shortly expressed a heightening level of dissatisfaction, even estrangement from each other and their common interests. At a family meeting, they each expressed the desire to maintain some giving autonomy, but also wanted to honor past family interests and ongoing interests. For instance, making a grant from each donor-advised fund to support a university that the family had supported for years seemed wrong somehow. It seemed to dilute their importance, ignored their common commitment, and avoided the value of reaching joint decisions. The perfectly easy solution was to set up another donor-advised fund for whom each was an advisor. Then, as they came up with common commitments, each donor-advised fund could make a grant to this family donor-advised fund, which would then make the single grant. This simple mechanism allowed for both individual and common decision making with less of the sturm und drang often present in family giving.

Other interesting examples exist:

Merger options. In mid-1999, the Charles E. Culpeper Foundation ($212 million in assets) merged with the Rockefeller Brothers Fund (approximately $472 million in assets). In his "Message from the Chair," Steven C Rockefeller noted, "At the RBF, 1999 will be remembered first and foremost as the year of the merger with the Charles E. Culpepper Foundation."[5] The message goes on to comment on the complex process of integrating governance (four Culpepper board members joined the RBF board), as well as the endowment and programs in a sensitive and inclusive way.

In June 2006, Warren Buffett pledged what was then $31 billion to the Bill and Melinda Gates Foundation over a number of years. One stipulation amounted to a spend-down of that amount over time. Starting in 2009, the Gates Foundation must spend at least the amount that was allocated for 2008, in addition to the amount that the foundation would be required to spend under federal tax law. This process would then continue until the Buffett gift is totally expended. Word has it that other donors made the same offer to the Gates Foundation but were declined. Whatever the nature of the offers, this suggests that there is a "market" for additional, competent, independent foundations to steward additional philanthropic funds.

On January 2, 2007, the Silicon Valley Community Foundation opened its doors and became the second-largest community foundation in the country with $1.5 billion in assets under management and 1,400 philanthropic funds. This was the result of a merger of the Community Foundation of Silicon Valley and the Peninsula Community Foundation. As the announcing press release noted:

> This community foundation has the opportunity to pioneer a new standard for civic engagement," said Dr. Emmett Carson, CEO and president of Silicon Valley Community Foundation. "Merging these two well-run and successful foundations is not only innovative and unique, but will better allow us to support, encourage and partner with leaders from the nonprofit, public and private sectors to advance the best ideas and solve problems across the region.
>
> With this final agreement we can officially bring together the knowledge, talent, networks and best practices of both foundations under one roof," said Patricia Bresee, vice chair of board. "The new foundation will be in a great position to more effectively capitalize on the innovation, creativity and entrepreneurship of Silicon Valley than the two parent foundations could alone.
>
> Many benefits will result from Silicon Valley Community Foundation's increased economy of scale. Others will come by blending the different, complementary strengths of each parent foundation — resulting … in a single organization that is greater than the sum of its parts. Based on research and collaboration, members of the board anticipate many advantages will stem from the merger, including:
>
> - Innovative programs and initiatives that result in a deeper and broader impact on the community;
> - Ability to educate and involve the public in key policy and community issues;
> - Greater capacity to engage donors in supporting causes locally and globally;
> - Streamlined grants programs and improved technical assistance for local nonprofits;
> - Greater program expertise and capacity;
> - Better investment options and management of assets, leading to greater donor satisfaction and increased giving; and
> - Increased efficiency in operations.

Intermediaries. There are also the very interesting nonprofit and commercial intermediaries that provide advice and services much deeper than simply consolidating the grantmaking process. This includes community foundations but also organizations like the Philanthropic Initiative and Rockefeller Philanthropy Advisors. There are others, more commercially operated that do the same thing. Some are consulting firms that have found different clients working on the same things, thus suggesting some coordination. The John D. and Catherine T. MacArthur Foundation tried some advisory services. There have been several efforts by the Edna McConnell Clark Foundation, including Blue Meridian Partners.

There are many ways to bring together different donors and foundations. Each of these examples is a variation on the theme of merging. While some are not exactly mergers, these organizational experiments may be the harbingers of exciting and useful organizational structures that do merge mission, endowment, and administration of different foundations in new ways of giving, thus illustrating ways of combining foundations for greater effectiveness and efficiency. There are myriad possibilities and iterations. The field as a whole would do well to focus creatively on the pros and cons of mergers and other such organizational forms. What about other examples? And where are the good "inside story"/how-to case studies? In fact, a valuable service would be performed if the Foundation Center or even the Center for Effective Philanthropy would report on the variations, their structures, advantages and disadvantages. There is something important hidden here. (Let us just not make a big deal out of all of this and market it as the next big thing in philanthropy!)

The history of "strategic alliance" efforts some pundits and foundations have sought over the years to foist upon nonprofits should serve as a cautionary note about all of this. Mergers in any sector are not simple panaceas. They are usually time-consuming, difficult, complex, and messy. They can be inappropriate and inefficient. Each of the above examples had its own difficulties. Mergers certainly have the potential for representing a loss of control or of family involvement. They can become takeovers where the original mission disappears in the bowels of the new entity.

Mergers can also be effective ways to stay true to mission and passion and values. They can substantially increase impact in communities or increase leverage for programs of importance. They can improve efficiency in operations and provide greater programmatic expertise. They can shake up the calcification of settled philanthropic practice while reviving and strengthening civil society, as discussed below.

Conclusion

Boardrooms, staff, scholars, and donors should think about variations of foundation structures that may better serve mission and effectiveness, with efficiency. They could drive impact in powerful ways. We need to experiment with the idea of new foundation forms and combinations. Of course, choosing perpetuity or spending down are relevant issues, just likely too uncreative. Focusing too narrowly on perpetuity versus spend-out is a distraction from the purposes — and the possibilities — of foundations.

The original version of this article was published as one of my contributions to the Smart Assets blog of Philanthropy New York while a Senior Fellow there, on February 8, 2010. Reprinted with permission from Philanthropy New York.

---

[1] Anita Nager, "Spend Out vs Perpetuity: Raising the Question," Philanthropy New York blog post, August 5, 2009.

[2] Jane Schwartz, "After We Say Goodbye," Philanthropy New York blog post, January 29, 2010.

[3] Loren Renz and David Wolcheck, *Perpetuity or Limited Lifespan: How Do Family Foundations Decide?* (New York: Foundation Center, 2009).

[4] John Thelin and Richard Trollinger, *Perpetuity or Limited Lifespan: How Do Family Foundations Decide?* (Washington DC: The Aspen Institute, 2009.) p. 36 and 37.

[5] 1999 Annual Review of Rockefeller Brothers Fund. (New York: Rockefeller Brothers Fund, 2000), p. 5.

4. The Spend-Out Presumption and the Value of Enduring Institutions

Foundations should always explicitly consider their lifespan options. As Richard Marker also wrote in response to this original blog:

> I am regularly surprised by the leanings of my clients toward one or the other approach. Often these leanings seem to run counter to the pattern of funding or content of their grantmaking. Whatever the objective arguments for or against spend-down/perpetuity, funders often make their decisions on the basis of very subjective preferences about their own legacy, perceptions of their own family's values, and experience with the organizations with which they have had direct experience over time. It is important, I think, to ... honor the legitimacy of both approaches — if thought through and made with self-awareness.

In the previous article on "The Spend-Out/Perpetuity Distraction and the Merger Option," I concentrated on the point that simply focusing on foundation perpetuity or spending out was, *per se*, a distraction, from attending to mission and effectiveness and from considering different and potentially productive philanthropic structures, such as foundation mergers. However, I remain distracted by two other things, that I want to address here:

- much of the discussion about foundation lifespan presumes the superiority of spend-out, and
- the value of enduring, independent philanthropic institutions to civil society is unfortunately ignored.

A Spend-out Presumption

For instance, some outsiders and policy people emphasize the advantages of spending out because they fear the independence of foundations; don't trust staff and boards to do the perfect thing; or desire getting the money out of foundation coffers now, no matter how productive that might be. Foundation staff may not admit it, but spending out may be in their self-interest, since it increases their "power." Some board members, foundation staff, and donors favor spending out because they believe only they can make the best decisions. They hate the idea of passing control to others, or they are flummoxed by how to negotiate the generational transfer of intent and governance. Spending more funds on particular issues now may hold the promise of greater immediate impact. But for many of the issues foundations address, spending more now may be a temporal illusion: the philanthropic version of the short-sighted, short-term thinking that plagues American corporations in search of profit.

These are not the only reasons to spend out, of course. My point is simply that the case for spending out isn't quite as obvious or neutral as it is sometimes portrayed; there can be some less attractive motivations for it. The presumption may also "crowd out" other options.

There are, of course, less attractive reasons for perpetuity as well. It is, for instance, the unthinking, default position for far too many foundations and donors. Sometimes, a false belief in donor immortality and control from the grave is at play. In any case, all motivations, good and bad, should be discussed before deciding whether spending out or a longer lifespan will best serve mission and effectiveness.

Taking the Long View

Nonetheless, I believe there are good reasons to take a longer-term view about foundation lifespan, one that is rarely raised. In an "exit interview" published in the December 13, 2007 *Chronicle of Philanthropy* before she left the Ford Foundation, Susan Berresford talked passionately about the importance of long-term institutions: "Our society values enduring institutions...we treasure them because they express and reinforce our values." And justly so.

Strong, diverse, and long-lasting institutions are a vital part of a sustained civil society. New foundations and other philanthropic formations constantly help to renew civil society, and that is a good thing. At the same time, foundations that have long histories, existing cultures, experience, and working capital are immensely valuable as well. As enduring institutions, foundations can represent significant, independent organizations within civil society. They are "countervailing" institutions, to use a phrase now out of fashion. They stand separate from governmental, corporate/commercial, and other special interests. They can cooperate with and influence these interests with legitimacy, experience, and an independent status that comes from their long-term knowledge and endowments. Centuries of history and many events in the last couple of decades — in the United States and internationally — should remind us just how important enduring and independent institutions can be to society. If one is going to talk about the public good, surely having long-lived foundations can be one such public good.

I wrote "can be" because one of the challenges for us is how to make sure long-lived foundations don't merely become calcified dinosaur bones. How can they remain vital and renewed, and use their history, knowledge, and cultures to enrich civil society and the causes for which they care?

Foundation mergers and exploring other organizational models may be some ways. Having regular discussions about mission and effectiveness — along with explicitly considering the time horizon for a foundation — can be another. Developing staff and board leadership (from within and without) with a comprehensive time horizon in mind is crucial.

We also need foundations with long-lasting commitments to issues that require long-term attention. All too often, the short-term belief that we can, for instance, eliminate poverty or cure cancer in ten years is supremely presumptuous and wasteful. Big money dropped on a cause or organization can be quite detrimental to both. It can be wasteful and less impactful than consistent funding over many years. Indeed, few issues addressed by foundations have been solved in a lifetime. While that is certainly partially due to foundation ineffectiveness, many problems are immensely complex and may even be part of the human condition. Foundations represent not only a workshop for passion and innovation, as many have remarked. They also represent the financial and human capital needed to address issues. And passion, fact-finding, innovation, and financial capital are sometimes best utilized with a longer-term perspective.

Assuming perpetuity as the default or presuming spending out in X years are both mistakes, because they are assumed and not thoughtfully decided. Spending out or enduring can both be legitimate strategies if they help meet a foundation's mission. In any case, the values to society of sustained and independent philanthropic institutions should be its own, explicit, part of what we consider when making that choice. I suspect individual foundations rarely think that way. Perhaps part of the "public" obligation of philanthropic institutions is to "think about" their larger and continuing role sustaining a robust civil society. I am not suggesting that this consideration should take precedence over all other considerations.

Perhaps, then, when one looks at perpetuity versus spend out, or mission and impact, one value to factor in is a foundation's role as an enduring, independent institution; as a long-term, committed philanthropic citizen; as a countervailing power within the complex workings of society, government and markets.

The original version of this article was published as one of my contributions to the Smart Assets blog of Philanthropy New York while a Senior Fellow there, on February 26, 2010. Reprinted with permission from Philanthropy New York.

CHAPTER 7

GOVERNANCE MATTERS

Board and troubled board have become almost interchangeable.... The board appears to be an unreliable instrument for ensuring accountability — the outcome society most wants from it. Behind every scandal or organizational collapse is a board (often one with distinguished members) asleep at the switch. And while it is true that a board is behind a very high-performing organization, it is often along for the ride, cheering and boosting the work of the executive and staff. — Richard Chait, William Ryan, Barbara Taylor

In a very real sense, then, boards exist — at least for now — to serve as the binding which holds together the "sticks" — political, economic, cultural, public, and private — that comprise public life. — Peter Dobkin Hall

The requirement of moral courage. It is not morally easy to make choices that respect the future against the past and the present. It is not morally easy to assert one's obligation of final judgement against a determined and skillful staff. It is not morally easy to defend choices that may not be immediately popular. It is usually very hard indeed to do what is right instead of what merely pleases the powerful. But this is what foundation trustees are for. — McGeorge Bundy

S hortly after I started at the J. M. Kaplan Fund, I had lunch with Margaret Mahoney, the legendary president of the Commonwealth Fund. We talked a great deal about foundation boards. She emphasized that I, as executive director, needed to cultivate board members to get the kind of board I needed to support and watch me. I appreciated the way she wove the importance of governance into my job description. Five years later, at my first board meeting as ED of The Clark Foundation, board member Cliff Wharton told me that if the board didn't reject 10 percent of my recommendations, I wasn't being creative enough. I was forever thankful for that benchmark and that clever expression of trust from my board.

I quickly learned that family foundation boards were complex, not least because the boardroom table erratically morphed in and out of being the family kitchen table where all manner of family wrangling played out. It was a sight to behold. On the doorknob of the Kaplan Fund boardroom I hung a pair of boxing gloves!

I also gained a tremendous level of respect for boards generally and a soft spot for family foundation boards. They are passionate and committed, come to quick — mostly thoughtful — decisions, and have a thirst for learning how to do it better. That doesn't mean that there aren't some pretty spectacular *faux pas* and dodgy behavior, too. I have seen some truly appalling behavior at other foundations and once resigned a board because of it.

Some of my most satisfying professional and personal experiences have been my longtime work on several boards (especially The Chamber Music Society of Lincoln Center, the Council on Foundations, and a small family foundation). Those experiences also taught me how crucial good governance is. Boards must especially learn the skill to continually think well into the future: What about possible executive transitions in the future? How will a board continually replenish itself of good executive staff and also train new board members?

Even so, most foundations pay slight attention to grantee boards or to the careful care and feeding of their own boards. As a result, I have seen foundations miss grantee problems and underestimate their needs. One foundation's million-dollar bet on an organization went terribly awry because they didn't include the grantee's board in initial project discussions. Over time, The Clark Foundation started asking that a grantee board member attend our site visits.

How, then, do we help ensure success for the nonprofit organization and for the board members themselves? How do we help lessen the chances of ineffectiveness and inefficiency? These articles just touch the surface of such important topics.

1. The Dirty Deed Is Done:
Reflections on Grantmaking and Governance

I am honored to be here. Thank you, David, Michael, and Governance Matters. I have learned so much from you all. Indeed, over time I have come to understand the importance of board governance, which undergirds everything I say tonight. I see now what I summarize as "Chuck's rule of thumb about governance" for both nonprofit and foundation boards: 80 percent of a nonprofit's success is enabled by or attributable to effective and engaged board members. And 80 percent of a nonprofit's failure is traceable to lack of oversight or leadership by the organization's board. Why, then, is board governance so often undervalued or ignored? How do we help ensure the board success for foundations and nonprofits and mitigate the inevitable failures? Those are heady topics. In keeping with tonight's vibe, I will meander through the woods of our business and come back to board governance later.

When looking at philanthropy writ large, I very much like an observation by Shakespeare, which I think captures the heady and oh so important nature of philanthropy:

> … a trade sir that I would like to practice in good conscience as a mender of *souls*.

When I read the first draft of my remarks, they were forty-five minutes long. Both Yancy and my better half, Carol, separately commented "Chuck, giving away money makes you charming but not that charming." I had wanted to weave together several stories (roadkill, if you will) along the yellow brick road from proposal to grant and then make some recommendations. Stories like:

- The job training grantee turned away two foundation program officers on a site visit because they were not appropriately dressed. (Haven't we all wanted to do that!) One would think that program officers knew that dress is an important part of preparing young people for the world of work. A few years later a young client of that same grantee was the doorman at the building where a big foundation had their offices. One day, I arrived ten minutes late for a meeting. The young doorman chastised me for being late, bless his heart. These two stories suggest how good that job training program really was. No doubt that nonprofit should also have a philanthropoid training program for the likes of us!

- A foundation in Chicago gave $10,000 a year to help solve the dropout problem in the public schools. After three years, it refused to make another grant because the problem had not been solved. On what planet?

- The community foundation head who said that an early $5,000 grant to Faneuil Hall justified claiming credit for the Hall's subsequent success. Oh, the hubris.

- A nonprofit, having a serious budget shortfall, sent out fifty desperate letters one snowy December seeking end-of-the-year grants — clearly not understanding that foundations can't act that quickly, but that is a different issue. The letters went from the Bronx to Manhattan-based foundations. But — wait for it — they actually sent those letters via FedEx First Delivery. You can't make this up.

- I don't think I have received more than a half dozen really good proposals in my career. It is a great irony that when The Clark Foundation undertook to build the technical assistance capacity of TA providers in New York City, a short and simple request for proposals from TA providers produced the dozen worst proposals we ever received. Makes one wonder.

- And one more: there was the program officer who said he had defunded a group because he had grown "bored" with them. I was left speechless.

Well, I have shortened my comments to four points about:
1. philanthropic hubris and the uneasy relationship between foundation and nonprofit organizations;
2. grantmaking in this — or any! — economic climate;
3. implementing good grantmaking; and of course,
4. how we are finally discovering that governance really does matter.

Hubris and "The Dirty Deed"

Over the last forty years, I have worked for nonprofits, started a book publishing company that, alas, became a nonprofit, and for many years ran and then sold a successful corporation. For the last twenty-five years, I have primarily been a member of the genus *philanthropoid*. I have worked for six foundations: one large independent foundation, three family foundations, one supporting organization and one large operating foundation. Inherently corrupting as it is, I expect to remain in this business for a while longer.

The day after I became executive director of the J. M. Kaplan Fund, historical preservationist, foundation watcher, and friend Kent Barwick sidled up to me and congratulated me: "That is great news, Chuck. But yesterday was the last time you will ever get a bad meal, ever tell a bad joke, or ever get an honest compliment." That rather stark prediction turns out to be largely true. Daily events remind me of this often because I have become a very important person.

For example, on a cold November 8th, eight years ago, I and The Clark Foundation were being recognized at a big and impressive event for United Neighborhood Houses. During the reception, the board chair and executive director of a long-term grantee came up to me. It was a love-fest about how wonderful I was, how wonderful The Clark Foundation was, and then more about how wonderful, understanding, helpful, handsome, and smart I was. It went on for what seemed like many minutes. It was extravagant, overdone, and, of course, well-deserved. I was very gracious about it all. As they left, thinking I was out of earshot, the chair leaned toward the executive director and whispered, "There, the dirty deed is done." So that is what a $100,000 yearly grant buys!

But the true impact of all this was less on how people would view me and more about how I and philanthropists generally start viewing ourselves. All meals started to taste good, all our jokes were hilarious to us, and the compliments I got were obviously sincere and deserved. And therein lies the care and feeding of philanthropic hubris. We are not nearly as special as we think we are. Let us get off our high horse, listen more, pontificate less (except in my case tonight), and learn from our peers in the nonprofit sector.

As much as philanthropy may derive from a love of mankind, and truly serves that purpose often, it is always eternally laced with self-interest, pettiness, and biases too numerous to count. Let us not kid ourselves. Remember back to the program officer who defunded a group because he was bored. Indeed, I think that the inexplicable in foundation behavior is often simply explained if one just acknowledges that helping nonprofits is not necessarily what foundations are about. My great-aunt unwittingly pointed this out to me. She is a wonderful woman from Holland. She loves the English language, is endlessly curious about it, but still struggles with it. Years ago, she asked me about my work. I told her I gave away money and was a "philanthropist." A bit later, she rushed back into the room with dictionary in hand. With a rather distressed look on her face, she asked, "Oh, Charlie, are you really a philanderer?" Humm. Having too many casual affairs with grantee organizations? Endlessly teasing them? Being self-absorbed? I wonder if she didn't get the picture partially right?

Let's admit that we are very often moved by whim and self-interests. That leads to the fickle natures of our decision making. We should always question our motives. We must guard against making promises and playing around with our grantee organizations. This is hard work: to listen, learn, and always be humble. Even the simple things count. If we are going to say no to a request, the earlier the better. Don't ask for proposals or final reports if we have no intention of taking it seriously.

As I have gotten older and more experienced, I have learned to distrust the grand schemes, the systems, and the lofty views of philanthropy. I tire of endless meetings and wonder if grand solutions really get us very far. There are too many unintended consequences that are negative. Instead, I more and more believe in hard, smart work, evidence, and cooperation, if it leads somewhere. I know all of this is rarer than we would all like to admit. Grantmaking is time-consuming and difficult to do well. Success, then, is about the little things, as many before me have noted. William James has this wonderful quotation:

> I am done with great things and big plans, great institutions and big success. I am for those tiny invisible loving human forces that work from individual to individual, creeping through the crannies of the world like so many rootlets ... which, if given time, will rend the hardest monuments of human pride.

Exactly! Get the little things right; they are really everything.

Grantmaking and Economic Excuses

Right now, foundations, nonprofits, and especially our ultimate clients are being buffeted by economic turmoil, uncertainty, and slow growth. In this economic climate much needs to be done, and hats off to the many foundations and nonprofits that have made very difficult decisions and have acted quickly and sensibly. But talk of the recession also feels like an excuse. I wonder about all the time and effort spent on this topic. Endless meetings, endless surveys, all to what effect?

This is the time to remind ourselves that the response to this economic crisis is simply about implementing good grantmaking, not about new ways to do grantmaking. What we as foundations and nonprofits should together be doing in response to this recession is exactly what *we should have been doing* over, well, forever: long-term general operating support, smart technical assistance, building management capacity, developing leadership, managing by results, fully costing out all programs, cooperating in substantive ways, and working with and developing strong boards.

It is a terrible insult to all that is important to us if we think we can simply change our ways of grantmaking now, in response to the recession. If that is the way we act and see things, we will have learned nothing and will go back to our old ways after the recession is over.

Of course, we must practice our crafts in the changing landscapes before us. Foundations are not the "warehouses of wealth" critics sometimes perceive. In fact, one of the dirty little secrets of foundation work has been that there are not enough good nonprofits to support. Hear me out on this. Several years ago, over a six-month period, I heard the same lament from five executive directors and senior program officers. Each person complained that there simply were "not enough good organizations and programs" to fund. I would add that I occasionally faced the same quandary. There are times when meeting the budgeted 5 percent payout meant that less effective organizations were funded. In addition, since the mid-1980s, when recessions or significant economic downturns showed up in reduced grant making budgets at many foundations, some staff candidly admitted that this was an opportunity to cull their grantee lists of those organizations they considered less effective.

What does that say about foundations and the efficiency and effectiveness of the nonprofit sector? Well, there is less to give away during the recession and its immediate aftermath. And however offensive this next observation may also be, I for one continue to believe that there are too many nonprofits. Several commentators have said that because of the recession, there will be 10 percent fewer nonprofits in the next year or two. This can be tragic and painful. And it is also potentially a good thing. But foundations must refrain from "encouraging" mergers, which make what should be strategic decisions into just plain old "funding opportunities." Nonprofits need to make those decisions themselves. It could lead to better uses of resources, more effective provision of services. It doesn't need to gut the community infrastructure we all value. Those are the challenges where implementing good grantmaking can play a salutary role. This is true all the time, not just in response to a recession.

One last thing about grantmaking excuses. I think staying the course can be a vastly underappreciated value, especially since we as grantmakers do jump on pretexts — good or not — to change directions, almost for their own sake. For instance, right after 9/11, many foundations made drastic changes in their funding priorities, which meant that fairly regular support to hundreds of nonprofits was cut. As I talked with grantees, it was clear they were worried and that many key support programs were in jeopardy. While we all have to make difficult choices, cutting support for these programs was a mistake in my view.

I proceeded to walk into board chair Jane Clark's office and mentioned the issue. To her great credit she immediately saw that we should maintain our current priorities and our general operating support for our grantees. This was the most important step we should take. We sent a letter to our 120 or so grantees telling them this. We received many notes of thanks and relief.

Implementing Good Grantmaking: 6 Things One Must Do

In this economic crisis – in any economic situation -- there is only good grantmaking, now and forever. Our job is to figure out how to implement good grantmaking, whether we are in foundations or nonprofits. It can be broken down into a "to-do" list of six practical suggestions. They should be requirements:

Exhibit humble, simple common decency. As Alan Pifer wrote years ago, when president of the Carnegie Corp., "...the human qualities of its staff may in the end be far more important to what a foundation accomplishes than any other consideration." Foundations need to respect boundaries. We don't know everything. We need to listen, help in ways beyond money, then step back and let our grantees do their work.

Foundation staff must have real experience and real skills. If you haven't met a payroll, don't apply. Practical and significant financial and other business training is crucial. All program officers should serve on one non-grantee board.

Make half the number of grants, give twice the size of grants for twice the length of time. For instance, at The Clark Foundation, we should have 60, not 120 grantees; we should have an average grant size closer to $180,000 per year and not $90,000. The grant term should be two years. All of this is contingent, of course, upon capacity and results. However, as we have found, this isn't easy. At The Clark Foundation, we are not shy about increasing or decreasing the size of a request. Alas, so often we simply don't feel comfortable doing so, based on the proposal and capabilities of leadership. The reasons are multiple, of course, and we are partially at fault too. We feel we must limit our risk.

Eighty percent of all grants should be negotiated general operating support. For The Clark Foundation, it is close to that. In exchange for clarity about how an organization defines success, measures success, and would know success, there should be considerable autonomy on how the organization implements a plan and spends the money. The devil is in the details here, of course. When we tried to do this, I immediately received a hastily handwritten note from Fran Barrett, ED of Community Resource

Exchange, that read: "Negotiated General Operating Support. Bullshit!" Only Fran would write that to a foundation grantor, I laughed! Or so I thought. When I called her, she assured me she had written "Brilliant." After further handwriting analysis and review by others, I think there is a 90 percent chance it did read "brilliant." That bad handwriting symbolizes how difficult GOS really is. Our experience has been decidedly mixed. That is due in part to our own failings. But I have almost never read a good rationale for general operating support from a grantee. Without a solid rationale you encourage crazy foundation behavior. One of my favorite — horrifying — examples is the foundation that wrote, "We do not fund any indirect costs. We fund identified specific project costs only and feel that the organization should fund its own indirect costs." What? Really? That is an incoherent statement!

Focus on and refine what it means for foundations and nonprofits to succeed. Results, results, results!

Ensure the right people are on the governance bus. Foundation and nonprofit boards hold the key to organizational success or failure. Board members, whether we like it or not, do make a very big difference.

Governance Does Matter

Finally, and crucially, board governance does matter. I am preaching to the choir of course. It either ties it all together or it leads to a fraying of effectiveness.

No one can read about contemporary problems at banks, Brandeis University, and the LA Museum of Contemporary Art and not know that governance really does matter. Within a matter of weeks of becoming the executive director of the J. M. Kaplan Fund, I had lunch with Margaret Mahoney, the legendary president of the Commonwealth Fund. We talked a great deal about foundation boards, which I later saw neatly distilled in one of her annual letters in the Commonwealth Fund's annual report: "Demonstrating that a foundation deserves trust begins with its board of directors consciously taking on the job of trusteeship…" Over time, that has proven to be all too true for foundations and nonprofits generally. Boards are not an afterthought or simply a legal nicety.

When Mahoney started beating this theme into our heads, boards were largely invisible or an ineffective distraction. They were rarely part of any due diligence process that foundations did. In at least one case in recent years, a foundation's nearly $1 million investment almost scuttled a significant nonprofit because the board was ignored in the grantmaking process.

Things are better now and there are extraordinarily fine boards. But foundation and nonprofit leaders are still not good enough at developing, using or managing their boards. One very effective nonprofit executive — contrary to this point — strictly ignores his board and is proud of it. We can understand that; it can be a pain. It works for him now. But I know that, as a result, his effectiveness will leave little legacy when the board needs to hire new leadership without the cooperative experience, knowledge and standards by which to do so well.

Boards are, of course, often quick to micromanage. They can be reticent and slow to apply the oversight, stewardship, and foresight that are their difficult job. If those are not done well, problems and ineffectiveness grow. Indeed, most problems that foundations and nonprofits have should have been seen first by boards. Michael Kaiser, president of Kennedy Center, recently said, "Most board members ... do not know how to fit a vision into an affordable structure." This, sadly, makes ineffectiveness more possible. And that is why good governance is so crucial. There may be no more highly leveraged task for foundations and nonprofit boards and staffs than to attend to the nature, care, and feeding of their boards.

Philanthropy as a Mender of Soles?

But wait, oh my goodness, I have made a terrible mistake. There is a misspelling in the Shakespeare quotation I gave you above! It should read:

> ... a trade sir that I would like to practice in good conscience as a mender of *soles*.

Much more appropriate. No hubris there! We in philanthropy are not so special and our grantees would be better off if we approached our work as simple cobblers. That work must include boards, for they hold — whether we like it or not — many of the keys to success.

Oh, and about that grantee who did the "dirty deed." Yes, they are still a grantee. The dirty deed is done ... and it can be undone.

This presentation was originally prepared as the keynote to the Governance Matters Annual Meeting, February 11, 2009. Governance Matters was an early, groundbreaking organization formed to provide nonprofit leaders with the governance resources they need to develop better boards that serve New York's communities. It was founded in 1969 by Brooke Mahoney who was ED and self-described "Innovator-in-Chief" for thirty-eight years. David La Greca had become executive director in 2008 and served in that capacity until 2016.

2. Call to Duty: Effective
Board Service for Nonprofits, Philanthropy and You

The reputation and impact of nonprofit organizations and foundations rise and fall on the abilities of their boards. Robert K. Greenleaf put it this way in his important book, *Servant Leadership*: "There is no other way that as few people can raise the quality of the whole American society as far and as fast as can trustees and directors of our voluntary institutions."

The ability to support a cause through a public charity, or the opportunity to be a steward of family wealth through a family foundation (or donor-advised fund), are why individuals join boards. Board members supply leadership. They give their invaluable knowledge and experience to philanthropic and nonprofit organizations, which makes those organizations more effective at meeting their missions over time.

Two characteristics typically distinguish board service between these two forms of nonprofit. First, foundations give away money and nonprofit organizations, as the term is usually used, raise funds for charitable programs and services. This is a significant difference though polls show most Americans don't get it. Most *private* foundation boards include donors or family members of the donors and are thus usually described as family foundations. The family overlay can be a source of great satisfaction and/or deep angst. For the purposes of this article, I include donor-advised funds, since many of them are taking on some of the governance trappings of private foundations. There are differences, but the importance of governance remains. That family overlay is a constant feature: As John D. Rockefeller is reported to have quipped, "Everything is relative, except relatives, who are constant."

Second, meaningful board service for a *public* charity, however, usually includes some level of financial contribution that doesn't apply as a board member of a family foundation. And fundraising is a major task.

Both types of organizations, though, require leadership. As Adrian Sargeant, a professor of fundraising at Indiana University, recently wrote in *Crain's New York Business*, "Today's donors don't want to be seen as piggy banks. They want to be seen as people who are active in the cause." With my nearly 30 years of experience in the foundation and nonprofit world, I have come to believe that 80 percent of nonprofits success is enabled by effective and engaged board members. And 80 percent of a nonprofit's failure is traceable to lack of oversight or leadership by the board. This is especially true, I think, with family foundations. How, then, do we help ensure success for nonprofits and foundations as well as a satisfying board experience for individuals? How do we help lessen the chances of ineffectiveness and inefficiency?

This article provides an introduction to nonprofit and philanthropic board service, with suggestions for how to make it a valuable experience for you and the organization. My four main points cover: asking the right questions before joining a board; understanding your duties and responsibilities; understanding the special nature of family legacy organizations; and driving the board's performance through leadership.

Before Joining a Board

An individual was recently asked to join the board of a nonprofit organization she cares deeply about. Upon review of its financials, several red flags became evident that could have signaled major problems. Everything turned out to be fine, but these were issues worth asking about before she made a decision that could have been a serious mistake.

Prior to committing to board membership, then, it is important to know what you are getting into. You may want to ask yourself the following:

- Is it a cause or organization I care deeply about?
- Do I respect the board members, board chair, and executive director, and see myself working well with them? For a family philanthropy, the question is complex: Do I get along with the donor and with what may be generations and branches of family?
- Is the organization financially sound? Has the board answered my organizational and financial questions clearly?
- Is there a statement of board members' responsibilities? Are the duties meaningful? Do the board chair, other board members, and the executive director share the same view of the role?
- Is the time commitment something I can reasonably meet?
- Are the financial obligations and fundraising obligations clear?
- How will I contribute to the organization beyond the financial?
- Does the organization have directors' and officers' liability insurance?

Additional things to think about when considering joining a board:

1. What areas interest you?
   - Arts and culture
   - Education
   - Environment and animals
   - Health and human services

- International/foreign affairs
- Public/societal benefit
- Religion

2. Where do you feel the most comfortable?
   - Grassroots or start-up organization?
   - Founder-driven group?
   - Transitional group?
   - More established board?
   - A turnaround situation?
3. What are your pragmatic requirements?
   - Near home or work?
   - Travel time?
   - Meet during the day, evenings, or weekends?
4. What role do you want to play?
   - A catalyst?
   - Part of a small pioneer group?
   - Member of a larger, established entity?
   - A comfortable, non-stress stewardship commitment?

For family foundations there is a very important additional consideration. Since most board members are family members, both nominators and prospective board members usually simply assume family members will — and indeed should — be board members because they are family. That assumption can be the beginning of conflict. It is doubly necessary, then, to ask the questions listed above and to discuss the duties and responsibilities enumerated below before making a decision. That applies to all family members, including original donors, family board members, and especially those of different generations, such as parents or cousins, and finally, the prospective board member. Simply being a family member should not be a guarantee to board membership.

Even if you have answered all the questions, be careful about the number of boards you join. Serving on multiple boards is a common, social temptation. Doing so may well limit the attention you can give to each and thus your personal satisfaction and effectiveness. There was an individual who joined a nonprofit board in his community. Five years later he realized he now sat on eight boards! While each "yes" had a good reason, he simply could not fully meet his responsibilities to any of the boards. He found the whole thing a burden. He quit all eight boards in frustration and then had to explain how his actions were not a vote of no-confidence in the nonprofit organizations. The lesson is that if you do join more than one board, do so with care, know which one is your primary commitment, and make sure the respective organizations know your priorities.

Duties and Responsibilities

Do you know what the board chair, other board members, and the executive director believe the board's role to be? When a family is involved, be aware of the donor's intent, if there is one. Be particularly sensitive to generational issues, since that can add a significant challenge to communication. Too many boards assume that their role is to rubber-stamp the decisions of the founder or donor, executive director, or board chair. When that is the case, it is clear that you are about to embark on a "meeting of the bored." You want to avoid this because it is both an abrogation of a board's legal responsibilities and a sign that your skills and leadership will not be appreciated.

A nonprofit organization or family foundation should have a written statement of board responsibilities and duties. In fact, many boards have a formal job description for their members, which each board member signs. I know of one family foundation that lists these legal responsibilities, other board obligations, and the organization's mission on a "placemat" that is set in front of each board member at meetings. It serves as a useful reminder about the board members' roles and how their work furthers the mission. When family members are involved, something like that can help keep the boardroom table from morphing into a "kitchen table," where family disagreements from the past can raise their ugly heads.

Each board has different expectations and duties; nonetheless, there are three primary legal duties:

The duty of care. Pay careful attention to the operations and finances of the organization. Be prudent; ask questions.

The duty of loyalty. You must set aside personal, professional, and family interests. Your loyalty is to the nonprofit or foundation over all other parties when organizational issues or opportunities arise. You must understand and avoid conflicts of interest and self-dealing: that is, actions personally benefiting yourself or others. Family foundations can pose particularly treacherous self-dealing situations. Questioning actions by other family members can be quite difficult. Some self-dealing rules are anything but logical. That doesn't matter. Knowing about self-dealing rules and being very careful about it is especially important.

The duty of obedience. Participate actively in the oversight of organizational activities through meetings, review of information, and other measures. Board members should exercise their own reasoned judgment, but they cannot act in a manner that is inconsistent with the organization's mission.

Perhaps there is no more important responsibility for a board member than to learn about the organization and to ask the difficult questions. There is an old adage that too many board members leave their brains at the boardroom door, particularly when it comes to financial acumen. I have seen this tendency exacerbated within family foundations. Maintaining the truly important family culture and avoiding upsetting family members can become excuses for ignoring uncomfortable, difficult issues. Promoting a family legacy, a good cause, and a social mission are all the more reason for board members to be hard-nosed and businesslike.

An Organization's Responsibility

Prospective board members should be carefully vetted; practically this is usually a haphazard process of who knows whom. New board members are then usually simply led to a seat at the table. Board membership is not a natural skill. There should be a formal board orientation to introduce them to their responsibilities and to the organization's history, culture, challenges and opportunities. Many boards also assign a "buddy" to new board members. This may appear hackneyed, but it helps bring new members up to speed and gives them a way to ask questions that might be passed over.

The lack of an orientation process is an invitation to poor board performance. For instance, a couple added their young adult children to the board of a foundation that was about to grow significantly. They wanted to introduce them to the joys and responsibilities of taking on this important legacy. Despite everyone's enthusiasm, there was no initial guidance. Different expectations led to nasty conflicts. A written "job" description, a board orientation, and a buddy system would have been very helpful.

The Shoals of Board Compensation

Board compensation has legal implications and complexities worth mentioning here. Most public charities and family foundations do not compensate board members. Board membership is seen as a privilege, a voluntary activity, and indeed a responsibility. However, compensation is permissible, as long as it is reasonable. Some people make the case that reasonable compensation is an important way to reimburse members for their time and expertise.

For family foundations, this can be a particularly sensitive issue. On the one hand, the board's work for a small foundation can take considerable time since there is often no staff. Family foundations can serve as a training ground by providing initial jobs for a family member. Reasonable compensation can make sense here, though most family foundations do not do this. On the other hand, self-dealing restrictions against private inurement must be very carefully followed. Working for a family foundation is not and should never be seen as a family sinecure. There are regular stories in the press of shamefully excessive compensation being paid that is against the letter and spirit of the charitable mission of foundations.

Many foundations use small annual discretionary grant allocations as an alternative way to thank board members for their time and expertise while continuing to pursue their grantmaking missions. This can make sense. Be careful not to let discretionary allocations replace a common focus, which can easily happen. Some family foundations have discretionary allocations tied to the amount a board member gives of their own money.

Family Foundation Boards Are a Bit Different

Best practices for boards apply to foundation and nonprofit boards alike. However, because many private foundations involve family, there are multiple ways that these family foundations are different.

It all starts, as one might imagine, with family dynamics. Potential joys and landmines abound. The wonderful, sustaining, and valuable qualities that can bring families closer together are set against the painful, complex, crazy, and conflict-producing qualities that can tear families apart. This mix makes board interactions more complicated for family foundations. It is a critical challenge to try to keep personal, family, and foundation issues as separate as possible. Don't let the boardroom table become a kitchen table free-for-all. Because family relationships can hijack governance within family foundations, it is worth repeating that serving on a board means you are running a business, not engaging in some family retreat!

Though not exhaustive, the following six points suggest some of the more important factors affecting family foundations:

Whose money is it? Public charity boards understand they are stewards for an institution's well-being and finances. Since there is a family connection with family foundation boards, there can be a tendency for board members to view the endowment as "their" money. It is not! They exercise significant control *not* by dint of being family but because they are trustees or directors of the institution, with all the attendant duties and responsibilities.

Board entitlement. There is often an assumption that a family member will simply become a board member. Not all should. Prospective board members should be vetted the same way, whether it is a family foundation or public charity. Prospective board members should make sure that they are comfortable with the mission and family goals of the organization.

Generational issues. Helping to govern and manage a family foundation can be a wonderful learning opportunity and a stepping stone for other endeavors. Bringing on and educating the next generation is essential to sustaining the family legacy. It will require patience, openness, and skill on the part of each generation. Simply putting a child or other family member on the board is not enough. Orientation and mentoring are key. Generations tend to feel and think differently, so developing listening skills is especially important.

Non-family board members. Whether to have outside (non-family) board members is often a complex issue. It is sometimes seen as a solution to family squabbles; it rarely accomplishes that. Having non-family board members can be a good or a bad idea depending on the circumstances. It is worth a careful, candid discussion. Then, if a foundation decides to do so, it is usually best to bring on two or more (so family members are less likely to "gang up" on the "outsider"). Including spouses has its own quandaries; family dynamics will determine whether and how to handle this.

No fundraising, but ... On the one hand, there is rarely a need to contribute or raise funds. On the other hand, you will experience significant outside pressure from prospective grantees and their board members as they solicit your help in getting a grant. That may even include being asked to join *their* boards. And remember that your personal financial commitments are *not* commitments of the family foundation.

Management experience. Finally, family foundations can be a good training ground for the next generation to learn about social responsibility and board governance. A family member may also be a staff member running the day-to-day operations of the foundation. Governance and management, however, are two different things. Board members need to respect and understand the differences. Many family foundations don't allow family staff on the board, or only in an *ex officio* capacity. I think that is a good rule.

Providing Leadership and Driving Performance

Good boards must balance oversight and leadership to move the organization forward. Oversight entails regular and fairly routine review of what the organization has done. Leadership is a higher and nonetheless necessary level of inquiry. The goal is to anticipate and then provide more active guidance into the future. For example, a client has now been a board member of two arts organizations for the last five years. Each organization had been languishing, but she has turned them around through her eye for detail and passion for planning ahead — an immensely valuable contribution.

The contributions you can make to a nonprofit organization often go well beyond any donations, as truly significant as that fundraising role is. Executive Director Cynthia Remec of BoardAssist, matches prospective board members with organizations and she sees this again and again:

> We find that most of our placements take on a leadership role within six months. And since leadership is rare, those skills, in whatever area, are very often more valuable to the organization than their financial commitment.

Once you have learned everything you can about the organization and the board, choose the way to get involved that best suits your skills and personality. That could be as a member of a board committee, lending your special expertise in finance, development or grantmaking, serving as a mentor to the executive director, or simply being a voice of reason and compromise. I have often thought that playing the role of "family therapist" was an important and high calling in family foundations. You can also use your connections to help the board and organization find the external expertise they need. Whatever the niche that works for you and your skills, don't stop there. Ask yourself about the added value you do bring and ask how the organization will benefit.

How best to think about focusing your leadership potential and contribution to the board you join? One way is to think about the list of common responsibilities many boards articulate for their members. Ask yourself, for instance, how you can promote and strengthen the nonprofit or foundation along one or two of these lines:

Know the organization's mission. Review it periodically for accuracy and validity. Are the mission and programs aligned? For family foundations, this also means understanding the donor's original intent and its ongoing role for the foundations (see the articles in Chapter 9).

Select, support, and assess the CEO. There should be a clear job description. Give the chief executive moral and professional support to do the job. Make sure to evaluate his or her performance periodically.

Ensure effective organizational planning. Participate in the overall planning process; set policies, operations, and practices. Advocate for and help organize a board retreat. Oversee a new strategic plan. Monitor its implementation and effectiveness. Ask what will the future look like and how will we get there?

Ensure adequate resources and manage them effectively. Exercise careful fiduciary oversight. The board develops the annual budget and must have proper controls in place. Does the organization have the resources to fulfill the mission? Engage all board members in fundraising: teach them how.

Help institutionalize a culture of learning and inquiry. Boards often don't know how to ask difficult questions. An atmosphere of false courtesy can stifle constructive debate. Learning to encourage asking and answering difficult questions will lead to sound and shared decision making.

Enhance the organization's standing. As an ambassador for your nonprofit or foundation, introduce the organization and its mission to others. Make sure the organization is consistent and transparent in its messages to its constituents, including acknowledging difficulties and mistakes. Always be clear about when you are speaking for the foundation and when you are speaking as in individual. They are not the same thing, especially for family foundations.

Ensure legal and ethical integrity. Adhere to legal standards and ethical norms. Create and uphold personnel policies, grievance procedures, and conflicts of interest policies, as well as bylaws and articles of incorporation.

Recruit and train new board members. Consider ways to energize the board through planned turnover and thoughtful recruitment. Succession planning for board and staff leadership is a very difficult and necessary responsibility to ensure long-term continuity for any foundation or nonprofit. Orient new board members to their responsibilities and to the organization's history, needs, and challenges.

Assess board performance. Get involved in the delicate but important process of evaluating the board's performance, as well as the self-evaluation of members.

Know when to leave. Finally, whether there are term limits for board service (and more boards now have them), there will be a time when your contribution is done. Even in a family foundation, one's value as a board member will come to an end. Perhaps that will be a time to let the next generation be fully in control. Knowing when it is time to leave a board is a unique form of leadership. This should be done thoughtfully as you unwind your commitments and make room for fresh leadership and that next generation that may be chomping at the bit.

Family foundations face two additional factors requiring special care and leadership:

Managing unruly board growth. As families grow, so does the pool of potential board members: cousins from the different family lines and perhaps spouses. In addition, at what age does one bring on new board members? Or for that matter, when does it make sense for members of an older generation to pass the reins, and how? These are sensitive issues that most people will want to avoid because they cause their share of turmoil for both the foundation board and the whole extended family. Helping to determine good rules about who can become a member of the board and how, as well as what board size is ideal, are long-term gifts for the foundation. I know of some foundations that give different family lines or different generations the responsibility for choosing their representatives on the board for a set term. That way, board size is managed.

Family legacy. Learn the family history and stories. What was the donor's intent: to specific causes or to a family philanthropic legacy generally? Contribute to the passing of that tradition to future generations by telling the stories and even writing them down. At the same time, ask the difficult questions about difficult issues, such as perpetuity versus spending down, and how mission stays relevant as both the world and the family generations change.

Resources

There is no one, right answer for any of these issues. My purpose with this short article is to raise issues, not to provide an answer when things don't lend themselves to the cookie-cutter approach. It is clear, however, that each board member and each board must think about these things carefully.

You are not alone as you try to reach your own conclusions regarding the many issues raised above about family foundation and/or nonprofit board membership. Many resources can help make those experiences satisfying and productive. Books and articles abound. More important, I find board members are quite generous in sharing their own experiences and challenges. So ask. We are all in this together. Board membership is an art worth learning.

For more information on various aspects of board membership, the following are a few good places to start:

- Board Source, www.boardsource.org
- Council on Foundations, www.cof.org
- Exponent Philanthropy, www.exponentphilanthropy.org
- Independent Sector, www.independentsector.org
- National Center for Family Philanthropy, www.ncfp.org
- Philanthropy Roundtable, www.philanthropyroundtable.org

Enjoying the Rewards of Board Service

Joining a public-charity board or a family foundation board can be a very satisfying professional and personal experience. You *can* make a significant difference for the causes you care about. You can make a significant difference to your family and its legacy. As a board member, you will have a new lens through which to see and learn about the inner workings of an organization. It is an excellent way to develop one's own leadership skills that can inform and enhance your life, your work and your community. It can be rewarding, fun, and productive.

However, we have all heard about board experiences that turned out to be nightmares. Add a family component and the nightmare can be particularly dark. There also seem to be nearly monthly exposés of nonprofit, foundation, and commercial board failures. Therefore, remember that board service is also an important legal and social responsibility. Finding your own answers and approaches to the many issues above can mitigate the risks and accentuate the successful fit.

Indeed, one could argue, as I would, that board service is simply an important element of both good citizenship and family leadership.

This article is based on "Call to Duty: Participating in Effective Nonprofit Board Service," which was originally published in Bessemer Trust's Perspectives on Wealth Management, *Issue V, 2011. A year later I prepared a revised version titled "Effective Family Foundation Governance" which broadened the discussion to include family philanthropy too. It appeared in the bimonthly* Family Foundation Advisor, *Vol. 11, No. 6 (September/October 2012), published by Civic Research Institute, 4478 U.S. Route 27, P.O. Bo 585, Kingston, NJ 08528. I thank the original publishers for use of portions of these two works in this single article.*

CHAPTER 8

PHILANTHROPY AND THE STATE:
THREE DIFFICULT CASES

Most of the Third Sector ... must henceforth live within the embrace of, and to a significant degree as dependents and instruments of, government.... there is no plausible basis for supposing that it can be reversed — or indeed that either party to the relationship wished to reverse it. The leaders of most of the major categories of the Third Sector institutions want more government money, not less, and are fully prepared to accept the regulatory consequences. — Waldemar Nielsen

It is becoming clear that we have confused the state's blustering eagerness to take responsibility with an innate capacity to exercise it.... The independent sector must come to see itself as elementally different from the state, with a prior, more powerful moral franchise than the state. Its means seem more fragile than the state's irresistible powers to tax and command, but they are in the long run more legitimate and powerful. The sector cannot fulfill its essential mission until it detaches itself from the state. — Richard Cornuelle

... a robust political economy of institutions and decisions seeks answers to the following three questions:

- *Which institutions perform best when people are not omniscient?*
- *Which institutions perform best when people are motivated by self-interest?*
- *Which institutions perform best when people have limited knowledge and are prone to self-interested behavior?*

... In a world characterized by uncertainty and imperfect knowledge, attempts to promote economic stability by centralizing powers in the hands of regulatory authorities are likely to increase the possibility of "systemic" failure. — Mark Pennington

These brief, older pieces look at three aspects of the intersection of government and philanthropy that remain relevant at all times. They acknowledge the siren song and occasional reasonableness of the intruding politicization of philanthropy: first, through regulation to stop abuses; second, through the estate tax, which supposedly encourages philanthropy; and finally, some brief notes on "whose money is it anyway?"

The point is not that politics or politicizing all issues is wrong in all cases. That is not the case. The point is certainly not to dismiss concerns about real problems. That is not true either. However, the extremely common assumptions that government intervention — almost no matter what — will be good for society and philanthropy are wrong. Those largely unquestioned assumptions about government action and their primarily positive outcomes are the stuff of public policy. They are embedded in our concepts and the words we use when discussing philanthropy. It is hoped that these short pieces suggest there are different and broader aspects to these issues that deserve fuller discussion.

Threads of these points also run throughout the articles in Chapter 2 and other articles in this collection. For the larger argument here, I would refer the reader to a very important book: *Robust Political Economy: Classical Liberalism and the Future of Public Policy*, by Mark Pennington (Cheltenham, UK: Edward Elgar, 2011).

1. Philanthropy and the "Intrusion" of Law

Introduction

The July/August 2004 issue of *Philanthropy Magazine* published "Philanthropy and the Law: A Symposium." Various egregious abuses and fears of new ones had led to hearings by both the House and Senate. Sweeping new regulations for nonprofits and foundations were under consideration. *Philanthropy* asked a dozen foundation heads, consultants, nonprofit leaders, academics, and politicians to respond. They were invited to address the larger issue by addressing as many or as few of the following questions as they wanted to in their short contributions.

- What abuses most need corrections?
- What are the two most important principles for reform?
- Is current law sufficient to address these abuses? If not, should the federal government or state take the lead in reform? What's the role for the IRS? For state attorneys general?
- Can and should the field self-regulate? If so, how precisely?
- Have the IRS and the state attorneys general done enough to enforce existing legal requirements? How could they improve?
- What should be done about abuses of donor intent?
- When is staff or trustee compensation unreasonable? Are existing laws adequate to protect against this?
- Do you favor the extension to foundations of Sarbanes-Oxley–style requirements for independent boards?
- Do you fear any legislative over-reaching in the current environment? What do you most fear?
- Should foundation perpetuity be allowed?

Years later now, little has changed on the abuse or regulation side. The debates about foundation and nonprofit regulation continue. The same issues are salient. And it seems even more clear to me that

1. The laws on the books are generally more than sufficient for dealing with nearly all abuses;
2. It is worth asking whether some regulations are superfluous, with worse unintended consequences (though it is very difficult to get rid of regulations);
3. Enforcement and transparency are key areas that do need improvements, and punishments should be carried out fully;
4. The impact of regulations on the independence and innovation of the sector is a genuine worry;

5. The impact of regulations on donors and the growth of philanthropy is an important related issue; and

6. We should all be more aware — and, yes, often suspicious of — the motives behind not just foundation and nonprofit leaders, but also of the commentators and politicians for whom new regulations may very well be in their self- or political interest to propagate.

I led off the discussion with this contribution.

Philanthropy and the Law

As we think about the controversy surrounding foundation abuses, we mustn't focus too narrowly or too indiscriminately. That is as true now in 2019 as it was in 2004. First, this discussion should be about the abuses — and the benefits — of the entire philanthropic, nonprofit voluntary sector. Some specifics may apply only to foundations, but we are all in this together, as is clear from the breadth of the hearings that Senator Grassley (R-Iowa) held in June 2004. Remembering this should inform our response to real abuses.

For instance, there were outrageous abuses then, ranging from ones by nonprofits like Hale House in New York City to those committed by charitable trusts and foundations as reported at the time in the *Boston Globe*. These can include disgraceful salaries, conflicts of interest, self-dealing, and fictional valuations for donated property. I think some such abuses should clearly be illegal and enforced. Others may be reprehensible and subject to publicity but perhaps not illegal. No doubt some significant abuses continue.

Make no mistake, most of these cases represent a failure of governance. Stupidity is no excuse. Board governance and directors/trustees carry real responsibilities. Looking back from 2019, I have seen several shady actions on the part of boards. Some might have been illegal. I have seen numerous stupid actions on the part of trustees and staff that might not cross the line, but… One can only hope that boards and perpetrators of such illegal abuses are brought before a "hanging judge" — the stocks at Williamsburg come to mind, too.

In general, however, the necessary laws are in place. The responsible public agencies must have both the capacity to enforce them and be held accountable if they don't. While we shouldn't engage in "blaming the enforcer," is it possible that they were asleep at the switch? There is also the likelihood that "regulatory capture" explains lax enforcement (economist George Stigler's observation that regulators often end up serving the interests of the regulated rather than the interests of consumers or the public). True, the responsible agencies have neither the systems nor the resources to do what they should have been doing. Thus, much of this focus on abuses should result in more resources and accountability for the enforcers, and oversight of the regulators.

Most new legislative solutions suggested to date involve significant cost-shifting and complex requirements that would be unnecessarily burdensome on an already struggling voluntary sector. The specter of negative unintended consequences of so many government solutions is real. As so often is the case, there is a tendency for policy wonks and politicians to invest in shiny new regulations rather than the nitty-gritty operational slog of effective implementation of what is already there. We should bear in mind that some of the reforms in 1969 did both intended and unintended damage to the sector, without demonstrable improvements. Perhaps the best reforms would be to assess and reform the extant regulations.

One can anticipate that some of the new regulations would be universal remedies that ignore nuances and eliminate honest and creative efforts in the sole interest of compliance. There might be requirements that have a chilling effect on board membership and good governance; that add significant costs and would reduce program funding; restrictions that would result in less philanthropy and public spiritedness. Extending some provisions from Sarbanes-Oxley requirements, for instance, might impose heavy restrictions while doing little to protect the public. The June 2004 "discussion draft" from the Senate Finance Committee even had a suggestion mandating that board membership be between three and fifteen. That is just silly.

After all of this, the voluntary sector and philanthropy could easily be less robust and effective. It is unclear how much wrongdoing would be caught or avoided by all of this, anyway — which would simply unleash another round of handwringing and more regulations. Looking back from 2018, I am even more convinced that effective enforcement and implementation is the key to both avoiding abuses and to allowing the voluntary sector to continue to benefit the public weal.

In the end, I just don't believe something is systematically wrong with the nonprofit sector or with philanthropy generally. There are some bad people, and they should be caught. There are some inattentive boards, and they need a continuing reminder of what is expected of them — perhaps a form of electro-shock therapy! But let's face it: we don't live in a perfect world; some abuses are inevitable. Markets, the nonprofit world, *and* government are vast information systems and learning communities. We need to encourage constant improvement and innovation, enable effective vigilance, and let it work.

Public access to information, transparency, and knowledgeable scrutiny are also crucial checks for the sector. Even here, these are complex issues;

one can have too much transparency in the form of silly and damaging regulations. Simply consider Florida's Sunshine laws. They exacerbate some problems. We need an educated press that can ferret out abuses *and* that also understands the sector. Public officials need to be better informed about the sector, too. We need to do a much better job of communicating the good stories, as well as the difficulties of finding and funding effective programs. We as a sector should do a better job of condemning the bad apples and discussing our failures. That, in turn, suggests that much, much more needs to be done on accountability, results, and outcomes. Similarly, we need more research on the true extent and nature of abuses (a few hours of public hearings don't make for good policy).

We as individuals and as a sector should not countenance abuse in our actions, public documents, or in our cocktail conversations. We need outspoken leadership taking the moral high ground with respect to the standards our sector expects, as well as with respect to the sector's importance and independence (some do still call it the independent sector). There is also room for self-regulation. I know that is a term deserving of some derision. However, the sector has several respected organizations in place that could retool and help provide that role, e.g., the Center for Effective Philanthropy and the Foundation Center. Perhaps we could see a reborn Council on Foundations or Independent Sector, though many of us have been waiting for that for a long time. Doing so could severely test their funders, but maybe even that is a good thing. It recalls, however, the question of who will regulate the self-regulators. Indeed, with self-regulation or government regulation, there is an ever-present danger of "regulatory capture," where the regulations and agencies are staffed by professionals from the field who then promote the narrower interests of the field.

As we work through these difficult issues, it may also be worth remembering that not all issues should be a matter of public policy, as much as policy wonks from the left and right would like them to be. Some things are best left to "private policy," where there is room for differing opinions and actions. Whether a board has three or fifteen members or has a quota are examples. There are good and bad reasons for foundation perpetuity. These and other examples are situational and can be complex. They should be left to donors and boards. Donor intent is a very important and complex issue, and it should primarily be left to donors and boards to work out, as well. Egregious abuses are just that — egregious — and are now subject to various legal remedies should that be necessary. Decisions to limit foundations to a minimum of $20 million (or $5 million) shouldn't be decided by legislative fiat; donors and families can have very good and effective charitable reasons for small foundations.

Unfortunately, one of the biggest regulatory worries is the rampant politicization of discourse and the nefarious uses to which regulation can be directed. Sometimes the terms of the debates about this sector have been commandeered by conservative and liberal critics who have made common cause (sometimes unintentionally, but nevertheless too often, in fact) against the voluntary sector. Much of the rhetoric promotes a "politicization" of the nonprofit sector and philanthropy — the notion that all problems must be and can only be solved by political action and legislation. But that politicization often morphs into political use by one side against the other. That is increasingly dangerous.

The history of philanthropy in the United States and Britain gives us too many lessons about how regulations diminish the charitable spirit in our communities. Have we forgotten that less than 70 years ago, much conventional wisdom held that there was little role left for private philanthropy and a voluntary sector? It is worth remembering Tocqueville's uncanny warning in 1835, which is just as prescient today:

> Among democratic nations it is only by association that the resistance of the people to the government can ever display itself; hence the latter always looks with ill favour on those associations which are not in its own power; and it is well worthy of remarking that among democratic nations the people themselves often entertain against these very associations a secret feeling of fear and jealousy, which prevents the citizens from defending the institutions of which they stand so much in need.

I have admittedly been surprised by some of the abuses. I have also been impressed by the level of concern and the efforts of a wide variety of nonprofit and philanthropic intermediaries to address the issues in a serious and effective way. While these efforts may seem disorganized, real progress is often messy and that is OK. I believe the value and independence of civil society (of which voluntary and philanthropic organizations are a major part) exceedingly important. Our increasing individual and collective vigilance about abuses within the sector should always include vigilance for the health and independence of the sector, too. There is often a default assumption among many — including philanthropoids, policy people, and politicians — that they have rarely seen a regulation they didn't like. Let us be sure that any unintended consequences of addressing these abuses don't harm the voluntary sector. Change is necessary, and it need not always be "political."

Future Considerations?

Finally, let me just note that there has recently been a renewed and sophisticated series of critiques on voluntarism, donor choice, and philanthropy generally. These are not primarily about addressing current abuses or taxes. As critiques of philanthropy, these are important books. But in multiple ways these books do question the very validity of the very nature of voluntary choices in philanthropy as a reasonably independent activity within civil society. They, in response to real and perhaps not so real but complex issues, assume away civil society and welcome the state with little concern. It seems a major thrust is to more completely subsume both civil society generally and philanthropy specifically under the state, even to the point of one author advocating very severely limited discretion for donor's and philanthropic institutions choosing how to give "their" money away. The net result would be the nationalization and politicization of more and more philanthropic choices. This seems to me to be Herbert Croly's *The Promise of American Life* on steroids.

Several examples include *The Givers*, by David Callahan (New York: Knopf, 2017); *Philanthropy in Democratic Societies*, edited by Rob Reich, Chiara Cordelli, and Lucy Bernholz (Chicago: The University of Chicago Press, 2016), and *Just Give: Why Philanthropy Is Failing Democracy and How It Can Do Better,* by Rob Reich (Princeton: Princeton University Press, 2018).

I mention this big issue as a "tickler" for serious consideration by others in the future. These are serious works that raise very important points that need serious discussion. For me, they are "bringing the state back in" in the name of some amorphous democracy. But doing so would ultimately decimate civil society and jeopardize democracy.

Originally published in the July/August 2004 issue of Philanthropy, *as the lead contribution to a symposium on "Philanthropy & the Law" by 12 nonprofit leaders. Reprinted with the permission of* Philanthropy.

2. Philanthropy and the Estate Tax

Introduction

When the National Center for Family Philanthropy did a special edition of *Family Giving News* in September 2003, it asked six "leading thinkers" to provide perspective and context for the ongoing debates about the estate tax:

> Those who support the estate tax feel that it is an effective tool for both "leveling the playing field" and for encouraging and motivating the very wealthy to make significant gifts to charitable organizations. Those that favor repeal feel that it is an ineffective tax that raises little revenue and has a significant negative impact on the economy — leading in the end to inefficient and reduced philanthropy. Most Americans, regardless of their opinion on the estate tax, believe in the importance of charity, and in a society that is essentially fair and equitable. The question is how best to achieve that result ... and here, as we all know, there is much less agreement.

John Edie, William Gates Sr., Mario Morino, Adam Myerson, Paul Comstock, and I were asked to comment. This was over twenty years ago. Much has changed. The 2018 tax reform bill doubles the federal estate tax exclusion to $11,180,000 per person, based on inflation adjustments. Few estates are this large, so for most the estate tax is effectively repealed. Nonetheless, I believe this issue remains salient:

- Many states have an estate tax;
- The nature and consequences (intended and not so much) of an estate tax need to be better known and researched because it is still a controversial issue; and
- Estate tax "reform" will certainly return to the policy agenda at some point. (After the 2018 mid-terms with all sound-bites focused on 2020, it looks like these issues will come back with a vengeance.) As this book is being published, the estate tax exemption is scheduled to go back to $3.5 million in 2025. No doubt before that the exemptions and rates will be whipsawed around by Congress.

The Estate Tax

Most discussions connecting philanthropy *and* the estate tax ignore donors and their families. They are merely a convenient source of funds for the benefit of government coffers or avoiding the tax for the benefit of foundations and nonprofits. This reminds me of a comedian's recent routine. After a moving ode to a very ill grandfather that is done in a mournful style, the song reaches a jarring hard-rock crescendo. We hear "die, die!" so that the young man can have his grandfather's money, be rich, buy a yacht, etc. This isn't funny coming from a relative, nor is it funny coming from public policy advocates.

Donors are not just the abstract creation of an abstraction called "society." They have many kinds of decisions to make about the use of the wealth they help create (whether it is a lot or not). While charitable giving may top other choices in my or your value system, it is not the only private good *or* public good. It should compete for the hearts and minds of an individual's and family's wallet with other values. It is incumbent upon those of us who believe in a myriad of charitable causes to make the best case.

For most who discuss the estate tax, the assumption had always been that it will increase the amount of giving to philanthropy. It turns out that to rest so much of the case for philanthropy on the presumed largesse bequeathed to avoid estate taxes is largely not true, for three reasons. First, an estate tax doesn't increase giving, at least not in recent decades. There is good data showing that a lower or eliminated estate tax results in more money being available to and given to philanthropy. Some studies had shown or predicted varying detrimental impacts to philanthropy of eliminating the estate tax, at least over the short run (see Jon Bakija and William Gale, "Effects of Estate Tax Reform on Charitable Giving," Brookings Institution, July 2003). Other studies showed little or no impact, causing Paul Schervish and John Havens to revise their assumptions about detrimental effects of eliminating the estate tax. This was also confirmed by their own survey data on the very wealthy. Current data tracking the changes in the estate tax exclusion towards effectively eliminating the federal estate tax for most hardly shows any sort of "devastating" effect. More current work needs to be done on this, but at the very least, the huge increase in giving by the wealthy would suggest that behavior does change, and values may be increasingly a bigger driver of charitable decisions.

Second, by emphasizing tax considerations, the sector and financial advisors do a disservice to the values that predominantly drive decisions for philanthropy. Paul Schervish and others have shown that the value of caring is not only limiting what families want to leave to heirs, but it also drives and increases what goes to philanthropy. It is incumbent on us and the field to emphasize the causes and values, not the questionable philanthropic draw of an inefficient estate tax. (For more on this, see "The Making of the Intergenerational Transfer" in Chapter 5.)

Third, there has been a tendency over many decades for parents to be careful about giving too much to heir. This means that "tax saving" due to no estate tax will increase the amount available to philanthropy.

Some call it a "death tax." I see it as simply a bad tax as much economic and social analysis has shown. It taxes productivity and savings while encouraging consumption; it discourages economic growth and preservation of family businesses; it is biased towards liquid assets. Ironically, the estate tax helps to ensconce the very wealthy, since they are best able to afford the expensive legal help that allows them to avoid paying their fair share. The personal and social costs of compliance are significant. It doesn't raise a lot of money for government coffers. What money is raised, and the costs of avoidance, would be better used to increase economic growth *and* philanthropy. And there is good evidence that it would.

Philanthropy and the estate tax are best not entwined. There are better ways to address the real problems of exorbitant wealth and economic inequality: overall tax reform, changes in the income tax, eliminating corporate welfare, a consumption tax, etc. This is an important and complex discussion for another place.

There is reason for some longer-term optimism. For instance, back when this review was written, over 350 quite affluent Americans had banded together in an organization to oppose repeal of the estate tax and its "disastrous consequences" to charitable giving. But clearly, then, they have very strong charitable values that would lead them to give big ... even without the estate tax! They should do that and encourage *that* behavior. The success of the Giving Pledge is further evidence.

It appears — in the parlance of economists — that the demand for family bequests is inelastic and that of charitable giving is elastic. More of a donor's wealth is going to charity as donors change their behavior: "Doing away with the estate tax would increase not only the amount of giving, but also the quality of giving," writes Schervish. I sense that it has. But has it?

The estate tax *and* philanthropy are each very complex issues. We need to know more about how donors react over time to changes. It is, however, possible to make a firm and principled case that the estate tax is a bad tax that is best permanently reduced significantly or repealed, *and* that society and philanthropy would benefit in many ways if it were. Most important, though, these are separate issues. To conflate and intertwine them in policy machinations or contortions does no one a favor. Those of us who believe deeply in philanthropy and the voluntary sector should redouble our own efforts to show more donors how and why they can give more (especially during their lives).

If our case is good enough, they will respond. The 2018 *Giving USA* report has noted that the last three years have been very strong for philanthropy. The renewed interest in the intergenerational transfer of wealth suggests that baby boomers will give generously, when given the right reasons to do so from nonprofits leaders. That means expressing the values and impact that organizations have. An estate tax doesn't have that power and deflects donors *and* nonprofits from focusing on their values and impact.

Published in the September 2003 issue of Family Giving News, *published electronically by the National Center on Family Philanthropy. Reprinted with the kind permission of the National Center on Family Philanthropy.*

3. On Controlling Philanthropy — Whose Money Is It Anyway? A Few Short Notes

What Comes First: Civil Society or the State?

For centuries, political thought has tended to revolve around ideas of public policy and the progressive politicization of society. This has seemed to many not only a natural progression but also the primary "option." Among other things, the reaction of Eastern Europe to the fall of communism reminded us of a different tradition that entails what I would describe as a more complex, robust and diverse way of seeing things. This tradition called to mind the preeminence a dichotomy. It could never be in theory or reality a hard and fast, absolute distinction. But as Thomas Paine expressed it so well at the beginning of *Common Sense*: "Some writers have so confounded society with government as to leave little or no distinction between them, whereas they are not only different, but have different origins." The difference is crucial. Simply put, the realm of civil society is voluntary action in all of its forms. Generally, the notion of public policy ignores the nature and dynamics of civil society by preferencing politics. It wasn't always that way, as Daniel Boorstin noted: "… in America, even in modern times, communities existed before governments were here to care for public needs." Similarly, Michael Novak movingly set the contrast as follows:

> When the limited state allows private persons to make private bequests of the substance they have earned, and thus to launch their purposes into the stream of future history, such a state declares in an unmistakable way that its own ambition does not exceed its own limited purposes, and that the state is not coterminous with society. It recognizes in practice that society is far larger in its sweep than the limited state, and that even the public good, the commonweal, exceeds by immense stretches the limited domain of the state. In a free society, the public good is in the keeping of all its citizens, well beyond the limited public order that it is the sworn duty of the state to uphold. As the rights of citizens are prior to the state, so also is their conception of, and their pursuit of, the common good. For the right to pursue their own happiness is not merely a privatized right. It includes the right to pursue their own conception of the public good, within which their personal good finds its proper place.

This perception of the relative uniqueness of civil society and the state (or government) is one of the major themes in the essays in this book. Philanthropy is a major element in civil society.

The Audacity of Politics

A sad fact of history is that civil society is constantly vulnerable to and subject to predations of the state. It is also hidden from the tunnel vision underlying the politicization of society, which denigrates and marginalizes private giving by trying to subsume philanthropy under the control and aegis of government. The following three quotations are suggestive:

> [I]s there any need to support private philanthropy when government is taking over more and more of the burden...? Should not the trend toward public philanthropy be encouraged, and should not private philanthropy be expected to retire from the scene ... — Solomon Fabricant, 1970

> ...very basic principle... There is nothing in American society which requires that foundations exist. Public needs can be defined by elected officials who are responsive to the people they serve. — Senator Vance Hartke, 1974

> Private giving for public purposes has regularly throughout American history been the subject of both pragmatic and ideological skepticism... Yet, if some aspects of philanthropy are reasonable grounds for concern in a democratic society, the implications of little or no philanthropy may be grounds for even greater concern in a pluralistic society" — *Giving in America*, 1975

Whose Money Is It Anyway?

Giving is a natural, voluntary transaction of individuals in civil society: a donor's own private money, given for charitable purposes. The money goes to recipients, nonprofit organizations, or foundations. In the latter cases, the funds are then "owned" by the governing boards and trustees, under clear limitations and "public" purposes. It is worth reemphasizing that this process is powered by individuals and donors who make private decisions based on their values, which in multitudinous ways serve many public interests. As many of the chapters in this book suggest from different angles, the giving and volunteering of philanthropy is a remarkable, robust and creative process. Our thinking about this has becomes muddled.

It seems to me that a multipart terminological sleight-of-hand (shall we call it a form of conceptual imperialism?) has taken place that confuses our understanding of the charitable transaction. Simply stated, private donations of one's own money are described as public subsidies, thereby politicizing the transaction and seeming to allow government a claim on those funds as "public" moneys. This is because of a tax deduction or exemption. It seems to me whether various deductions or exemptions are a good thing is an important question, but it seems a logical *non sequitur* to have that confer an ownership interest to government (which itself may not express the public interest). A tax deduction does not change the ownership relationship of the donated amount. It is/was still the donor's money. In what ways exactly does providing an exemption or deduction turn a person's personal funds into government-controlled money? It must have been the government's to begin with, it seems; that seemingly logical extreme is exactly the cornerstone of authoritarian governments from the divine right of kings through the totalitarian tragedies since.

Society *and* government see philanthropy as such an important and robust process that deductions and exemptions often become part of the social contract. But does that convey ownership of those funds? See, for instance, Michael Novak's quotation above. That sleight-of-hand has opened the door for a *de facto* transformation of charitable giving into a form of government subsidy. Whose money *is* it?

Philanthropy as a Government Subsidy?

Accepting that giving and philanthropy are really a subsidy (even if "only" partially) totally politicizes such a major aspect of civil society. There is a long history of efforts to politicize philanthropy along those lines, from left and right. Here are a few views on this contested notion:

> Corporations and foundations are tax exempt. Therefore, part of the money they spend is my money. — *Giving in America*, 1975

> It has been often asserted, that to exempt an institution from taxation is the same thing as to grant it money directly from the public treasury. This statement is sophistical and fallacious. — Charles William Eliot, 1870s

> IS believes that charities' disclosure obligation derives from their role in serving public interests, not from their tax treatment....

These tax benefits do not justify mandatory disclosure… —
Independent Sector Comments on Joint Committee on Taxation

[C]harities are fundamentally private entities and as such are
entitled to a substantial zone of privacy with respect to their
internal decision-making process…. IS takes issue with the JCT
Report's characterization of tax exemption and the charitable
deduction as government subsidies and the Report's view that the
receipt of those subsidies creates a strong presumption in favor
of increased disclosure. — Independent Sector Comments on
Joint Committee on Taxation

For instance, *Criteria for Philanthropy at Its Best*, published in early 2009 by
the National Committee for Responsive Philanthropy makes much of this
point (see also Chapter 4, "Can We Still Improve Philanthropy?"). If, as it
writes, "generous tax subsidies provided to donors and to foundations
make the government and the public partners with philanthropists in
pursuit of the public good," then this concept must apply to the entire
third, nonprofit, or independent sector. Does "partially public" mean
distributions of some percentage should be allocated by a government or
bureaucracy? At one point, *Criteria* floats the idea that "at least 45 percent"
public is a good percentage to go with. What does that mean?

It seemed to me contrary to logic. Indeed, must not this view of tax
subsidies also apply, then, to the mortgage deduction and tax breaks of any
kind? Surely the mortgage deduction doesn't make, say, 37 percent of a
house public property (the bathroom, the second bedroom, one of the
garage spaces and the finished basement?).

This view has now been institutionalized in government budgetary
considerations. For instance, calculating the "cost" of a deduction or
exemption has come to imply an ownership relationship where the cost is
the portion that is presumably part of the government's largesse, i.e. owned
by the government. It is extended and combined with the "public purpose"
reason for charity to become the argument that all foundation funds and
giving *are* public giving and thus should be controlled politically. "Public"
has been twisted to mean "political," rather than part of civil society, which
was one of the more common older meanings. The old saw that the power
to tax is the power to control (paraphrased) can be crudely expanded so
that anything *not* taxed (by dint of a deduction or exemption from taxation)
is still, by implication, public money.

This is a crucial issue that can't just be assumed away; it is not simply
wordplay. It is firmly embedded in much philanthropic and public policy
discourse. It deserves the full and careful unpacking of these ideas and
assumptions. See, for instance, the discussion and critique in *How Public Is*

Private Philanthropy: Separating Myth from Reality, by Evelyn Brody and John Tyler (Washington DC: The Philanthropy Roundtable, 2009 and 2012), as well as the edited transcript of a Hudson Institute/Bradley Center discussion, "How Public Is Private Philanthropy?" held June 19, 2009. Elements of this "public" argument also have become important parts of significant — though I think wrongheaded — critiques of private philanthropy, such as in *Philanthropy in Democratic Societies*, edited by Rob Reich, Chiara Cordelli, and Lucy Bernholz (Chicago: The University of Chicago Press, 2016).

These considerations have led to some policy and academic discussions about whether eliminating the tax deduction and exemptions are ways to protect private giving by eliminating the "public money" argument. What impact would that have? There is evidence of various sorts that the deduction is not the major determinant of giving for many wealthy donors. Certainly, some exemptions may not make sense. (For instance, The Clark Foundation where I was executive director, owned considerable property in Cooperstown which was tax exempt. The Foundation regularly paid Cooperstown the equivalent of the exemption value.) But deductions and exemptions do have a value and impact for many. (I know of one very large donor who has eschewed both deductions and charitable institutional status for their philanthropy. He felt the flexibility would enhance the effectiveness of his charitable activities.)

Eliminating tax exemptions and deductions might be a good overall strategy, or not. But it should be discussed on its merits. In any case, there would remain ways the "public money" argument could still be used. The suspicions of private giving from left and right will find new rationales for political control of the ill-named "public purposes" for which giving is meant. The term "public" is imbued with the implication that it can only be politically determined and disbursed. And yet civil society is a voluntary "public." Thinking about eliminating deductions and exemptions won't fix the perceptual belief that all things should be politically controlled. Trying to address what I earlier called the sleight-of-hand directly may be the best option we have.

On Controlling Philanthropy

Foundation and nonprofit board governance is so important but too often invisible. It gets neither the respect nor the accountability it deserves. For instance, in 2003, the Urban Institute conducted what it called the first "comprehensive exploration of foundation attitudes." But the focus was on interviewing CEOs and executive directors, not board members. Since this was written, that has been changing. It is not surprising, for instance, that Warren Buffett highlights the importance of board governance by conditioning his contributions to the Bill and Melinda Gates Foundation with "at least one of you must remain alive and active in the policy-making and administration of the BMG." The role of governance is so important for what it can accomplish and what damage bad governance can do.

The idea of the public subsidy of donations and exemptions can also have very long tentacles beyond denigrating donors and their decisions. It also extends into the boardroom. It can lead to politicizing even those decisions. Could boards lose all or most of their independence — by dint of the presumed "government" money that is seen as a significant portion of their income and endowments? Do they thus become mere agents of the government and subject to every whim of bureaucrats and fickle political interests? These are truly perfidious perceptions. (This is not a screed against political majorities from whatever direction. It is an acknowledgment of the role of self-interest in politics, of the multiple and diverse public goods that can't be summarized by a political majority, and the roles of a broad diversity of institutions both political and civil.)

Could the government be within its rights to restrict partially the use of foundation giving, depending, for instance, on whether people have voted for or against such formerly divisive issues as gay marriage, stem cell research, etc.? (And in our current time of political dysfunction, that list could be endless. The diversity and independence of the sector — and of civil society — would thereby be throttled and destroyed. When the Bush administration banned federal funding of stem cell research, wouldn't this assumption have given that Administration an excuse to ban 45 percent of private foundation funding for the same? These may seem like silly examples, but I am afraid there are those who would, and will, eagerly use similar excuses for their purposes, whether on the left or right.

Joel Fleishman has written that foundations are "the least accountable major institutions in America." He means this in part as positive in the sense that they are independent institutions, not fully accountable to government interests. Myriad foundation watchers including Wally Nielsen, Brian O'Connell, and Dick Cornuelle have noted this crucial independent characteristic for the well-being — and effectiveness — of philanthropy and civil society. Boards can and should be accountable and abuses punished of course. The point is simply that among the "myths" afflicting philanthropy — and by implication civil society — the idea that its funding is somehow public money is wrong. It is not just largely incoherent. It has potentially disastrous implications for the independence and responsibilities of both donors as well as foundation and nonprofit boards.

PHILANTHROPY AND THE STATE

The Philanthropic Enterprise held a conference June 25–28, 2009, in Westchester, New York, titled "Re-Imagining Philanthropy: Myths and Opportunities." Many of the papers were later published in Conversations on Philanthropy, *V. 7, 2010. In her introduction to that volume, editor Lenore Ealy explained, "The myths that surround philanthropy are many, but they are not tame.... What are the myths, creative and destructive, that shape these beliefs and open or foreclose to us various forms of philanthropic action?"*

I was a participant at that fine conference and used a version of the short notes above, in lieu of a finished paper. I was never able to go back to these miscellaneous thoughts and develop a full paper. However, I continue to feel this issue is of wide-ranging importance. Perhaps this short miscellany will be suggestive and helpful to others.

CHAPTER 9

DONOR INTENT, LEGACY, AND IMPACT

The care with which a donor disburses philanthropic funds is something over which donors have complete and absolute control and for which they should be held accountable. — Peter Frumkin

[My family foundation] is a vital closure on my life and as important a part of my legacy as my professional career. — distinguished NYC business leader (anonymity requested)

Just after Lucile Packard died in 1987, Dave was quite sick. During his time in recuperation, he wrote out an outline of what he wanted the foundation to look like in the future. He then sent it to the trustees and me. Within a few months he had changed it and then he dropped parts of it. Within two years it was very out of date. A few years later when he was asked by his attorney to write down his thoughts for the future, he refused. He felt that the world changes too much to try to leave specific recommendations for the future trustees. What David and Lucile left were their values. The foundation has written these down and we discuss them with the staff often. These are enduring values that will be as important and appropriate 50 or 100 years from now as they are today. — Cole Wilbur, then president of the David and Lucile Packard Foundation

When we tell our stories, we are offering three invaluable gifts to the next generation: 1) we are giving them a better understanding of who we are and the forces that shape the values we're trying to transmit; 2) we are giving them an opportunity to explore who they are and how they want to form their own journey; and 3) we are giving them the tools to continue passing on the family's legacy. — Ellen M. Perry

My interest in donor intent and family philanthropy started as a scholarly and professional one. I had the very good fortune to get to know Bob Payton and the folks at the Indiana University Center on Philanthropy, where I worked for a while. They took donors seriously because they were the lifeblood and spiritual basis for philanthropy. The stories, big and small, were often inspiring.

One couldn't help but also notice the petty and venal behaviors of some donors and families as well. The inefficiencies and ineffectiveness of philanthropy weighed on us all. But I was so impressed that this was reason enough for donors, families, boards, and consultant to work harder at getting it right.

A personal side developed as well. In 1994, Carol and I set up a very small family foundation as our "ethical will" for our young boys. We used to joke that we should have named it "Instead of a Summer Cottage in Maine Foundation." It has been very rewarding, capped by the comment of one son, now in his early 30s, that he feels honored to maintain this family philanthropy and will do so.

The transition from those experiences to subsequently running several family foundations and working with numerous donors seemed grounded and seamless. I have helped grant close to $300 million over my career. I was very active on the board of the Council on Foundations (particularly with the Committee on Family Foundations). The influence of Ginny Esposito was palpable to us all. My engagement with her later National Center for Family Philanthropy in putting together *Living the Legacy* was important. I got to know so many wonderful people working *in* family philanthropy, many various family members of foundations small or gigantic. Jason Born at the National Center, Cole Wilbur of the Packard Foundation and the remarkable consultant Alice Buhl stand out, though there were really so many others.

These personal experiences and ongoing reading have deepened for me an appreciation for how important donor intent and family philanthropy are for philanthropy generally and for our civil society. I have seen how donors and families do care so deeply. It is their money initially and their commitment and vision. They give meaning and vitality to so much that is noble and necessary in both family and social life. It is something to encourage, improve, and protect. Sadly, family philanthropy and donor intent don't have the nuanced advocates they once had. I can only hope these four articles and this volume overall will add something to the discussion.

1. Introducing Donor Intent:
Building a Legacy of Impact Through Partnerships

Donor intent matters. A bevy of articles, consultants, and examples are available on how to craft donor intent statements and how to communicate them. Whatever the content and form, they should be dynamic, reciprocal learning tools that engage donors (if still living), family members (as board members), *and* grantees. Great care needs to be applied so donor intent is not a one-way, power relationship. At its best and most effective, it is a shared connection that embodies mission, cooperation, mutual exchange, and honest give-and-take through time.

Engaging Grantees

Too often, donors (and philanthropoids) wrongly see no need to listen to grantees. Heaven forbid. The idea of "strategic philanthropy" in practice frequently fosters donor conceit and that stale old "I know best, so I'll go it alone" attitude. Donors are still so easily seduced by the hubris endemic in philanthropy, which "has no natural predators," to use Tony Proscio's wonderful phrase. This produces very poor relationships indeed. It usually generates anemic results and unsustainable change.

We live in a world of complex and evolving social needs. We are buffeted by rapidly changing methods to address these needs: some astonishing and some snake oil. These are knowledge problems no donor or foundation can surmount alone. Good intentions and complex logic models simply don't reach impact without a cooperative commitment, humility, and hard work. The good news is that in my experience, many donors and family foundations do understand the difficult nature and remarkable ability of these reciprocal relationships with grantees to translate *intent* to meaningful societal *impact*.

Engaging Generations

Building reciprocal relationships with grantees is difficult. Consider, then, the terror and euphoria of different generations around the family kitchen table! When I was the executive director of one family foundation, I symbolically hung boxing gloves on the board room door. This is a different kind of partnership of serial reciprocity, because the connection is passed from generation to generation. Each subsequent generation reaffirms, changes, adapts, and finally passes on what becomes an ongoing *family legacy.*

Donors almost always desire some form of legacy. They often have values and tasks they want to live past them. Or they desire to hand down a general philanthropic commitment. And yet, too often, donors and their statements are barriers to a viable legacy (in the same ways they can work against impact with grantees). They demand inflexible adherence, dismiss questions and discussion, and thereby poison the trust that makes generational relationships productive.

Family members, in turn, almost always desire a donor's guidance — not strident lecturing or a deaf ear. I have seen them go to great lengths to seek it here, there, and everywhere, even rummaging through decades of checkbook stubs to find out a donor's values and priorities.

In these efforts to build a legacy, donors (or the current "head" of a family) have a special obligation to express their personal views clearly, openly, and with great sensitivity. They need to respect the same for the next generations. Subsequent generations have a similar obligation towards donors and their own successors. In doing so, one begins to model cooperative behaviors. It has struck me anecdotally that family foundations with a strong generational legacy often also have the relationship skills to work more in partnerships with grantees/ beneficiaries.

Partnering for Better Accountability

In the end, the reciprocal relationships that drive both *impact and legacy* have something to tell us about a more inclusive and healthier element of accountability.

Although everyone wants accountability for foundations, the problem is who are the deciders? Commentators on foundations often worry that foundations do not have shareholders (owners) or customers in the usual sense. Nor do they have voters as our democratic institutions appear to have. A self-perpetuating board or untethered executive director, then, can be open to the charge of self-interest and unsupervised play. The scrutiny of journalists and the oversight of governmental agencies is too easily uninformed or simplistic. And philanthropic policy wonks often fail to understand the motivations or the realities of philanthropic practice.

By contrast, the first level of accountability should be: Are we — as grantors *and* grantees — pursuing the intent and impact we have set for ourselves? This is a question all donors, board/family members, and recipients should continually ask, and ask in unison. The donor/grantor and grantee sides of the reciprocal relationship are jointly accountable, which requires a robust, ongoing discussion about mission, objections, results, and the future.

A family philanthropic legacy is also accountable to and through the reciprocal relationships that cascade across generations. It is relevant to ask and even judge a donor's intent and a family foundation's legacy by its handling of its development over time. The point is not that foundations have to abide by a specific donor intent, though that is a relevant consideration. The point is that donors and families should be able to communicate how they think about their philanthropic legacy over time. How do they handle the difficult generational discussions about change, evolving social needs, grantee partnerships, and their future hopes for that legacy? Are they also as good stewards of values and intent as they should be with the endowment?

We simply can't ignore donor intent (or its iterations). But, it requires authentic, two-way partnerships — within families and with grantees — for the knowledge and skills to attain genuine results. Together, these variegated reciprocal relationships encourage real learning from the past, the present, and into the future. The future growth and effectiveness of the core American tradition of family philanthropy probably depends on just how well we juggle all of this.

Originally published in the online PhilanthroFiles, *by Exponent Philanthropy, August 3, 2017. Reprinted here with their permission.*

2. A Living Legacy for Family Philanthropy

Family foundations give modern philanthropy its dynamic character. Founded by a donor within a family context, they are independent foundations where the original donor(s) or family members are still active on the board. Each family foundation has its own rich heritage of values, goals, and experiences, whether it has just been formed with an active donor at the helm (though "donor" is often a misnomer, since most family foundations are the combined initial efforts of at least a couple and increasingly of a whole family) or has just gone through complex succession planning for, say, the fifth generation of siblings and cousins. Whether constant or constantly changing, this individual heritage is the legacy of a family foundation.

This article focuses on the legacy that is family philanthropy. For instance, consider the actual thinking behind a family foundation set up in 2006:

> For the founder, the question was, "How do you leave a legacy?"

> In a letter to his daughter, he wrote, "You are my legacy."

> The daughter reflected seriously on the responsibility: "I am going to be the legacy of the foundation."

Legacy expresses and continues the values of the donor and the family through multiple generations. Sometimes that family legacy — as we will often call it — is the continuation of a donor's intent, which has either been clearly expressed or extracted from historical records and recollections. In other cases, it is a more general commitment to philanthropy that is affirmed by each generation in changing and expanding ways.

Some people worry that the values and priorities of deceased donors and distant generations (a so-called "dead hand of the past") are determining the future directions and grantmaking of many contemporary family foundations in rigid and unrealistic ways. Others view those values and priorities as sacrosanct, and even legally binding, elements of a donor's intent. Both perspectives are rather static views of how foundations actually carry on their work and of what donors and successor trustees usually want. It is precisely the ongoing legacy of values, vision, and giving that holds family foundations together (or may tear them apart), propels them creatively into the future, and is the basis of their positive impact on society. The narrow idea of donor intent has received important attention over the last decades. It is hoped that the more robust idea of a living legacy will receive much more attention in the next several decades. Legacy is not a "dead hand". It is, instead, a living, "helping hand" that is entrusted to and guides succeeding generations of family trustees and foundation staff.

The Legacy of Philanthropy

Giving in America continues to be a booming part of American society. As reported in *Giving USA, 2018*:

> Americans achieved a philanthropic landmark in 2017: for the first time total charitable giving … surged to an estimated $410.02 billion, an increase of 5.2 percent over the previous year. Americans gave generously, and the growth was virtually across the board.[1]

A thriving economy helps, of course. But giving is also pre-eminently about values. While there will be ups and downs in the economy, there is a growing recognition of the importance of donors, family foundations, and the idea of a legacy. These will continue to change the nature of family philanthropy. It may help, then, to start with a little historical context: What is the legacy of American philanthropy?

When historian Daniel Boorstin commented that "in America, even in modern times, communities existed before governments were here to care for public needs," he went on to write that "philanthropy has arisen in America out of our poignant and pressing sense of community."[2] What Boorstin noticed at our founding is what we have come to call the independent sector, that critically important web of voluntary associations and nonprofit organizations that help provide for many needs and public goods. That societal legacy of voluntary action has gone through great periods of expansion and contraction. By 1993, author Richard Cornuelle, who originated and popularized the term "independent sector," saw that a revival was underway: "I am more than ever certain that the revival of the independent sector is essential to the survival of American society."[3]

The current growth in the independent sector is fueled in many ways by the remarkable growth of new family philanthropy. The number of foundations has more than doubled between 1980 and 2000, from approximately 22,000 to 58,000. They gave more than $20 billion in that latter year. Nearly all of these foundations start as family foundations and most remain so for some time. Family foundations start small and most remain small. There are those examples, though, of the creation of wealth in this economy that has led to very large foundations. Some are large from the inception — the Bill and Melinda Gates Foundation being only the most famous example. Others start small and may grow gigantically over time. At the death of an original donor, or upon the sale of a family business, there can be significant increases in the endowment. When this article was originally written, some optimists thought that this growth in the number of foundations would continue. A 2000 book by Joel Orosz predicted that there might be as many as 250,000 foundations by 2050![4] The vast majority of them would be family foundations.

In fact, current numbers show Orosz to be a piker! *Foundation Stats* of the Foundation Center (accessed August 2018) reports the following numbers for 2014:

- Number of foundations: 86,726
- Gifts to foundations: $57 billion
- Giving: $60 billion
- Assets: 865 billion

There were nearly 285,000 donor-advised funds in 2016. Since these can be counted as equivalent to foundations, for my purposes here, the total number of philanthropic organizations is over 370,000, nearly 50 percent higher than Orosz's prediction, reached 34 years *before* his 2050 timeline. Consider as well that adding foundation and donor-advised fund numbers for "gifts to," "giving," and "assets" bump up the other numbers above a great deal too. That is truly remarkable.

And to complete the thought: counts for the number of *family* foundations have always been imprecise. But *Foundation Stats* reports these estimates:

- Number of family foundations: 42,000
- Gifts to family foundations: $28 billion
- Giving by family foundations: $26 billion
- Assets of family foundations: $401 billion

Donor-advised Funds as Family Philanthropy

As noted above, donor-advised funds (DAFs) are increasingly popular giving vehicles for families. As the late founder and executive director of the Donor's Trust, Whitney Ball defined them:

A donor-advised fund begins with a donor contributing cash or assets to a public charity, which in turn creates a separate account for the donor, who may recommend disbursements from the fund to other public charities. Technically, the charity that sponsors the fund has final say on the disbursements, and it is legally required to ensure they go only to charitable purposes, but in normal circumstances the original donor's requests will be followed.[5]

The New York Community Trust started the first donor-advised fund in 1931. But it wasn't until 1992 that Fidelity Investments started the first commercial donor-advised fund: the Charitable Gift Fund. There was considerable controversy among certain ingrained philanthropic interests about whether DAFs should be considered charitable vehicles. Several IRS rulings put that to rest. The resulting outpouring of funds to DAFs is changing the philanthropic landscape. And is it ever! The National Philanthropic Trust's *2017 Donor-Advised Fund Report* reported the following 2016 figures:

- Number of donor-advised funds: 284,965
- Contributions to donor-advised funds: $23 billion
- Average donor-advised fund size: $299,000
- Over $85 billion in assets
- Grants made of over $15 billion
- Payout of over 20 percent
  Note: There is double-counting in some of these figures due to unknown amounts and numbers of transfers between donor-advised funds or between foundations and donor-advised funds.

There is a sense in which donor-advised funds were originally simply a variant of a charitable checkbook, with tax advantages. Over the last several decades, however, families are treating them more as a family philanthropy vehicle just like a private foundation. This happened as donor-advised fund sponsors, in particular community foundations, liberalized the role of advisor. Most now permit current advisors to list successor advisors, often in perpetuity. Once that was possible, more families started acting as if donor-advised funds are their vehicle for family philanthropy: including having family meetings, writing legacy statements, etc. (There are still significant differences, however, between the two vehicles, with attendant advantages and disadvantages for each approach to family philanthropy.)

Taking Donors and Family Philanthropy Seriously

This stunning growth of and prospect for family philanthropy still bemused most commentators. Indeed, it is worth remembering that there was a time, not so long ago, when philanthropy itself was thought to be unimportant and on the way out. In an early scholarly look at philanthropy in America, economist Solomon Fabricant asked in his introduction "Should not the trend toward public philanthropy [government payments that might be considered "philanthropic"] be encouraged and should not private philanthropy be expected to retire from the scene"?[6] The donor and family in the philanthropic equation tended to be pesky interference. When Arnold Zurcher wrote in 1972, he raised important issues while also clearly being suspicious of "founder-donor and family influence at the primitive foundation level."[7]

Thus, it is not completely surprising that the role of donors, families, and family foundations was for many years nearly invisible. The mega-donors like Rockefeller and Carnegie were historically given attention, of course. Little attention had been paid to current donors or family foundations until the 1980s. For instance, when the annual "Taking Fundraising Seriously" symposia of the Center on Philanthropy started in the late 1980s, they were virtually unique in taking donors seriously. The Philanthropy Roundtable, which began as a national association of donors, was not founded until 1987. The larger nature, future, and challenges of family philanthropy escaped most public attention until the Council on Foundations inaugurated the Program on Family Philanthropy in 1994.

Several factors have influenced the dramatic increase in family foundations besides the booming economy. There have been some key changes in the tax code. Many of the newly wealthy are quite young and there is a greater propensity for charitable giving at a younger age. The new range of giving vehicles and their ease of use have encouraged greater philanthropy as well. These and simple demographics have fueled more interest in the oft-discussed intergenerational transfer of wealth that portends a golden age of philanthropy. LOCUS Impact Investing presented very optimistic projections in April 2018[8]:

For the 10-year period 2018–2027:
- estimated wealth transfer of $8.5 trillion
- charitable potential of $424 billion

For the 50-year period 2017–2067:
- estimated wealth transfer of $89.7 trillion
- charitable potential of nearly $4.5 trillion

The most important, factor, however, is a social and psychological shift that may be affecting this country in significant ways not yet fully understood. Commentators have long discussed with either approval *or* disapproval the changes in the social contract such that government is supposed to do less *or* more. The real change is the feeling that individuals, families, and communities should do more. There is a great awakening of a more profound sense that problems can be addressed philanthropically, voluntarily by us, directly.

Individuals and families are feeling newly empowered to take on precisely the responsibilities that Boorstin and Cornuelle alluded to. Robert Putnam reminds us that "Your extended family represents a form of social capital"[9] and is a means by which we can help society. Years ago, Paul Schervish and John Havens conceived of the growth in giving in prescient ways that are still robust today:

> Although it is impossible to project with certainty the horizon of material wealth, we do believe it will be substantially large and that greater wealth accompanies a general proclivity toward increased charitable giving in general and for individuals… Apparently something more profound than tax aversion and tax incentives is generating a greater predilection for philanthropy. This more profound factor, we believe, is at least in part a growing public culture and personal spirituality of care.[10]

One shouldn't underestimate this still inchoate "growing public culture and personal spirituality of care." They presage "a golden age of philanthropy" while urging us all to focus on charitable values.

It is no surprise, then, that donors and families are forming foundations — and other family giving vehicles — at a quickening pace. They want to be involved in ways previously unknown. They believe that they can and should be heard. We don't know how this attitude will continue to develop over the next several decades, but it underlies much of the desire of donors and families to do philanthropy differently and to pass on a legacy of values to their next generation and to society.

Family foundations are both the incubators of organized American philanthropy and a reaffirmation of a great American legacy that giving with purpose, goals, and a vision is a responsibility and opportunity to effect change. For this amazing growth to be better grounded, more focused, and increasingly effective, donors and families are beginning to attend to the legacy that propels their giving. Let us look now at three major legacy themes:

Family Legacy: the legacy of values that underlie family philanthropy.

Donor Intent and Donor Legacy: the importance and limitations of a donor's original actions and intentions in starting a family foundation.

Living the Legacy: the ongoing effort of donors and succeeding generations to discover, maintain, and develop an ongoing family legacy.

Family Legacy

The distinguished sociologist Edward Shils once likened tradition to "an old building, lived in and used and modified over the years, continuing to be similar to what it was and to be thought of as still being the same building."[11] What a fitting image for the tradition of a donor and family legacy. The essence of family philanthropy over time is exactly like that: a home filled with memories and mementos, pictures and stories. Values that seem explicit and obvious coexist with those that may be more ambiguous or contentious. One can almost see a kitchen table laden with food around which stories are told, values disputed, and decisions made.

Over time, rooms are added, renovations made, etc. In the collection I edited, of which this essay was the introduction,[12] a variety of rich examples are given of how memories and events symbolize values and lessons for the donor, succeeding generations of family trustees, staff, and the community at large. (Most of the examples below come from this volume and, as necessary, they are referred to in this text as *LL* collection) An account of the McKnight Foundation mentions how a new generation of family members and prospective trustees discovered the foundation and the values of the family at family meals. Bill Graustein tells a number of marvelous family stories that resonate through the workings of the William Caspar Graustein Memorial Fund. These and other stories illustrate how values get passed on and changed within the inner workings of family foundations and how they animate their giving programs.

Not enough stories are being told. Sadly, the values that stand behind the decision to form a foundation too often get forgotten. For all the emphasis given to tax planning, it is usually a secondary consideration when a donor or family makes such an important philanthropic decision. And yet the values and purposes that underlie family philanthropy — the family legacy — get lost as various immediate legal, organizational, and accounting matters get pushed to the forefront. That is a shame, which impoverishes our understanding of a foundation's mission and its future.

It is true that intent and values are not easy to discuss, especially when money, power, and family dynamics are also part of the equation. Open conversation is a challenge. Making those founding values as explicit as possible, though, is one of the most important tasks in establishing and maintaining a philanthropic legacy. It is always better if these values and purposes are formulated and communicated at the beginning, when the donor is alive. Thankfully, it is also more common today to see new family foundations facing this issue head on. Both donors and other family members are more likely to engage in early discussions of family values and legacy.

Even when there appears to be no donor intent or legacy, the values embedded in the family provide continuity and flexibility to address the needs of the future. One foundation in New York City, for instance, has no explicit mission or donor's intent to fall back upon. But family member trustees did have such a strong family culture and common values that it has fitfully sustained its focus through three generations. Each generation has worked through different approaches to similar problems based on a generally common core of values. In that way, change over the years becomes an opportunity to recommit to old values in new ways.

A philanthropic legacy doesn't, of course, have to begin or end with an organized foundation. Nor is such a journey a straight line. For instance, two donors set up a small foundation in 1993 as their "ethical will" to their pre-teen sons. By 2000, they decided to spend out. The foundation was but one tool they used to help their children develop meaningful values of their own. They saw that the foundation had become unnecessary because their children had developed their own values and desire to "do the right thing," whether that meant someday starting their own small foundations, or just leading a good life. And yet, in 2017, one of the sons touchingly told his parents that he wanted the foundation to continue: better, he said, to leave most of any small estate to the foundation and not to him! One child and his wife have now taken a lead in the foundation and want to continue this philanthropic family legacy as their own.

"My family is my #1 interest!" exclaims H. D. Leighty, echoing a sentiment common among both donors and family trustees of succeeding generations. The idea of a family philanthropic legacy is about communicating and transmitting values across generations. Even with the most explicit intent, over time, the donor's legacy becomes a family legacy. While family legacy for a foundation doesn't stop with a statement of donor's intent, the issue of legacy does start with the donor. How much better if there is clarity from the beginning.

From Donor Intent to Donor Legacy

New donors draw on the inspiration and lessons of their family, their personal and professional mentors, lifetime influences, interests, and skills. Sometimes they draw on the experience and legacy of other foundations, as Ronald Austin Wells points out in his article in the *LL* collection. Nonetheless, donors have a critically important role as "institutional" founders transmitting values. Their intentions matter. What has come to be known as donor intent is merely the beginning of what can become an ongoing and robust family foundation legacy.

There are several examples throughout the *LL* collection of original donor statements, variously called a preamble to founding documents or a statement of donor legacy. The first, most basic, purpose of such a statement is to express the values, purposes, and grantmaking goals of the donor. It is their money and they are making a charitable commitment that may serve specific purposes or be a general charitable commitment in perpetuity. Second, a clear statement provides a benchmark by which to measure grantmaking success. Is it helping to accomplish the stated goals and values the donor set down? It can help protect a foundation and its funds from being used in ways that would be inimical to the donor's wishes. Third, and most important for an ongoing family legacy, a donor's statement offers a crucial starting point and guidance to family trustees and staff as they take the reins of the grantmaking program. Consultant Mary Phillips has described the opportunity taken by the donors and family of the Stoneman Family Foundation to develop a legacy statement prior to the death of the donors: "Such a statement could ease any lingering doubts or anxieties family members might have about giving away inherited wealth or assuming responsibility for more of the foundation's grantmaking ..."

Any statement of donor intent or legacy is like life: it is a work in process, first for the donor, and then for succeeding generations as well. It is far better to set down what one knows and feels now. It can and arguably should change as experience matures one's values and intentions. The costs of not doing so, or of not being clear, are manifold. As foundation critic Waldemar Nielsen has written, it all starts with donor intent: "Very serious problems exist involving departure from donor intentions as well as in the activities and operations of many foundations. On the whole, I believe that most of those problems derive from faults and failures of donors."[13]

Unfortunately, donor intent has been turned into a loaded, often ideological, term by advocates and critics. The real difficulties of defining and maintaining donor intent transcend — or afflict — all political viewpoints. On the one hand, some people defend donor intent as the only way to save foundations from wandering. Even with the clearest documents delineating donor intent, however, interpretations can vary widely. One large foundation started in the 1950s has a detailed "Liberty Fund Basic Memorandum" of nearly 150 pages and yet there is much public and private controversy over whether that intent is being maintained. Some people suggest that a donor's intent is best protected only during the lifetime of the donor and the next generation, who presumably knew what the donor wanted. Who is to say that a donor's intent will even survive that generation?

Some commentators have advocated sunsetting provisions to protect a donor's intent. There is certainly nothing wrong with sunsetting, as long as it is a "private policy" decision by the donor or trustees, and not some sort of public policy requirement. In fact, most donors want a family legacy in perpetuity — as a general philanthropic value or for specific causes — so requiring sunsetting usually contradicts a donor's wishes. It could also have a very detrimental impact on the long-term institutional capacity of civil society and the independent sector to be effective and independent. Some of my articles in Chapter 6 of this book explore a few of those issues.

Sunsetting can also be an excuse by current trustees to spend out rather than be more careful stewards of the legacy for future generations. In the end, care for the ongoing legacy and vision of a donor and foundation is an uncertain but important goal. Who can be certain, for instance, that the final grantees of a sunsetting foundation will appropriately maintain the intent presumably behind their grants?

On the other hand, some people dismiss donor intent quickly as the "dead hand of the past." One donor expressed it thus: "It is immoral to have others do your work for you when you are gone." Do those that worry that adhering to a specific intent will limit the creativity of succeeding trustees or staff want to offer *carte blanche* to trustees and staff without any reference to the donor's views? That seems hubristic and churlish at best. Several legal cases have shown that ignoring a donor's intent can cause serious legal complications, if the donor was clear in the beginning. There is also the moral issue. The original donor made the money and decided to set up a foundation to advance particular values and views. Aren't trustees and staff in some sense accountable for following the donor's intent if it is set forth clearly? Or at least for taking it seriously? These are difficult issues and none of this is an argument for iron-clad donor intent.

There is a third way instead of a crass either/or choice. Establishing a donor's intent at the beginning clarifies the values and purposes to the donor(s) and offers valuable guidance to succeeding generations. By itself, donor intent is a limited concept that ignores the extraordinary and difficult family and generational dynamics that animate family foundations over time. Family donor intent is very important. It is just the beginning of a multi-generational process that develops and honors a dynamic family legacy. Family foundations should start with a sense of the donor's intent or the family's values. But it doesn't stop there.

Developing a Living Legacy

In fact, the key element of a useful donor intent is the commitment of donor and family to ongoing candid discussions, which allows for understanding and change across generations. Providing the guidance of a statement of donor intent then, is not the "dead hand of the past" as many claim. As a "helping hand," donor intent can provide insight into the values, vision, and purpose of the foundation. As Will Close has noted about the Spring Close Foundation: "For our fiftieth anniversary, we had a two-day retreat to examine the future of the foundation. Although we made some fundamental changes in the way we make grants, I cannot overemphasize the importance of donor intent and the work of the past generations in our thinking." Over time, the donor's intent becomes a beginning, enriched by subsequent generations.

What if there is no statement of the donor's wishes, as is so often the case? After the death of a donor, children and grandchildren are often at a loss as to what to do without some guidance from the founding donors. They usually want both to honor the past and use the past to look to the future and make the foundation their own. Succeeding generations typically don't want a blank slate; they want guidance from the donor or earlier generations of trustees. One of the questions raised by many family members is "How can one discover or reconstruct what is often a lost and vague intent and then nurture a legacy over time?" Several stories in chapters four and five of my *LL* collection give fascinating examples of how different foundations and family trustees have rediscovered a usable philanthropic legacy when the donor was silent on the topic.

Each successive generation within a family foundation is faced with the exciting task of respecting and passing on what becomes a family legacy. It is sometimes surprising — and certainly heartening — to see how hard many family foundations work to discover their pasts. Succeeding generations of trustees must engage in inquiries of various kinds to determine the legacy of values and goals left by those who came before. When those stated purposes are too general, the actions of a donor during his/her life are vivid sources for determining a donor's legacy. One foundation sought to unearth a deceased donor's values and interests by systematically reviewing years and years of tax returns and checkbook stubs. Even when a donor's intentions are quite specific, succeeding generations may be left adrift if specific grantees disappear or issues become irrelevant. Once again, the question is how do trustees and staff determine, revive, adapt and apply the values that animated such specific goals? There is no single or simple answer, but each donor and each family trustee should attend to a culture of listening and conversation that facilitates this.

As Tom Lambeth, past executive director of the Z. Smith Reynolds Foundation has noted, "The only thing more dangerous than having the conversation is not having it." Many factors can make this conversation easier or harder, such as whether there is a statement of legacy, the size of the family and board, and the size of the foundation. Other influences could include the foundation's relative importance compared to a family business, the wealth and talents of succeeding generations, geographic proximity or dispersion of family members, cohesiveness of values, sibling and cousin relationships, and changing times. Whatever the unique features of a family foundation, spending time on the issue of legacy is an important and rewarding effort.

Unfortunately, it seems that passing on what is known about a foundation legacy is often ignored. At the 2000 Family Foundations Conference of the Council on Foundations, for instance, trustees and staff were asked if the board had a plan for educating the next generation of foundation leaders. Over 50 percent responded no. Recent survey data from foundation members of Exponent Philanthropy suggest the situation may be better, but there is much more trustees and donors can do to make the process a productive one. Katherine Tyler Scott describes in my *LL* collection an ongoing educational process to develop a strong sense of trusteeship based on the foundation's history, mission, publics, and future. Dr. Robert Lynn elegantly put it this way: "An institution whose leaders are out of touch with its movement through time — its trajectory — is often in serious difficulty."

Discovering and communicating a legacy requires a careful, balanced eye. Discussions of donor and family legacy should avoid two extremes. The first is the tendency for foundations to lionize the founder and his or her legacy. We have all seen examples of hagiographic family or foundation histories that serve little purpose. At the other extreme are cases of subsequent generations of foundation trustees that seek guilt-ridden contrition for the sins they see in the actions of the founders. They so abhor the way the money was earned, or the uses to which it was put, that they overreact and likely miss out on understanding some of the nuances that may be there and may still impact the family legacy of values.

Legacy and Accountability

A foundation's legacy can also play two important roles as the foundation world addresses calls for accountability: both for a foundation itself and for the community of foundations as well. We all say we want results and accountability for foundations. Almost by its nature, significant results must be based on clear goals and must be seen in the long term. A focus on the legacy of a foundation provides a lens by which to assess how we have all done, from the donor's original values and purpose through the continuity and change provided by the family legacy of succeeding generations. If a foundation is unconnected with its past and changes direction every few years, for instance, meaningful impact and assessment are more difficult. The resulting grantmaking may be more dilettantish than strategic. Reference to the donor and a family legacy is one of the primary ways we can assess how it is doing: "Is the foundation following its mission and values?"

Legacy and accountability are also related when it comes to the foundation world as a whole. Commentators on foundations have worried that they don't have shareholders (owners) and customers in the usual sense. These stakeholders do exert tremendous power on commercial organizations. Nor do they have voters as our democratic institutions do. A self-perpetuating board, then, can be open to the charge of self-interest and unsupervised play. The oversight of journalists is often uninformed and phrased in sound bites. Governmental oversight by legislation and by the state's attorney general are saddled with the same problems. And neither have any interest in looking for or thinking about whether an ongoing legacy of values exists or is relevant. In fact, surveys show that legislators in particular know little about foundations and often don't believe in that form of voluntary action anyway.

As Colin Campbell, former president of the Rockefeller Brothers Fund, succinctly put it, "telling our story" may be the most persuasive response to both the internal and external needs for accountability:

> Accountability means giving an account of yourself — put simply, it means telling your story... One thing today's family philanthropists can do is to tell their stories more publicly and openly, to circulate widely the values, lessons, and examples that will inspire and enable tomorrow's family donors to follow in their footsteps... By becoming storytellers, family foundations speak not only to new generations of their own donor families but also to others who will be in a position to inherit or dispose of substantial wealth.[14]

In our process-oriented world, exploring a family foundation's legacy is not merely a useful internal exercise for trustees and staff. It adds depth and content to grantmaking programs. A sense of family legacy adds significantly to a foundation's "bottom line," by identifying the impact it wants to have on its chosen areas of interest. It provides another, longer-term way of asking how foundations are doing. Telling the story of how a foundation and its trustees are actually "living the legacy" reminds us of exactly how foundations — here family foundations — act in a manner accountable to their origins, their values, their impact, and to their future.

Conclusion

Returning to Edward Shils' metaphor of tradition as a building, it is generally better to restore and renovate than simply to tear down and build anew. As family foundations take their past into account, they build a living, family legacy. It may be loosely tethered to the past. It can change and adapt as future generations participate and have their own discussions about legacy and the future. If there was a specific intent from the donor, maintaining and communicating those values across generations — across the kitchen table — makes them an integral part of a broader, ongoing family legacy. If there was no clear statement, discovering that heritage of values and interests through family stories and records in dusty trunks may help build a similar family legacy. Finally, and inevitably, each generation makes changes. They adapt and add their own values and viewpoints. In all such cases, the legacy is important not as a concession to the past, but as a "helping hand," a vital and rich part of the present that shows the way to the future. Paul Ylvisaker wrote that

> There is something distinctive and precious about family foundations that suggests they should remain as they are: a unique opportunity for families to make and leave their mark on the society around them, to share with others the fortune they have enjoyed and the creative energies they so often possess.[15]

Articulating, discovering, maintaining, adapting, and carrying out a family legacy from a donor's intent through multiple generations helps build dynamic, values-based family philanthropy and foundations. Living the legacy of a family foundation is also a powerful way to strengthen the larger societal legacy that is our responsibility. It is certainly not too much to hope for both results. Now that is a legacy worth pursuing!

This article was originally published as the opening essay to Living the Legacy: The Values of a Family's Philanthropy Across Generations, *edited by Charles H. Hamilton (Washington DC: The National Center for Family Philanthropy, 2001). Reprinted with the permission of The National Center for Family Philanthropy. I have made some revisions and added endnotes.*

[1] *Giving USA: The Annual Report on Philanthropy for 2017*, (Indianapolis: The Giving USA Foundation, 2018), p. 17.

[2] Daniel J. Boorstin, *The Decline of Radicalism: Reflections on America Today* (New York: Random House, 1969), pp. 46 and 68.

[3] Richard C. Cornuelle, *Reclaiming the American Dream* (New Brunswick: Transaction Publishers, 1993), p. 182.

[4] Joel J. Orosz, *The Insider's Guide to Grantmaking* (San Francisco: Jossey-Bass, 2000), p. 266.

[5] Whitney Ball, "Interview on The Future of Donor-Advised Funds," *Philanthropy*, September-October 2005.

[6] Solomon Fabricant, "Philanthropy in the American Economy: An Introduction," in Frank G. Dickinson, *The Changing Position of Philanthropy in the American Economy* (Washington DC: National Bureau of Economic Research, 1970), p. 29.

[7] Arnold J. Zurcher, *The Management of American Foundations: Administration, Policies, and Social Role* (New York: New York University Press, 1972), p. 22.

[8] See "Understanding Transfer of Wealth: 2017 National Analysis," LOCUS, April, 2018; and "$9 Trillion and Counting: How Charities Can Tap into the Transfer of Wealth," *The Chronicle of Philanthropy*, April, 2018.

[9] Robert D. Putnam, *Bowling Alone* (New York: Simon and Schuster, 2000), p. 21.

[10] John Havens and Paul Schervish, "Millionaires and the Millennium," Boston College, Social Welfare Research Institute, 1999, p. 20.

[11] Edward Shils, *Tradition* (Chicago: The University of Chicago Press, 1981), p. 46.

[12] Charles H. Hamilton, editor *Living the Legacy: The Values of a Family's Philanthropy Across Generations* (Washington DC: National Center for Family Philanthropy, 2001). Referred to in the text of this article as *LL* collection.

[13] Waldemar Nielsen, "The Donor's Role in Donor Intent," in *Donor Intent* (Washington DC: The Philanthropy Roundtable, 1993), p. 15.

[14] Colin Campbell, *Telling Our Story: Accountability for Family Foundations*, (Washington DC: Council on Foundations, 1996), and excepted in my *LL* collection.

[15] Paul Ylvisaker, *Conscience & Community: The Legacy of Paul Ylvisaker,* edited by Virginia Esposito (New York: Peter Lang, 1999), p. 375.

3. Donor Intent and Real Impact: How Your Family Can Have Both

Takeaway 1: Donor intent matters today. It places values and purpose at the beginning of a philanthropic journey.

The phrase "donor intent" has entered the hallowed halls of philanthropic folderol and empty disputation: "the soulless, devitalized, pretentious means we use to confuse words with things, opinions with truths, intentions with results" (as Michael Bailin described philanthropic jargon in his introduction of Tony Proscio's great little book, *In Other Words*). For some donors and others, donor intent is an unchangeable diktat. Others believe it is a pesky nuisance, obstructing their better ideas, or becoming a "dead hand of the past." It can be those things, of course. But both positions obscure how donor intent can and often does cultivate success for real impact and a viable philanthropic legacy. We need to have those conversations.

Donor intent matters in many ways. Donors (often a couple or broader family action) are moved by passions, purposes, and values to start a foundation (or a donor-advised fund, major gift agreement or another philanthropic vehicle). Otherwise, one is engaged in willy-nilly philanthropy. A donor's intent is like an early mission statement. It may stress general values or a specific issue.

It may be flexible or not so much. It often envisions an evolving family philanthropic legacy through generations. It may favor spending down in X years or seek an elusive perpetuity. Mission and purpose may also be relegated to others (lawyers/accountants, professional philanthropoids, or future generations). John D. MacArthur famously told his board "I made the money; you guys will have to figure out what to do with it."

Donor intent statements exist as letters, stories, videos, or as a few pithy sentences on the back of an envelope. Pierre F. Goodrich left a painfully long statement of 143 pages including index, with tolerably successful results for nearly sixty years, so far. There are a bevy of articles, consultants, and examples available elsewhere on how to communicate donor intent.

Whatever its content and form, a donor intent statement is only one vital, but static, step. Indeed, it matters most when it is a dynamic learning tool that really engages family members, grantees, and others. Philanthropy, after all, represents those kinds of quintessential reciprocal relationships, connecting the ones giving (for instance, a donor) and the ones receiving (for instance, grantee organizations, institutions, "next gens," or trustees). Great care needs to be applied so this is not a one-way, power relationship. At its best and most effective, it is a shared connection that embodies cooperation, mutual exchange, and honest give-and-take. How, then, do these genuine reciprocal relationships help donor intent achieve impact and legacy?

Takeaway 2: Engaging grantees. Intent only counts when it can achieve impact. Donors and families must engage in two-way conversations with grantees.

If donor intent statements do not intend and lead to impact, well then, they are just words, words, words, right? Most donors are not going to pen treatises on achieving results. But, they can encourage involving grantees and others in those reciprocal partnerships that lead to implementation and impact.

Too often, however, donors (and philanthropoids) wrongly look narrowly to themselves to achieve impact and, alas, see no need to listen to grantees. For instance, the idea of "strategic philanthropy" in practice frequently fosters donor conceit and that good old "I know best, so I'll go it alone" attitude. Philanthropy in general and donors are easily seduced by the hubris endemic to giving away money (which "has no natural predators," to borrow Tony Proscio's wonderful phrase). This produces very poor relationships indeed, not just with grantees but with family too. I remember a sibling of a founder whose admittedly impressive grantmaking as ED was also imperious regarding the other siblings and grandchildren. Eventually, they had had enough and threw her out.

My experience has been that many donors and family foundations understand the difficult nature and remarkable ability of these reciprocal relationships to translate donor and family intent to societal impact. Sometimes, talk of engaging in these partnerships is simply dismissed as so much politically-correct hooey. But, the fact is that we live in a world of complex and evolving social needs. We are buffeted by rapidly changing methods to address these needs: some astonishingly useful and some merely snake oil. It is a challenging knowledge problem no one donor or foundation can surmount with mere theories of change or intent. Donor intent and successful impact can flourish when a healthy, reciprocal, two-way relationship exists between: 1) the passions, values, and money of a benefactor/donor, and 2) the needs, unique insights, unparalleled local knowledge, and practical skills of a grantee. Good intentions simply don't become impactful without this cooperative commitment, humility, and hard work.

A cautionary word about sunsetting a foundation. By itself, this can be a worthy goal and strategy. But it is not, as sometimes promoted, a quick fix to protect intent and provide impact. It may relieve donors and boards of the responsibilities of doing the difficult work of building both authentic partnerships with family and with committed grantees. There are simply too many blatant examples of grantees ignoring a donor's intent and directing money to their priorities. Sunsetting requires the same candid relationships, clear agreements, and verifiable outcomes with final grantees as are required for a meaningful transfer between family generations. You choose, but do either one well.

Takeaway 3: Engaging family. A robust philanthropic legacy happens only when donors and families affirm, change, and adapt together.

Building reciprocal relationships with grantees is difficult, rewarding, and necessary. Consider, then, the terror and euphoria of different generations, and then future generations, around the family kitchen table! When executive director of a family foundation, I symbolically hung boxing gloves on the board room door. This is a different kind of partnership, often called serial reciprocity because the connection is successively passed on from generation to generation. First, the donor's values and vision, whether explicit or merely implicit and emotionally understood, are the starting place. Each subsequent generation then reaffirms, changes, adapts and finally passes on again what becomes an ongoing family legacy. Much has been written about how to do legacy statements, and there are numerous fine examples of such statements.

Donors almost always desire some form of legacy. They may have specific values and tasks they want to live past them. Or they may mostly desire to hand down a general philanthropic commitment. Many may even hope a legacy will help keep families together over generations. That hope borders on whimsy, except for a few durable exemplars, like the Rockefellers. And yet, too often, donors and their statements work against a viable legacy in the same ways they work against genuine impact. They demand inflexible adherence and dismiss discussion, thereby poisoning the trust that makes generational relationships productive. Building and sustaining a family legacy takes hard work, sensitivity and great listening skills.

Similarly, family members almost always desire a donor's guidance — not strident lecturing or a deaf ear. I have seen them go to great lengths to seek it here, there and everywhere: conversations with donor, grantees, and friends; a donor intent statement; family stories; and even rummaging through decades of checkbook stubs. They want a "helping hand of the past" that assists them in their own deliberations and decisions.

I have been in meetings with multiple generations struggling with a family philanthropic legacy. Sometimes, the generations just can't find a common voice and don't want to. Other times, the desire for common ground is palpable and filled with compromise and hard-won trust. There are those remarkable times when goodwill and some common values trump disagreement as generations make a viable, flexible, living legacy that is their own. I once worked with two very contentious generations with almost opposing viewpoints. But they maintained a shared commitment to New York City and to key social values. They found a real but shaky common ground. The means and grantees chosen to achieve those commitments often differed. This led to some seemingly contradictory grantmaking. For a time, though, there was a coherent, successful legacy that made a valuable impression in New York City, which continues twenty years later. The challenge will soon be how they bring on a new generation of trustees. In another case, parents reluctantly agreed to discuss charitable giving with their grown children shortly before their small family foundation would receive a huge influx of funds from the sale of a family business. They wisely asked a consultant to help. By the end of the day of discussion, the parents saw that the children had a deep commitment to charitable giving through the family tradition of tithing. The children realized that there was common ground about several causes. Parents and children differed in the means they thought would best serve those causes. But they walked away from that meeting with a higher level of trust and lessons in how to communicate, listen, and compromise. They seemed up to the hard work ahead.

Finally, a donor wished to avoid family divisiveness. So, he set up separate $1 million donor-advised funds for each of the six adult children. At a retreat where the father announced this plan, the children appreciated the separate charitable vehicles. But surprisingly for all, they also expressed deep regret that long-term family values and commitments would not become a common family legacy going forward. They wanted that kind of involvement. The seven of them proceeded to set up a largely unfunded *family* donor-advised fund. The children and father would contribute to it from their funds and make joint legacy commitments: What a great example that out of separateness can come a common commitment to family legacy.

Through it all, building a philanthropic legacy requires the most intimate and difficult of reciprocal relationships. I don't think we give that process the attention it needs. John D. Rockefeller is reported to have quipped, "Everything is relative, except relatives, who are constant." That is the joy, sorrow, challenge, and opportunity of family philanthropy. This is a situation where outside consultants can frequently bring some objectivity/civility, direction and brakes to a generational discussion. In these efforts to build a legacy, donors (or the reigning heads of a family) have a special obligation to express their personal views clearly, openly, and with great humility. They need to respect and be flexible about the views of the next generations, as do the subsequent generations towards donors and their successors. Everyone needs to listen! In doing so, family members can begin to model cooperative behaviors. It has struck me anecdotally that family foundations with a strong history of family cooperation and a generational legacy often have the relationship skills to work successfully in partnerships with grantees.

After all the wrangling, tears and agreements, family members can't forget that they must get up from the kitchen table and take on their responsibilities around the boardroom table *as* trustees. The responsibilities and practices of foundation governance and implementation happen there. One is a trustee with its attendant responsibilities and constraints outside of family ties.

Takeaway 4: Family philanthropy is accountable through its (a) ability to develop impact, (b) relationships with recipients and (c) legacy with successive generations.

Finally, the reciprocal relationships that drive impact and legacy have something to tell us about accountability in ways that are real and relevant to family philanthropy. They suggest a simple, more inclusive and healthy element to accountability.

Everyone wants accountability for foundations. The problem is who are the deciders? Commentators on foundations often worry that foundations do not have shareholders (owners) or customers in the usual sense. Nor do they have voters as our democratic institutions do. A self-perpetuating board, then, can be open to the charge of self-interest and unsupervised play. The scrutiny of journalists and the oversight of governmental agencies can be important. But it is too easily uninformed or presented in simplistic sound bites.

By contrast, the first level of accountability should be: Are we — as grantors and grantees — pursuing the intent and impact we have set for ourselves? This is a question all donors, board/family members and recipients should continually ask themselves. Note that looking at it this way means both the donor/grantor and grantee sides of the reciprocal relationship are jointly accountable. The two-way partnership should encourage a robust, ongoing discussion about results, accountability and the future. These are extremely important points, with huge implications for the nature of philanthropic effectiveness that, sigh, can't be fully discussed here.

A family philanthropic legacy is also accountable to and through the reciprocal relationships that serially cascade across generations. It is relevant to ask and even judge a donor's intent and a family foundation's legacy by its handling of its development. History and a sense of continuity matter too. The point is not that foundations should abide by a specific donor intent, though that is a valid option. The point is that donors and families should be able to communicate how they think about their philanthropic legacy. How has this commitment and grantmaking developed over the years? How do they handle the difficult discussions about change, evolving social needs, grantee partnerships and their future hopes for that legacy?

Takeaway 5: A philanthropic legacy that both engages family and welcomes grantees to the discussion will validate donor intent and sustain real impact.

Philanthropy is by its nature deeply relational in many ways barely touched on here. Contrary to much that has been written, we simply can't ignore donor intent (or its generational iterations). Nor can we ignore the role of partnerships. Donor intent requires authentic, two-way conversations if it is to have the knowledge and skills to attain results. Similarly, the most particular of relationships — family across generations — sustains philanthropy. A family philanthropic legacy both validates donor intent and sustains it over time.

Perhaps most important, the partnerships we must nurture with care ensure family philanthropy remains relevant. They allow for changes and improvements that are connected both to intent, but also to the evolving social needs of and knowledge about this world. Reciprocal relationships encourage real learning from the past, the present and into an unknown future.

The conversations need to continue. We can see that usable donor intent, real impact, and a responsive family philanthropic legacy are all of a piece. The growth and effectiveness of this core American tradition of family philanthropy probably depends on how well we do this.

This essay was originally written as a Summit Essay for the National Summit on Family Philanthropy: Donor Intent & Real Impact: Can Your Family Have Both? (San Francisco, February 20–21, 2017), sponsored by the Dorothy Johnson Center for Philanthropy, Grand Valley State University. Reprinted with the permission of the Dorothy Johnson Center for Philanthropy.

4. Legacy: The Helping Hand of Family Philanthropy
Co-authored with Jason Born

John D. Rockefeller is reported to have once quipped, "Everything is relative, except relatives, who are constant."

That is the joy, sorrow, challenge, and opportunity of family philanthropy. Given their inherent ongoing connection to the donor and the many individual interests that family members develop over time, how can family foundations avoid the outcomes of either chaos or rigidity that make succeeding generations lose interest in philanthropy? Helping these foundations (and now, increasingly, donor-advised funds as well) develop and share their family philanthropic values — their legacy — will likely become key to the future growth and effectiveness of this core American philanthropic tradition.

The number of foundations in the United States has more than doubled in the twenty years since 1980 (when this article was originally published), from approximately 22,000 to 58,000. Foundations then gave more than $20 billion annually. Growth in the number of foundations is expected to continue. Joel Orosz's 2000 book *The Insider's Guide to Grantmaking* (Jossey-Bass) predicted that there might be 250,000 foundations by 2050. In fact, current numbers show Orosz' estimates to be woefully low! *Foundation Stats* of the Foundation Center (accessed August 2018) reports the following numbers for 2014:

- Number of foundations: 86,726
- Gifts to foundations: $57 billion
- Giving: $60 billion
- Assets: 865 billion

There were also nearly 285,000 donor-advised funds in 2016. Since these should be counted as equivalent to foundations, for purposes here, the total number of philanthropic organizations is over 370,000, nearly 50 percent higher than Orosz's prediction, reached thirty-four years *before* his 2050 date! Consider as well that adding foundation and donor-advised numbers for "gifts," "giving," and "assets" bumps up the other foundation numbers a great deal too. That is truly remarkable.

The vast majority of these foundations will start as family foundations and most will continue to operate as such for some time. Each will go through different stages of development with different generations involved. Other popular family philanthropic vehicles — including supporting organizations and donor-advised funds — are increasingly being governed in a manner similar to family foundations, and they are increasingly faced with challenges and opportunities like their family foundation cousins.

Intent and Legacy: Beyond the "Dead Hand"

Some people believe that the values and priorities of deceased donors and past generations — the "dead hand of the past" — should not determine the future directions and grantmaking of family foundations. Others believe that these values and priorities are revered elements of the foundation's mission and purpose. When rigidly held, both perspectives on a donor's original intent lead to rather static, one-dimensional views of how foundations actually develop and carry on their work. Neither view reflects what donors and successor trustees usually want or how they commonly act.

That brings us to legacy. Each family foundation has its own rich heritage of values, goals and experiences. This is true whether it has just been formed with an active donor at the helm (though "donor" is something of a misnomer, since most family foundations are the combined initial efforts of at least a couple and increasingly of a whole family) or whether it has just gone through complex succession planning for, say, the fifth generation of siblings and cousins. Whether constant or constantly changing, this heritage is the legacy of a family foundation.

Family foundation trustees and staff often recognize that donor intent is very important, however it may change over time. It at least represents an initial grounding. Founding values and purposes should be formulated and communicated early on, preferably while the donors are active in the work of the foundation. But legacy only starts with a donor's explicit or implicit intent; it doesn't stop there. It is precisely the ongoing legacy of values, vision, and giving that holds family foundations together (or may tear them apart), propels them creatively into the future, and is the basis of their positive impact on society. Legacy is not a "dead hand;" it is, instead, a living, "helping hand:" one that is entrusted to and guides succeeding generations of family trustees and foundation staff.

Family foundations that sustain a family's involvement over time often do so because of their ability to develop and communicate an ongoing legacy to which both the donors and successive generations of family members contribute. The *donor's legacy* — the founding values and vision of the donor, whether explicit or merely implicit and emotionally understood — is a necessary starting place for future reflection and consideration. Over time, succeeding generations may reaffirm the founding vision or may choose to adapt and change it. Each generation within a family foundation, then, is faced with the exciting responsibility of respecting, adapting and passing on what becomes an ongoing *family legacy*.

Several promising strategies for reflecting and passing on a family legacy are described in *Living the Legacy: The Values of a Family's Philanthropy Across Generations*, published in 2001 by the National Center for Family Philanthropy. Many of the stories and quotations in this article come from that collection. Two of the most important strategies are described here. The first is to collect and tell stories about the values, vision, and actions — myths and allegories — that uniquely capture what philanthropy means to a family. The other, a bit more focused, is to move past a narrow donor's intent. It is to develop, share, and build upon a living legacy statement regarding what moves the donors, trustees, and family members and the philanthropy that results.

Telling and Listening to Stories

One Ohio-based family foundation sets aside time at each annual board retreat to tell stories. Family members listen to audiotapes of the founders (the now deceased grandparents of the current senior trustees). The family gathers together after dinner to listen to these "oral histories." Individual members of the family then share their own personal stories about the founders, and their own relevant family experiences. In this way, trustees and other family members remember and continually reinvigorate the values that animate their giving.

More family foundation stories need to be told. Even when the values that stand behind the decision to form a foundation are clear in the mind of the donor, they too often get set aside from the beginning. Financial incentives, tax planning, and organizational matters get pushed to the forefront. Stories remembered and handed down can make a dramatic difference by reinvigorating and refocusing on the values and mission that animated the founding.

In the late 1980s, the William Caspar Graustein Memorial Fund experienced a rapid increase in assets, during which time the board decided to set a new direction for what had been "a small and sleepy family foundation." Board chair Bill Graustein recalled the stories of his own childhood as one way to help guide this process:

> The outward labor of guiding this transition was mirrored by an inward process of coming to understand as an adult the stories of my family that I heard as a child. These stories came to be touchstones for guiding the Memorial Fund's work.

Graustein shared several of these stories in a series of annual reports for the foundation, helping grantees of the foundation and others get a better perspective on the principles and legacy that drive the fund's work.

New stories reinvigorate the values behind a family's philanthropy. However, it takes commitment and practice to record stories, tell one's own stories, and learn to actively listen. The Russell Family Foundation, based in Washington, sets aside time at each board meeting to share stories and historical family pictures, and to build on family heritage and history. Sarah R. Cavanaugh, trustee and former executive director of the foundation, says that the family "treats this time as sacred."

Developing a Legacy Statement

Many foundations undertake a more formal process by developing written (and in some cases audio or video taped) statements of family legacy. Doing so can serve several purposes. First, it clearly expresses the values, purposes, and grantmaking goals of the donors. Second, a legacy statement offers crucial guidance by one generation to the succeeding generations of family trustees and others as they take the reins of the grantmaking program. Third, each generation in turn can develop their own statement, which builds on and adapts the vision and values passed down to them. In this stepwise fashion, a legacy statement preserves a "usable past" while also allowing for a renewal of values for the future. Finally, a clear statement provides a benchmark by which to measure grantmaking: Is it helping to accomplish the stated goals and values of the donor and family?

Foundation advisor and lawyer Paul Rhoads recommends that donors consider developing a statement as they establish the foundation: "It should not be put off until later, because it may never be completed. Do it at the beginning, with the knowledge that as your philanthropy matures, you can modify it." Items to address in such a statement may include:

- The donor's life and accomplishments;
- The causes in which the donor is interested (in general or with reference to specific organizations), growing out of that background;
- The values, traditions, and perspectives that animate both the donor's life and giving history;
- The resulting specific intent of the donor for the foundation; and
- The way the donor wishes succeeding generations of trustees to perpetuate this legacy over time.

A statement of legacy, however, derives its greatest importance and strength when it manages to engage successive generations. In some cases, this simply means helping the family reaffirm the donor's and family's original goals and values over time. It can also mean that a new generation adapts and builds upon those values to "make the foundation their own."

Consultant Mary Phillips describes the opportunity taken by the donors and family of the Stoneman Family Foundation, prior to the death of the donors: "Such a statement could ease any lingering doubts or anxieties family members might have about giving away inherited wealth or assuming responsibility for more of the foundation's grantmaking." In this instance, The Stoneman Family Foundation Statement of Donor Legacy was adopted in 1997 and said in part:

> As the foundation's donors, we would like to think that the foundation will always be rooted in the values and traditions of our family. As you know, we have established a tradition of giving over the years that reflects our interests and who we are. We would like this tradition of family values and giving to be part of The Stoneman Family Foundation into the future. The purpose of this document is to convey this wish to current and future members of the board of directors.

> Part of the Stoneman family's identity and interests has been in the Jewish community. Our participation in this community has been an acknowledgement of our own roots and has never promoted sectarianism.... We would like our family foundation to acknowledge and continue this participation in the Jewish community into the future...

> Secondly, the Stoneman family has its roots in Boston. Generations of the Stoneman family made their homes here, starting with Sidney's father who emigrated from Russia to the United States many years ago.... We would like The Stoneman Family Foundation to continue to have a Boston presence, with a preference but not a requirement that the foundation annually allocate a significant portion of its grant funds to organizations in the Boston area....

> And lastly, The Stoneman Family Foundation certainly is, and always has been, a family affair.... It is our hope that Stoneman family members will constitute a majority of the board in perpetuity. Failing that, we would request liquidation of the foundation. This being said, we make no further presumptions about representation of different branches and generations of the family, except to say that we expect that the foundation directors

will establish policies relating to board membership that are inclusive and equitable.

After the death of a donor in a family foundation, children and grandchildren usually want to honor the past while at the same time looking to the future. For many families and foundations, a profound sense of loss is felt when there is no direction from donors. The past seems empty and unhelpful. Succeeding generations typically don't want a blank slate; they want some guidance from the donor or earlier generations of trustees. Legacy statements and stories are important ways to give some guidance. And as each generation passes their legacy on, a new generation sets down the legacy anew and tells their own stories.

Legacy and Accountability

A foundation's explicit legacy can also play an important role in addressing calls for accountability. Everyone wants results and accountability for foundations. Measuring significant results can only be accomplished when one has clear goals and a long-term outlook. If a foundation is unconnected with its past, the resulting grantmaking may be unfocused and awfully dilettantish, rather than strategic and targeted. Referring back to the donor and family legacy through stories or a specific statement is one of the primary ways to assess how a foundation is doing: "are we pursuing our mission and values?"

Legacy and accountability are also related when it comes to the foundation world as a whole. Commentators on foundations often point out or complain that foundations do not have shareholders (owners) or customers in the usual sense. Nor do they have voters as our democratic institutions do. A self-perpetuating board, then, can be open to the charge of self-interest and unsupervised play. The scrutiny of journalists and the oversight of governmental agencies can often be uninformed and phrased in sound bites. For instance, neither would look back to consider generational legacy issues.

By contrast, foundations communicating the beliefs that animate their mission and grantmaking can be a very persuasive response to both the internal and external needs for accountability. As Colin Campbell, then President of the Rockefeller Brothers Fund, succinctly put it in *Telling Our Story: Accountability for Family Foundations*:

> Accountability means giving an account of yourself — put simply, it means telling your story…. One thing today's family philanthropists can do is to tell their stories more publicly and openly, to circulate widely the values, lessons, and examples that

will inspire and enable tomorrow's family donors to follow in their footsteps.... By becoming storytellers, family foundations speak not only to new generations of their own donor families but also to others who will be in a position to inherit or dispose of substantial wealth.

The Helping Hand of the Past

We have seen the importance and vitality of family philanthropy grow dramatically in recent decades. It is continuing though family foundations and other family-friendly philanthropic vehicles. It will remain vital and useful only if it is grounded and motivated by values, rather than by important, but secondary, legal and tax considerations. While commentators will endlessly discuss with either approval or disapproval the changes in the social contract such that government is supposed to do less or more, something else is also going on. There is a feeling that individuals, families, and communities should do more and can do more. Family philanthropy is a big part of that change.

One shouldn't underestimate this fledgling and still inchoate "growing public culture and personal spirituality of care," as described by Paul Schervish and John Havens ("Millionaires and the Millennium", 1999). Individuals and families are feeling newly empowered to express their diverse philanthropic values and to take on precisely the responsibilities of citizenship that Robert Putnam reminds us of in his powerful book *Bowling Alone* (2000), "Your extended family represents a form of social capital."

It is surprising — and certainly heartening — to see how hard so many family foundations work to discover their pasts. Succeeding generations of family foundation trustees must engage in inquiries of various kinds as they try to determine the legacy of values and goals left by those who came before. When those philanthropic purposes are too general, the *actions* of a donor during his/her life become hints and answers; they are an expression of values and a vivid source for determining a donor's legacy. For instance, one foundation sought to uncover a donor's values by systematically reviewing years and years of tax returns and checkbook stubs to unearth a deceased donor's giving history, and, by implication, her values and interests.

Providing the guidance of stories or of a legacy statement need not be the "dead hand of the past". As Will Close, then president and trustee of the Springs Close Foundation, founded in 1942, reported, "For our fiftieth anniversary, we had a two-day retreat to examine the future of the foundation. Although we made some fundamental changes in the way we make grants, I cannot overemphasize the importance of donor intent and the work of the past generations in our thinking." In cases like this, telling stories and preparing legacy statements are ways to help harness the "constant" in family philanthropy. They communicate, preserve and expand the larger story of the values that have grounded American philanthropy and promise to move it forward.

Crucially, that past and guidance becomes a shared responsibility of all those touched by family philanthropy. As foundation trustee and historian Ronald Wells puts it:

> Legacy then ... is an organic, living entity.... [Legacy] encompasses not only the donor's original statement of intent, but also all of the subsequent work and accomplishments of the foundation and its grantees. Like all living things, legacy constantly changes, thriving under favorable conditions and waning under those that are less so. And as with all living things, legacy can be nurtured or starved. As time passes, the legacy may become anachronistic, something that has petrified into a fossil fit only for a museum; or it may, treated with sympathy, compassion and intelligence, evolve into a perpetual monument to the human spirit. It is the clarity of the donor's instructions, infused with a trust in the wisdom and good will of succeeding generations that will decide what the donor's legacy will become.

Indeed, is it not the ethical responsibility of all who are involved in the foundation's work — trustees, family members, staff, and grantees — to vigorously nurture the foundation's legacy through their work over the decades?

Legacy is important not as a concession to the past, but as a helping hand, a vital and rich part of the present that helps show *us* the way to the future.

Originally published in Foundation News & Commentary *(January/February 2002), published by the Council on Foundations. Reprinted with the permission of The Council on Foundations and the kind permission of my co-author Jason Born, one of the most effective and long-term advocates for family philanthropy.*

Jason has been intimately involved with family foundations and family philanthropies for decades. He has authored or edited more than 60 publications and reports. He has been for many years the valued vice president for programming at the National Center for Family Philanthropy. I first met him when he was on the staff of the Council on Foundations in the 1990s. He was my editor — and more — when I put together the volume Living the Legacy *for the National Center for Family Philanthropy in 2001.*

ACKNOWLEDGMENTS

I am indebted to many publishers for permission to use the articles in this volume, and for finding value in my efforts at the time of publication. The original source information is listed with each article.

Numerous people encouraged these on-and-off efforts over the years. Most directly, I especially valued the support and comments of Robert Payton, Dwight Burlingame and Warren Ilchman of the Indiana University Center on Philanthropy. They offered me a place to hang my hat, amazing intellectual stimulation and encouragement, and a small grant. Peter Dobkin Hall at the Program on Non-Profit Organizations at the Institution for Social and Policy Studies at Yale supported some of my off-beat ideas by challenging me. And for two years I had a parking pass and a library card; how great is that! Ginny Esposito, Jason Born and Alice Buhl of the National Center for Family Philanthropy each enlightened me about the beauties, power and angst of family philanthropy.

Dick Cornuelle, Phoebe Boyer, Lenore Ealy, Dick Magat, Brooke Mahoney, and Michael Moody were among those who kept giving me practical and intellectual fodder for thinking about these issues. Numerous Foundation and nonprofit colleagues continually showed me how passion, competence and a voluntary sector can "muddle through" to some amazing results, while hubris can scuttle anything.

The J. M. Kaplan Fund, The Clark Foundation, The Chamber Music Society of Lincoln Center, Bessemer Trust, and Liberty Fund each provided an institutional home. They helped me hone my practical skills.

Implementation of any project counts for so much. The special typing and eagle-eyed copyediting skills of Kathy Kestler, production expertise of Sue Khodarahmi, the indexing acumen of Lorin Driggs, and cover design by Doris Halle were so important. Stefania Civitella at Borgo di Vagli near Cortona, Italy, has over the years provided respite and time for reading and writing overlooking Tuscan landscapes. And she helped me work with Francesco Campanoni who did the wonderful and whimsical cover illustration.

Finally, the authors who write about civil society and philanthropy showed me why what I have done could be so important. Even more important, the practitioners in philanthropy and nonprofits showed me how to make a difference by listening and putting ideas into action. Each perspective inspired and influenced these reflections and a life in search of impact. It remains an intellectual adventure. What I have made of such support and influence is my own doing. And I can't thank each and every one of you, named and unnamed, enough.

ABOUT THE AUTHOR

Chuck Hamilton's career has focused on philanthropy, voluntarism, and the importance of civil society: through his foundation and nonprofit work, board experience, and consulting. And in the interstices, he has undertaken varied research projects, written extensively, and edited the works of others.

Moments

At age 12 — In 1958, with that certainty a twelve-year-old has, I decided ordinary Christmas gifts were silly. On a snowy day I trudged to the post office. I bought two $10 money orders, probably for the Red Cross and the Salvation Army. Those were my gifts to Mom and Dad. They were gracious but disapproving. It didn't much matter to me; I had done the right thing in my view. Therein began a lifelong commitment to the voluntary sector.

At age 18 — As a high school senior in 1964, we were shown a professionally produced film called *The Apacraticans and the Republic of Apathy*. It has disappeared from history. In it, a presidential election is won by the Apacratican Party, which claimed all those who did not vote. That was more people than voted Republican or Democrat. As a cautionary tale about apathy and the importance of voting, it was effective. It was also so uninteresting to me. I saw a different civics lesson with intriguing questions: What did it mean that they "controlled" government? Did they also control society? How would things get done without a functioning government? And what alternatives were possible for a functioning society? To a young mind it was a vivid and exciting introduction to civil society as opposed to political society. A few years later, I came to believe that Thoreau had it right: "Even voting for the right [thing] is doing nothing for it."

At age 25 — As the Vietnam War dragged on, I felt I had to take a personal stand. I refused to pay federal income tax in 1971. I mailed my signed tax form stapled to a 24-inch square poster with a Thoreau quotation: "How does it become a man to behave toward this American government today? I answer, that he cannot without disgrace be associated with it." I was later visited by two IRS agents from central casting: black hats, ties, and suits. I refused to pay. The IRS then took the funds from an account at Marine Midland Bank that was not mine. So, just like Thoreau who didn't pay his poll tax arrears, I never paid my tax that year.

At age 26 — In 1972, I obtained a heavily redacted copy of my FBI file. It noted my name and added "aka Chuck"! After consulting unnamed informants, it concluded, "In view of the lack of subversive or radical activity ... it is recommended that no further investigation be conducted in this matter, pending the receipt of additional information indicating a more concrete basis on which to predicate a full and complete security matter investigation." That is it? So silly and yet so scary too.

At age 32 — When a Nazi party attempted to march in Skokie, Illinois, a town where many Holocaust survivors lived, the American Civil Liberties Union defended their right to march as a free speech issue. As offensive as that march was, I thought the ACLU had made a difficult and profoundly correct decision. Later, I read that the ACLU had lost approximately a third of its members for taking their position. I immediately became a Life Member (#967). Sadly, like many other observers, I have since watched the ACLU often waffle on a nuanced absolutism for free speech.

Education

1979–1983: New York University, Graduate School of Business Administration, NYC. MBA in Management and Corporate Strategy.

1970–1973: Union Graduate School, Yellow Springs, OH. Individually designed Ph.D. program in economics and social history. Drs. Roy P. Fairfield and Paul Avrich were advisors. I met the M.A. requirements, but left the program to start Free Life Editions. I took courses by simply approaching professors at various universities directly; they always welcomed me. Courses included the first-year graduate economics program at Columbia University; History of Economic Theory with Israel Kirzner at NYU; economics with Murray Rothbard at Polytechnic Institute; two history colloquia at the City University; and reading tutorials with Paul Avrich (Graduate Center CUNY and Queens College) on anarchism, social history, research methodology, and independent education. I also did a four-week project on Auberon Herbert at the British Museum and Amsterdam International Institute of Social History.

1969–1971: New York Theological Seminary, NYC. Urban Year and Metropolitan Intern Program. Program for "doing divinity" outreach and courses leading to a Master of Divinity. I was sponsored by the New Eden Baptist Church, Brooklyn. I did not finish the program.

1968–1969: City College, NYC. Masters Program for Urban Schools offered by the Board of Education. Earned 12+ graduate education credits for preliminary certification as an elementary school teacher.

1964–1968: New College, Sarasota, FL. B.A. Triple major in history, philosophy, and political science. Thesis on the origins of Social Security: "Politics in Process: Old Age Insurance During 1934–35."

Professional Experience

2011–2013: Bessemer Trust, NYC. Director of Philanthropic Advisory Services & Principal.

2009–2011: Consulting. Clients included Bessemer Trust, WT Grant Foundation, Robertson Foundation, Strive/Per Scholas, Social Enterprise Program at Columbia Business School, Rensselaerville Institute, Pumpkin Foundation.

2009–2010: Philanthropy New York, NYC. Senior Fellow.

1999–2009: The Clark Foundation, NYC and Cooperstown. Executive Director and Secretary. Also secretary of two other foundations.

1995–1999: The J. M. Kaplan Fund, NYC. Director, Chief Operating Officer, and Secretary.

1985–1996: Market Projects: Strategy and Research for Nonprofit Organizations, Carmel, IN, and Wilton, CT. Consulting clients included The J. M. Kaplan Fund; The Philanthropy Roundtable (as director of Planning and Program Development); The IU Center on Philanthropy (as adjunct research associate); and The Institute for Humane Studies.

1987–1992: Liberty Fund, Indianapolis, IN. Director of Publications and Program Officer.

1984–1986: The Foundation for Economic Education, Irvington-on-Hudson, NY. Director of Publications and Editor of *The Freeman*.

1984–1985: The Albert Einstein Institution, Cambridge, MA. First ED and member of the Board. Founded by Dr. Gene Sharp to "advance the worldwide study and use of strategic nonviolent action."

1977: *Libertarian Review*, NYC. Publisher and Associate Editor.

1972–1983: Free Life Editions, NYC. Founder and Editor. Independent publishing house that published nineteen nonfiction titles, including three that received the front-page review in *The Sunday New York Times Book Review*. Titles were widely reviewed in *The New York Review of Books*, *Times Literary Supplement*, academic journals, etc. Reprint rights were sold here and abroad, various titles translated into six languages, and several titles were offered by book clubs. When closing the operation, I edited several titles and sold them to other publishers, notably Universe Books.

1970–1972: *libertarian analysis*, NYC. Publisher and Editor.

1969–1972: One-Stop Community Center, Ocean Hill Brownsville, Brooklyn, NY. Teacher and Director.

1969–1970: Public School 192M, 500 West 138th, NYC. Assistant teacher, math and reading specialist, and substitute teacher.

Research Experience

1994–1996: Institution for Social and Policy Studies (Program on Non-Profit Organizations), Yale University, New Haven, CT. Visiting Fellow.

1992–1996: Indiana University Center on Philanthropy, Indianapolis, IN. Adjunct Research Associate.

1979–1980: Liberty Fund, Indianapolis, IN. Research Consultant.

1970–1972: Research Foundation of the City University of New York, NYC. Research Assistant to Dr. Paul Avrich.

1967: Federal Reserve Bank of New York, Financial Statistics Division, NYC. Research Assistant.

Board Memberships

2016 to present: New College Foundation. Sarasota, FL, as a vice-chair.

2016 to present: La Musica, Sarasota, FL.

2016 to present: Bessemer Trust: Bessemer National Gift Fund, NYC. Special Fiduciary.

2006–2013: Civitella Ranieri Foundation, Umbertide, Italy, and NYC.

2006–2016: Chamber Music Society of Lincoln Center, NYC. Vice Chair, 2007–2015.

1997–2003: Council on Foundations, Washington, D.C. Also Chair, Committee on Family Foundations, 1999–2001.

1996–1998: Association for Research on Nonprofit and Voluntary Action (ARNOVA), Indianapolis, IN.

1995–1998: New College Foundation, Sarasota, FL.

1994 to present: The Hamilton Foundation, Founder and Trustee.

1993–1997: New College Alumni Association, Sarasota, FL.

Shorter-term board memberships include JobsFirst, NYC, 2010–2011; The Albert Einstein Institution, Cambridge, MA, a founding member, 1984; Center for Libertarian Studies, NYC, 1976–1980; One-Stop Community Center, Brooklyn, NYC, 1969–1972.

Family Business Experience

1971 to present: Variously trustee, partner, or president of a dozen entities: charitable funds, investment trusts, hotel properties, and small businesses.

Books and Publications

Radical Portraits: Seeking Liberty, by Charles H. Hamilton (Free Life Editions, 2019).

A Matter of No Curiosity, by Albert Jay Nock, edited with an afterword by Charles H. Hamilton. Collection of Albert Jay Nock writings on The State. (Cornucopia, WI: Michael Coughlin, Publisher, 2010).

Valerio: An Extraordinary Ordinary Man, edited by Michael Coughlin (Cornucopia, WI: Michael Coughlin, Publisher, 2005). Authored essay: "A Tattered Paperback and Valerio."

Donor Legacy: The Values of a Family's Philanthropy across Generations, edited by Charles H. Hamilton. (Washington, DC: National Center for Family Philanthropy, 2001). "Introduction: Legacy: The Helping Hand of Family Philanthropy" and several case studies.

The Conservative Press in Twentieth Century America, edited by Ronald Lora and William Henry Longton (Westport, CT: Greenwood Press, 1999). Author of articles on *The Freeman* (1920–1924); analysis (1944–1951); and *The Freeman* (1950–).

New Directions for Philanthropic Fundraising (in two volumes), edited by Charles H. Hamilton and Warren F. Ilchman. (San Francisco: Jossey-Bass Publishers, 1995): *Cultures of Giving I: How Region and Religion Influence Philanthropy*, #7, Spring 1995; and *Cultures of Giving II: How Heritage, Gender, Wealth, and Values Influence Philanthropy*, #8, Summer 1995.

The State of the Union: Essays in Social Criticism, by Albert Jay Nock, edited and a foreword by Charles H. Hamilton. (Indianapolis: Liberty Fund, 1991).

Benjamin R. Tucker and the Champions of Liberty: A Centenary Anthology, edited by Michael E. Coughlin, Charles H. Hamilton, and Mark A. Sullivan (Minneapolis: Michael Coughlin, Publisher, 1986). "Introduction: The Evolution of a Subversive Tradition."

Fugitive Essays: Selected Writings of Frank Chodorov, edited, with an introduction by Charles H. Hamilton. (Indianapolis: Liberty Fund, 1980).

The State, by Franz Oppenheimer, with an Introduction by Charles H. Hamilton. (NYC: Free Life Editions, 1975).

A TIME Guide to the Draft, by Charles H. Hamilton (NYC: TIME Education Program, 1969).

Miscellaneous

2007: Guest Conductor: Stamford Symphony Orchestra, Stamford, CT.
1978: Life Member: American Civil Liberties Union.
1970: Honorary Life Member: The Nature Conservancy.

PHILANTHROPIC LANDSCAPES

INDEX

Made in the USA
Columbia, SC
03 November 2019